MW01672708

The Commands of the Prophets

EXTRA LARGE PRINT

God's handbook to raise families, communities, and nations of sons and daughters to walk with him in righteousness

Assembled and with notes
by Michael Phillips

These are the commands, decrees and laws which the Lord your God directed me to teach you to observe in the land that you are to possess, so that you, your children and their children after them may fear the Lord your God as long as you live by keeping all his decrees and commands and so that you may enjoy long life. Hear, Israel, and be careful to obey so that it may go well with you and that you may increase greatly in a land flowing with milk and honey.

Hear, O Israel: The Lord our God, the Lord is one. Love the Lord your God with all your heart and with all your soul and with all your strength. These commandments that I give you today are to be on your hearts. Impress them on your children. Talk about them when you sit at home and when you walk along the road, when you lie down and when you get up. Tie them as symbols on your hands and bind them on your foreheads. Write them on the doorframes of your houses and on your gates.

(Deuteronomy 6: 1-9, author's paraphrase)

The law of the Lord is perfect...
The testimony of the Lord is sure...
The precepts of the Lord are right...
The commandment of the Lord is pure...
The ordinances of the Lord are true...
Psalm 19

The three volumes of *The Commands* and the five volumes of *The Eyewitness Bible* present a unity of vision and outlook on God's work and purposes through history and in the individual lives of his people. Their themes and messages form a single tapestry-perspective of the Bible as God's revelation. They are most profitably read in conjunction with each other, and with that overarching unity in mind.

The Commands of the Prophets
The Commands of Jesus
The Commands of the Apostles

The Eyewitness Old Testament, Volume 1
The Eyewitness Old Testament, Volume 2
The Eyewitness New Testament, Volume 1
The Eyewitness New Testament, Volume 2
The Eyewitness New Testament, Volume 3

Special Editions:
The Commands of the Prophets Extra Large Print Edition
The Commands of Jesus Extra Large Print Edition
The Commands of Jesus Journal Edition
The Prayers of the Commands
The Commands of Jesus Pocket Edition
The Commands of the Apostles Pocket Edition

9-23-25

The Commands of the Prophets
by Michael Phillips
© 2024 by Michael Phillips
Published by Sunrise Wise Path Publishers, 2024
Extra Large Print Edition, 2025

Scriptures are taken from the Revised Standard Version unless otherwise noted.

ISBN 978-1-969924-04-0

Cover design by Joseph Dindinger

CONTENTS

The Commands of the Prophets

1. Wisdom

1. Listen to your father's instruction.
2. Love, cherish, seek, and pray for wisdom.
3. Though it cost all you have, get understanding.
4, Let wisdom, understanding, and discretion protect you.
5. Exercise prudence.
6. Don't act or speak hastily, and listen before speaking.
7. Do not speak thoughtlessly, or carelessly pass on gossip.
8. Trust God with all your heart, and do not rely on your own understanding.
9. Acknowledge God in all your ways.
10. Find a husband or wife of noble character.

2. Choice and Consequence

11. Love God with your whole heart, soul, mind, and strength.
12. Seek God diligently.
13. Take heed not to forget God's commands.
14. Choose this day whom you will serve.
15. Walk in obedience to God's commands.
16. Do what is right and good in the sight of the Lord.
17. Do not let your heart become proud.
18. Do not be afraid or discouraged.
19. Remember blessings and consequences and choose life.
20. Set the desires of your heart Godward.

3. Authority

21. Acknowledge God's authority.
22. Embrace command.
23. Choose obedience.
24. Walk with God.
25. Do not let sin beguile you.
26. Run from sin.
27. Honor marriage and family.
28. Separate from the world.
29. Keep covenant with God.
30. Live as a manifestly distinct righteousness-choosing people.

4. Command

31. Worship no other gods than the Lord your God.
32. Make no idols.
33. Do not speak the Lord's name carelessly.
34. Observe the Lord's rest.
35. Honor your father and mother.
36. Do not kill.
37. Do not commit adultery.
38. Do not steal.
39. Do not speak falsely about others.
40. Do not covet what you do not have.

5. Obedience

41. Love your neighbor as yourself.
42. Show kindness to widows, orphans, strangers, and aliens.
43. Help and be kind to the poor.
44. Keep your camp pure.
45. Work diligently and cheerfully in what you undertake.
46. Respect the property of others.
47. Make restitution for wrong.
48. Bear no grudge, seek no revenge.
49. Lend without interest.
50. Exercise wise stewardship over God's provision.

6. Separation

51. Be strong and courageous not to walk in the world's ways.
52. Watch yourself closely so the world does not ensnare you.
53. Do not yield to the world's enticements.
54. Do not associate with worldly people.
55. Make no friends of fools.
56. Do not bring sin into your home.
57. Do not covet or imitate what the world's people have or do.
58. Women do not wear men's clothing, men do not wear women's clothing.
59. Do not be lured into worshiping false gods.
60. Do not follow others into sin.

7. Watchfulness

61. Keep watchful by knowing God's commands.
62. Read and re-read God's law.
63. Fix God's words in your mind and store his commands in your heart.
64. Apply your heart to understand God's purposes.
65. Do not help an evil man or woman.
66. Do not let sin become a thorn in your side.
67. Seek counsel, guidance, and advice.
68. Meditate on God's precepts.
69. Humbly listen and heed wisdom, insight, instruction, and correction.
70. Live by the truth you know.

8. Righteousness

71. *Pray with David:* Search me, O God, and know my heart. Try me and know my thoughts. See if there be any wicked way in me, and lead me in the way everlasting.
72. Incline my heart to your commands.
73. Teach me your ways.
74. Give me understanding and wisdom in my secret heart.
75. Help me not to stray from your commands.
76. Give me wise judgment and knowledge.
77. Protect me from falsehood, keep my steps steady, let no sin get dominion over me.
78. Create in me a clean heart and put a right spirit within me.
79. Guard my life—may integrity and upright-ness preserve me.
80. Guide me, lead me, and help me walk in truth.

9. Judgment and Forgiveness

81. Confess sin.
82. Forgive when you have been wronged.
83. Judge others fairly.
84. Overlook offenses and weaknesses in others.
85. Repent of unintentional sin.
86. Be honest and truthful in dealings and relationships.
87. Turn away anger with gentle speech.
88. Wear a cheerful countenance.
89. Spread peace.
90. Keep your word.

10. Renewal and Restoration

91. Be still and know God.
92. Consecrate yourself.
93. Circumcise your heart.
94. Continually renew covenant with God.
95. Destroy potential idols.
96. Make no rash decisions.
97. Do not chase fantasies.
98. Avoid people who talk too much.
99. Keep knowledge to yourself.
100. Do not engage in meaningless worship.

11. Legacy

101. Live a peaceable, responsible, domestic, and upright life.
102. Speak truth.
103. Claim and pass on your inheritance in God.
104. Instruct your children in God's commands.
105. Show respect to the elderly.
106. Succeed by planning.
107. Walk in patience.
108. Cultivate love for the Lord's statutes and commands.
109. Walk in integrity.
110. Act justly, love mercy, and walk humbly with your God.

12. Purity

111. Be pure in thought and behavior.
112. Do not be the cause of allowing sin to spread.
113. Engage in no sexual relations outside marriage.
114. Hate falsehood and do not circulate potential falsehoods.
115. Guard your tongue.
116. Purge temper, anger, bitterness, resentment.
117. Use honest weights.
118. Turn from all hint of impurity and impropriety.
119. Purge evil from your life.
120. Welcome God's furnace of purification.

Stand at the crossroads and look;
ask for the ancient paths,
ask where the good way is, and walk in it.

—Jeremiah 6:16, NIV

The Commands of the Prophets
The Commands of Jesus
The Commands of the Apostles

Author Note:

This book is one of a trilogy of titles on the commands of the Bible. Much like *The Chronicles of Narnia,* there are two ways to read the three commands books—in their chronological order, or in the order in which they were written. *The Commands of the Prophets,* though first in biblical sequence, was actually the last of the three to be written. In the same way that *The Lion, the Witch, and the Wardrobe*, though sequentially not the first in Narnian history, is the foundational title of the series, so too is *The Commands of Jesus,* as first written, the foundational book of commands. It is therefore the book I recommend readers new to the series begin with. The books are independent and can of course be read in any order. However, *The Commands of Jesus* is the anchoring centerpiece of the whole. Both the other two books of the series will have more meaning and be more easily understood with that foundation in place.

INTRODUCTION TO
The Commands of the Prophets

How *Command* reveals God's high purposes in the universe, and is the mechanism for man's specific instructions for life

However one reads and interprets the Old Testament, one fact is clear: It is the earliest, most detailed, and therefore most important record of God's first direct attempt to communicate personally with man, and of man's attempt to understand who God is and what he was saying.

THE OLD TESTAMENT'S ESSENTIAL MESSAGE

All the rest about which people debate and disagree—the *Genesis* timetable, were Adam and Eve real people, how old is the earth, evolution, are the "days" of *Genesis* twenty-four hours in length, how reliable is Old Testament history, where did Cain's wife come from, is Noah's ark fact or fable, is the Bible "inspired," did Moses write the first five books, were the Jews a chosen people or merely a conquering nomadic group of tribes, did the exodus from Egypt take place as recounted, did God forgive sin on the basis of shed blood or was the sacrifice borrowed from primitive paganism, did a man called Jonah really get swallowed by a whale…these and a thousand other controversial points are essentially side issues. They are not fundamental to the *message* of the Old Testament. Taken out of context, made too much of—analyzed, debated, and argued about—they become distractions which often *prevent* an accurate reading of that essential message.

Throughout the course of history there have been tens of thousands of books written about the Old Testament, analyzing all these disputed topics at great length, and every other disputed point you can think of. There are so many doctrines, theologies, and historical opinions—Jewish, Christian, and Muslim—put forth based on the writings of the Old Testament that they muddle and obscure what I will again call its *essential message*. It is a remarkable thing that the analytical religious mind nearly always tends to make spiritual things more complicated than they are.

This is *not* a book of doctrine or theology. Neither is this primarily a book about the history of the Old Testament except as providing the contextual backdrop for what that history is intended to *mean*. Instead, we will attempt to isolate the *essential message* of the Old Testament, and the *purpose* underlying why God inspired it to be written.

No agenda lurks between the lines other than to get to the bottom of the fundamental and practical meaning and intent of the Old Testament writings. Hopefully this book will be able to speak uniformly to Christians and Jews, and Muslims too if they are interested in the wisdom of the ancient patriarchs. It may even speak to those who do not consider themselves spiritual at all. It is intended for any and all who are in earnest about knowing what the Old Testament is all about.

Is it too ambitious to think that we will be able to understand the root message of the Old Testament in a little over two hundred pages, when so many theologies and histories written over two-and-a-half millennia have *not* been able to achieve that goal?

The attempt to understand the essence of the Old Testament is only impossible to those who do not understand how the message of its ancient texts come to us. Once we grasp how that message has been delivered—by God, by Moses, by priests and prophets and kings, by poets and men of wisdom—it will not be remarkable to find the hidden significance of the Old Testament unfolding itself with surprising practicality. Obviously people will disagree with much in that message, just as everyone responds differently to the claims of Christ which came later. Not everyone, therefore, will want to *follow* and *order their lives* according to the precepts of the Old Testament's message. That's another thing altogether. But the message itself isn't so very hard to understand.

The fundamental starting point is relatively straightforward:

How does the message of the Bible come to us? How has it been delivered, first to the ancient Hebrews, and now in modern times to us who read it today?

THE THREE PRINCIPLES OF SPIRITUAL PHYSICS THAT GOVERN THE UNIVERSE

To answer that question, we have to back up a bit. Before we can get to the answer, we must recognize three underlying principles that govern the entire created universe. It is these fundamental presuppositions that will allow us first to discover, then to understand, the answer to the above questions.

Beyond all the complex interplay of stars and planets and gravity and black holes, God established creation to function according to these three laws. Just as physicists base much of their understanding of the physical world on what are called the three laws of thermodynamics, so too there are laws which govern the spiritual realm of God's creation.

These are the three fundamental laws of *spiritual physics.*

They are principles of the *spirit* world. Their undergirding importance also carries over and, for those with eyes to see it, becomes a ruling dynamic of the *physical* world as well.

These principles lay the foundation for understanding the essential message and purpose of the Old Testament.

- PRINCIPLE ONE: *Universal Fatherhood*

God is a personal being, not an abstract entity. He thinks, he makes choices, he has goals, he feels emotions. He is in all ways personal. His intrinsic life has existed forever. His essential nature is goodness and love. Out of the characteristics of that essential nature flows his Fatherhood. God creates because he loves as a *Father* loves.

God is the Creator and Father of the universe and everything in it. His is not a neutral or impersonal Fatherhood, it is a *good* Fatherhood and a *personal* Fatherhood. He is a good and *loving* Father. It is his Fatherhood that gives life and makes life a good thing.

Personal and universal Fatherhood is thus the essential energy of creation—not life force, not intelligent impersonal design, not random evolution, but *purposeful Fatherhood.*

Physicists identify two components that make up the entire universe—mass and energy. At the moment of what is called the Big Bang, both were united in *infinite* energy. When that energy exploded, the universe was created. That infinite energy was God himself. Because he was a Father, he created a *living* universe.

As a creating and *energetic* Father, God created every living human man and woman, not just to float through space on a unique planet designed for life, but to be his sons and daughters. Our relation to the world and the universe is therefore defined and given meaning by the relationship of children to their Father. We are not independent, autonomous beings who just "happened" to evolve into a mass of atoms. We are eternally bound in a relation of childship to our Creator. We may not acknowledge or do anything about it. We may ignore it.

But we cannot escape it. We are created children of a creator-Father.

- PRINCIPLE TWO: *Command and obedience.*

God established the universe to function according to the interrelated harmony of *authority* and *response to authority*, lived out through *command and obedience.* This is the natural order between a Creator and his universe, and between Fathers and their children.

For most of the world's history, the institutions of man functioned by authority, command, and obedience. This principle in God's economy has thus been generally understood. Many of those living *under* authority may not have been fond of it, but most accepted the principle of authority as intrinsic to life. They were therefore able to grasp the truth that God created the universe with a foundation in place in which he is the ultimate authority because he is the creating good of the universe.

The truth of authority as intrinsic to the created universe and the life of man, however, is no longer recognized by modernism. This shift toward the autonomous independence of individuality, explains why the principles of God's order in the world are increasingly difficult for modern men and women to grasp. On every side they are being inundated by the anti-Fatherhood, anti-authority outlook of progressivism. Spiritual physics has been dropped from modernism's curriculum.

Rejecting Fatherhood and the primacy of authority, modernism cannot understand how the universe was intended to function. All its theories about how humanity is intended to live are therefore flawed. Spiritual physics explains how the world works, and how humanity works. With it dropped from the curriculum, is it any wonder the world is a mess and most people have no idea what life is supposed to mean?

- PRINCIPLE THREE: *Free will.*

In order to enrich the interconnection between created and Creator, and to give authority and obedience reality and growing substance, God gave to his highest creature a priceless gift found nowhere else in creation—the gift of free will. He gave man power to choose, to make decisions that carry consequences, to order his life and make of it what he will. His intent was that we use the gift to live in harmony to his will—that we *choose* to be children of his Fatherhood...*good* children because he is a *good* Father.

The impersonal stars and galaxies and planets *must* obey the laws of physical physics by which God ordained that they function. We don't know and understand all those laws. But we know that the physical universe has no choice but to obey them. The lower animal kingdom, too, was created to function without determinative power of choice. It is ruled instead by the instinct of each creature-species.

But God desired a race of men and women that lived by *chosen* obedience to the authority of his loving Fatherhood. In man, therefore, he placed *spirit, soul, intelligence* and *volition*—the capacity to *become, grow,* and *enlarge* as spiritual, relational, intelligent beings. He designed the gift of free will as the inborn human power by which that growth would take place, with command and obedience as the mechanism through which man's spirit, soul, intelligence, and volition would develop.

By freely choosing to fall in with God's created order, free will was to be the life-giving vehicle that would make it possible for God's children to grow into the fullness and destiny of their personhood. It was intended as the means through which an ever-deepening relationship with God as Father would mature mankind into his sons and daughters.

Thus, in his own creative act, God allowed risk into his creation. By giving man the opportunity to decide for himself whether or not to live according to his authority and command, at the same time God gave man the power to reject it.

Spiritual physics is therefore different than its physical counterpart. We have been given the choice whether or not to live by its laws.

This divine risk, the sin that resulted, and the consequences of both, can be seen as the characterizing foundation for all human history. Modernism *does* recognize and embrace this third foundation-stone of the universe. Doing so, however, absent its intrinsic linkage to the divine Fatherhood, the "free will" of modernism is afloat on a foundationless sea of self-seeking independence and gratification. Anchored to no ultimate purpose, pleasing the *self* has become its own meaning. In our time, the consequences of using free will to reject the very source from which it came, demanding independence rather than childship, has become the defining characteristic of our world.

HOW THE MESSAGE OF THE OLD TESTAMENT COMES TO US—*COMMAND*

At last we are in a position to answer the question posed earlier: How does the essential message of the Bible come to us?

It comes to us by *command*.

The authority of God's universal Fatherhood works itself into life, and *sustains* life, by command. Those under authority are expected to obey. Good children are supposed to obey.

We may not like it. Modernism positively hates it and therefore rejects it. Children often don't like it. But we cannot escape it. Authority and command—not DNA or RNA or amino acids or carbon and nitrogen and hydrogen and oxygen—are the true building blocks of life. Indeed, life *began*, not by accidental electrical and chemical reactions, but by *command*.

Authority and command, and the obedience that energizes them, are the basic building blocks of spiritual physics. Everything is built out of these three elements.

As we have seen, command is accompanied by free will. It is a two-sided coin. There are always two responses to command—obedience and disobedience. We have the option to *choose* whether to obey. We are free also to choose *not* to obey.

It is a curious state of affairs, that an all-powerful Creator, who loves the children of his making and who desires intimacy with them, would create those children with the capacity to turn their backs on him. Yet this is where we find ourselves. Though we are the offspring of God's creation, we must *choose* to grow into his obedient sons and daughters.

Sadly, most men and women throughout history have chosen not to do so. The almost anarchist and often depraved lust for independence from authority that so defines our time is ironically the result of the very gift God gave his human creation.

This is why command in the Old Testament is often accompanied by the simple word *if.* Many of the commands of the Old Testament are phrased as *if-then* propositions. They lay out the two sides of the obedience coin, then spell out the inevitable consequences of obedience and disobedience.

No clearer example exists than in Moses' farewell address to the Israelites in Deuteronomy 30 at the end of his life. Moses issued this final command to the Israelites. It is a "command," but the *if* and its consequences are stark and clear.

> *"I have set before you this day life and good, death and evil. If you obey the commandments of the Lord your God which I command you this day, by loving the Lord your God, by walking in his ways, and by keeping his commandments...then you shall live and multiply, and the Lord your God will bless you...But if your heart turns away, and you will not hear, but are drawn away to worship other gods...I declare to you this day that you shall perish...I have set before you life and death, blessing and curse; therefore choose life, that you and your descendants may live, loving the Lord your God, obeying his voice, and cleaving to him; for that means life to you and length of days."* (Deut. 30: 15-20)

THE BIBLE'S EQUATION—COMMAND AND PROMISE

Many Christians in our time focus largely for their scriptural diet on the promises of the Bible. Entire organizations and churches exist whose primary emphases are the *promises* of God. Bibles are printed highlighting its promises. Promises are memorized and categorized so that for every life-situation one can produce a corresponding promise to meet the need.

Curiously, however, many of those who dwell on the promises do not actually live to a great extent in the *reality* of those promises. They are more *hoped for* and *prayed for* than experienced.

The reason for this disconnect is abundantly clear. The Bible's promises are part of an overlooked scriptural equation. God's promises do not stand alone. They are not free. They are linked by cause and effect to certain conditions. These conditions must be met before the promises can be fulfilled.

The promises represent the second half of a compound sentence. They occupy the "then" half of an "if-then" equation. Without the *if*, there can be no *then*.

The commands are scriptural if-hinges upon which God's promises function. Promise is always linked to command, exactly as in the words of Moses above. We also see this *if-then* progression clearly throughout the book of *Proverbs*.

> *IF you accept my words and store up my commands within you…applying your heart to understanding, and*
> *IF you call out for insight and cry aloud for understanding, and*
> *IF you look for it as for silver and search for it as for hidden treasure,*
>
> > *THEN you will understand the fear of the Lord and find the knowledge of God…*
> > *THEN you will understand what is right and just and fair—every good path. For wisdom will enter your heart, and knowledge will be pleasant to your soul. Discretion will protect you, and understanding will guard you.*
> >
> > —Proverbs 2:1-5, 9-11, NIV

This is surely one of the towering and majestic promises in the Bible. But its fulfillment is not automatic. The IF-hinge looms large. The determinative IF explains why many do *not* walk in understanding, knowledge, wisdom, and discretion. They have filled their heads with knowledge, but they have not set themselves to become the kind of people in whom wisdom is able to flourish according to the first two chapters of *Proverbs*.

It is not a neutral if-then equation. *Command* is included in the IF. We are *commanded* to get wisdom: *Do not forget…Get wisdom; get insight.* (Proverbs 4:5)

The *if-then* equation of *Proverbs* is usually easy to see. The *if-then* linkage in Moses' charge to the Israelites is equally clear. But many of the Bible's promises do not come to us phrased in such linear if-then statements. We often have to search to discover the *command* or principle that governs the function of a given *promise*.

It is nearly always there. Some *command* stands as the foundational root out of which every biblical *promise* grows. If we desire to see the promise manifested in our lives, we must discover and live by the command attached to it.

The promise is the fruit. The tree that grows that fruit is the tree of command and obedience. If the tree is not flourishing in the garden of daily choices over many years, the promised fruit will not grow.

God's commands to man proceed out of his ultimate will for the universe. He purposes for mankind to grow progressively capable of living according to his eternal will. This we do first by obeying at the lower levels of command. Out of obedience to specific lower commands emerges insight to perceive higher principles.

Discerning higher principles and obeying loftier commands, wisdom gradually illuminates the heart and mind toward still higher truths. Obedience is the soil out of which understanding and wisdom grow. As George MacDonald phrases it, "Obedience is the opener of eyes." *

Some of the principles of God's eternal will are difficult to apprehend when looking into the distant future. There is much within God's overarching plan that remains for eternity to clarify. Yet other elements of God's will he *has* made clear. The general principles of work, wisdom, understanding, knowledge, selflessness, choice, foresight, growth, order, predictability, accountability, humility, and so on, can be seen throughout the book of *Proverbs*. It is one of Scripture's pivotal books in which the universal themes of God's eternal will are translated into very specific instructions for daily life, relationships, attitudes, personal habits, and general outlook.

The book of *Proverbs* is literally a guidebook, an instruction manual, for discovering how to live the high and holy thing called God's Will.

For this reason, we will begin with the wisdom of *Proverbs* and the challenges of Moses from *Deuteronomy*. Our purpose is to look at *themes* not recount Old Testament history with sequential precision. Though out of order in the historical flow of the Old Testament these two groupings of commands truly lay the foundation and set the tone for everything that follows.

Then we will backtrack to *Genesis* and follow a general historical sequence through the remainder of the groupings. Those preferring to follow a strict chronology may wish instead to begin with Authority, Command, and Obedience and consider the Wisdom commands following the prayers of David in the Righteousness commands.

In whatever order we read them, in the commands we unlock the essence of the Old Testament's message—the very revealed Will of God. Beyond all the history, theology, doctrine, and disputed questions, the commands of the Old Testament reveal God's purpose for mankind. That purpose will only be illuminated into the hearts and minds of those who make it their life priority to *obey* those commands. That's the *energy* of spiritual physics.

What we will try to do in this book is isolate the most important of those commands and try to uncover how we can personalize and live their principles in our lives. The commands are grouped into twelve series of

---

* George MacDonald, *Unspoken Sermons, Second Series,* "The Way."

ten commands each. The groupings are not intended in every case to place similar commands together. Sometimes this is done, but not always. Occasionally mixing up various commands in unexpected ways can actually be beneficial in keeping the big picture in view.

Though reversed from the scriptural sequence, the first two books in this series—*The Commands of Jesus* (2012) and *The Commands of the Apostles* (2014)—came before this compilation of the Old Testament commands. Nine years have now passed, during which time I hope I have grown and continued to deepen in my understanding of the Bible's commands. The challenge presented by the massively greater amount of material to consider here has required some adaptations to my approach, and in the structure of this volume. This explains why you will find it slightly different from the two New Testament books.

In general the 120 Old Testament commands are organized similarly. However, a few features are distinct. I have felt it appropriate to expand the introductions to each of the series in order to provide a loose sequential panorama of the historical flow of the Old Testament—something that was not so necessary in the two New Testament books. As mentioned, the commands themselves are not intended in every case to be grouped precisely according to their series themes. Those especially originating from the book of *Proverbs,* and others from the Levitical Law, are scattered throughout.

These changes have resulted in a longer book than the other two volumes. The expanded introductions, lengthier devotional thoughts in some cases, and added material, may make treating the 120 entries as a "daily devotional," so to speak, more challenging. Hopefully the benefits will outweigh the difficulties.

A Final Introductory Post Script

I have worked hard in grouping and phrasing the commands in this book, trying to be attentive to God's voice before offering my own thoughts. *The Commands of the Prophets* has taken almost nine years from start to finish, being laid aside for long stretches because I did not feel I was hearing clearly from God what form it should take, and what commands the book should focus on. I have been seeking to hear God's whispers about these commands and these entries for a long time.

This lengthy process highlights that the Old Testament is an enormous book. The magnitude of coalescing its message, themes, and in particular its commands, is daunting in the extreme. This will therefore be far from a perfect or complete selection of commands. I will have passed over many that others consider important. Though I have tried to bring to light the main themes into which most of the commands fit, the overlap, even repetition of those that seem paramount meant that others could not be included. I continued to tweak, modify, combine, omit, and add as I went. This process continued all the way through. Not wanting to over-spiritualize it, I prayed for insight, illumination, and guidance before every entry. Some commands from my original compilation were taken out, others added, some combined. I did my human best to sense from the Holy Spirit what commands should be included, and what to say about them.

I recognize, however, that my human best to hear from God is limited by the myriad deficiencies of self that we all share. The window through which I try to see God's truth, and the inner ears with which I try to hear him, are like the man's perceptions in Mark 8:22-25 who was *beginning* to see but did not yet see everything clearly. We're still little children who do not understand our Father as well as we would like. At some point, however, one has to commit his efforts to print and hope that God's hand has been at work in all those decisions and details.

Along with my own imperfect humanity which in this life is capable of perceiving God's high truths only as through a glass darkly, I am conscious, too, that I come at this effort, as I did the previous two volumes, from my *own* perspective, from my range of experiences and insights and Bible study and my own years as a Christian.

I am a great believer in the individual practicality and application of the Bible's multi-layered truth and wisdom for each of our lives. What speaks to you personally will probably not speak in exactly the same way to me, and vice-versa. That is what makes the Bible the unique book it is, and why, with good reason, it is almost universally called by most Christians God's Word. The Bible *speaks*. It speaks individually, personally, privately, corporately. It speaks truth, it speaks leading and direction, it speaks hope, it speaks comfort, it speaks revelation, it speaks wisdom.

And it speaks in all these ways both *universally* and *individually*.

This, therefore, represents my attempt to speak out of the reservoir of *my* individuality what I believe to be some of the universal truths and themes contained in the Old Testament. But there remains one missing element to that equation—the individuality of *your* insights and perspectives and what God has made real in his Word…to *you*.

I therefore encourage you as you read, to add those commands, promises, truths, insights, and passages that have special meaning to you as God's Voice has spoken into *your* heart. I often encourage readers to write their own books, taking what I offer merely as a door leading into their own thoughts and observations. You may not publish a book on the commands of the Old Testament. (Though one of you may, who can tell!) But you can and should write your own personalized addition to these thoughts of mine. Whether it takes the form of your favorite verses, or insights God has shown you, or commands that are especially meaningful and challenging to you that have not been included, or promises from *Psalms*, for example, that have drawn you closer to God. Your personal book of thoughts, commands, promises, and insights might take any form. *Psalms* and *Proverbs* alone could yield twice as many entries as I have not had the space to include! The truths in God's Word are inexhaustible.

Personalize this book by writing your own!

Michael Phillips, 2023

Direct my footsteps according to your word.
Let no sin rule over me. Teach me your decrees.
The unfolding of your words gives light,
Direct me in the path of your commands,
Teach me knowledge and good judgment,
Give me understanding to learn your commands
so that I may keep your law and obey it with all my heart.
Psalm 119

Series One

Wisdom

Get Wisdom, Get Understanding

Walking in wisdom over a lifetime

God's gifts can be squandered if we do not obey the wisdom he gives us

More even than for his wealth and lavish lifestyle, Solomon is remembered for his wisdom. 1 Kings 3 is one of the truly remarkable chapters in the Bible, with enormous practical application for every one who chooses to follow the example of Solomon's prayer.

It may seem incongruous to begin with one of Israel's kings who was not technically a "prophet." I do so because the wisdom God gave Solomon undergirds the message of the entire Bible. Wisdom itself is the prophetic message of eternity. The universe will ultimately be drawn up into the very wisdom and being of God himself. Solomon can therefore be viewed as prophetically endowed by God to deliver the high thing—God's wisdom—to mankind in the down-to-earth garb of simple, living, do-able proverbs that can be practiced by any man or woman, anywhere, anytime. If we want to know what comprises the character, behavior, and thought patterns of a Godly man or woman, succinctly and practically, we find it in the book of *Proverbs*.

We are told: "Solomon loved the Lord, walking in the statutes of David his father." In hindsight we know that throughout the remainder of Solomon's life, *loving* the Lord did not necessarily translate into *obedience*. The wording of this verse is intriguing, Solomon walked more in the *example* of his father than in the statutes of God his father wrote about in Psalm 119.

Nevertheless when his first major test came as king, Solomon did well. God appeared to him in a dream and said to him, "Ask what shall I give you."

Solomon's answer is beautiful. It is worth quoting almost in full as a basis for a prayer we should all pray with regularity, a prayer I learned to pray from my faithful childhood pastor, the very prayer referenced by the Lord's brother in James 1:5:

> *"And Solomon said, 'Thou hast shown great and steadfast love to thy servant David my father, because he walked before thee in faithfulness, in righteousness, and in uprightness of heart...And now, O Lord my God, thou hast made thy servant king in place of David my father, although I am but a little child; I do not know how to go out or come in...Give thy servant therefore an understanding mind to govern thy people, that I may discern between good and evil; for who is able to govern this thy great people?'*
>
> *"It pleased the Lord that Solomon had asked this. And God said to him, 'Because you have asked this, and have not asked for yourself...but have asked for...understanding to discern what is right, behold, I now do according to your word. Behold, I give you a wise and discerning mind, so*

that none like you has been before you and none like you shall arise after you. I give you also what you have not asked, both riches and honor...And if you will walk in my ways, keeping my statutes and my commandments, as your father David walked, then I will lengthen your days.'" (1 Kings 3:6-14)

What a prayer: *Give me an understanding mind.*

What is so remarkable about this prayer and God's answer is that we possess the practical fruit of both prayer and answer crystallized in the book of *Proverbs*. It is a book that stands alone in Scripture for it proceeds directly out of God's answer to Solomon's prayer for wisdom.

Accompanying his wisdom and administrative ability, however, Solomon had an Achilles heel—he was too fond of the good life. His reputation as a womanizer with more than seven hundred wives is well documented. But the downfall of the kingdom after his death resulted from more than moral failings and spiritual disobedience. He built up such an opulent court and personal lifestyle, along with his temple building project, that the amount of money and labor to sustain his reign became crippling.

When we get to the other side, I believe that one of the most humble, soft spoken, Christlike saints of old we will meet may be Solomon. The grief and remorse of his failure to live by his own injunctions will have so purified his heart in the fire of God's loving forgiveness that he will be a humble and radiant reflection of that eternal Love. We may drink deeply from the waters of wisdom God gave the world through Solomon during his brief earthly sojourn, recognizing the flawed man he was, yet equally recognizing the humble child of God he was becoming. Would we not all say the same of ourselves? Flawed, weak, disobedient, often confused we are. But like Paul we keep our eyes on the high calling of what God may be able to make of us in the end.

The word "proverb" (Hebrew, *masal*) comes from a root meaning "to be like" or "to represent" or "to be compared with." Obviously its basic meaning is as a simile or analogy or allegory. Most proverbs are concise statements, usually of two lines, expressing a contrast between good and bad, wise and foolish, etc. Many general observations are given, however, without the corresponding contrast. Some are phrased as commands: "Do not love sleep or you will grow poor."

The use of figurative language is common: "Like cold water to a weary soul is good news from a distant land." In chapter 25 alone, as but one example, eleven verses begin with the comparatives "like" or "as." Such similes add to the pithy and vivid power of the proverbs. Many are also humorous or sarcastic: "Like a gold ring in a pig's snout is a beautiful woman who shows no discretion." The metaphors throughout the book are almost breathtaking, not only with the truth they speak but the picturesque imagery: "The teaching of the wise is a fountain of life," and "the tongue that brings healing is a tree of life."

Proverbs is the original *Life's Instruction Book*—a father preparing his son for life. Diligence and hard work are persistent themes. Wealth is usually seen as the fruit of righteousness. Wisdom, understanding, insight, discretion, honesty, uprightness, and justice are praised. Pride, arrogance, and foolishness will come to ruin, and the drunkard is the epitome of a fool.

By the admission of the text itself, Solomon did not write all the proverbs. The book has come to us as an assembled collection of wisdom from diverse sources.

One of the interesting features of *Proverbs* is the parallel—both in message and style though they appear dramatically different on the surface—with *Deuteronomy*. The so-called "deuteronomist" perspective follows a predictable sequence—God gives commands, consequences follow obedience or disobedience to those commands. Blessings follow as cause and effect to righteous living and spiritual faithfulness. Probably no book in the Bible so thoroughly underscores those actions, attitudes, and outcomes as the book of *Proverbs*.

The obvious difference between the outlook of *Proverbs* and Moses' commands in *Deuteronomy* is that the specific commands of God are not the driving force behind most of the proverbs. In a sense, they are impersonal—not spiritually driven but *life*-driven. The end result is the same—a dual set of opposite consequences which follow predictably from the actions and attitudes of either wisdom or foolishness.

- Moses said, *Choose life.*
- Solomon said, *Get wisdom.*

Proverbs rekindles Moses' message removed from the context of Israel's history and spiritual heritage. Here is the "Choice and Consequence Code" of *Deuteronomy* which we will consider in the second series of commands, stripped of its spiritual overtones, translating the principles into everyday life, common sense, relationships, and human character.

I view *Proverbs* as the "gospel" of the Hebrew Bible. By that I mean that it is the most practical book of the Old Testament, as I believe the gospels are in the New. The teachings of *Proverbs* resemble the principles of the Sermon on the Mount.

The wise man built his house on the rock…
The foolish man built his house on the sand…

We see the same pattern in *Proverbs*. Jesus, however, usually expands the core principle into a short story, while Solomon simply gives the essence of the thing and lets it stand.

Solomon states the principle:

The plans of the diligent lead surely to abundance, but every one who is hasty comes only to want. (21:5)

Jesus expands it into a brief story:

For which of you, desiring to build a tower, does not first sit down and count the cost, whether he has enough to complete it? Otherwise, when he has laid a foundation, and is not able to finish, all who see it begin to mock him, saying, "This man began to build, and was not able to finish." (Luke 14:28-29)

The proverbs, like Jesus' parables, are intended to be personal. They require a response. Which direction will we choose—wisdom or foolishness?

Its unmistakable gospel-practicality explains why I read the proverbs as commands. Most of them are not phrased in the format of command as are some of Jesus' words: *This is my commandment, that you love one another.*

But when I read,

When words are many, sin is not absent,
A man of understanding holds his tongue,
A fool delights in airing his own opinions,
Avoid a man who talks too much,
Listen, my son, and be wise,
He who heeds instruction is on the path to life,
The hand of the diligent will rule.

I take those as direct scriptural commands no less than what Jesus says in the Sermon on the Mount. I thus translate those proverbs to read:

Don't talk so much.
Hold your tongue.
Do not air your opinions.
Avoid long-winded people
Listen.
Heed instruction.
Work hard.

I take the liberty of such a lengthy introduction to this wisdom series of commands because, as I have mentioned before, more of the commands distributed through this volume come from *Proverbs* than any other biblical book.

The injunctions of *Proverbs* are intended to infuse and inform all aspects of our lives and our character with their truths. They are not to be isolated, but circulated, spread, disseminated throughout *everything* we do and think. The truths of *Proverbs* have equal weight and importance whether we're considering Moses or Malachi. They are whole-life, entire-Bible commands.

Proverbs is the most *practical* book in the Old Testament, if not in the Bible.

Series One

Wisdom

1. Listen to your father's instruction.

2. Love, cherish, seek, and pray for wisdom.

3. Though it cost all you have, get understanding.

4. Let wisdom, understanding, and discretion protect you.

5. Exercise prudence.

6. Don't act or speak hastily, and listen before speaking.

7. Do not speak thoughtlessly, or carelessly pass on gossip.

8. Trust God with all your heart,
and do not rely on your own understanding.

9. Acknowledge God in all your ways.

10. Find a husband or wife of noble character.

1. Listen to Your Father's Instruction

Hear, my son, your father's instruction…Hear, O sons, a father's instruction. (Proverbs 1:8; 4:1)

If the book of *Proverbs* could be succinctly summarized into a single command, it might read something like this: *Humbly listen and heed wisdom, insight, instruction, and correction, be prudent and diligent in all your affairs, speak with discretion, and choose relationships wisely.*

In other words:

Live wisely, responsibly, diligently, considerately, and with integrity.

Do we really need any more instruction for life than this?

Solomon begins with what is not a very politically correct command in today's cultural climate.

Listen to your dad.

His assumption is that fathers have used their life experiences to become men of sufficient wisdom to pass on good instruction—pointing to wisdom, responsibility, diligence, consideration, and integrity to their sons and daughters. Though nearly a quarter of *Proverbs* (the first seven chapters) is addressed to "sons" (which we read as "sons and daughters"), by implication they are equally directed at fathers (which we read as "parents").

If parents expect children to pay attention to Solomon's instructions about honoring and listening and heeding their advice, those fathers and mothers had better be living lives of wisdom, responsibility, diligence, consideration, and integrity themselves. Because the foundation that enables those qualities to be infused by teaching is parental *example*.

After a brief Prologue to open the book, Solomon begins in earnest at verse 8 of Proverbs 1:

"Hear, my son, your father's instruction, and reject not your mother's teaching."

The next six chapters all begin by addressing sons and exhorting them to listen. No age limit is specified. Children are to listen and heed their parents all their lives. Conversely, a heavy responsibility rests on fathers and mothers to *live* by wisdom. They are to pass on *wisdom*, not opinions rooted in character flaws, immaturities, and selfishnesses.

Solomon commands that *instruction in wisdom* be passed from parent to child, not *instruction in opinion.*

In other words, the command to heed a father's instruction is given validity in the integritous *life-example* and *wisdom* of that father.

When I read, *Hear, O sons, a father's instruction*, as chapter 4 begins, I think not only of my own sons, I also think of my father and *my* responsibility to continue heeding *his* wisdom in my life even though he has now been gone for a quarter century.

There is no end-point at which the command, "Hear, O sons, a father's instruction," no longer applies. I am seventy-seven. I am conscious every day of my prayerful desire to be an honoring *son* to the father God gave me as a window into his divine Fatherhood.

Though I love both fatherhood and Fatherhood, and emphasize them in every book I write, my sonship is more self-defining to my personhood than my fatherhood. Yet along with my sonship, I also reflect daily on my earthly fatherhood, and my responsibility to inculcate wisdom, truth, and character into my sons.

This rich command is full of a twofold exhortation:

- To earthly *sons and daughters* toward their parents all their lives.
- To earthly *fathers and mothers* to be wise and worthy transmitters of wisdom.

I am continually moved by Solomon's example as we have it in 1 Kings 3. A grown man and now king of Israel, had he been a modernist Solomon would have said, "No more parental shackles! I'm my own man now!"

But his words give a wonderful and loving tribute to his father, then acknowledge, not his kingship, but his *childship*:

> *O Lord my God, thou hast made thy servant king in place of David my father, although I am but a little child; I do not know how to go out or come in.*

What an example Solomon set before us in that moment!

It is upon this foundation—*I am but a little child*—that Solomon embarks upon the *Proverbs*. He is able to speak with authority because he understands both halves of the holy relationship. He understands *fatherhood* and the role of the wise father to transmit wisdom to his sons and daughters. And he understands his own *sonship* as a recipient of wisdom from both his earthly and heavenly fathers.

It is out of that dual reservoir that Solomon speaks with such power in the opening chapters of *Proverbs*. George MacDonald states this truth that originates in the Godhead in many ways throughout his writings:

> Nobody knows what the relation of father and son may yet come to…For is it not a reproduction in small of the loftiest mystery in human ken—that of the infinite Father and infinite Son? If man be made in the image of God, then is the human fatherhood and sonship the image of the eternal relation between God and Jesus.
>
> The relation of the Father and the Son contains the idea of the universe…
>
> The child-relation is the one eternal, ever enduring, never changing relation.*

* George MacDonald, *The Hope of the Gospel,* "The Yoke of Jesus," and *Warlock O'Glenwarlock*, ch. 24.

Understanding fatherhood *and* sonship, Solomon understands wisdom.

I thank you again, God, from the bottom of my heart, for the dear father you gave me. He did not possess the nature of a teacher, nor was he a vocal, expressive, or outwardly spiritual man. Instead you gave me the privilege of learning to discover where his fathering wisdom was hidden in more elusive aspects of his character. You taught me how to receive from him in subtle ways—how to feed upon, learn from, and grow to appreciate the virtue his example instilled in me. I thank you for what that learning and discovering process taught me about your Fatherhood. Even though he is now with you, help me to continue learning from him, from the man he was. Imbue my memories with the instruction you have for me as my heavenly Father, through my earthly father. May I always be listening, and may my spirit never cease receiving wisdom from both my fathers.

2. Love, Cherish, Seek, and Pray for Wisdom

Get wisdom; get insight…The beginning of wisdom is this: Get wisdom. (Proverbs 4: 4, 7)

Echoing his father's abiding love for God's statutes, precepts, and commands, Solomon not only speaks repeatedly of *love* for wisdom, he *commands* us to love wisdom. We will never attain anything in life that we don't love enough to pursue. Loving wisdom is therefore the starting point for growing into wisdom.

Obviously this command originated in Solomon's own heart. He loved wisdom above all things he could have asked God for.

Most people would say they would like to be wise? *Sure, that would be nice…why not…yeah, I guess I would like to be wise.*

It doesn't work that way. Wisdom comes to those who ask God for it, and then who pursue it diligently, living by what they know of wisdom, all their lives. Wisdom only comes from seeking it with all one's heart.

The significant life-question, then—one of the most important character-defining questions every human being faces in some way, however subtle it comes, however unrecognized it may be—is a simple one:

If the genie (who is God!) gave me *one* wish he would grant…what would I wish for?

One thing…*one* wish.

How many would give the answer Solomon gave?

Do I love wisdom enough to pursue it as one of my highest life priorities?

The wisdom of Christlikeness is truly life's ultimate pot of gold. Yet how many are seeking it, praying for it, learning to walk in that wisdom as life's ultimate attainment? Christlikeness and wisdom are two sides of the same coin. Christlikeness is the New Covenantal gospel-flowering of wisdom.

One of the magnificent verses in the Bible, one of my top five, is found in Proverbs 4:7.

The beginning of wisdom is this: Get wisdom.

These words have been hanging in my office for twenty years on a hand lettered plaque given as a gift from my son Gregory, who knew them to be among my favorite verses. The circular wording always sends me into a tailspin of humorous and prayerful introspection. How do you grow in wisdom? By getting wisdom. How do you get wisdom? By getting wisdom.

This injunction is truly remarkable in its simplicity. The wording is strangely incongruous, beginning with a declarative, then climaxing with the command. The normal parallelism of *Proverbs* is missing. It seems grammatically off, yet is so brilliantly succinct. Circular reasoning is usually a flawed approach to understanding. But in this case, by a brilliant contradiction, Solomon's phrasing of this mighty truth hits the bull's eye dead center.

His words are not accidental. He repeats them over and over. Wisdom has to be pursued, loved, and diligently sought. To get it you have to…*get* it.

There is a miraculous God-infused component to wisdom's growth in any man or woman. But that God-infused aspect of wisdom only grows in those who pray for and set their heart's compass toward wisdom. This setting of the heart's compass begins with the previous command:

When I was a son with my father…he taught me and said to me,
"Let your heart hold fast to my words; keep my commandments, and live;
do not forget, and do not turn away…
Get wisdom; get insight…
The beginning of wisdom is this: Get wisdom." (Proverbs 4:3-5, 7)

If only these first two commandments were foundational to the world's outlook, how different might be the condition of humanity upon the earth.

For the Christian, wisdom is the highest personal character attribute that can be sought. So many spiritual principles are vague and nebulous. Paul rates faith, hope, and love as the three highest things. But faith is an elusive commodity. You cannot simply *get* faith. We are commanded to abide in Christ. Likewise, the abiding life is elusive. Humility, meekness, righteousness…all these are both objectives and fruits of the Christlike life. But they grow slowly.

Wisdom, however, is different. We are not commanded to wait for it to permeate our hearts and minds by osmosis. We are commanded to *get* it.

Jesus' words echo Solomon's. Wisdom must be loved enough to be sought, prayed for, pursued, and lived: "Ask, and it will be given you; seek, and you will find; knock, and it will be opened to you."

Wisdom is infused into character in two stages.

- First we *ask.*

James writes: *If any of you lacks wisdom, let him ask God who gives to all men generously.* (James 1:5)

This is exactly what Solomon did. He *asked* God for wisdom.

- Then we *live.*

We live wisdom. We live the proverbs. We *do* wisdom.

The proverbs were written precisely to give us common sense guidance in exactly that ask-then-live sequence.

> *The proverbs of Solomon...that men may know wisdom...*
>
> *My son, if you receive my words and treasure up my commandments within you... if you cry out for insight...and search for it as for hidden treasure, then you will understand... the knowledge of God. For the Lord gives wisdom... Then you will understand righteousness and justice and equity, every good path; for wisdom will come into your heart.* (Proverbs 1:1-2; 2:1, 3-6, 9-10)

When I work hard, listen, take advice, avoid airing my own opinion, give generously, refuse to chase fantasies, avoid drink, walk in humility, act cheerful, avoid the foolish, seek friends of character, and am patient...I have been wise.

There is no waiting. I have *done* wisdom.

And as one continues to live and do wisdom through countless obediences, slowly over many years the high thing permeates more and more corners of character.

When I was in college visiting my childhood pastor, our conversation turned toward wisdom. I asked him a simple question, "But *how* do you grow in wisdom?"

His answer was so quick, so spontaneous, and so simple that it almost shocked me.

"Ask God for it! Just like James says."

His words struck deep. I began praying Solomon's prayer that same day. I have been asking God to develop wisdom within me ever since. My earthly eyes see little fruit. But I live in the belief and expectation that all our deepest longings that we have sent by prayer into God's heart will be fulfilled in eternity. In that knowledge I continue to pray, and am quietly at peace.

I renew my prayer for wisdom, God. I cherish wisdom and I desire to live by it. I cry out for it. With Solomon I say, I am but a little child; I do not know how to go out or come in...Give me therefore an understanding mind. Give me insight into wisdom, help me daily to do wisdom and live in wisdom. And may you, heavenly Father, though my efforts are so small, infuse wisdom by degrees into my deepest character and being.

3. Though it Cost You all You Have, Get Understanding

The beginning of wisdom is this: Get wisdom.
Though it cost all you have, get understanding. (Proverbs 4:7, NIV)

Praying for wisdom, even sincerely, is the easy part. I meant it with all my heart when I first prayed for wisdom at just over the age of twenty. But I was young. I had no idea what I was in for. It was one (of many!) idealistic prayers of my youth.

Such prayers are important at whatever season of life they come—whether at twenty, forty, sixty, or eighty. They set the compass. They orient our earthly life directions, whether we have a lifetime before us (at twenty) or are looking ahead to eternity (at eighty). They establish personal and character objectives.

Then the hard work begins.

Thus Solomon adds this hugely pivotal corollary which is intrinsic to wisdom. There's a cost involved. It may cost you everything.

Wisdom and understanding don't come cheap. You don't find wisdom and understanding on life's bargain table.

They may begin in idealism, but they grow in the soil of practical reality, sometimes in pain, and *always* through difficult decisions and unexpected circumstances. Not only do we have to love and seek and pray for wisdom…we have to *do* wisdom, *be* wisdom, and *choose* wisdom in the crucibles, pains, and disappointments life throws at us.

Wisdom costs.

As I have reflected on and tried to live in the challenging reality of the first four chapters of *Proverbs*, I have been fascinated by the complex interplay between wisdom and understanding. They seem interchangeable. Yet Solomon does not use them precisely as synonyms. Both have fascinating nuances. Only the wise can truly understand the deep things of God. In that sense they are so linked as to be almost synonymous.

Yet it is possible to "understand" certain aspects of life in a wisdom-less vacuum. How many scientists, politicians, psychologists, and economists, not to mention progressive modernists and even theologians, *understand* the facts within their respective fields without a clue into the eternal realities that make the universe tick.

They possess *knowledge*, and with that knowledge comes some true level of *understanding* within their fields. But *what* do they understand? Does their technical understanding reach to life's highest, most important, and eternal truths?

Splitting analytical hairs is not my intent, but to come to grips with the intricate connection between wisdom and understanding. To put it in Solomon's logically circular phraseology, we might say:

To understand wisdom we have to understand wisdom.

This is why wisdom is so lacking in the world, and even in the church—because so few are seeking to understand life's *highest* truths and principles. They are satisfied with knowledge, but rarely look higher to the Author of knowledge. They don't ask what story that Author is writing in their various fields of knowledge, or what story that Author desires to write in their own lives.

Not asking what knowledge *means*, how can they understand and grow wise?

The high understanding that rises above knowledge and leads to the inner sanctum of wisdom, to the front of the tapestry, to borrow an image from George MacDonald, cannot be got at intellectually. Intellectualism, indeed, is a sterile soil, yet is the soil in which most of the world's knowledge grows, though in truth it leads to many *false* understandings that masquerade as the real thing.

True *understanding* comes from seeking the Author's high story of life.

> We are here in a region far above that commonly claimed for science, open only to the heart of the child and the childlike man and woman...For things as they are, not as science deals with them, are the revelation of God to his children...neither fact nor law is there for the sake of fact or law; each is but a mean to an end; in the perfected end we find the intent, and there God—not in the laws themselves, save as his means. For that same reason, human science cannot discover God; for human science is but the backward undoing of the tapestry-web of God's science, works with its back to him...Doubtless it thus makes some small intellectual approach to him, but at best it can come only to his back; science will never find the face of God; while those who would reach his heart...will find also the spring-head of his science. Analysis...discovers a little of the way God walks to his ends, but in so doing it forgets and leaves the end itself behind...the very process of his work...is a following back of his footsteps, too often without appreciation of the result for which the feet took those steps...If the man could find out why God worked so, then he would be discovering God; but even then he would not be discovering the best and the deepest of God; for his means cannot be so great as his ends.*

The highest Understanding, like Wisdom itself, comes from learning to see from the Author's perspective. He set the ways and means of the universe in motion. How else can we understand them but by seeing what he sees, that is, turning from the back-strings of the tapestry to behold the glory of what God is weaving that all the universe will one day behold in its fullness.

I have not had to pay a high price for my faith, Lord God. My walk with you has not cost me all I have. You have blessed me beyond measure. Yet my understanding of your ways is still so small. I hardly know myself well enough to know if I am willing to pay the cost of everything I have to understand you more fully. But I want to be willing. Help me to be willing. Deepen my understanding whatever the cost.

---

* George MacDonald, *Unspoken Sermons, Third Series,* "The Truth."

4. Let Wisdom, Understanding, and Discretion Protect You

Wisdom will enter your heart, and knowledge will be pleasant to your soul.
Discretion will watch over you and understanding will guard you. (Proverbs 2:10-11)

Solomon is so exquisitely elegant, first in his exhortation to wisdom, then in describing the character fruits and life blessings of wisdom, that it is beyond belief how he could have allowed his morals to deteriorate as they did. Proverbs 2 must surely stand alongside 1 Corinthians 13 as among the poetic masterpieces of Scripture. Solomon is a peerless writer. God gifted him with more blessings than wisdom.

The first eleven verses are worth setting down in full as conveying Solomon's wisdom with far more profound insight and stylistic grace than I could.

My son, if you receive my words and treasure my commands within you,
tuning your ear to wisdom and inclining your heart to understanding,
if you cry out for insight, seeking it like silver
and searching for it as for hidden treasure,
then you will understand the fear of the Lord and find the knowledge of God. For the Lord gives wisdom,
and from his mouth come knowledge and understanding.
He stores up wisdom for the upright
and is a shield to those who walk in integrity.
Then you will understand righteousness, justice, and equity, every good path.
Wisdom will enter your heart, and knowledge will be pleasant to your soul.
Discretion will watch over you and understanding will guard you.
(Proverbs 2:1-11, author paraphrase)

The book of *Proverbs* is about wisdom. It describes how wisdom lives, behaves, thinks, talks, and relates to people. It thus describes the *character* of a whole, integrated, mature man or woman. Solomon repeatedly emphasizes seven attributes that combine to make up the high thing of wisdom. Taken together, these characterize the man or woman walking in wisdom:

- *Understanding.*
- *Knowledge.*
- *Integrity.*
- *Discretion.*
- *Insight.*
- *Prudence.*
- *Righteousness.*

We find these seven attributes throughout *Proverbs* characterizing the wise man, and their opposites characterizing the foolish man. We are told to *get* wisdom, and to let these qualities of character guard and protect us.

Proverbs 9:1 reads, "Wisdom has built her house, she has set up her seven pillars."

Though that verse does not specify what the pillars are, I take some interpretive liberty by reading the above character qualities as exemplifying the pillars that uphold the house of wisdom. They support the dome that overspreads the individual proverbs. The specifics of all the proverbs give colorful, pithy, often humorous individual practicalities to illuminate how wisdom and these seven attributes are to be lived within the house of wisdom. Then they reveal evidences of either living by them or their opposites.

How, then, do we "let" them protect us? In the same way that we "get" wisdom.

By *doing* them.

- *Do, live, be, choose understanding.*
- *Do, live, be, choose knowledge.*
- *Do, live, be, choose integrity.*
- *Do, live, be, choose discretion.*
- *Do, live, be, choose insight.*
- *Do, live, be, choose prudence.*
- *Do, live, be, choose righteousness.*

The following passage from George MacDonald's *The Marquis of Lossie* illuminates this *do* as the doorway into the seven-pillared house of wisdom. Without this *do*, all attempts to understand God's perspectives will fail. In the story, a searching young lady asks a pastor why a young fisher lad understands God's truths, while so many more educated religious types do not.

> *"There is a far more important factor concerned than this exceptional degree of insight. Understanding is the reward of obedience...Obedience is the key to every door. I am perplexed at the stupidity of the ordinary religious being. In the most practical of all matters, he will talk, and speculate, and try to feel, but he will not set himself to do. It is different with Malcolm. From the first he has been trying to obey...If a man may not understand the things of God whence he came, what shall he understand?"*
>
> *"How, then, is it that so few do understand?"*
>
> *"Because where they know, so few obey."* *

Elsewhere MacDonald elaborates:

> Our business is not to think correctly, but to live truly; then first will there be a possibility of our thinking correctly. One chief cause of the amount of unbelief in the world is, that those who have seen something of the glory of Christ, set themselves to theorize concerning him rather than to obey him....More eager after credible theory than after doing the truth, they have speculated in a condition of heart in which it was impossible they should understand; they have

* George MacDonald, *The Marquis of Lossie,* chapter 53, "A New Pupil."

presumed to explain a Christ whom years and years of obedience could alone have made them able to comprehend. Their teaching of him, therefore, has been repugnant to the common sense of many. *

Men would understand: they do not care to obey;—understand where it is impossible they should understand save by obeying...They delay setting their foot on the stair which alone can lead them to the house of wisdom, until they shall have determined the material and mode of its construction. For the sake of knowing, they postpone that which alone can enable them to know, and substitute for the true understanding...a false persuasion that they already understand...It is on them that do his will, that the day dawns; to them the day-star arises in their hearts. Obedience is the soul of knowledge...† Obedience is the opener of eyes. ‡

Guide me and protect me, Lord, according to your wisdom. Give me discretion and understanding to walk in your ways and to obey your commands. Keep the seven pillars of wisdom ever before me. Deepen their multi-faceted truths into my subconscious even when I am not thinking of them. Build them into my character. Infuse them into my motives. Spread them through my being as I sleep, remind me of them when I wake. May my relationships, my words, my thoughts, my responses, my expressions, and my heart's desires be informed both consciously and subconsciously by understanding, knowledge, integrity, discretion, insight, prudence, and righteousness.

5. Exercise Prudence

Learn prudence...I, wisdom, dwell in prudence...and discretion. (Proverbs 8:5, 12)

It would obviously be simplistic to say that all the proverbs of *Proverbs* could be incorporated under the heading of "prudence."

So I won't say it. But I will *hint* at it.

Prudence is but one of the seven pillars, yet it is singularly down-to-earth and practical, exactly as are most of the proverbs. Understanding, integrity, knowledge, and righteousness all point to ideals that are not always easy to translate into reality in the next five minutes.

But prudence is easily the most practical of the seven pillars. If we look hard enough, we can probably detect prudence in most of the proverbs. This is not meant to be a catch-all generalization, but an important summarizing outlook and perspective illuminating how prudence protects us from foolish decisions.

Unlike the other pillars, when I walk out the door, prudence is *instantly* do-able.

* George MacDonald, *Unspoken Sermons, Third Series,* "Justice."
† George MacDonald, *The Hope of the Gospel,* "Salvation From Sin."
‡ George MacDonald, *Unspoken Sermons, Second Series,* "The Way."

—Is it starting to sprinkle? I had better go back for an umbrella or raincoat. *Prudence.*

—Do I have an appointment scheduled this afternoon? I had better plan out my day so I am not late. *Prudence.*

—Is a pointless argument brewing with a cantankerous know-it-all? I should graciously excuse myself and walk away. *Prudence.*

—Is my car's gas tank a quarter-full with two busy days facing me? I had better fill up today rather than trying to squeeze it in tomorrow. *Prudence*

—Is a new acquaintance acting foolishly and crossing ethical lines? I had better not draw closer into friendship. *Prudence.*

—In a discussion with friends, do I have no wisdom to offer? Then it would be wise for me to keep silent rather than entering the back-and-forth exchange of opinions. *Prudence.*

—Am I planning a project that will involve financial costs? Then I had better consider those costs so I am able to complete it. *Prudence.*

—Is my weak knee acting up? I had better not take the walk I was planning over rugged terrain, and choose a different route. *Prudence.*

—Have I been given a word of counsel from one I trust? Then I had better consider his or her advice carefully. *Prudence.*

—Am I being pressured to join in something everyone else is doing? I had better consider my steps warily before following the crowd. *Prudence.*

—Am I suddenly aware that I am monopolizing a conversation? I had better shut up. *Prudence.*

—Am I facing a difficult decision and am puzzled about which way to go? I had better seek counsel from wise people I trust. *Prudence.*

The need for prudence comes at us all day long from every direction. It is a favorite topic in Thomas Kempis's 15th century classic *The Imitation of Christ.* Kempis's work could have been taken straight from *Proverbs*:

> The more humble a man is in himself, and the more subject to God; so much the more prudent shall he be in all his affairs.
> Grant me prudently to avoid him that flatters me.
> It is no small prudence to keep silence in an evil time.

Dictionary definitions, so often stale and lifeless, in this case offers down-to-earth practicality:

> Prudence: Wisdom in handling practical matters, the exercise of good judgment and common sense, care about one's interests and conduct, circumspection and discretion.

The ancient Latin root that stems from "foreseeing" adds yet another layer of insight. Prudence *foresees* and plans accordingly.

When I taught our sons to drive, I emphasized always being on the lookout for potential dangerous situations—watchful, careful, scanning right and left and back, trying to anticipate and foresee what other drivers might do, driving warily and defensively.

This sums up prudence—cautiously, carefully, and watchfully anticipating potential outcomes and responding wisely.

Keep me from thoughtless imprudence, Father. Slow me down enough to see the need for prudence ahead of time. Give me good judgment, common sense, circumspection, and discretion to be conscious of potential hazards that may lie in my path. Give me prudent wisdom in decision making. More than this, I ask you to use my prudent behaviour and decisions to weave prudence ever more deeply into my character. Grow me into a prudent man.

6. Don't Act or Speak Hastily, and Listen Before Speaking

Do you see a man who is hasty in his words? There is more hope for a fool than for him…
To answer before listening…is folly. (Proverbs 29:20; 18:13, RSV, NIV)

I speak frequently in my writings about the tendency to react quickly and hastily rather than calmly and circumspectly. I emphasize it because it represents such a fundamental component of wisdom on the one side (calm, deliberate circumspection in behavior, decisions, and speech habits) and foolishness on the other (rash behavior and decisions, and inappropriately random, opinionated talk). I also stress prudence in speech because I know how much I need to be reminded of it myself!

Wisdom waits, considers, weighs options, and listens.

Foolishness reacts, jumps ahead, does not weigh options, and talks too much.

Proverbs is full of examples illuminating the contrast.

- "A wise man is cautious." (14:16, RSV)
- "He who restrains his lips is prudent." (10:19, RVS)
- "To answer before listening—that is folly and shame." (18:13, NIV)
- "A fool uttereth all his mind, but a wise man keepeth it in. (29:11, KJV)
- "Do you see a man who is hasty in his words? There is more hope for a fool than for him. (29:20, RSV)

And also from Solomon's *Ecclesiastes*:

- "Be not rash with your mouth, nor let your heart be hasty to utter a word. (Ecclesiastes 5:2, RSV)

I emphasize these opposite patterns of behavior and speech because the Bible emphasizes them, and because my own experience bears out exactly what the Bible says. James and Solomon are scathing in their condemnation of loose-tongued speech.

These are not idle and insignificant personality distinctions. Loose speech is a sin. Talking too much is selfish and insensitive. Making rash decisions may cause harm to many people.

These are *serious* character flaws that too few people take with the thoughtful-mindedness they deserve.

Obviously living the proverbs requires balance. Along with individuals whose lives are characterized by one foolish and hasty decision after another, I have known others who are so indecisive that they are fearful to make decisions at all. Decisions are intrinsic to daily life. To be cliché about it, it's the *haste* that makes waste.

Nor are we to *stop* talking. Conversation and mutual dialogue are the lubricants of relationship. But how different are the speech patterns of the wise and the foolish.

The wise:

- "The mind of the wise makes his speech judicious." (16:23, RSV)
- "Wisdom is found on the lips of the discerning." (10:13, NIV)
- "Gracious words are…sweet to the soul." (16:24, NIV)
- "A word fitly spoken is like apples of gold in a setting of silver." (25:11, RSV)

The foolish:

- 'The babbling of a fool brings ruin." (10:14, RSV)
- "A fool is right in his own eyes." (12:15, RSV)
- "Fools…delight in airing their own opinions." (18:2, NIV)
- "A fool's lips bring strife." (18:6, RSV)

The intriguing point is that *everybody* knows this, but few make a concerted or lifetime attempt to change it in themselves. They might try to watch themselves more carefully for a day or two, but then slip back into the same habit patterns.

I happened to bring up Thomas Kempis to a particularly loquacious friend recently, having no idea whether he/she had ever read a word of *The Imitation.* I was surprised at how knowledgeable she/he actually was. Interestingly, she/he then referenced Kempis's many injunctions to silence. "I know I talk too much," he/she said…and then went on talking for ten more minutes without a break, moving from topic to topic to topic without coming up for air. When the conversation ended and our friend left, I hadn't offered a single word to the conversation after my initial mention of Kempis.

Not that I had anything profound to add. Kempis speaks for himself. But the response was so intriguing—"I know I talk too much...so I will just keep on talking and talking."

Most talkers have little interest in listening. They are singularly skilled at changing directions in their monologues without so much as an intake of breath. No one else has a chance to squeeze in a word between topics.

Knowing they ought to be better listeners, most inveterate talkers simply don't care enough to make the effort to address the habit.

Of course habits are hard to change. But bad habits that ignore the Bible's commands are serious scriptural business, with serious character consequences.

Having brought Kempis into the discussion, let me add that his admonitions are as pithy and timeless as when he wrote them 650 years ago.

- Our own opinion and our own sense often deceive us, and they discern but little.
- Do not give ear to every suggestion, but...leisurely...ponder things according to the will of God.
- Be not too confident in your own opinion; but be willing to hear the judgment of others.
- Each one's opinion may be good; but to refuse to yield to others...is a sign of pride and stiffness.
- Often I wish that I had held my peace sooner than have spoken.
- You will be more glad that you have kept silence, than that you have talked much.
- It is no small prudence to keep silence in an evil time.
- How truly profitable has grace been...preserved in silence.
- It is great wisdom not to be rash in your proceedings. *

Wisdom waits, ponders, thinks, and prays to know the will of God. Wisdom is not rash in its responses, its words, its reactions...nor in all its proceedings.

Close my mouth, Holy Spirit, and open my ears. Sting my awareness before I make a hasty response. Give me wisdom to wait, ponder, think, and ask what is your will. Give me wisdom not to be rash in reacting to news, to stressful situations, even to crisis. Keep me calm. Remind me to be quick to listen and slow to speak.

* Selections from Thomas Kempis, *The Imitation of Christ.*

7. Do Not Speak Thoughtlessly, or Carelessly Pass on Gossip

Whoever…spreads slander is a fool. A perverse person stirs up conflict, and a gossip separates close friends. (Proverbs 10:18; 16:28, NIV)

Just like the prayers of Solomon's father David, the proverbs are *intensely* personal. They hit us profoundly in the deep places where we live with God. Solomon isn't concerned with enemies and idols and war as were Moses and Joshua, but about how we behave and talk and relate to those around us every day.

It doesn't get more personal than that! This is down-to-earth life.

Gossip comes in many forms. The word is so specific that it is easy to assume, "Oh, I'm not a gossip. I know better than that!"

Solomon, however, warns against a wide range of careless speech habits that may not technically fall under the heading of *gossip*, but that we nevertheless thoughtlessly fall into. It may seem like a strange message for the Old Testament, but careless speech, foretelling James's warnings in chapter three of his New Testament letter, is one of Solomon's most repeated cautions. Careless speech is always identified with foolish people, and always leads to bad results.

Two other words Solomon uses that we may also dismiss too casually are *slander* and *falsehood*. Again, the easy response is, "I would *never* slander or spread falsehoods."

But gossip, slander, and falsehood are examples of a more general sin: *Talking thoughtlessly and carelessly about others.*

How often do we pass on thoughts and observations, colored with subtleties that imply character flaws or failings? In a general sense, true or not, that is slander.

If what we convey isn't *completely* true? Then we may be guilty of spreading falsehoods. It doesn't matter that it may be unintentionally. We've put a falsehood into the mind of whoever has been listening to our careless words. It may go on from there and be spread to others. My loose and careless tongue may set a whole string of falsehoods in motion.

This is an enormously imperative spiritual principle. Yet it is as ignored as it is imperative. As clear in Scripture as they are, are even these two successive commands (#s 6-7), coming at it from different angles, enough to stem the tide of careless speech habits in God's church?

Talking frivolously about others is so common we don't think twice about it.

Years ago, Judy and I were convicted by the simple prescription: "If you're not part of the problem, or part of the solution, it's none of your business. Say nothing"

Yet listening to and passing on tidbits of news about others is one of the delicious spices of life. "The words of a gossip are like a choice morsel," writes Solomon in Proverbs 18:8. The impact of his insight can be devasting, because, as he continues, "they go down to the inmost parts."

People don't forget what they've heard—whether true or not!

Worse, careless words separate, create dissension, suspicion, judgment, and division. Good never results. *A perverse person stirs up conflict, and a gossip separates close friends.* (Proverbs 16:28, NIV)

It's impossible to escape the swirl of gossip from news-mongers. People *love* being "in the know." Being the *first* to know is the greatest prize of all!

They especially love disseminating everyone else's news. People have dog ears that perk up toward every wind of suggestion that floats by from loose and careless tongues eager to spread those suggestions and flame the fires of newsy gossip. This is no mere minor character habit. This is a serious, faith-numbing, *chosen* pattern that is dangerous to spiritual growth. Passing on news is nothing less than a disease.

Recognizing this, Judy and I have made it a high priority to recognize that other people's news and business, and the doings of their lives, are *not* ours to share. We give each other a scissors-sign when one of us is getting too talkative. When something comes into our hearing of another's business, it's hard not to pass it on. It's easy to forget that doing so is sin. The Scriptures command against it. Other people's business is *their* business. To whom does the "news" belong? They and they *alone* have the right to share it. We even apply this to one another when we refrain from telling each other everything we chance hear about someone else. In a sense, we try to protect each other from forming potential wrong judgments about others.

It's all the more important not to talk about people because not everything you hear is true. I may pass on a falsehood without realizing it. Not all gossipy news is true.

Thomas Kempis counsels "not to believe everything which you hear…" He then adds the forceful admonition applicable in our lives a dozen times a day: "…nor…to repeat again to others what you have heard."

That is such a powerful injunction that it bears repeating:

Nor to repeat to others what you have heard.

The point is not that it is *never* appropriate to speak seriously about important ideas. Kempis is warning against haste, carelessness, and fleshly responses. Having gobbled up gullibly "everything we hear," the foolish man or woman turns *presently* and rushes out to repeat it to the next person they meet, without waiting to find out whether it's even true.

Minding our own business is one of Kempis's signature tunes in his *Imitation of Christ.*

- We might enjoy much peace, if we would not busy ourselves with the words and deeds of other men…with things which appertain nothing to our charge.
- Meddle not with curiosities.
- If you will withdraw yourself from speaking vainly, and from gadding idly, and also from hearkening after novelties and rumors, you shall find leisure enough and suitable for meditation on good things.
- If you had not…hearkened to idle rumors, you would the better have preserved a happy peace of mind.

- Grace cares not to hear news.
- He that diligently attends unto himself, can easily keep silence concerning others.
- Do not busy yourself in matters which appertain to others, neither entangle yourself in their affairs.
- O how good is it and tending to peace, to be silent about other men…nor too easily to hand on reports.
- Neither entangle yourself with business not committed to you.

Help me, God, not to be curious about others. Keep me from a meddlesome curiosity and from the desire to insert myself in business that is not committed to me and is none of my business. Alert my conscience the moment I begin carelessly to pass on something I have heard about another. Please rid me of the cancer of gossip. Whatever it takes, help me learn silence.

8. Trust God with All Your Heart, and Do Not Rely on Your Own Understanding

Trust in the Lord with all your heart, and do not rely on your own insight. (Proverbs 3:5)

From what is surely one of the most practically down-to-earth commands in this book, we turn in a dramatically different direction—to a deeply private, spiritual, inner command that can be obeyed only in the depths of our hearts and minds. I would not call it *impractical*. In our individual responses, we can discover practicality in all God's commands. At the same time, we would all admit that learning *how* to "trust God" in our daily lives presents challenges in its moment-by-moment application.

I speak of the two halves of Proverbs 3:5-6 together (commands #8 and #9) because this passage, and God's promise to direct our paths when we trust and acknowledge him, has deep and personal meaning for me. As a young man, in the process of developing a growing personal faith of my own, God used this promise in a vivid way to say very dramatically to me:

"I really am here…I am watching out for you…I am listening…and I *will* direct your paths."

A friend and I were on our way in Germany to a city of 60,000 to meet the third of our summer's European work-and-travel trio. He was visiting an acquaintance, but we had no address, no phone number, and did not know how to spell the family's name which we had only heard by word of mouth. Nor did our friend know when we were coming. Obviously we weren't paying much attention to the prudence and wise planning proverbs! But sometimes God teaches us one lesson at a time.

Imprudent as it may have been, I was full of my newly burgeoning life with God. I simply took these verses as written. We did not need to do more than trust God, acknowledge him, take the promise at face value that he would lead us…and off we went. I had supreme confidence that God would indeed direct our paths and lead us straight to our friend wherever he happened to be amid that sixty thousand!

We drove into the center of the city, walked into one of the city's governmental buildings and began asking questions…and an hour later were with our friend. I still look back on the series of events with awe. It has been a reminder all my life that God really means what he says.

Our steps were…*led.* Our path was…*directed.*

Ever since I've lived in the confidence that God *means* the composite truth contained in these two verses. With all my heart I believe that Solomon wrote these words inspired by God to convey to his people a promise that can and *will* orient their lives Godward if they live by the magnificent truth it contains.

It is an *If-Then* promise, exactly as we discussed in the introduction. It is comprised of four parts. The *if* has three components. Then follows the *promise*:

If you:

- *Trust God…*
- *Don't rely on your own understanding…*
- *Acknowledge him…*

Then:

- *He will direct your paths.*

I love this progression. It describes a full-life orientation, and the outcome of living by that perspective. Proverbs 3:5-6 might be said to succinctly summarize the entire Christian life. Jesus, of course, adds much specificity to what it means to trust and acknowledge God and not rely on oneself. But the general foundation is found in these two verses.

Knowing *how* to live within this overarching life-perspective, however, is difficult and complex. That's why we have the gospels. That's why we have the rest of the Bible's commands—to add specificity to the *how.*

Trusting God is a deeply personal exchange that takes place in the heart between myself and God, an exchange, a yielding, an acknowledgment, a laying down, that involves no one else but myself and God. It takes place in the "secret heart" spoken of by David when he prayed for wisdom in Psalm 51:6.

I can't tell you how to "trust God" in *your* secret heart any more than you can tell me how to do so in mine. Those are revelations God gives us…quietly, individually.

They don't usually come as dramatically as God's promise was made real to me that day in Germany in 1969. That took place over fifty years ago. I've never had quite such a singularly dramatic experience of God's leading since. If we're fortunate, God might give us one or two of those experiences in our lifetimes to remind us, "Hey, I'm here…I'm listening!"

They are meant to point to something deeper—a moment-by-moment orientation of trust and non-self-reliance. The lifetime purpose is not so that he will miraculously intervene, but so that our hearts will be established in a *continual* inner attitude, even if unconsciously, of yielding trust.

I thank you again, Lord, for that memorable day when you taught me the practicality of trusting you. May it be more than a memory. Though I may not see such visible outcomes, I desire to trust you with all my heart. It is not easy to keep from relying on my own understanding. Self-reliance is the default of humanity. But my understanding is not always to be trusted. Remind me that one of my life purposes is to kill that default within my heart and brain, and to default instead to trusting you. Help me slow down, still my brain, and yield in trust to your leading.

9. Acknowledge God in All Your Ways

In all your ways acknowledge him, and he will direct your paths. (Proverbs 3:6, RSV & KJV)

The third element of the "if" which leads to the then-promise of Proverbs 3:5-6 comes in verse 6. In some ways *acknowledging* God might be easier to understand than *trusting* God. It is equally easy to *mis*understand. While "trust" can be mistaken as a one-time event (praying a prayer to "trust Christ for salvation") rather than a lifetime's heart attitude, *acknowledging* God can be mistaken as external, visible, and vocal—carried out with bumper stickers, witnessing agendas, church involvement, and other external identifications of your profession of belief.

But *one-time trust* and *visible acknowledgment* miss the mark intended by these two magnificent verses by a country mile.

The telling phrase "in all your ways" clearly indicates something far more profound and lifelong. *All your ways* can't be accomplished with a one-time prayer or a bumper sticker. The impossibility of the *all* is the same impossibility as Paul's *pray without ceasing*. For these two commands—

In all your ways acknowledge him,
Pray without ceasing,

—to have practical meaning, they have to reach beyond external evidences, manifestations, words, or actions. On the conscious level of thought, both the *all* and the *without ceasing* are impossible. Their scope lies beyond our conscious minds altogether, probing into far deeper regions of personhood.

Those deeper regions are the domains where motive and heart's desire set the directionality of life focus. We find ourselves again at the all-important anchor-point, if I might glance briefly ahead, of command

#20—setting one's internal compass. That orientation of heart is not dependent on the mind's continual awareness of it.

That said, acknowledgment is bolstered by regularly *re-setting* the compass. Life direction doesn't function on auto-pilot. Continual *reaffirmation* of that direction is imperative to keep the needle pointing North. The "Morning Prayer" found in several of my small devotional volumes represents a daily expression of "acknowledgement" I use in committing my days to God.

A portion of that prayer is found below, acknowledging God as Father, prime mover, and regulator of my life…*even when I am not consciously thinking of him.* I pray this prayer, not to remind God…but to remind *myself* where I am bound, which direction my compass is pointing, and to ask God to help me move steadily toward his North all my days. He doesn't need reminding…but *I* need reminding.

From this foundation, other perhaps more visible manifestations of acknowledgment rise to the surface. That prayer orders and informs how I live and behave and relate to people, how I think, what I believe, how I function in but not of the world, not as a hermit but as one engaged in the world around me and acknowledging whose child I am.

Acknowledgement *may* at times be visible and vocal. That foundational prayer may require it. I have recently written a book that addresses the current political and cultural quagmire in which we in 2020s America find ourselves. It is an outspoken acknowledgment of my beliefs in a more open way than I have ever been led to do before. I felt my faith required this bold step, this outward acknowledgment and public stand.

The Old Testament prophets stood tall and boldly acknowledged their faith in many ways that are probably not appropriate for us today. God calls his people to acknowledge him in all their ways personally. His leading will likewise be uniquely individual.

That leading is one of the results of the promise that follows…

And he will direct your paths.

I give myself this day to you. I acknowledge myself your son. I affirm my intent and desire to relinquish selfish motive, yield independence of spirit, and to abide in your will not my own. Remind me constantly of this affirmation. Keep me centered in the quietness of your perspective, renouncing the world's values, and oriented toward my eternal citizenship. Imbue me with your wisdom. Reveal yourself ever more fully to my understanding. Whisper to me out of the Silence. Still my heart and brain to remain attuned to your Voice. Focus my senses within the Center. Awaken me every moment to the commands. Press and urge your words upon me. Bring your precepts continually alive to my consciousness. Give me courage, meekness, and wisdom to model my attitudes, behavior, and life priorities after the Lord's example, eyes to see people as he saw them, and a heart to love as he loved.

10. Find a Husband or Wife of Noble Character

A wife of noble character is her husband's crown.
A wife of noble character who can find? She is worth far more than rubies.
(Proverbs 12:4; 31:10 NIV)

What a wonderfully powerful phrase Solomon uses to describe the kind of wife every man should seek, and by inference the kind of husband every woman should seek.

Noble character.

Not "noble" in any hierarchy of social standing, but a man or woman who walks in nobility of *character.*

One wonders what the man who eventually was said to have seven hundred wives was thinking when he wrote "a wife" in Proverbs 12:4 in the singular. It is probably no accident that the 31st chapter of Proverbs was not written by Solomon. His credibility to speak about marriage is a little shaky. Yet this phrase, used by both Solomon and Lemuel, author of Proverbs 31, is weighty with import.

In the matter of husbands and wives, there is not a word about beauty, intelligence, sex appeal, or falling in love.

Only one biblical standard identifies the foundation for a lasting and fruitful marriage—*nobility of character.*

How the world would scoff at such a notion. And it is true that Solomon may be a puzzling oracle to convey this imperative. So perhaps we should base our conclusions instead on Lemuel's observations, gleaned from his own mother, in the final chapter of *Proverbs.*

Not only would the world scoff, the words "nobility of character" will sound as little more than nonsense in the world's ears. Even few Christians take this command seriously. (For so I take the words of these two proverbs—as instructions, precepts...*commands,* for a fruitful and happy life and marriage.) Christians in our time are no less intoxicated than is the world by the immature allure of looks, personality, and that most deceiving of emotional snares, falling in love. What deceptively unreliable foundation stones upon which to build a marriage!

Of course such love exists. I am not hesitant to speak of "falling in love" with my wife Judy. But falling in love is the caboose of the love-train. The engine is nobility of character, followed by the cars of many virtues, all of which combine to elevate falling in love as it follows to a lofty and wonderful level of stature and significance. When falling in love is the engine, trouble lies waiting further along the tracks when the engine runs out of steam.

Many in today's world, however, are so in love with themselves that they have no desire to listen to the wisdom of the ages. They know best. They know what they want. They are "in love." Nothing will persuade them it isn't the real thing, and that God has not ordained it. A lifetime of bliss awaits!

The foolish hubris of youth is nowhere more evident than in the shortsighted foolishness of marital choices. Failed and unhappy marriages by the millions are the result.

Lemuel has pinpointed both the crux of the problem, and the godly key to a good and fruitful marriage, in the three powerfully important words: *who can find?*

Who indeed? What young people in today's world even try? Falling in love is enough. Why try to *find* anything beyond that?

Lemuel insists that nobility of character must be *found.* It won't just happen. Falling in love does indeed usually *just happen.* It's more accidental than purposeful. Two people meet and the sparks fly. Where are depth of character, life purpose, selflessness, orientation of inner compass, spiritual maturity, and motive and heart's desire in the equation of falling in love?

Who is even thinking of those things when emotions are speeding the train down the track? The wise individual who desires a Proverbs 31 life partner and friend needs to remember the difference between *finding* and *falling.* The price of not heeding Lemuel's wisdom may be a life of misery when the train of love hits the mountains.

Nobility of character doesn't come along randomly nor is it perceived with a fluttering heart. It is a quality of personhood that must be sought with eyes open to the undependability of emotions, looked for with prudent wisdom, discovered and found slowly, and tested in the soil of virtue where the world is incapable of discerning it.

Find a wife.

Find a husband.

When found, nobility of character is worth far more than rubies...priceless indeed.

What can I pray, heavenly Father, but to thank you yet again for leading me to find a Proverbs 31 wife, and for giving me the good sense, as young and immature as I was, to recognize in her the noble character of a woman of God in the making.

Series Two

Choice and Consequence

Life's If-Then Equation

Blessings, curses, and fruitfulness in life

Deuteronomy's Equation for Life: the Soul of the Old Testament

All Scripture is profitable. But not all is of equal importance. Some portions of the Bible rise to a loftier level than others. While we can glean truth from all its books, these high peaks of Scripture are more than once-a-year-entries in a Bible reading schedule. They ought to stay with us as constant daily sources of light, wisdom, truth—the clearest written windows we have been given into the mind, heart, and purposes of God.

They illuminate our daily affairs, regulate behavior and thought patterns, affirm and clarify and remind us of our priorities as Christians, encouraging us to walk our faith with courage and single-mindedness.

They give us our moment-by-moment marching orders. Theology and history, poetry and prophecy, all have their place. But these bright-beacons within the pages of Scripture show us our path today, *right now*, in the next five minutes...and they do so *every* day, all our lives long.

Deuteronomy stands at this apex of importance along with *Proverbs* and a few other books and passages. Even in considering *Deuteronomy* itself, much of it is comprised of a lengthy and rambling historical review of the Israelites' history. It is important to isolate out of Moses' reminiscences those particular segments that precisely and unequivocally set down God's purposes for his people. It is these forceful and fundamental exhortations that challenge the people he has led to the promised land to live by God's commands and decrees, exhorting them not to forget those principles. They also set down the consequences of following God's purposes in obedience...or, on the other side of the choice-coin, *failing* to follow them. *

These clarifying high-points of *Deuteronomy* come chiefly in chapters 4, 6-8, 11, and 30. They establish for all God's people who will follow over the next three thousand years (and beyond) what I call the "Choice and Consequence Code." They lay out God's equation for life as transmitted to humanity by his chief Old Testament prophet.

I often call the commands God's "bull's eye" as representing the primary focus and most important essence and core and *center* of God's revelation to man. In considering these commands of the Old Testament, we recognize that one of the prophets understood *command* more lucidly

---

* Because a few readers may be interested, I will set down some of my personal mountain-top passages. Everyone, of course, will have their own particularly meaningful passages of Scripture. These happen to encompass most (not quite all) of mine, chosen for their practicality and daily challenge to keep God's commands ever before me. Selected portions from them form the basis of my *Pocket Memory Book*, and *Book of Daily Memory Reminders*. They are: Deuteronomy 4, 6-8, 11, 30, Psalms 51, 91, 119, 139, Proverbs, Matthew 5-7, John 13-17, Romans 12:1-2; 9-19, 1 Corinthians 13, Philippians 4:4-8, Colossians 3, and James. There are obviously also individual verses that I would include (Malachi 3:2-3, Ephesians 2:21-22, Philippians 2:10-11, 1 Timothy 4:12-16, and *many* more). But these more lengthy passages form the bedrock of my understanding of my walk with God and my daily life as a Christian man.

and eternally than most of the rest. Consistently he pointed the Israelites straight toward the bull's eye.

That was Moses. His unwavering clarion call to the Israelites serves as the foundation stone of the entire Old Testament.

His message was a simple one:

Choose this day.

Choose life.

Choose obedience.

In some ways, *Deuteronomy* and its Choice and Consequence Code may be the most politically incorrect book of the Bible. The secular world can even tolerate Genesis 1-3 simply by calling the account an ancient myth. But *Deuteronomy*, with its stringent and unyielding focus on right, wrong, obedience, disobedience, all founded in command…these high truths are an absolute anathema to the relativism of modernity. It hates the very notion of accountability as much as it hates the idea of command. Independence is the god of our age. No one will tell *me* what to do! No one will lay a command on *me!*

From deep out of the past, Moses rises bold and courageous as God's prophet to proclaim, "Oh yes I will tell you what to do! I will *command* you what to do, because God commands his men and women to live by his decrees. If you don't, you will suffer the consequences."

The nature of a command requires obedience. A "command" is not a "suggestion." A command is a *command*. Obedience is compulsory. And yet…there remains such a thing as *dis*obedience.

That is why it is a *Choice* and Consequence Code. The coin of command has two sides.

The Bible focuses these two paths from beginning to end—always highlighting that the choice between the two lies within the will of the human mind and heart. We *choose* whether to obey or disobey, we *choose* light or darkness, we *choose* whether to live by God's principles or disregard them, we *choose* whether to exalt ourselves or deny ourselves. We each make that choice a hundred times every day.

At the end of his life, drawing together and summarizing what he has emphasized in chapters 4, 6-8, and 11, Moses issued this charge to the Israelites:

> *I have set before you this day life and good, death and evil. If you obey the commandments of the Lord your God which I command you this day, by loving the Lord your God, by walking in his ways, and by keeping his commandments…then you shall live and multiply, and the Lord your God will bless you…But if your heart turns away, and you...are drawn away to worship other gods…I declare to you this day that you shall perish…I have set before you life and death, blessing and curse; therefore choose life, that you and your descendants may live, loving the Lord your God, obeying his voice, and cleaving to him; for that means life to you and length of days.*
>
> —Deuteronomy 30: 15-20

Not only does modernity hate this fundamental message of *Deuteronomy*, antiquity hated it too. The Israelites hated it and frequently chose the wrong side of the coin of command. David often chose the wrong side of the coin. Solomon chose the wrong side of the coin. Most of the nation of Israel, and later Judah chose the wrong side of the coin.

And they all suffered the consequences. *God* did not curse them for their disobedience. They brought the consequences of disobedience down on themselves. The "curse" spoken of so often by Moses is self-inflicted.

In many ways, the above passage represents the heart of the Old Testament. But history reveals that it is a message to the few not the many. Though addressed to the whole of Israel, and in the Bible to all Jews and Christians who have ever lived, only a scant few will hear and heed and live by God's bull's eye of command and will *choose* obedience. The same will be true centuries further along in Israel's history when we come to Josiah and Ezra. They will address their call to repentance to the whole nation of Israel, which by that time will be represented primarily by the tribe of Judah. But disobedience will continue to thrive. Their challenge, like that of Moses, and as will be that of Jesus, will sadly turn out to be a challenge heeded by the few not the many—those with eyes to see, ears to hear, and the humility to embrace the bull's eye of command, and *choose* to obey the Choice and Consequence Code.

Because this Code lies at the heart of the biblical message, much within it is repeated over and over throughout the Old Testament. We will encounter Moses' exhortations time and again. This explains why certain seeming repetitions crop up in these selected 120 commands of the prophets, while other more obscure commands are not mentioned at all. These are the commands of the Choice and Consequence Code that undergird all the rest:

- Be careful.
- Do not forget.
- Take heed.
- Remember the commands.
- Walk in obedience.
- Watch yourselves closely.
- Be careful, be watchful, take heed not to forget.

Yet the majority of Jews and Christians *do* forget. They do *not* take heed. Moses' challenge does *not* form the bedrock of their daily lives. Thus they continue to embody, following the pattern of many who have come before, the wrong side of the coin of command.

Thus, the Choice and Consequence Code, and the entire bull's eye of command, will always be embraced, not by the masses, but by those with eyes to see and ears to hear.

SERIES TWO

CHOICE AND CONSEQUENCE

11. Love God with your whole heart, soul, mind, and strength.

12. Seek God diligently.

13. Take heed not to forget God's commands.

14. Choose this day whom you will serve.

15. Walk in obedience to God's commands.

16. Do what is right and good in the sight of the Lord.

17. Do not let your heart become proud.

18. Do not be afraid or discouraged.

19. Remember the blessings and curses and choose life.

20. Set the desires of your heart Godward.

11. Love God with Your Whole Heart, Soul, Mind, and Strength

"You shall love the Lord your God with all your heart, and with all your soul, and with all your might." (Deuteronomy 6:5)

I confess that all my life I have silently struggled with this command, what Jesus identified as the first and greatest of all commandments. It is expressed in many ways in both Old and New Testaments, from the preeminent human prophet, Moses, to the divine Son of God prophet, Jesus himself, and in some way by all the prophets.

The components of the command vary—heart, soul, mind, strength, etc.—but the command is universal: Mankind is commanded to love God entirely, completely, with its whole being. *Nothing* is to be a higher and more paramount priority in life than love for God.

Yet whenever I heard people speak of their great love for God, in my heart of hearts I harbored a terrible secret—I didn't share their enthusiasm. I could not honestly say that I felt the same passionate and fervent *love* for God everyone seemed to be talking about. For most of my early Christian life, therefore, I wondered if there was something wrong with me in the greatest-commandment department.

Did I really love God at all…I mean really and truly and deeply and passionately *love* him?

I honestly could not give a resounding *Yes!* to that question. I could not say that I loved God with the same emotion and fervor and intensity with which I loved my wife and sons, for example, or with the same level of warmth and bonding of heart I feel deeply for my close friends, or even with the delight that can make me soar to the heights of joy when doing what I love—sharing life with Judy, working hard, exerting my physical energies to make things, creating with my hands and mind, running and cycling to the limits of my endurance, writing, grappling with lofty ideas, thinking high thoughts into unexplored regions of spirituality. All these, and the individuals who imbue them with even more meaning and purpose (wife, sons, friends, even readers whom I might not have met personally) fill me with nothing less than the soaring joy which can be described as nothing less than *love*.

But *God* is not included in that list.

My feelings toward him are more abstract, hard to define, distant. It's been an inward quandary for much of my life. Every time I hear the Great Commandment cited, my doubts as a young man when I wondered if I was a second-class Christian because I didn't speak in tongues—or was even a Christian at all!—come whispering back into my mind telling me there is something wrong with my walk with God and my entire belief system. I've never openly expressed this inner secret so candidly before this moment.

Before I began this morning, a deep, sober, quiet, prayerful sense came over me of the eternal significance of what I was about to attempt—to place the first and greatest commandment into practical perspective for those seeking reality in their daily walks with God. Who was I to speak about the greatest commandment when my own "love for God" raised such questions at the core of my own faith? With Moses, I wanted to cry, "But…but God…why me…I can't…"

I pray every day as I write. But today that prayer was personally urgent, and more imperative than ever. I hesitate to over-dramatize it, but it was an intensely real prayer.

I prayed:

"What do you have for me today? What do you have for me to communicate from your heart today to your people? May I be a conduit to speak out of your heart into the hearts of your men and women whose heart's desire is to hear what you would speak into their lives."

I *meant* what I prayed. I knew that I could not write a word unless God answered that cry of my heart. In myself I did *not* understand love for God as much as I longed to. I could not simply try to fill up the page with words. If there was anything to be said, it had to come from *him*. God had to be the one to illuminate what love for him meant, and *how* he wanted his people to love him.

As my eyes fell again on the words, "…with your whole heart, soul, mind, and strength," a sudden revelation burst quietly upon me. I say that tentatively. I am not one to bandy lightly the words, "The Lord showed me…" or to claim answers to prayer every day or two. God's operations in my life are undramatic. God sends me no telegrams. I live my life, and try to do so faithfully. But there are no fireworks, dreams, visions, revelations, prophecies, mountain experiences, or spiritual exuberances. Life goes on. Life is hard. God's people have to live life in the trenches not on the summits.

Therefore, I do not necessarily claim divine inspiration for what followed. I will leave you to make your own determination. I can only say that I prayed the words as I have written them, then my eyes again read the command at the top of the page, and suddenly the following insight burst into my mind.

For me, it came as a profound revelation—one that personally answered the quandary that has plagued me for years, and at last put many years of uncertainties to rest. If it helps anyone else, I can only quietly be thankful. Now life will go on. But for me it will go on with a new sense of quiet peace in the particular corner of my life where love for God dwells.

As I read again Jesus' restatement of Moses' words in Mark 12:30, the four words Jesus used jumped off the page at me—*Heart…Soul…Mind…Strength.*

I saw that they emerged out of and defined different aspects of our humanity.

- *Heart*—the center of feeling, emotion, joy, love, where so much in human experience and relationship begins—marriage, friendship, companionship, honor, respect, community, even nationhood…all reflecting the infinite Heart that beats at the heart of all creation and all the universe. Though it is always listed first, it may in some sense be that this component of love emerges as a result of the outworking of the other three.
- *Soul*—the spiritual center of being where God has placed himself, where our in-his-imageness separates us from the rest of creation, where he has placed conscience and the ability to know right from wrong, and where he has placed the seeds of hunger for him, for good, for righteousness.
- *Mind*—the thinking, mental, intellectual component of the human make-up which has been endowed by God with the power to think, analyze, draw conclusions, dream, create…all energized by a brain far more complex than that of any other life form or living being, given its unique and unfathomable power by virtue of the fact that God placed within it, at its source, a small reflection of his own infinite Mind, thus continuing the reality that man was purposefully created in his image. The mind is also the center of being where volition dwells, the repository of that determinative power to choose, to make decisions, all of which are fruits of that greatest gift given by God to man of free will…itself a reflection of its Maker and the source and power of chosen obedience to direct and regulate the maturing of man's abundant gifts, talents, and abilities.
- *Strength*—man's physicality, the power of the human body, in conjunction with the creative and analytical gifts and power of the mind, to make and do and build—to subdue the earth and, for every man and woman, his or her corner of it…again reflecting God's own creative and unending and unlimited power and strength and outpouring creativity which created man and the world.

All four together are reflections of God himself. He created us in his image. These aspects of his Being are intrinsic to who he is, and are intrinsic to who man is, linking us in our most basic essence to God in his most basic essence.

Out of all four centers of being that define our fourfold essence, God wants us to return to him. He wants us to give back what he gave us.

I saw that what I had always expected "love for God" to mean—an emotional, even passionate *feeling* of love such as might exist between a man and woman—was only one small component of this fourfold whole. And in truth the least important part of it.

Volition of Soul—using the determinative power of free will to *choose* to live by God's principles—is a far more important and decisive life-regulating instrument to determine how we live and whether we grow into the sonship and daughterhood for which we were created than emotion or feeling.

Similarly, all the powers with which our minds and our human capabilities of strength are imbued—creative, intellectual, analytical—working in harmony with volition and choice, these all contribute more to determine the kind of people we are than feeling and emotion

The enormity of the command suddenly struck me with a forceful truth I had never beheld:

Loving God with the *Soul, Mind,* and *Strength* had nothing to do with a *feeling* of love such as I had unknowingly expected.

To *love* with the mind means using my free will to make good choices, to choose righteousness, to choose to live by God's principles. When I *choose* to obey God, to walk by one of his commands, in that moment I have demonstrated "love for God" with my mind.

To *love* God with the mind means using all the intellectual and creative power and mental gifts God has given me to think his thoughts, to think in harmony with his perspectives and priorities, to turn my mind and brain in directions in which God himself thinks, to use my mind to understand him and his ways more completely.

Those who say spirituality is not intellectual are wrong. The intellect is pivotal in what love for God means. I love God with my mind and intellect when I set my brain and thoughts Godward.

To *love* God with my strength means using my hands and body and the physical capabilities he has given me, in harmony with my mental and intellectual powers and creativity, to choose activities and life directions that synchronize with God's priorities and perspectives.

I love God with my strength when my physical capabilities reflect aspects of God's nature and are neither selfish nor contrary to what would be God's will.

I saw that in truth feeling and emotion play but a tiny role in the totality of what it means to love God with our heart, soul, mind, and strength. My hands, my bodily strength, my intellect are expressing equal love for God when I use them to the full.

Love must be practical. Loving God over a lifetime with the fourfold components of our humanity draws up into it the totality with which we bring heart, soul, mind, and strength to point ourselves Godward.

When I write...I am expressing an aspect of my love for God. When I ride my bike hard...I am expressing an aspect of my love for God. When I make something for Judy...I am expressing an aspect of my love for God. When I wrestle and pray and think through some thorny theological conundrum in order to understand God's nature more fully...I am expressing an aspect of my love for God. And when I set my head to pillow in the darkness of night and quietly whisper, *Thank you...*I am expressing an aspect of my love for God.

We are commanded to love God with the entirety of our in-God's-imageness. We are commanded to live in, draw life from, and love the source of our life, then to return to that source with our whole beings. We recognize that our hearts, souls, minds, and strength all reflect who God is. They are ours because they came from him. Thus we yield them back to him.

The command completes the circle of creation—sending back, in love, the very essence and fulness of my being which was created out of his heart.

As I ponder this high truth, I pray that God will continue the revelation, expand it in my heart and mind, and increase my understanding from this beginning.

And I am at peace.

God, what can I do but thank you for this revelation. Thank you for my heart, for my soul, for my mind, and for my strength, all of which are able to love you in their unique ways, exactly as you created them to reflect your nature. I thank you for creating mankind as you have...and for creating me just as I am. Thank you.

12. Seek God Diligently

"You will seek me and find me; when you seek me with all your heart." (Jeremiah 29:13)

Though as we progress we will loosely follow the Old Testament story to give a historical context for the commands emerging out of that story, we're not trying to adhere to that historical progression with precision. Starting with *Proverbs*, looking back at *Deuteronomy*, we now gaze forward briefly at a command found in *Jeremiah*. Making these commands relevant for our lives today occasionally requires both a fluid sequence, and a wider application of the commands than might have been applicable 3000 or 3500 years ago.

This command to *Seek God diligently* is especially interesting in that regard. These words would have been filled with so many different implications at various times in history. To the ears of modernism, they are essentially meaningless. To the ears of many Israelites leaving Egypt during the exodus, they probably meant sojourning to the promised land where at long last God would be with them as a nation. To many Jews of Jesus' time, seeking God no doubt was associated with traveling to Jerusalem and the Temple at Passover.

Jeremiah was closer to the mark when he wrote of the inner, personal, and spiritual implications inherent in the words he prophesied, speaking out what he believed was God's heart-cry to humanity: "You will seek me and find me; when you seek me with all your heart."

This verse embodies Moses' charge as well as Jeremiah's. Though Jeremiah doesn't phrase it as coming from God's mouth exactly as a command, it clearly lies at the foundation of God's intent for mankind. God *wants* man to know him, to understand him, to walk in fellowship with him. He *wants* us to seek him. We are *supposed* to seek him… seek to know him and understand him… seek fellowship and relationship with him.

For most of the ancient Israelites first receiving the law from Moses, these words would not have had the same deeply personal meaning they did later for Jeremiah, or for us today. They were at such a primitive state spiritually that Moses had to begin earlier in the spiritual progression—*Do this, don't do that.* True, the command to *Love God with your whole heart* was fundamental to Moses' instructions. But initially, as given in the Ten Commandments, even "love God" was phrased as *Worship the Lord your God*, with the specifics of that "worship" laid out more in legalisms than in the heart-response of Jeremiah 29:13.

In reality, *seeking God* often precedes *loving God*…especially loving him with our whole hearts. So called "love at first sight" doesn't usually apply to God. First thoughts of God do not usually cause us instantly to fall in love with him. Those initial thoughts are often laced with a multitude of conflicting and false ideas, along with doctrine, tradition, early-life teaching, fear, anger, confusion, and for a great many in our time, indifference. These and a great many more hurdles must be overcome before we get within miles of being able to truly *love* God.

The trouble is, however, that these roadblocks of doctrine, false ideas, anger, and indifference, usually prevent people from wanting anything to do with God. They don't *want* closer association with him. The very idea of "seeking God" represents a gigantic disconnect, a meaningless if not repellant idea. It may be that deep down, elements of this same disconnect exist in the subconscious minds even among many who are dedicated Christians. We may not be aware of it. But subtle and unconscious erroneous ideas may be pulling us both toward God (knowing we're *supposed* to love him) and *away* from him by some of the same doctrinal and emotional falsehoods that keep the world from knowing him.

Seeking God diligently, then, often begins, not with *love* or *worship*, but with the determined *decision* to get to know who God really is…to *understand* him.

Why some people come to a point in life when they *want* to know God, while the majority of men and women couldn't care less, is a mystery. Speaking for myself…

I believe that:

- It is incumbent upon the human species, with the brains and emotions and the power of volition we possess, to seek to know where those gifts came from…and *why* we possess them.
- It reveals a weakness of character, a squandering of the capacity of the intellect, even an inherent self-centeredness, *not* to desire to

know whether or not God exists and not to *seek* that knowledge with all the heart.

- If there is a God, it is incumbent upon humanity not only to know he exists, but to *understand* him truly, and, understanding him, to relate ourselves to him as we are meant to relate to him.
- Not seeking to understand God, we cannot in any sense consider life having been fulfilled.
- The imperative of seeking and knowing God is essential to our humanity.
- Not fulfilling this imperative, we cannot complete and realize the totality of what personhood is intended to mean.
- Not fulfilling this purpose, we will never be *whole* men and women.

The world will obviously scoff at these presuppositions. I stand by them. We are *supposed* to seek God and understand him.

It is central and basic to our role, our function, our responsibility, our duty, our legacy as human beings. We fail as human beings when we do not seek to know and understand God humbly, truly, and accurately—not as defined by doctrine or church teaching, but understand him as he defines and reveals himself.

God, my Creator and Father, I believe in you and know in my heart that you are real. But I want to know you and understand as much about you as you will reveal to me. Put within me a hunger, a seeking heart, to know you more fully. Reveal yourself to me. Never stop revealing more of yourself to me. Reveal who you are and what are your eternal purposes. Especially reveal your purposes for me, and help me fall in with those purposes every day.

13. Take Heed Not to Forget God's Commands

Take heed lest you forget the Lord…Be careful lest you forget the LORD your God, by not keeping his commandments. (Deuteronomy 6:12; 8:11)

He commanded our fathers to teach to their children; that the next generation might know them, the children yet unborn, and arise and tell them to their children, so that they should… not forget the works of God, but keep his commandments. (Psalm 78:5-7)

From an expanded, and for myself a liberating perspective of the first and greatest commandment, we encounter a key reason why such a more encompassing outlook is important. Here we have what might be characterized as entirely an *intellectual*, mental, cerebral command.

To obey this command is to love God with the *mind*. This command cannot be obeyed with the feelings or emotions of the heart. Neither will strength accomplish it. Volition certainly plays a role. But even deciding, "I will not forget God's commands," won't necessarily get it done.

Obedience here is mental and intellectual. Here we must love God with the intellect—not *feeling* love, but forcing ourselves to remember. To obey requires engaging the brain, working hard mentally, studying, thinking, remembering, and *continuing* in all these ways to keep God's commands at the forefront of the mind. This command forever eliminates the myth that Christianity and love for God aren't intellectual. They are!

This is a lifetime command. We might work hard at it for ten years…even twenty. But if we get lazy and stop engaging mentally…forgetfulness will set in. In a few years, everything I once remembered will have receded so deep into the recesses of the gray cells that at some point I will have to start over.

That feeling and emotion have almost entirely hijacked the *love God* command is surprising. The command to use the *intellect* in faith is one of the most frequently given in the Old Testament. Intellectual mental obedience is commanded by God and his prophets over and over. Moses commands the Israelites nine times in *Deuteronomy* not to forget God's commands, exactly as often as he issues the command to love God.

How, then, do we practically obey the command not to forget? Are we intended to memorize every biblical command? That would obviously be a good thing, but for most a bit too lofty a goal.

To get at the heart of this command, I hearken back instead to the preliterate days in which these first commands of the prophets were delivered. In a culture in which history and law and tradition were passed down through the generations orally, memorization was certainly important. Mostly it was a matter of repetition—keeping the commands front and center in the national and spiritual consciousness. The commands of God were intended to represent a national focus, a central undergirding theme regulating activities and relationships.

This is the basis for Moses' words: "Talk about them when you are at home or out walking, when you stand and when you sit." The message was a simple one: *Keep God's commands forefront.*

That's what it means for us personally, and also in our families and church communities. It should be a matter of repentance and shame that God's commands are given so little attention in today's Christendom.

People use many aids to remember—the watch worn backwards, the string on the finger. We do what works for us. Through the years I have made numerous small printed reminders to carry with me. Judy still carries one in her purse that I made for the five of us thirty-five years ago when our sons were young. *We are commanded not to forget God's commands.* So we must take this more seriously than *hoping* the commands will come to mind now and them. There is some serious brain work required here.

I often ask, "When was the last time you heard a sermon preached on the commands?" That we have to stop and think about it reveals the sad state of modern Christian leadership, and a clergy far more obsessed with doctrine, theology, politics, experientialism, worship, and music than in turning God's people toward remembrance of his commands.

If we are serious about making the commands a thematic focus of life as Moses commanded, then the commands of God should be read and re-read, thought about, discussed, yes and memorized too, and preached about often. They should be the subject of Bible studies, the focal point of prayer, both personal and corporate. They should be the bedrock and grounding foundation of Christian families, the subject matter of our personal devotions, the most oft-underlined verses in our Bibles.

You and I may not be able to change the misplaced priorities of the church and its leadership. But we can make this important command a focus in our own lives.

Keep God's commands forefront.

Give me mental focus, Lord God, to prioritize the commands in my mental library. Amid a thousand distractions in my life, return my thoughts constantly to your commands. Help me keep them forefront. Give me self-awareness to apply myself diligently, mentally, intellectually, and to be careful not to forget.

14. Choose This Day Whom You Will Serve

Choose this day whom you will serve…but as for me and my house, we will serve the LORD.
(Joshua 24:15)

This well-known phrase was spoken by Joshua as his end of life charge to the Israelites after they had subdued the land of Canaan. It echoes the overarching message of *Deuteronomy* with precision:

Choose life!

"I set before you life and death, blessings and curses.
Therefore, choose life!" (Deuteronomy 30:19)

Daily *choice*…the regular decision to obey or not to obey God's commands and instructions, is the foundational legacy of Moses and the core theme of *Deuteronomy.*

In his final challenge to Israel (Joshua 24:15), in seven succinct words Joshua summed up everything he had learned from his mentor. His final charge was almost identical to that of Moses.

Choose!

The sequence of commands from *Deuteronomy* now takes a decided step up to a higher plane of personal involvement and accountability. These words are so familiar, it is easy to miss the enormity of their import. These seven words distill and focus the entire message of the Bible!

From deciding to seek God…
from loving him…
from diligently remembering his commands—
—it is now life-decision time!

What will we do about the three prior commands of this series? Will they make a difference in how we live?

A new and highly-charged word has now entered the equation—*serve.*

Loving, seeking, remembering...these can all remain abstract. To some degree we can obey all these commands intellectually, but *only* intellectually. This is important as far as it goes, but in itself it is not enough.

To *serve* suddenly raises the stakes. This is hands and feet. This is daily life. This is *doing*. This is *servanthood.* This is cleaning the toilet. This is caring for the sick and dying. This is cups of cold water to the thirsty. This is food to the hungry. This is sensitivity to the hurting.

The implication is enormous—having *loved, sought, remembered*...are we prepared to enter God's *service*...as his servants, his disciples, his sons and daughters? It is still possible, as Moses constantly put before the Israelites, to say *no.* The decision is always two-sided.

This is the *choice* before us. Seeking, loving, and remembering culminates in chosen servanthood. Without chosen servanthood as the flower blooming atop seeking, loving, and remembering, those plants will ultimately go to seed and die without accomplishing their purpose.

Servanthood to *God* is clearly what Joshua means. Yet instantly that servanthood expands toward every man, woman, and child we meet *today*...in the next five minutes. Whose servants are we?

Four of the words in Joshua's charge are huge in their implication:

Choose...*this day*...whom you will *serve.*

The servanthood-choice is one that we make, or don't make, *every* day.

- Whom have I *chosen* to serve?
- Who will I serve *today*?
- Whose disciple am I?

The response of the people to Joshua's charge was enthusiastic. But as history will tell us as we continue, enthusiasm without ongoing obedience doesn't last very long.

> *The people said to Joshua, "...we will serve the Lord." Then Joshua said to the people, "You are witnesses...that you have chosen the Lord, to serve him." And they said, "We are witnesses." He said, "Then put away the foreign gods which are among you, and incline your heart to the Lord, the God of Israel." And the people said to Joshua, "The Lord our God we will serve, and his voice we will obey." So Joshua made a covenant with the people that day, and made statutes and ordinances for them at Shechem. And Joshua wrote these words in the book of the law of God.* (Joshua 24:21-26)

I want to be your servant, God—a disciple of Jesus. I dedicate myself in service to you. May my obedience be daily and lifelong, not the enthusiasm of a moment. Give me more staying power than the Israelites had.

15. Walk in Obedience to God's Commands

"I am God Almighty; walk before me and be blameless. (Genesis 17:1)
Walk in my statutes and observe my commandments and do them. (Leviticus 26:3)
You shall walk in all the ways which the Lord your God has commanded you. (Deuteronomy 5:33)

The Deuteronomy progression now reaches its climax.

One can seek God knowing little or nothing about him. One might seek him while filled with many false ideas about him. Such in part would I characterize my own spiritual journey as a young man. Like me, MacDonald also had to seek God…seek the *true* God from amid the myriad obscuring doctrines that had shrouded his boyhood.

We will not be able to love him rightly until we escape the suffocating fogs of false ideas—unfortunately passed into the historical consciousness of western civilization by much in the Old Testament story because of the unbelief and wrong interpretations of the Law by the Israelites. Only with falsehood gone can we begin truly to know God's nature as our loving Father.

Knowing him accurately, we are commanded to *love* him with our whole being. Most of the Israelites did not know God truly. Yet in spite of the incompleteness of their understanding, they were commanded to obey him anyway They were to do so through command and obedience.

Thus, the next stage of the progression—at *whatever* stage may be our understanding and knowing—is to recognize, and thus *remember* what God's commands are. We can't obey them unless we know and remember them.

This remembering may take many forms. For the ancient Israelites it was largely oral—repeating, reciting, studying, discussing, memorizing, passing the commands down to children and grandchildren. We of today are able to read the commands as well as memorize and discuss and think about them.

Then comes the moment of choice and decision—*choosing…now…today*—whether we are prepared to place ourselves in the service of God as his servants of obedience to the command.

And yet…there may still be a disconnect between the *choosing* and the *do*.

How many through the years have made a "decision for Christ," perhaps sincere, often tearful and repentant and full of good intentions, even enthusiasm, yet who have lapsed into old ways.

The *choosing* was sincere.

But there was no lasting *do*.

The passage at the end of *Joshua* in which the people pledged their commitment is precisely repeated at thousands of evangelistic altar call services. Enthusiastic commitment…yet where is that enthusiasm and commitment in ten years?

This order of the first five commands of this series—*love, seek, remember, choose, walk*—is one which might be equally understood with the order reversed.

Obedience to the commands also comes first. Obedience may actually be what produces the heart-hunger to seek and love God.

Unable to love him, we still obey. These five commands all work in complex harmony. In truth, they are not separate at all. We consider them in sequence to help focus our thoughts on certain progressive themes in which God works among us. The heart that hungers for God and chooses to be good *will* live in obedience to the commands, *will* do what is right and good even before it is aware that doing so is one of Moses' commands to the Israelites. Obedience will itself fuel love for God as a fruit of obedience.

Though circular reasoning is a principle of flawed logic, many of God's principles are intriguingly circular in revealing deep truths. In this case, curious as it may sound, obedience to the commands fuels the dedication to choose obedience to the commands.

The life of obedient discipleship is thus a complex symphony of many themes, choices, and heart-motives, all spreading their thematic melodies through the growth of Godly character in intricate interplay.

It might be said that the essence of all spirituality emerges out of follow-through. Words are not enough, love is not enough, remembering the commands is not enough.

Choosing *is* enough, but only if the choosing is repeated every day. The life of faith is lived in the *follow-through.* From knowing and remembering the commands, the faithful man or woman now *walks* in them.

Note the huge difference between *choosing* and *walking*. A "choice" may be made in an instant. A choice can be made in church, seated in a pew, at rest, going nowhere. Here we are commanded to get up and *walk* in obedience to the commands. This takes the sequence of obedience to another level. A lifetime opens before us. Life cannot be lived sitting down.

We might have phrased it:

Walk in obedience to God's commands over a lifetime.

This is what the command means. This is what God intends. No superficial commitments that are gone by day's end. Obedience is lifelong. No weekend warriors need sign up for Joshua's army, or in Jesus' discipleship-army.

We are commanded to *walk with God*...with Noah, with Solomon and David, with Moses and Joshua...over a lifetime.

Give me strong spiritual legs, God, to rise from the chair of enthusiasm, and follow through on that commitment every day. May my legs be strong to walk with you as Moses and Noah and Joshua did. May it be said of me on my deathbed, he/she walked with God over a lifetime.

16. Do What is Right and Good in the Sight of the Lord

And you shall do what is right and good in the sight of the Lord. (Deuteronomy 6:18)

These words from Deuteronomy 6:18 have been deeply embedded in my consciousness since boyhood. I saw them on a small piece of paper, typed by my mother and scotch-taped to the old white refrigerator in our kitchen. With the deepest gratitude and love I honor my mother for starting my sisters and me out in life with such a profound focus of spirituality and life orientation in front of us on that little strip of paper literally every day.

I probably lapse into superlatives more frequently than I should. That is one of the consequences of discussing, or "majoring in" the commands of the Bible as readers of my books might term it. The commands themselves, collectively, *are* Scripture's superlative. They represent the pinnacle and essence of the Bible's message. You'll have to forgive me, therefore, if it seems that I am continually saying, "This is *really* one of the important commands!" Because they all are.

Yet among the Bible's commands, there are indeed a handful that rise above—the superlatives of all the superlatives.

I like to think in terms of superlatives—the best of the best. That's why I have produced so many books of quotes and compilations from authors I consider important—isolating the high point of their thought, collecting selections that focus and distill the *essence* of their life-perspectives.

As scriptural superlatives go, Deuteronomy 6:18 is certainly in my top ten, probably in my top five. Here is the essence and core of God's intent for humanity—to *do* what is *right* and *good*. It's as plain as Moses could make it. Not to theorize about it or analyze it or study it or preach it, but to DO it.

"Ah," says the analyst, the theorist, the theologian, the biblical scholar, Mr. Facingbothways, as MacDonald calls him, "but what *is* right and good? How are we to know?

Let's discuss it.

Let's analyze it.

Let's look the two words up in *Strongs* and compare all their scriptural uses.

Let's compile a list.

Let's put a bumper sticker on our car that reads "Deuteronomy 6:18."

And of course before we can possibly know what is right and good we must make sure that our beliefs are correct. So let's immerse ourselves in Christian doctrine to be sure that our rightness and goodness are not merely human attempts to achieve goodness in our own fleshly strength, for we must never forget that before a holy God our goodness is as filthy rags. So let us walk carefully, because rightness and goodness may not be as simple as we think." (Please forgive my sarcasm, but these responses are used by Christians every day.)

Such reasonings are absurd. To nonsense in this vein, Dorothy Sayers bluntly replied, "Balderdash!"

Let's stop playing games with Christianity. We either are or aren't serious about obeying the commands. All humanity knows what *right* is, and what *good* is.

We know it in our hearts.

We know the difference between *selfishness* and *kindness.*

We know what being *nice* is.

We know what *unkindness* and *meanness* are.

We know the difference between *graciousness, courtesy, gentleness, generosity, sympathy, forgiveness,* versus *thoughtlessness* and *irritability, suspicion, nastiness, cruelty, rudeness, anger,* and *spitefulness.*

We *know.*

God placed that knowing within the human mental and emotional DNA when he created us. It's called conscience. Knowing, if we do not *do,* what else can it be called than mocking God—mocking his creation (our knowing) and his command (the doing).

Will we *do*?

That is the only question here. *Do*...now...in the next five minutes.

One of my sisters once said, "You know, being a Christian mostly just boils down to being nice."

I have never forgotten her words. I think she was right.

She grew up looking at that refrigerator every day too.

Thank you, heavenly Father, for this wonderfully concise, simple, prescription of obedience. What insight you gave dear Moses. Leaving aside all the doctrine and theology and so much about the Bible that is hard to understand, even things about you that are hard to understand, I just want to be good. Help me, Father, do right. Help me to be nice to everyone I encounter. Give me grace, wisdom, selflessness, and an obedient heart to do what is right and good in your sight today.

17. Do Not Let Your Heart Become Proud

Be careful that you do not forget the LORD your God, failing to observe his commands...Otherwise, when you eat and are satisfied, when you build fine houses and settle down...and your silver and gold increase and all you have is multiplied, then your heart will become proud and you will forget the LORD your God. (Deuteronomy 8:11-14, NIV)

This command could obviously go anywhere in the book. The entire Bible resonates with injunctions against pride. Pride is the original sin—the sin of Satan, the sin of Adam, the sin of Cain, the sin of Saul, the sin of David and Solomon and all the kings who did evil in the eyes of the Lord, the sin of the Pharisees, the sin of James and John when they wanted to rain fire down on their adversaries, the sin of Judas, the sin of Paul when he spoke publicly against Peter, the sin he wrote about so perceptively in

Romans 7, and the potential sin that lies in your heart and mine every moment.

Considered as intrinsic to the Choice and Consequence Code, it is obvious why Moses warned so persistently against pride. Pride is the enemy of the commands. Pride's entire motive is to undermine the commands.

Obedience requires *submission*—that word so despised by modernity. To obey requires the acknowledgement that we stand lower, in submission to, responsible to, accountable to, in the service of...Another.

Pride acknowledges *no* other but self. Pride is an independent entity unto itself, answerable and accountable to no one.

Pride sits on its own throne. Obedience relinquishes the throne.

Obedience to the commands is the mortal enemy of pride.

To survive, therefore, pride *must* circumvent, dilute, weaken, explain away, and ultimately *destroy* the commands.

Pride and obedience cannot coexist. They are mutually exclusive. For one to live, the other must die. For pride to live, this book I am writing, and that at some future time you are holding, must be rendered meaningless by a thousand subtle reasonings into heart and brain.

Pride says: A book like this, and all messages that point to obedience, must *not* be taken seriously and practically in moment-by-moment life.

Moses recognized this persistent danger—that pride is the mortal enemy of obedience. His warnings over and over—*Remember...don't forget...be careful...watch yourselves closely...walk in obedience...choose life*—all stated this command in slightly different ways:

Don't let pride kill the commands.

Pride, however, is the most cunning internal enemy we face in walking with God. Satan knew *exactly* where to target Adam and Eve's mutual pride to kill God's command in their hearts. Then he knew exactly where to target Cain's pride to kill God's commands and his own brother in the process. He knew where to target Solomon's pride that even Solomon's wisdom was not sufficient to overcome.

There is a huge lesson here. Pride targets each of us differently in ways that will cause us to kill the commands in our *own* hearts.

My pride-target will be different than yours. Your pride-target will be different than mine. I will probably be able to see *your* pride easily...all the while remaining blind to my *own*. Pride will whisper a thousand subtle reasonings to blind us to our own pride, and supply all the excuses we need not to take the commands seriously.

Therefore, Moses says: "Do not let your heart become proud." Don't let pride kill the commands.

Oh, God, I am sorry for my hidden pride that I do not see. I know I must learn to see it, and confront it, then kill it. I don't even want to pray to see it, but I know I must. Reveal to me my pride. Give me wisdom what to do and how to root it out. Give me grace and humility to know that you want to answer this prayer because you love me, and because this is the doorway into yet deeper obedience to your commands.

18. Do Not Be Afraid or Discouraged

Be strong and of good courage, do not fear or be in dread…for it is the Lord your God who goes with you…be strong and of good courage. (Deuteronomy 31:6-7)
Be strong and courageous. Do not be afraid; do not be discouraged, for the Lord your God will be with you wherever you go. (Joshua 1:9, NIV)
Fear not, for I am with you, be not dismayed, for I am your God; I will strengthen you, I will help you, I will uphold you. (Isaiah 41:10)

Most of the Bible's commands are straightforward, binary, black and white. We obey or don't obey. Others, however, are fuzzy and nebulous. Obedience is less easily defined. The choice isn't straightforward.

This is one such command. I find it troublesome and difficult, not just at times to obey, but even to know what obedience should entail. The difficulty is compounded in that it is one of the most oft repeated commands in the Old Testament. Obviously God considers it of great importance.

Yet *how* do we obey?

I am terribly prone to discouragement. In my life, I do not face the kinds of enemies the ancient Israelites faced that strike *fear* into the heart. I am rarely in fear for my life or the lives of my family. (Except a time or two in airplanes when it was a little too bumpy for comfort!)

Discouragement, however, is another matter. Sometimes discouragement and despondency so overwhelm me that I am powerless to keep from sinking into a hole of depression and despair. I can tell myself I'm not *supposed* to be discouraged. I can tell myself that I am *commanded* not to be discouraged. I can tell myself that I have no *reason* to be discouraged (which usually I don't). I can tell myself that I am greatly *blessed* in a thousand ways.

None of it helps. Discouragement is not rational. I cannot reason my way out of it. At such times, I don't know *how* to obey. This command stares me in the face, yet I am powerless. How do I simply *stop* being discouraged?

In almost sixty years since my first serious bout with debilitating discouragement and depression, and with dozens of subsequent episodes…that question remains unanswered. Simple obedience provides no solution to the dilemma of the "Ds" that has been my persistent thorn in the flesh. I have to look elsewhere for an answer.

I often speak of the importance in the life of faith of *motive*. Later in command #20 we will consider this in more detail—establishing the inner orientation of motive and heart desire toward God's perspective and purposes.

For me this is an incredibly practical principle. I may not always be capable of perfect obedience to some of the nebulous commands. Who can altogether keep from *fretting about trifles,* for instance? I fret about trifles as often as I get discouraged!

Then I remember that my *motive* and heart's desire is to obey. I remind myself that fretting and discouragement are abnormal. They are not what God wants. They are contrary to Christlikeness.

I don't know if fretting and discouragement are technically sin. We are commanded against them. But they may not quite rise to the level of *sin.* They are, however, weaknesses of my flesh, character flaws that the Spirit of Christ wants me to resist and battle against.

That battle is ongoing. I mustn't lay down and succumb to these persistent tendencies. Knowing this, I call on the Lord's help, asking for strength to endure the season of discouragement with fortitude, asking for courage to stand as God's man in spite of the fact that everything looks black around me. Perhaps most importantly I try to remember to thank him—though it can be really hard!—knowing that I am also commanded to give thanks in seasons of trial. The discouragement itself, provides opportunity to obey another command that is not the least bit nebulous—giving thanks.

Perhaps the answer to the quandary is not *giving in* to the discouragement, not *accepting* it, recognizing it as *contrary* to the life of Christ in me yet perhaps having been given me, like Paul's thorn in the flesh, for purposes I cannot see. Though as I say, it is hard to do, the prayer of gratitude in the midst of discouragement may provide a key to understanding what is otherwise a difficult command.

Remarkably, in the seeming *inability* to obey this one command, the opportunity to obey a half dozen other commands suddenly rise into prominence: thankfulness, patience, endurance, perseverance…not being anxious…trusting God…being at peace…taking up my cross…being glad in all circumstances. The failure in one area results in a many-fold greater opportunity for obedience!

As in all God's principles, fruitfulness abounds when, even in our human weakness, we set the direction of motive toward obedience.

I thank you God for the many and varied opportunities you give me to understand and obey your commands. It is hard to thank you for being discouraged, though I will try. But at least I can thank you that discouragement provides rich soil for so many other good things to grow. Remind me of this truth the next time I sink into a hole.

19. Remember Blessings and Consequences and Choose Life

I have set before you this day life and good, death and evil. If you obey the commandments of the LORD your God which I command you this day, by loving the LORD your God, by walking in his ways, and by keeping his commandments and his statutes and his ordinances, then…the LORD your God will bless you in the land…But if your heart turns away, and you…are drawn away to worship other gods…I declare to you this day, that…you shall not live long in the land…I call heaven and earth to witness…this day, that I have set before you life and death, blessing and curse; therefore choose life, that you and your descendants may live.
(Deuteronomy 30:15-19)

Moses' commands, *Remember, do not forget, watch yourselves closely that you do not forget,* stated in diverse ways, are perhaps the most oft-repeated theme in *Deuteronomy.*

In chapters 4-8, Moses hammers the Israelites with variations on this theme over and over. These few snatches are taken only from those five chapters. But they are repeated in *many* ways throughout the entire book, and brought to a climax in chapter 30.

—And now, O Israel, give heed to the statutes and the ordinances which I teach you, and do them…

—Only take heed, and keep your soul diligently, lest you forget…

—Therefore take good heed to yourselves…

—Beware lest…you be drawn away…

—Take heed to yourselves, lest you forget the covenant of the Lord your God…

—You shall be careful to do therefore as the Lord your God has commanded you…

—Hear therefore, O Israel, and be careful to do them; that it may go well with you…

—Then take heed lest you forget the Lord…

—You shall therefore be careful to do the commandment, and the statutes, and the ordinances, which I command you this day…

—All the commandment which I command you this day you shall be careful to do…

—You shall remember…

—Take heed lest you forget the Lord your God…

—You shall remember the Lord your God.

There is a reason why God and Moses beat this drum so constantly. It is human nature to forget, to get lazy, to drift in dedication and commitment. Culminating this persistent message as he climaxes his farewell address, Moses frames the distinction by drawing an unmistakable line in the sand:

- *Obedience vs. disobedience.*
- *Life vs. death.*

- *Blessings vs. curses.*

We have to take a stand on one side or the other. Therefore, Moses says, *choose life.*

The curses of which Moses speaks are not punishments. They are natural consequences. Certain things happen when we follow God's principles. Good things. Blessings. Other things happen when we live, think, behave, and walk through life contrary to God's principles. Things that do *not* produce good and blessings in life.

The word *curse* is unfortunate. It conveys the mistaken assumption that God's curse is a punishment for disobedience. The word *consequence* conveys the meaning more accurately. We bring consequences upon ourselves by the way we think and behave and live.

This principle is found throughout *Proverbs.* Rather than speaking of "curses," Solomon emphasizes the natural fruit, benefits, blessings, and *consequences* of either living or not living by God's principles: *Do this...and you will...*

Using many specifics, analogies, images, and life-situations, Solomon is expanding upon Moses' words. Moses and Solomon speak the same message.

During my lifetime study and reflection on the commands, I have long been struck with how "unspiritual," so to speak, many of God's commands are. The commands of Jesus are remarkably down-to-earth. Many act as brief exclamation marks to those of Moses.

Moses:

- *Now what I am commanding you today is not too difficult for you or beyond your reach. No, the word is very near you; it is in your mouth and in your heart so you may obey it.*
- *See, I set before you today life and prosperity, death and destruction.*
- *I command you today to love the Lord your God, to walk in obedience to him, and to keep his commands, decrees and laws. Then you will live and increase, and the Lord your God will bless you in the land.*
- *But if your heart turns away and you are not obedient, and if you are drawn away to bow down to other gods and worship them, I declare to you this day that you will certainly not live long in the land.*
- *This day I call the heavens and the earth as witnesses that I have set before you life and death, blessings and curses. Now choose life, so that you and your children may live and that you may love the Lord your God, listen to his voice, and hold fast to him.*

—Deuteronomy 30: 11, 14-17, 19-20

Then Jesus adds his summarizing punctuation:

- *Be careful and watchful.*
- *Remain alert and on guard.*
- *Take heed to yourselves.*

The command, *Remember,* lies at the heart of all the commands. Without the mental diligence to remember, taking care not to forget, spiritual laziness sets in. Spiritual lethargy, and ultimately spiritual death, begins with not making the effort to remember.

Holy Spirit, I invite you to stir up my brain to remembrance. I invite you, I entreat you to act as an internal alarm clock when I begin to go to sleep spiritually. Wake me up. Jolt me out of my lethargy. Bring the commands ringing loudly into my brain. Help me remember!

20. Set the Desires of Your Heart Godward

"Trust in the Lord, and do good…delight yourself in the Lord,
and he will give you the desires of your heart.
Commit your way to him and trust in him, and he will bring it to pass.
And he will bring forth your righteousness as the light.
Rest in the Lord and wait patiently for him." Psalm 37:3-7

In the introduction, I spoke of the Bible's promises representing the second half of an *if-then* equation—God's *promises* being the fruit of *obedience* to his commands.

We now bring the "Choice and Consequence Code" to its fulfillment with a beautifully complex multi-layered if-then progression. It is one of the most profound if-then sequences in the Bible. But because it is not set down linearly, at first glance the progression is a little difficult to lay hold of. I encourage you to give it the prayerful time needed to unravel its intricacies. I think I can guarantee that you will be rewarded with what might be life-changing insights.

I call the command-promise principle embodied in the passage quoted above setting one's *Internal Spiritual Compass Godward.*

The direction in which our lives grow is regulated by an internal character compass whose needle and directionality we each determine for ourselves. Circumstances and luck don't determine what we make of our lives and ourselves. We do.

You and I decide toward what North our compasses point.

The promise found in Psalm 37:4, "Delight yourself in the Lord, and he will give you the desires of your heart," is one of my lifelong favorite verses. This promise has sustained me through some difficult times. It has been one of the foundational anchoring truths of my spiritual life. As I look back over more than fifty years of walking with God and attempting to communicate truth to God's people, I am blessed beyond expression to see how God has fulfilled that promise.

But the fifteen words of this verse cannot be taken out of their larger context and read simplistically as promising that God will give us whatever we desire. More depth is contained in Psalm 37:3-7 than a mere promise. We must also ask what exactly are the desires of the heart he promises to give? This is the question that forces us to the deepest foundations of who we are.

As we dig deeper, we discover increasing layers to the *if-command*. Exploring these layers forces us to probe deep into the marrow of personhood where our most basic "heart's desires" dwell.

The full passage of Psalm 37:3-7 illuminates a sweeping series of "ifs" that drive us to the all-important question each of us must eventually face:

What *is* my deepest heart's desire? Is it the *right* heart's desire?

That right heart's desire, the heart's desire God wants us to cherish, is *righteousness*. That is the direction toward which my internal compass is supposed to point toward, with *righteousness* as my heart's desire.

The verses of this passage lay out the sequence—the deepening layers of the if-command—of setting one's internal compass:

- Trust God.
- Do good.
- Delight in him.
- Commit your way to him.
- Set righteousness as your heart's desire.
- Rest in God.
- Wait patiently for him.

...and he will give you the desire of your heart.

We find the forceful *command* half of the equation in verses 3 and 5: "Do good...commit your way to him...trust him."

This is the hinge point linking *command* and *promise*. This is the command inherent in Psalm 37. It is foundational to all the commands. It lies at the heart of the Choice and Consequence Code. The "if" hinge.

Do good...commit your way to him...trust him.

Then follows the blessings half of the if-then equation? Will God give us *anything* we desire? Obviously not. We have to desire the right things.

Verse 6 tells us what heart's desire will fulfill the promise—*righteousness*.

When righteousness is the desire of the heart, and we commit ourselves to growing in righteousness, he will fulfill that heart's desire.

Not *any* desire of the heart. But *that* specific desire of the heart.

That is the promise, the fruit, and the blessing. If righteousness seems a long time coming, we may "rest patiently for him" to bring it about.

In speaking of the heart's desire of righteousness, David is pointing toward a higher prize even than the wisdom sought by his son. For the dedicated follower of Jesus, this highest of all desires is fulfilled in Christlikeness.

Yet with the righteousness of Christlikeness at the North of the compass, other desires may be drawn in and fulfilled along with it. As God blesses his people with righteousness, other blessings often follow in its wake. The promises of *Deuteronomy* about a land flowing with milk and honey are not idle promises. But the heart's desire of righteousness is always the door that opens into that land.

The phrase *commit your way* in verse 5 is forceful. It implies determination and dedication. We have to *know* what our character North is, and keep the compass pointed toward it.

Periodic self assessments and *re-settings* of the internal spiritual compass are intrinsic to that commitment. I *choose* in what direction my life will go. I have to re-choose that direction every day. If I am not paying attention, the needle of my character-compass may begin to waver.

The command *Delight in the Lord* on the surface seems at first glance like a feeling or emotion that we may not be able to control. But I believe, however, that this "delight" can be chosen whether we're feeling it or not. David's expansive expressions of love for and delight in God's commands in Psalm 119 are our roadmap for *choosing* to love God's ways, his principles, his precepts, his outlook…his commands.

There are dozens of substitutes toward which the life-compasses of the multitudes point. Most people aren't even aware what direction they are moving. Taking life as it comes, they've never bothered to set the direction of their compass at all

But righteousness and Christlikeness never develop in human character by auto-pilot, but by continually *reaffirming* and *re-pointing* one's internal compass Godward.

Of course the reality seems slow in coming. I am dishearteningly aware of my weakness. But God is building eternal character over a lifetime. What lies to me is to keep my compass pointed Godward. The earlier in life we begin, and the oftener we reaffirm its direction, the more and sooner will God be able to fulfill the promise.

Moses calls this realignment process *taking heed to yourself.* George MacDonald places in the mouth of his characters the words: *I had better watch what I am about.*

They're both saying the same thing: Keep your compass pointing North.

God, I desire more than anything to be your obedient son, to grow in righteousness. To my earthly sight I am light years from anything approaching Christlikeness. But I trust that you know what you are doing. I can only point my internal compass toward that eternal hope that is in me, and ask you to mature me in your own way and in your time. Thus I commit my way to you.

Series Three

Authority

Let There Be!

The foundation of creation, the universe, humanity, and truth

God's First Two Prophet-Types:

Authority revealed in two historic lives of early *Genesis*: We are all Adam, but we are called to emulate Noah

Innumerable theories exist about everything. But about *ultimate* beginnings, the *first* Cause from which all later effects spring, the *beginning* of beginnings, there is only one explanation on the market. It is found in Genesis 1 and 2. Thus far, no Albert Einstein or Steven Hawking, no brilliant physicist or philosopher or theologian, has offered a credible alternative to the *Genesis* account of how the universe and life originated out of pure nothingness.

In exploring the Old Testament commands, we will do our best not to get sidetracked by contested points, nor attempt to unravel what is by definition impossible to fully understand. Our purpose is different. It is to see what the Bible tells us about life, God, ourselves, and how we are supposed to relate to this One about whom we know so little but whom there is no other word to describe than our *Creator*. Mysterious as it is—if we follow causes and effects back far enough to *ultimate* beginnings, there is no alternative than to say that you and I were "created" too.

Scientists take exception to the word *creation*. But what other idea or concept or theory are they going to use in its place? *After* Genesis 1-2, *after* the atoms and energy and matter were formed, made, or "created," at that point there are hundreds if not thousands of theories about how the universe and life as we know it flowed from those ultimate "creative" beginnings. But creation is the *only* logical word to conceptualize ultimate beginnings, what came *before* the Big Bang.

Though not everyone agrees with their dating conclusions, physicists, astronomers, and religious skeptics now date "beginnings" to what is called the "Big Bang" when scientists conjecture that the universe was formed. Tracing its present expansion backwards, it is mathematically computed to have occurred between 13.8 and 14 billion years ago, when all the condensed matter (or we might call it *pre*-matter) of the universe was comprised of pure infinite energy, then exploded outward. It has been rushing in all directions ever since, eventually giving rise to galaxies and stars and solar systems, and of course our own sun and its system of planets, our earth, and finally to life itself. All this is assumed to have somehow occurred "naturally" or by accident.

Fair enough. Except for those last two words. If you trace causes and effects back far enough, *nothing* truly happens by accident. *Everything* has an originating causal beginning.

The Achilles heel of science, and all scientific theories, the great blind spot of scientific academia for the past three hundred years, is that it does not trace cause and effect back far enough. As brilliant as many scientists are, men like Steven Hawking—one of the pioneers in establishing the Big Bang as the accepted model of so-called "beginnings"— almost universally allow this glaring blind spot to infect the credibility of their underlying assumptions, and thus the theories that grow from their hypotheses. They rarely inquire into *ultimate* beginnings.

Where did the condensed matter come from? Where did the infinite *energy* to ignite the Big Bang come from? Where did the atoms and sub-atomic particles to make matter come from? What set off the Big Bang? What was going on *before* the Big Bang?

These are far from merely theoretical questions. Everything hinges on how we answer them. Nothing comes from nothing. There are *always* causes and effects, all the way back to beginnings, all the way back…well, to nothingness—to the beginning of beginnings.

The mystery of "creation" is deepened by the almost mythical nature of the *Genesis* account. Nobody was there to record the events. The debate is all the more heated on the basis of the date added to millions of King James Bibles declaring that the creation of the world took place in the year 4004 B.C. This date has lodged deeply in the minds of many, setting up an unfortunate divide between science and religion about the origins and age of the universe.

What does that mean for us? Now, today? That is the inquiry before us. For the purposes of this book, I hope we can lay aside the many dating and factuality and historical arguments that rage about the *Genesis* account, and join together by digging deeper than those questions reach, and discover practical, daily reality for ourselves and how we live.

The biblical account of *Genesis* does more than give an account (nebulous, unspecific about timing and means and methods) of *ultimate* beginnings. It also records (equally fraught with debate, controversy, and uncertainty) humankind's earliest beginnings and responses to its role on the earth and in the "created" universe.

Those first responses center on authority. Mankind's initial exposure to authority—the authority of God, the authority of "Let there be!" by which the universe came into being—is embodied in the man *Adam.*

Adam is without doubt the most debated and enigmatic personality of the Old Testament. The quandary boiled down to its essence is this:

Was Adam a factual and historical man who lived at a certain time in history?

Thus the next question is whether or not the *Genesis* account of Adam's creation and life in Genesis 1-4 is accurate history exactly as written. Is that account fact, or is it intended to give an *interpretive* and *legendary* account of mankind's beginnings? The latter in no way compromises either the divine inspiration or the veracity of Scripture. The Bible is full of *interpretive* but equally *inspired* accounts which point toward truth no less than factually precise events.

We don't know how to thread the needle between *factual* and *interpretive* in the Bible. Though the debate between the many possibilities is heated, and those on both sides *claim* to know the answer with certainty, we simply *cannot* truly know. Honesty demands that we acknowledge ambiguity. The Bible contains historical *facts*. And the Bible contains interpretive *legends, parables, prophecies,* and *stories*. These different narrative types, or genres, are not always easy to distinguish and differentiate from each other. They flow and intermingle fluidly. The account of Adam and Eve is one of the most difficult to fit specifically into one category or another.

In the text of *Genesis*, two different Hebrew words are used for "man":

- *âdâm*—man, humankind, man in a general sense, the race of men and women;
- *iysh*—man, a single, specific, individual human male.

The distinction is seen in how the Bible speaks differently of Adam and Noah. In Genesis 6:9 ("Noah was a just man *[iysh]*...") Noah is an individual specific man. We can assume from this that his life was historically *factual*. The word *iysh* places him in that *fact* category. We cannot necessarily say that every tiny detail about him is precisely factual as recorded. It may be, it may not be. We simply cannot know. But the *iysh* makes Noah *himself* a factual man of history.

This is not the case, however, with Adam. He is *not* spoken of in this specific sense. Nothing in the text of Genesis 1-4 distinguishes *âdâm,* the race of "mankind," from a certain specific *individual* of that race. English translators render the word *âdâm* differently—*man, the man,* and *Adam*—as they choose to translate it. But the original Hebrew text itself makes no such distinction. Every mention of Adam is *âdâm.*

The word used does not indicate a specific historical individual, but a race of beings.

Noah is an *îysh*—a historical individual man. But Adam is *âdâm*—a race of beings.

For example:

Genesis 1:27— "So God created *âdâm (man...the race)* in his own image."

Genesis 2:18— "The Lord God said, 'It is not good for *âdâm (the man)* to be alone. I will make a helper suitable for him.'"

Genesis 2:20— "But for *âdâm (Adam)* no suitable helper was found."

In the Hebrew text, they are all the *same* word. So does the text indicate *mankind* as *the human race* of men and women, or does the writer at some point intend us to begin reading the word *âdâm* differently? Does the writer intend us to make a transition from interpreting the word *âdâm* as a race of beings to *a single specific man* named Adam?

How did the translations of *âdâm* in Genesis 1-3 gradually shift from *man*—mankind, humanity, humankind, the human species—to *the man*...and finally to *Adam*?

We can imagine how these legendary beginnings coalesced. As stories from the past were told from father and grandfather to son and daughter, passed along in a continuous succession, the Hebrew word for "man" or "mankind" gradually became the name of a *certain* man. Compounding the same progression, did early translations of the Hebrew—first into Greek, then Latin, and finally English—turn *mankind* in Genesis 1-3 into the individual man *Adam* by a mistake of translation?

The point is not to answer this conundrum, but to highlight the important fact that the question of how to read early *Genesis* presents a fundamental and unanswerable conundrum. The Bible *itself* does not specify *âdâm* as a specific factual historical figure. Adam *may* have been a factual man of history like Noah. But the Bible itself doesn't say so. Many people believe he was. But the Bible doesn't specify him to be.

To read *Genesis* accurately we have to do so with minds open to the bigger picture of its message. That message begins with *Authority*, then proceeds as mankind, and/or Adam as a specific individual, responded to that authority.

We all must, in a sense, place ourselves in that story of beginnings. *We are all Adam.* In our humanity, we are both *âdâm* and *iysh.*

We are mankind, *and* we are specific men and women of humanity and of history.

The resounding authority of *Let there be!* sets up man's most important response to creation, life, the world, God, and ourselves. You and I follow in *âdâm's* footsteps (the earliest men and women of our race) in trying to determine who we are, where we came from, and how we are to live in the world.

The quest for truth, knowledge, self-knowing, and God-knowing begins with Authority.

In a personal way, however, God's reality, presence, and authority were vague, ambiguous, and undefined after the creation. The Bible indicates that God *spoke* to *âdâm* and Eve and Cain, but we really don't know what that means.

The first five chapters serve as a Prologue. There will continue to be debate about them. But the real story begins at chapter 6. That's when the vague and fluid pre-history of a race of created beings called humanity spreading throughout the earth (some of it probably factual, some probably legendary) morphs into *factual history.*

Authority now becomes personal.

God becomes personal.

The first mighty Prophet-*Iysh* steps onto the pages of Scripture in Chapter 6. Noah is not an *âdâm,* he is a real man, a *specific* man linked to real definable history. There was a catastrophic flood. That is an indisputable archaeological fact. When it took place, whether it was regional or worldwide—these specifics will continue to be debated along with the Bible's first five chapters. But the *facts* remain:

- Noah was a *real* man.
- There was a *real* flood.
- God spoke personally to Noah.

In the life of Noah, authority became *personal*. Therefore, obedience also became personal. Noah did what God told him to do.

Out of the vague mists of pre-history, Noah emerges with clarity as a man (a factual man of history) with whom God related in a new and personal way over a lifetime.

Noah is the prophetic forerunner of all humanity that will follow him, and that will spread out and people the earth. Along with *âdâm*/Adam, though more personally and with undeniable factuality of existence, Noah is a human-father of mankind.

Both are prophet-types through whom God established the initial guidelines specifying the relationship he wanted to have with his created beings.

We are told, "Noah was a righteous man, blameless in his generation; Noah walked with God." (Genesis 6:9)

This is one of the most remarkable statements in the Bible. It sets up all that is to follow in humankind's long history. It establishes God's purpose for his created men and women of humanity

We were created to be righteous and to walk with God.

Series Three

Authority

21. Acknowledge God's authority.

22. Embrace command.

23. Choose obedience.

24. Walk with God.

25. Do not let sin beguile you.

26. Run from sin.

27. Honor marriage and family.

28. Separate from the world.

29. Keep covenant with God.

30. Live as a manifestly distinct righteousness-choosing people.

21. Acknowledge God's Authority

"Let there be..." (Genesis 1:3)

Contrary to prevailing modern thought, the answers to many, probably most, of life's quandaries are rooted in the first three chapters of the Bible. While Christians and secularists, Jews and atheists, traditionalists and modernists expend great mental energy debating the endless complex historical, theological, archaeological, and spiritual issues raised by Genesis 1-3, none of these unanswerables point us practically toward how we are supposed to live.

Nothing matters more than how we *live* day to day. How we treat others. How we relate to our Maker. The men and women we are, and the men and women we are *becoming*. None of the metaphysical conundrums of early *Genesis*, even if answered perfectly, are capable of producing maturity and wisdom of personhood.

For that we need to explore the *meaning* hidden deep between the lines of these three chapters. The *meaning* is the same whether one believes the universe is fourteen billion years old or six thousand years old. The *meaning* of Genesis 1-3, if we can be diligent to discover it, is the same for everyone.

What matters is that the universe was created by Almighty God. It was created out of nothing. It was created by the power and intrinsic beingness of his infinite Authority.

This is the foundational essence, the *meaning*, of the opening verse of the Bible: *God created.*

Sheer Authority.

Let there be...and there was.

- Let there be a firmament...and it was so.
- Let the waters be gathered...and it was so.
- Let the earth...and it was so.
- Let there be light...and it was so.
- Let the waters bring forth...and God saw that it was good.
- Let the earth bring forth...and it was so.
- Then God said, "Let us make man..."

As we continue our exploration into the commands of the Old Testament, now looking back to the ultimate beginnings where those commands originated, the first, primary, essential, imperative foundation stone upon which everything that follows in the entire Bible—Old and New Testaments together— is the resounding Truth revealed in every line of Genesis 1-2: *Authority.*

Though passive, even to a degree what we might call intellectual rather than visibly practical, the first essential command out of which all truth and understanding of life and the world grows, is the simple recognition of the resounding truth of God's originating authority.

- We were created by God's authority.
- We live under God's authority.
- We are answerable to God's authority.

Gone is modernism's futile yearning for autonomous independence, the utopian fancy that we are free and self-ruling agents answerable to no one but ourselves. Such independence is a mirage.

The foundation of life's meaning begins in Genesis 1, with the acknowledgment of God's supreme and ultimate authority. His authority extends over all creation, over the universe, over every living thing, over every man and woman and child, over you and me.

He created us. God is our Father.

Therefore, we are his children.

Truth begins, meaning begins, wisdom begins, personhood begins, in the acknowledgment of his Fathering authority. The first prayer, the beginning of all prayer, the originating cry of humanity into the vast heaven of creation, bowing in our created childness, is simplicity itself: *I acknowledge your authority.*

God, I acknowledge your creating and Fathering authority over the universe, and over me. May your originating command, "Let us make man in our image," be real and personal in my life—a reminder that you fashioned me and knew me even before I was born. I owe you my life. I owe you everything. I bow before you, and acknowledge you as the supreme creating good of my life

22. Embrace Command

"Be fruitful…multiply…fill…subdue…have dominion." (Genesis 2:28)

What does that infinite, creating, Father-Authority *mean*? What does Authority imply?

First is the recognition that *command* is intrinsic to *authority*. Authority expresses its will by command, not suggestion, debate, explanation, discussion, or persuasion.

Authority is the noun, command is the verb by which authority acts.

God *commanded* creation. *Let there be!* is the ultimate statement of command.

And the command of authority was obeyed: *There was light.*

The very fact of authority necessitates the essential imperative of *command* as the mechanism by which authority delivers its will. Authority does not attempt to talk its subjects into doing its will. It *commands* obedience to its will.

God commanded the universe and all matter in it, the heavens and its galaxies and stars and planets and moons, the earth and its waters and inanimate growing things, its laws, its motions, its science, its changes and growth and expansion and evolutionary development.

And all the universe obeyed. The universe obeyed the command of creation.

God *commanded*. The universe *obeyed*.

We may likewise recognize in the animals of creation a similar obedience to Authority's creation-command. The natural instinct possessed by the lower animals, in a vivid and real sense, embodies their "obedience" to the unique command given them, obedience which was implanted within their essential nature to define each species' unique "personhood," so to speak, its individuality and animalhood. Like the inanimate creation (stars and planets, rocks and rivers, oceans and trees), the lower animal kingdom obeyed because it could do no other. It *had* to obey. Trees, rivers, horses, plants, and atoms *have* to abide by (obey) their intrinsic createdness.

God commanded…and it was. Cows obeyed their essential innate created cowness. Crocodiles obeyed their innate created crocodileness. Mosquitos obeyed their innate created mosquitoness. Fish obeyed their innate created fishness. Birds obeyed their innate created birdness. Whales obeyed their innate created whaleness. Obedience followed command.

Then follows that wonderfully simple yet mysterious, and infinitely debated statement: "So God created man in his own image…male and female he created them."

Into mankind God placed something other than raw innate compulsory instinct. He placed in man that mysterious and unfathomable thing the writer of *Genesis* simply calls his *image*. What does it mean when God said that he would make man "in his image?"

As we ponder the great mystery of it, we immediately see what happened next. God began to issue his new higher creation *commands*. He told his man and woman what he wanted them to *do*, what he expected of them: "Be fruitful and multiply, fill the earth and subdue it, have dominion…over every living thing that moves upon the earth."

We might have used the parallel wording "acknowledge command." After acknowledging God's authority, however, merely *acknowledging* command, even acknowledging the *imperative* of command, is not enough.

Mankind was intended to do more than acknowledge. Humanity was intended to step into the living *reality* of command.

God commanded. He expected the men and women created in his image to acknowledge his authority, to acknowledge his right as their Father and Creator to command them, then to *embrace* command, and *live in* command as the governing decree placed upon their lives.

Embrace it…*hold close to command* as the essence of life!

Mankind's second imperative prayer, therefore, yielding yet more fully to the reality of his God's-image childness, becomes:

God, I embrace command as the mandate of your authority upon my life. Give me the wisdom and humility not only to acknowledge command but to welcome it. As your created child, I invite you to command me.

23. Choose Obedience

"You may freely eat…you shall not eat." (Genesis 2:16-17)

Progressing yet deeper into the practical *meaning* of Genesis 1-3—beyond its complex debatable issues of factuality, historicity, and timing—we discover that neither acknowledgment of God's authority, nor embracing command as the ruling mechanism by which the universe was set in motion and is designed to function, are sufficient to explain what came next.

Whatever were the far reaching and eternal implications of the fact that he had created mankind "in his image," the first consequence was immediately apparent—man was utterly distinct from the rest of animal creation. Not just more skilled, more intelligent, smarter, more dexterous and capable. His men and women were another kind of being altogether. Cows and whales obey their cowness and whaleness by instinct. God wanted man to *choose* its manness, its womanness, its humanness.

By his originating command he placed his humans above—in charge of—the earth-portion of his creation and its growing things (subdue the earth) and its lower beings (have dominion over every living thing). In their chosen humanity, God's men and women were tasked with stewardship over the earth. God gave the management of his world into the hands of the unique species of his final creation—created in his own image to enable them to do the job skillfully and faithfully.

But in the middle of Genesis 2, God's command-mandate took an unexpected (and perilous) turn. He set before his highest creation, a new kind of command—a prohibition.

All his commands up to this point were positive: *You may.*

Suddenly here was a difference: *You shall not.*

Notice the singularly important word *may.* "You may eat freely of every tree in the garden, but of the tree of the knowledge of good and evil you shall not eat."

May adds a subtle new twist to command. It is a word in which both permission *and* prohibition are implied. But the *shall* not, is definite and unyielding. The "may" is still operative, but the "shall not" carries an unmistakable warning. Adding further to the intrigue of this shift in God's command-mandate, he seems intentionally to tantalize man's curiosity by placing in the garden a tree from which he forbids him to eat.

Calling *everything* good, and giving man *every* tree for food, this is most curious. Suddenly we encounter something not good at all—*evil.* Or rather, we should probably clarify, containing the *potential* for evil. Why God did this, why he seems to tempt man in this way, is a great mystery. Somehow God wanted to convey that joy and fruitfulness in life would be the result of *chosen* obedience to him rather than mere animal instinct. For reasons we do not entirely grasp, this was his way to do it.

What a gift he gave us in free will! With grateful hearts, we should desire with our whole beings to choose wisely, to choose goodness!

At the seventeenth verse of Chapter 2, the entire narrative shifts on its axis. Not only are good and evil introduced as opposites. The specter of *death* enters creation, with the chilling warning following the prohibition, "In the day that you eat of it you shall die." This is a titanic swing in tone.

Up till now it would be possible to read the account by viewing "man" simply as the highest of the animals, or in post-Darwinist terminology, as occupying the highest rung on the evolutionary ladder—not as intrinsically *different in kind* but as the true "king of beasts," the greatest lion-king of all, a spectacular species with huge brain and far more cleverly "evolved" physical and mental and emotional capabilities. But still an animal.

Genesis 2:17 throws all that out the window. Animal *instinct* cannot explain what comes next.

In the "may" of verse sixteen, God takes a step back. In the following verse he takes another step back, handing man a gift nothing else in creation possesses.

To mankind, and *only* to mankind, the Creator gives determinative *choice* to regulate, influence, and define his life-direction, even alter his intrinsic personhood—to choose the nature of his own becoming. It is a stunning development. Stunning because verse seventeen reveals that man has even been given the power to *disobey* the command of his creator-Father.

God has truly stepped back—leaving man alone with his decision. He will command obedience, he will invite obedience, but he will not *compel* obedience.

Choice will forever after represent the fulcrum of life-direction.

Again comes the question why. *Why* God gave his men and women this extraordinary power is one of the great theological conundrums of the ages. In doing so, God *removes* his authority from mankind's inner epicenter of will. He gives man complete *freedom* to choose what he will do, how he will behave, and who and what he will become.

God truly steps away. He issues his command, then gives his men and women the power (not permission, but the power—the "may" is a coin with two sides) either to obey or disobey.

The entire history of mankind, the history of every man and woman, your personal history and mine, thus rests on the hinge point of the implied command of Genesis 2:17: *Choose obedience.*

The prayer of personhood, therefore—for ancient man (though perhaps *feeling* it and *sensing* it and falling in with its life-direction more than articulating it as I do here) as well as for you and me—reaches its threefold culmination as a prayer of *choosing*.

It is a prayer that not every man and woman—neither ancient nor modern—will choose to offer. Yet it is the only doorway into the full flourishing "manness," "womanness," or *humanness* if you like, for which each of us was uniquely created in the image of our Maker.

These first three principles—authority, command, obedience—establish the foundation for all that will follow, and for all the commands of the Old Testament. If this seems like a theological history lesson, it is because all the commands of the prophets—those we have already considered, and those yet to come—emerge out of this threefold foundation.

My creator and Father, I acknowledge your authority, I embrace command as your mandate upon my life as your son or daughter, and I choose obedience to your word, your will, your authority, and your command. Embed this foundation so deep into my consciousness that it becomes the basis for my worldview, and the moment-by-moment practical foundation for everything in my life. Remind me constantly that to choose obedience to you is the essence of life.

24. Walk with God

"They heard the sound of the Lord God walking in the garden in the cool of the day, and the man and his wife hid themselves." (Genesis 3:8)

A reminder here is in order, one that may have to be repeated again to counter the red herrings of factuality that always persist in a discussion of this nature. The deeper truths of our quest are independent of and disconnected from the factitude of every jot and tittle of the biblical account. Whether one reads *Genesis* literally or as a fictional myth, whether one reads evolution into the narrative or takes all the elements of creation as occurring instantly by fiat from God's authoritative command, whether one reads the day of creation as indicating twenty-four hours or eons of years—differences of interpretation do not change the *meaning* inherent within these chapters.

The truth that comes from certain myths and fables is no less powerful than truth emerging from fact. It is *truth* we seek however it is implanted into our minds and hearts. That is not to say that questions of factuality and timing are not significant, even imperative, for other reasons. They most definitely *are* important—for scientist and theologian alike. Some of the issues raised by the *Genesis* narrative are of exceeding import. But the answers to those questions are not central to *this* particular inquiry into the commands of the Old Testament. I am on a quest seeking the practical *meaning* of the narrative at deeper levels than factuality, timing, and historicity.*

As the early *Genesis* account continues, the next two commands take their wording from the pivotal third chapter, in which human history takes a disastrous turn.

In the eighth verse, presenting another of many evocative yet mysterious biblical images, we find God "walking in the garden in the cool of the day." We cannot know exactly what is meant by that image. We do know, however, that the man and woman were *not* walking with him.

We know why. They had disobeyed the command of Genesis 2:17. They had exercised the free will of choice and had chosen foolishly. Instead of walking *with* God, as obedient children, happy and content, looking up to their Father, living in obedience to his commands, *embracing* his commands, holding his hand in the cool of the garden, they now made a second foolish choice. They tried to hide from him.

They had indeed sinned by eating from the tree they had been commanded against. Even then, however, it was not too late to walk *with* their Father again. But fear had entered their hearts. Instead of running *to* their Father, they ran *away* to hide. Not only had their disobedience brought *sin* into the world, in its wake came *fear* of their only safety, comfort, and refuge—mankind's loving Father.

It will be obvious to the discerning reader at this point that I have taken interpretive liberty in my phrasing of this command. God did not directly command Adam and Eve to walk with him. I am always seeking the intent of God's heart in his revelation of himself to man. For this discussion to have meaning, we have to look to the big picture of God's *purposes.* Doing so often requires reading the Bible from a higher perspective than literality. The landscape is more fully visible as a whole from an airplane than a camera on the ground.

Not only must we obey God's commands, we must *discover* his commands. We must discover the practicality of command even when it may not be immediately visible from a literal reading.

In the *Genesis* account, therefore, I take it as God's purpose that he *desired* to walk with his man and woman. He had created them to enjoy fellowship with him. That was his intent and purpose. Thus I discover in the account what I call an *implied* command.

Mankind is supposed to *walk with God.* That was his intent and purpose.

Yet here God was walking in the garden alone. Something was wrong with the picture. Adam and Eve were *not* with him. They had distanced themselves. They were supposed to walk *with* him in the garden in the cool of the day. But they were walking *apart* from him.

All the subsequent pains and fears, discouragements and terrors, frustrations and disappointments of humankind's long sojourn in a hostile world could have been put to rest—and can this very day be put to rest in

---

* I emphasize this because I have addressed many of these debatable issues in the volumes of *The Eyewitness Old Testament,* and to a lesser degree *The Eyewitness New Testament.*

the heart of one who reaches up to the waiting hand—had men and women heeded the deep meaning of Eden's cool breezes.

Rightness is always just a moment away. Rightness is born the instant men and women turn from their foolish desire for independence and choose to *walk with God*. It is never too late to take the hand of the Father. He is always waiting for us to walk with him.

When he says, "Where are you?" that is the moment to reply:

Here am I, Lord. I have not obeyed you as I should. Forgive me. Help me henceforth to choose obedience to your commands, and walk with you, not hide from you, because you are my Father.

God, give me wisdom to see myself in the ancient Genesis story. Show me where I have broken off from you and gone walking on my own. Forgive me for doing so. Give me humility to return to you, to reach up and take your hand, and walk with you again in the cool of this day in which I find myself.

25. Do Not Let Evil Beguile You

"The serpent beguiled me, and I ate." (Genesis 3:13)

If we can avoid the distraction of the hot-button topics of *Genesis*, we discover in these chapters an absolute wealth of practical wisdom. Whoever wrote this account—Moses, an unknown scribe, or multiple historians and scribes through the centuries whose work was gradually collated into a single account (many associate Ezra with this editorial role)—the wisdom of these early chapters has no explanation other than divine inspiration. The creation account itself in Genesis 1 is breathtaking. The profundity of the next two chapters is almost beyond comprehension.

Taking another significant verse from Genesis 3, we encounter a word laden with rich and important meaning. Eve's response to God's question, "What have you done?" is as profound as anything that has come before, exquisitely illuminating the entire history of humanity.

If C.S. Lewis is right, we all know right from wrong. * We are perfectly aware of what he calls "the higher standard" of righteousness. Adam and Eve knew it was wrong to eat from the tree. But they were lured, tempted, persuaded to eat anyway. They used the gift of choice they had been given, and *chose* to disobey. Then, instead of confessing and asking forgiveness, they tried to excuse what they had done by blaming someone else. Having disobeyed and being called to account, they instantly passed the buck. "It was the woman's fault," says Adam. "It was the serpent's fault," says Eve.

The word Eve uses to defend herself slams with magnum force into our own lives. "The serpent *beguiled* me."

* Such is the basis of the early chapters of Lewis's classic apologetic for the Christian faith, *Mere Christianity*. It is also the basis of Paul's argument for the universal knowledge of God's moral and ethical standards in Romans 1.

This is *always* how evil gets a toe through the door of our minds. It beguiles us. We follow Eve's pattern. The all-important open door to evil comes the moment the question is posed (and sometimes which we put to ourselves): "Did God say...no, that's not true—you *may* eat. You *won't* die."

Beguilement comes in a thousand disguises from a thousand sources, giving us counterfeit permission to disobey. We are willing accomplices. We *want* to be persuaded because, like Eve, we *desire* it. We *want* to believe that we can succumb to the beguiling voice, eat the fascinating Turkish Delight,* the fruit "good for food and a delight to the eyes." Because we *want* to believe, we choose to convince ourselves that no harm will come of it...that we will "not die."

Such moments of beguilement can be seen in movies and on television every day. They are instructive in helping us recognize them. The exchanges may *seem* perfectly innocent. Two or three people are talking and a question or invitation is posed. "No, I don't think we should..." replies the one of the group whose conscience is active to what is going on. Then the others chime in, "Aw, come on...it'll be fun..."

It's seldom so obvious as, "Come with us, we're going to rob a bank...we're going to shoot someone." Beguilement against our better judgment is always subtle and comes in small doses. We convince ourselves they're not so serious. Peer pressure makes the beguilement all the more powerful, especially when a hint of wrong or danger might be involved.

"What, are you chicken? Are you *afraid*?"

The serpent knows exactly which individual buttons to push to make beguilement impossible to refuse. Giving in is easy. Turning to walk away from the beguiling temptation takes courage.

The tactics of beguilement can be devious and condescending, made harder to resist when the serpent speaks through those closest to us. It is a rare and precious friend who tries to help us grow in *virtue*. Most of those we encounter in the world unknowingly beguile us to cut corners with right, wrong, purity, and integrity. They try to take us *down* in virtue, not lift us up into *higher* virtue.

We see such cinematic exchanges onscreen all the time. Though fictional, they may be more real than they seem. We watch as the teenager, or man or woman, hesitates, the pressure on, knowing they shouldn't give in to the downward lure of unvirtue. The doubt in their eyes reveals the struggle. Eve is facing the tempter. A pivotal moment of choice has come.

Genesis 2:17 lives! Strength of character is on the line.

Every choice carries consequence. Every time I give in to the beguiling voice, I die an infinitesimal death. No matter how tiny the choice, how thin the wedge into the seat of volition, when evil wins over conscience I am changed. When I choose wrong against right, even if but for a moment, evil enters.

---

* Borrowing from C.S. Lewis again, "Turkish Delight" is the magical candy used in his first book of the Narnia series, *The Lion, the Witch, and the Wardrobe,* to beguile a young boy into the service of the White Witch.

All day...every day...two choices are always before me. They come at me over and over and over.

- A choice for *wrong* produces a momentary death to virtue. The will is weakened. I will be *less* able to resist the next time.
- A choice for *right* grows virtue. The power of the will is strengthened. I will be *more* courageous to resist the next time.

Will I slam the door in the face of beguilement? Or will I allow the seductive voice to continue its lure of what is "a delight to the eyes."

God's men and women, determined not to let evil through the tiniest crack in the door, are those who rigorously train themselves to recognize beguilements a dozen times a day.

God rarely shouts his warnings. But if we have trained ourselves to listen, we will hear his still small voice whispering, "Do not let evil beguile you."

Heavenly Father, open my eyes to the beguilements around me. Though others may consider the moments of choice between right and wrong as innocent and insignificant, give me courage to recognize when my own virtue is on the line, to see even the smallest of virtue choices as moments when my future character is on the line. Give me strength not to bow to Satan's subtle beguilements. Give me wisdom to choose virtue.

26. Run from Sin

"Sin is crouching at the door; its desire is for you, but you must master it." (Genesis 4:7)

The first use of the word "sin" in the Bible comes in its fourth chapter after Cain becomes jealous of his brother Abel. More deeply, however, Cain is angry against God. He thinks God favors Abel. So anger builds toward them both. Though the biblical story has just begun, this incident reveals much that will follow in the lives of God's humanity. Not willing to live by the threefold foundations God established (Fatherhood, command and obedience, free will), man wants God to leave him alone.

However this is the one thing God *cannot* do. He cannot simply create out of the abundance of his Fatherhood-love, and then turn his back on the sons and daughters he has birthed. To do so would go against the very love that defines his being. But wanting to be left alone, mankind has been nursing anger against God ever since.

God gives Cain a chilling caution. It is another wonderfully worded biblical passage containing inexhaustible depths of meaning we will spend the rest of our lives trying to plumb.

"*Why* are you angry?" God asks, then follows with his warning and a command, "Sin is crouching at the door; its desire is for you, but you must master it."

The imagery is powerful. To Adam and Eve, the disobedience of evil came in the form of a serpent. (Whether literal or fictional does not change the import of the moment.) To their son it comes as a crouching beast. And now the evil takes on a new name—*sin.*

Eve desired the fruit. Now the desire of evil has turned around. The subtle beguilement that lured Eve has become a sinister force that *desires* Cain, presumably to destroy him. God's command is clear: *You must master it.*

If I was adhering to strict literality, I would word this command, "Master sin." It is true enough, of course, that perhaps the most important charge to mankind—more important than be fruitful and multiply, more important than subdue the earth, more important than have dominion over everything that moves—is the charge to *master sin.* God is clear: You *must* master it.

Yet what exactly does that mean? Without practical help knowing what we are actually to *do,* the idea of mastering sin is vague and difficult to lay hold of. What can I *do* five minutes from now to *master* sin? It's too huge—as if sin even *can* be mastered.

In 1 Peter 5:8, perhaps harkening back to this very moment when God confronts Cain, Peter writes, "The devil prowls around like a roaring lion, seeking whom he might devour."

Peter increases the stakes considerably. Sin is not just crouching…it is on the prowl to devour us!

Paul tells Timothy *exactly* what to do against this prowling lion:

Flee.

After cataloging a litany of sins, Paul writes, "But you, man of God, flee these things, and pursue righteousness." (1 Timothy 6:11)

In other words, when sin is lurking, crouching, prowling…when evil beguiles with enticing whispers, when others try to persuade us against our conscience—turn tail and run!

I don't have to conquer *all* sin. I only have to run from the one sin in front of me. Sin does not assault us in clusters. One may lead to another, but they come at us one at a time. Every sin-moment is individual. I cannot master all sin in my life. But I can turn from the one facing me *right now.*

We master sin a single beguilement at a time.

How? Slam the door in its face and run. If Cain had been paying attention to what his anger portended, he should have turned and fled for the hills until it had passed. Not to hide like his parents, but to pursue righteousness.

Yet he ignored the warning. He did not even *try* to resist. Instead, he invited Abel out to the field, and allowed sin to have him.

Adam and Eve set the precedent, and their son followed their example. It's human nature—when told we *can't* have or do something, we want it all the more. Eve eyed the tree, and *desired* it. She was no unwitting victim. She *wanted* to eat. She did not *run* from the temptation, but inched gradually closer, her mouth watering.

Recognizing her desire, her safety would have been to run *away* from evil in order to pursue righteousness, to seek God where he walked in the garden.

She did not run until it was too late. Then she ran in the wrong direction. She and Adam ran *from God* instead of from evil. God was still their refuge. There was but one safe haven—running *to* him, not away from him! It was not too late to seek their Father's forgiveness, to step again into the childness in which they were created. But because they had not *run from sin,* they were afraid to run *to* their Father, and in his loving embrace to become again his children.

Sin changed the imperative of *run to* him to *hide from* him. Mankind has been running the wrong direction ever since. The story of Cain's sin ends with the ominous words, "Then Cain went away from the presence of the Lord." Such is the inevitable fate of all who do not run from sin.

He went *away.* He chose not to *walk with God.*

The ancient story of Adam, Eve, and Cain is timeless. Its truths are powerfully alive. This very day, the moment when I rose from my bed, sin was crouching at my door desiring to have me. I am commanded to master it.

There is only one way to do so. When its beguiling whispers begin, to slam the door in its face and run from sin.

Lord God, give me eyes to see how close sin truly is, crouching at my door. Give me wisdom not to take it lightly, to recognize the reality of Cain's example, that sin desires to have me. Give me courage for the battle. Strengthen me to master it one beguilement at a time. When sin is in front of me, spur me, goad me, kick me, remind me not to delay…and to run!

27. Honor Marriage and Family

"This is the book of the generations of Adam. When God created man, he made him in the likeness of God. Male and female he created them and he blessed them and named them Man when they were created." (Genesis 5:1-2)

Following the story of Cain and Abel, the narrative diverges into a sweeping panoramic chronicle of mankind's spread through the Middle East. As absorbing as are the dating and diverse theories of antiquity—not the least of which is what was occurring throughout the rest of the planet, and how mankind came to occupy every continent and corner of it—these fascinations are not our primary concern. *Wherever* mankind went, and *how* and *when* our species developed, our focus is how the men and women of God's creation are commanded to *live.*

The history of *Genesis*, as pure "history" of necessity drifts into the background as we read. Daily life (*my* life, *your* life) gradually takes center stage. As it does, however, the lives of our biblical forebears continue to provide a wisdom-rich backdrop by which to uncover God's purposes and the commands associated with them.

As mentioned earlier, not all the Old Testament's commands are spoken as "Do this," or "Don't do this." When we dig deeper to discover how God wants us to live, we often find ourselves following one of Scripture's many interconnected, though often hidden, veins of gold.

Genesis 4-6 reveal such a vein. There we find an enormously important series of family-related *implied* commands. Their import is so obvious it almost goes without saying: *God's ordained pattern for family roles and relationships establishes the foundational institution of humanity.*

Family comes before cities, commerce, technology, religion, government, temples, or churches:

- *Men*—husbands and fathers.
- *Women*—wives and mothers.
- *Children*—sons and daughters.

All three are created and commanded to live and grow together as a family unit.

Drawn up into this triad is of course marriage. Upon that basis, the extended family of grandfathers and grandmothers, and the ever-widening legacy of family stretching in both directions and the tracing of lineages to preserve that legacy—are the fundamental building-blocks of humanity's spread over the earth. It is how mankind was meant to live.

Mankind's history is defined by:

- Family.
- Heritage.
- Legacy.

These roles, relationships, and their diverse extensions through humanity and through time are not just important to God. They provide the very *foundation* for what it means to be a human being created in God's image. The honor in which God holds the nuclear family unit is apparent literally from the Bible's first chapter, with myriad timely applications throughout history and for our own time. From birth to death, humans are nurtured by family.

God created *male* and *female*. There are no other options. That creative choice is not ours to make. It is made by God and no one can alter it.

God's men and women were to join in marriage—*one man and one woman.* God made woman as "a helper" to man. She was called "his wife." There is no plurality. The *his* is singular and masculine, the *she* is singular and feminine. *One* man. *One* woman. "Therefore a man [singular] leaves his father and his mother and cleaves to his wife [singular], and they become one flesh [singular]."

There is, therefore, no polygamy, adultery, divorce, homosexuality, or gender fluidity in the divine plan. Many of the Old Testament's disobedient men had multiple wives. Many committed sexual indiscretions. But such was never God's intent nor command. Marriage was defined, and is still intended, to be monogamous and characterized by lifelong fidelity. There are no alternate forms of God-ordained marriage.

Children were likewise the offspring of one man and one woman, to be loved and raised and nurtured by that *one man* and *one woman* in *one family,* and to mature under their oversight.

All the genealogies and lineages of the Bible flow from these underpinnings. God *honors* maleness and femaleness. He *honors* marriage as he ordained it. He *honors* the threeway nuclear family. He *honors* the legacies that spring from those foundations—generation unto generation.

These are unbreakable links between humanity and its Creator. No culture, personal preference, or permissive legality can erase them. To break these God-man links blasphemes the character of God and transgresses his authority, his intent, and his command.

Heavenly Father, I thank you for family! I love my family. I love my wife and sons and grandchildren, my parents and grandparents. What an ingenious relational fabric you established to nurture your divine Fathering life into us. I thank you for the family legacy into which you chose to give me life, and for the grandparents and parents you gave me to nurture me and guide me into the life you have given me. Help me to be a more loving father, a more loving husband, and more loving son. And looking in the other direction in your divine plan, I pray for my grandchildren, and my great-grandchildren and all those who follow in the family legacy of which I am privileged to be a part. May we be a legacy that reflects the goodness of your divine Fatherhood throughout all the corners of life where you take us in the years to come.

28. Separate from the World

"Noah walked with God." (Genesis 6:9)

The power of Genesis 6:9 is breathtaking:

Noah was a righteous man, blameless in his generation;
Noah walked with God.

What a tombstone epitaph!

By Noah's day, the human tree had grown and progressed far and wide. According to archaeological evidence in the Near East, a catastrophic flood occurred about that time. Noah probably lived between 3,000 and 4,000 B.C.

Again, though there is disagreement about the dating of mankind's early history, it seems apparent that mankind had been alive, wandering the earth and building villages, cities, and cultures, for a long time. The global population of *homo sapiens* is estimated at about one million in 4,000 B.C., three to four million in 3,000 B.C., and perhaps twenty million in 2,000 B.C. From the biblical account we must assume that by far the largest percentage of that number had followed the example of Cain. (These population numbers, of course, have great bearing on the date and extent of the flood.)

It is doubtful that Noah was the *only* good man on the face of the earth. The Bible doesn't tell us the history of every people, every tribe, every continent. But in the Near East where we find him some five thousand years ago, down the multi-generational legacy tree from Cain's and Abel's younger brother Seth, Noah's goodness and relationship with God (the tantalizing specifics of which we can only guess at in awe) were obviously extraordinary. The remarkable statement about him we find in Genesis 6:9 was surely unique within humanity.

With Noah, God initiates a major change in the oversight of his creation. Like all commands that originate in *Genesis*, the command to separate from the world will prove foundational to the entire human story. Its consequences echo down through time all the way to you and me today. The relevance of separation is so timely and practical that the implications assault us every time we leave our homes.

Up till now, mankind has been a unity. Mankind is God's creation—disobedient, it is true, but a *single* human (very dysfunctional) family. God now institutes something new. His human creation has become *so* evil that God is forced to recognize a distinction between the rebellious and *wicked*—whom he now, in Old Testament parlance, cuts off and blots out of his family—and the *righteous*, as embodied by Noah and his family.

Henceforth God's *true* family will be separate from the evil and wicked world about them. Choices matter. Forever after there will be *two* humanities.*

In a sense, God disinherits the wicked (which even in their sin, he did not with Adam or Cain). To the humanity of evil and wickedness he says, "You are no longer my children. Henceforth I will build my family through the offspring and generations of righteousness."

Then turning to his righteous son, he adds, "Separate yourself and your family from the corruption and evil in the world about you, and live in faithfulness to my commands. This is how I want you to begin separating yourself from the world: Build an ark of gopher wood…"

---

* With the future perspective of New Testament truth, we know that God blots no one out of his created family. His Fatherhood is universal and eternal. In light of eternity there are not two humanities at all. Such is but a temporary distinction. But in seeking to understand truths that gradually unfold through the Old Testament, the temporal message of Noah's story is important in initiating the imperative distinction between "the world" and God's family of obedience. Thus I have used Old Testament terminology, though the deeper perspective that will become clear as Scripture progresses reveals that the distinction is between those of his created beings who chose *not* to walk with him, and those who choose to walk with him in obedience. But he remains the Father of both his obedient and his wayward children.

Separation between the two branches of humanity now becomes a dominant theme within God's plan. It will continue as another foundation stone to all the commands of both Old and New Testaments, and is intrinsic to the gospel message of Jesus.

Will some future archaeologist one day find Noah's ark? I hope so. I wrote an entire novel fictionalizing its discovery. * But it hardly matters. The enormity of truth contained in the chronicle of Noah's life is not dependent on how precisely factual it is or whether the ark one day surfaces. †

Elaborating on his word to Noah, we can easily read ourselves into God's exhortation:

"Come out of the evil around you and live in righteousness. To do so you will have to withdraw from everything in the world. If you obey, I will take you out of the world. I will separate you and establish my covenant with you. You and your family and those who come after you are henceforth my people. You will be separate and distinct because you are my family, and because you walk with me. Therefore, be fruitful in righteousness, and fill the earth."

The separation between "the world" (of disobedience) and "God's family" (of righteousness and obedience), began with God's command: *Separate yourself from worldliness.*

God, give me insight to see the imperative of separation from the world in my own life. The divide is not as clear as it was in Noah's time between righteous and wicked. But if separation is such an imperative part of your plan, I need to see it. Give me eyes to see what separation means today.

29. Keep Covenant with God

"I am God Almighty; walk before me and be blameless.
And I will make my covenant between me and you." (Genesis 17:1-2)

More generations pass in Seth's lineage. The biblical narrative continues to focus the racially diverse and by now global human enterprise into an account of the one particular lineage which God separated from "the world" through Noah. That lineage eventually comes to rest on the man, according to the biblical genealogy, who might have been Noah's nine-times great-grandson: Abraham.

We know little about those intervening years or the men and women of those generations. After four chapters with Noah, the following two chapters (10-11) mostly comprise lists of fathers and sons (with the tower

---

* *Rift in Time,* 1997.

† Noah's story, like that of creation, is told twice in Chapters 6 and 7, set into the historical narrative of the Hebrew people by two ancient scribes (the *Lord*/YHWH and *God*/ELOHIM versions). The two accounts were thoroughly collated here, the uses of "God" and "Lord" intermingling fluidly (as in 7:16.)

of Babel in their midst), until eleven generations later Abraham is born. His life story is then recounted in such detail that it is difficult to call him a "righteous" man by today's standards. We know his failings all too well. It seems clear that Abraham did not walk with God with the same level of obedience that his many times great-grandfather Noah had.

Yet in God's eyes, at that primitive time, he must have been as remarkable in his own way as was Noah. Because with Abraham, God took the world-separation covenant to a loftier level.

In a sense, the covenant God established with Noah in Genesis 9 was one-sided. We might think of it as a *pre*-covenant. It was not a two-way compact. We know that Noah was righteous, and *did* obey. But the covenant spoken by God (9:9) was all on God's side saying what *he* would do.

With Abraham, however, God makes another major change—the covenant becomes *mutual*. It contains the resounding command that is God's intent for all:

"I am God Almighty; walk before me and be blameless.
And I will make my covenant between me and you."

Abraham has been drawn into a binding *me and you* contract with the God of creation.

God's promise regarding the family and the people he has separated out of the world, now becomes vaster in scope. Indeed, it is now an *eternal* compact.

"And I will multiply you exceedingly...and you shall be the father of a multitude of nations...and I will give to you and to your descendants after you, the land of your sojournings, all the land of Canaan, for an everlasting possession; and I will be their God."

The mutuality is established so there can be no doubt:

"As for you, you shall keep my covenant,
you and your descendants after you throughout their generations...
So shall my covenant be...an everlasting covenant."

As God commanded creation, he now *commands* obedience to the covenant.

At its basic-most essence, it is not merely a covenant with Abraham. It is a covenant with *all* men and women who embrace command and choose obedience.

We follow in that lineage. The covenant is with those who make themselves God's sons and daughters. It is a covenant of *command*. It is straightforward and unambiguous. "Walk before me and be blameless." You *shall* keep my covenant.

How do we keep covenant with God? Just as Noah and Abraham did—by *walking* with him, being *righteous*, and *obeying* his commands.

- God commanded Noah: "Make yourself an ark."
- Noah obeyed: *"Noah did…all that God commanded him."*

So significant is his obedience that it is repeated, to leave no doubt who it was that he was obeying:

"And Noah did all that the Lord had commanded him."

Imagine what it means for such things to be said of a primitive man who lived in the midst of more evil and wickedness than we can fathom. Noah must indeed have been a remarkable man.

Don't let the little word *all* escape notice. That all tells us everything we need to know about Noah, and why it was said of him that he walked with God.

- God also commanded Abraham: "Go to the land that I will show you."
- Likewise Abraham obeyed: *"So Abram went."*

Spirituality isn't rocket science. It pretty much boils down to doing what God tells us. He is our Father. We are his children. We're supposed to obey.

What was said of Noah is supposed to be said of us too. "Noah found favor in the eyes of the Lord…Noah was a righteous man…Noah walked with God…he did all that God commanded him."

This is the essence of the two covenants made by God with Noah and Abraham—*Walk with God and do what he says.*

That it isn't said of us is not because God hasn't made his instructions even more clear than they were to Noah. His instructions are crystal clear. It isn't said of us that we walk with God because we don't walk with God.

We don't do *all* that God commands us.

I have all the commands of Jesus before me. I have the example of his life. I have the commands of the apostles before me, and the example of their lives. I have the commands of Moses, David, Solomon, Josiah, Ezra, and many more. Noah had none of the advantages I have.

We possess God's commands in abundance. Why then are such things not said of us?

Keeping the covenant by obeying God's commands is not necessarily easy. But it is simple enough:

Walk before me and be blameless. Obey my commands. Keep my covenant.

The idea of covenant, God, is somewhat strange in my ears. In my Christian life I have not been taught to think of my life with you as a covenant relationship. I see now that your revelation to humanity is anchored in your covenants with these two ancient men. I am part of them in more ways than I realize. Give me wisdom and insight to understand my role in your ancient covenants with mankind, and to understand my personal covenantal relationship with you as I seek to walk in Noah's and Abraham's footsteps.

30. Live as a Manifestly Distinct Righteousness-Choosing People

"I will establish my covenant between me and you and your descendants… for an everlasting covenant…and I will be their God." (Genesis 17:7-8)

The history of the Old Testament now narrows and comes to rest almost exclusively upon the nation of Israel—whose people were later called "Jews," a word derived from Judah (one of the sons of Abraham's grandson Jacob). Most Old Testament studies center upon various spiritual lessons based on the assumed thematic thread running through it that the Israelites were God's "chosen people."

In one sense, of course, we may interpret the account as God's having *chosen* Noah and Abraham with whom to establish his covenant relationship with mankind. But the great Achilles heel of Judaism, and the cause of most anti-Semitism through the centuries, has been a grievous misunderstanding of what "chosen" was intended to mean. Often assuming themselves more worthy than the rest of humanity (a fatal flaw carried forward into Calvinism's doctrine of the "elect"), the Jews have tended to think too highly of themselves. Much of the world has hated them for it.

As we now conclude what we might call the *Genesis* commands, we can say that by the end of the Bible's first book God's covenant is prepared to go global. It's not just that the book ends with God's little covenant family in Egypt, but that from Jacob's twelve sons will grow a nation which, in only a few hundred years, for a brief shining moment will be the greatest nation on earth.

Therefore it is time to step back for an overview of what this means, what this gradually expanding worldwide covenant implies—not only for the Jews but for the rest of humanity.

Why did God appear to "choose" one man, then another single man, and their families, then the nation that would arise from them?

What was God's purpose?

Was it merely to bless Abraham's physical bloodline and posterity?

That it was originally based on the obedience and righteousness of the two men who walked with God gives us huge insight.

In one sense, God did not choose them at all. They chose themselves. They lived by the twenty-third command—they *chose* obedience. *Noah and Abraham were the choosers.* In selecting them, God was but ratifying *their* lifetime of righteousness-choosing.

His purpose was not to single out their posterity any more than that of any other generational lineages. His purpose was infinitely larger. It is this eternal purpose that the descendants of Abraham have been slow and stubborn to apprehend. God's purpose was for *all* mankind to walk with him.

This is not merely a "New Testament" truth revealed by the coming of Jesus. This was *always* God's purpose, even in Abraham's lifetime. The covenant "choosing" was not the choosing of a bloodline, it was a covenant of righteousness which *mankind* was supposed to choose. The covenant "choice" is man's not God's. It was a covenant choice offered, and *intended*, for all humanity—for every man and woman who has ever lived, and will ever live. It is the compass-setting choice of command #20 to make righteousness the heart's desire.

We will understand the covenant much better by modifying the term to "God's *choosing* people."

God purposed to grow and develop a *choosing* people—a people who could choose to walk with him.

God set Noah and Abraham and their descendants apart as a "type" for all mankind, for *every* man and woman to follow—an example of faithfulness and righteousness. An example of *choosing*. The purpose was for Abraham's posterity to be so visibly and manifestly distinct in its righteousness-choosing that the wickedness of the world, requiring separation during Noah's time, could be redeemed.

God's objective was not to enrich one man's posterity, but world redemption. What later grew into a misplaced Jewish pride in being "the chosen people," should instead have produced profound humility. To the Jews was given the honor and responsibility of exampling righteousness-*choosing* to the world. Through them would the covenant bring fallen mankind back into union with its Creator.

Genesis climaxes, however, leaving us scratching our heads wondering if God has selected wisely. Surely it is a self-motivated and dysfunctional family with whom he has entrusted this high and holy calling. Neither Joseph nor his eleven brothers seem up to the task.

Looking back, however, viewing the full panorama of the *Genesis* story, we nevertheless see clearly—more in the figure of Noah than Abraham—what was God's intent: that a family, then a nation, then an entire race, would grow in obedience, becoming in time so visibly and practically unique from the rest of the world that God's covenant would ultimately expand to encompass all mankind.

Let us therefore look to this high purpose for the culminating command of *Genesis*. To us, as to Noah, Abraham, Isaac, Jacob, Judah, Joseph, and all who followed, God imparts his divine will by the command, implied though it may be:

Become and live as a manifestly distinct, holy, righteousness-choosing people, a people in covenant with me, in order that the whole world may be drawn into the obedience of righteousness by your example and your faithfulness to this mutual covenant.

God, I have little to pray other than asking you to help me become, as you want all your men and women to become, a humble righteousness-choosing man, distinct from the world and in covenant with you as my good and loving Father.

Series Four

Command

The Ten Commandments

God's fundamental precepts for human life

God gives man specific instructions how to live

The account of the Israelites in bondage in Egypt, the birth and career of Moses, and the events of the exodus and their forty years wandering in the desert before Abraham's descendants reached the land of Canaan…this dramatic progression tells what is probably the most well-known story in the Bible. No need exists for further summary of those events that brought the Israelites to the foot of Sinai where Moses received the Ten Commandments. Our purpose is to unearth veins of command-gold. Turning a significant corner in the biblical story, therefore, we must ask what had become of God's covenant family during their four hundred years in Egypt. Where does the covenant stand?

Essentially it is in tatters.

It is fascinating that with both Noah and Abraham, God gave so few instructions about what "Keep my covenant…walk with me…be righteous," actually meant. Remarkably, Noah seemed intuitively to know what being a good man meant. He knew that he was *supposed* to be good. At least this intuitive *knowing* seems to be the case, unless there occurred more interaction between God and Noah than what we are told.

The innate righteousness that apparently ruled Noah's life, however, did not take root in much of humanity, nor in the family of Abraham's descendants. The chosen people did not become the *choosing* people.

They were not getting it.

The Noah model—a man *choosing* from within himself to be good, to be righteous, to walk with God, intuitively knowing what that required—was apparently not going to work for most of the human race.

Something more direct, practical, and straightforward was needed.

So God used his delivery of the Israelites out of their enslavement as the opportunity to give them more explicit instructions. Hopefully greater specificity of command would get them on the right track toward the *Genesis* commands:

- *Embrace Command.*
- *Choose Obedience.*
- *Keep the Covenant.*
- *Live as a Manifestly Distinct Righteousness-Choosing People.*

Moses, the first of what are called God's *prophets*, was the man destined to lead mankind forward into a new era in its covenant with God.

That next stage in the covenant's development, in truth, was a step backward. God's intent was that his men and women would *know* righteousness and *desire* righteousness and *choose* righteousness and *live* by righteousness simply because they were made in his image—as Noah knew it and lived it. Their very humanity should have made righteousness apparent.

This was *always* God's ultimate purpose. As one of his later prophets would write, speaking on God's behalf, "I will put my law within them, and I will write it on their hearts; and I will be their God, and they shall be my people." (Jeremiah 31:33)

But that reality was not yet. The Noahs of humanity were few and far between.

Therefore God instituted Plan B.

He set up an intricate system of laws and commands that would regulate all aspects of life down to the tiniest detail. If they were too obstinate to figure out goodness and righteousness on their own as Noah had, he would give them directives and guidelines that would point in that direction.

Such a specific system of laws and regulations would not be as good as Plan A—intuitive goodness. But hopefully it would prevent his human children degenerating into the depravity of Noah's day. Plan B would inaugurate a lengthy process of growth toward what, in time, could become a level of righteousness from which God could indeed write his purposes on the hearts of his men and women.

Beginning at the rudimentary level of *Do this...don't do this,* God thus began laying the groundwork for what would come later—virtue, truth, selflessness, purity, compassion, honor, integrity, and humility.

Ultimately his high Law would be written on hearts that would *choose* the goodness inherent in walking with God. For now, however, that Law would be written on stone tablets.

He therefore initiated Plan B with ten foundational life-regulating commands given to Moses on Mount Sinai. They represented the summit, the pinnacle, the overarching crown atop the system of laws and regulations that would follow.

These Ten Commandments set the Hebrew people and the later Jewish nation apart from all peoples on earth. In straightforward simplicity and eternal profundity, they became the most influential basis for law, government, and human behavior in the history of the world.

Three and a half thousand years later, however, though their power is undimmed, God is still awaiting the day when the deeper covenant of righteousness toward which they point will truly be written on the collective heart of humankind.

Series Four

Command

31. Worship no other gods than the Lord your God.

32. Make no idols.

33. Do not speak God's name carelessly.

34. Observe the Lord's rest.

35. Honor your father and mother.

36. Do not kill.

37. Do not commit adultery.

38. Do not steal.

39. Do not speak falsely about others.

40. Do not covet what you do not have.

31. Worship No Other Gods Than the Lord Your God

"I am the Lord your God, who brought you out of the land of Egypt…
You shall have no other gods before me." (Exodus 20:2-3)."

The phrase, "You shall have no other gods…" may not strike modern readers with the same impact that would have resounded through the ancient world at the words.

This was a revolutionary command. The peoples of antiquity worshipped numerous "gods." There were gods of every imaginable kind and for every conceivable purpose. Each tribe, nation, and race had its own pantheon of deities. They were of different ranks, wielded unique power over various aspects of life, and were prayed to for different reasons—fertility gods, rain gods, sun gods, gods of war, bless-our-crops gods, health gods, healing gods, and more.

When God said *No other gods,* he was establishing a hugely momentous command. This uniqueness was bolstered by his name, YHWH—unpronounceable in Hebrew—from which the Hebrew God came to be known simply as "the God with no name." This command, therefore, shouted loud and clear to the rest of the world that the Israelites were distinct from other peoples because their *God* was different. Their YHWH rose above all the myriad gods of other peoples.

We know how difficult it was for the Israelites to obey this first command. The multiple-god obsession was endemic to ancient man, the Israelites included. Whenever their faithfulness to God's laws began to waver, this was the first command to go—they began bringing idols of the gods of the peoples around them into their homes and places of worship. The golden calf in the desert was but one of many examples that continued to undermine the obedience of God's people throughout the Old Testament. When this first command lost its force, the rest of the commands followed. The entire spiritual fabric—in individual lives first, then of an entire nation—unraveled.

When the prophets rebuked the people and called them to repentance, their first order was always, *Smash and destroy the idols to other gods.* It was a command the prophets were forced to repeat over and over. For reasons that are somewhat mysterious to us today, the people were *compelled* to worship multiple gods. They simply couldn't handle the idea of a single God.

Thus, this first command of "the Ten," reinforced by the *Shema* from Deuteronomy 6:4-5—Hear, O Israel: The Lord our God is one; and you shall love the Lord your God with all your heart, and with all your soul, and with all your might."—was more radical in its impact in the ancient world than may appear.

Its very simplicity underscores its uniqueness: *God is ONE.*

Ever after the Israelites were known as the people with a single God, the *one* God, the God with no name. It was the first indication that they were different, separate, that their covenant to their God was unique.

The purpose of this devotional is to focus on the *personal* living application of the commands. This first of the Ten Commandments, however, is unique in also being a group, corporate, even *national* command. It is certainly very personal—just how personal we will see in the command that follows. But its national component was enormously significant for the ancient Israelites. God was not merely giving instructions for individuals, but for the *nation* he was establishing—a nation that would learn, through many ups and downs, to walk in righteousness.

Observing twenty-first century parallels, the relevance of our national worship of a myriad of false gods suddenly jumps off the pages of *Exodus* with stunning force. They are not idols most people build statues of and pray to. But they are equally powerful false gods that undermine virtue, morality, integrity, and prevent the worship of the true God.

It is hardly necessary to enumerate the multiple false gods of our time—money, power, sex, violence, racial resentment, drugs, alcohol, gender sameness, liberalism, conservatism, abortion, militant feminism, social justice, gun rights, fashion, leisure, food…we could go on and on. Good things in many cases—there are good liberal ideas, good conservative ideas, justice is good, sex in marriage is good, respecting women as man's equal in personhood-value is good, leisure is good (it is the basis of the fourth commandment), food is good.

But all are capable of being worshipped in place of the *one* God. Our nation has substituted all these, in unique ways, for the "God of our Fathers." More than 3000 years have passed, yet we are no different than the ancient Israelites. We have abandoned the covenant of obedience to God's commands in favor of false and substitute gods.

A very personal question thus looms as we personalize this uniquely national command. Which of these false gods—or others—do you and I tacitly embrace just as the Israelites were beguiled by the golden calf? Though one man or one woman may not be able to change the political course of a nation, that one man and one woman *can* determine not to join in the worship of its false gods.

Lord God, our Creator and Father, give me single-minded devotion to call you, and only you, the God of my life. May you be the sole object of my worship and my obedience. Open my eyes to the false gods of modernism, to the false gods of my nation, to the golden calves of progressivism, and give me courage not to follow the crowd in bowing down to them.

32. Make No Idols

"You shall not make yourself a graven image, or any likeness of anything that is in heaven, or that is in the earth…you shall not bow down to them or serve them." (Exodus 20:4-5)

From the national, it is imperative that we zero in on the personal. Nations are made of *individual* men and women. Obedience to the commands always reduces in the end, not to what the rest of the country is doing, but to you and me standing alone before the probing mirror of the commands.

The link between the first two Ten Commandments is clearly evident. They present two faces of the same command, repeated differently for emphasis. Some commands are so foundational they need repeating. Thus this second commandment is a corollary to the first. "You shall not bow down to them or serve them" is simply another way of saying, "You shall have no other gods."

These commands were delivered to the Israelites a long time ago. How do you and I personalize them today? It's easy to skim over these words. Most of us reading this second of the Ten Commandments may not immediately think "idol worship" has much to do with us. You and I don't "make idols" or "worship idols."

We would be wrong. This command has *everything* to do with us.

Because of the imperative of practicality, I do not read the previous command as a prohibition against worshiping the "gods" of alternate religions—Buddha, Mohammed, Brahma, Shangdi, or Tian. Nor do I read this command as warning against kneeling before inanimate statues like the golden calf or a Buddha doll. That would be too easy.

I have to personalize the command against my *own* individual idols. I may not *worship* them as we think of the word. Yet daily I fall victim to the subtle whispered beguilements of my own golden calves that I erect in the invisible shrines of my mind and heart where I pay homage to them.

They are out of sight so deep in the private sanctuaries of my inner being that I may not even be aware I have made idols of them. Some are national idols of our times. How many have made their political liberalism or political conservatism nothing less than a god to be worshipped—or this or that component of political fervor, whether it be social justice, gun rights, constitutional originalism, or gender neutrality.

Most of our idols, however, probe deeper into the marrow of our beings than political and cultural idols, as powerful and destructive to serious discipleship as the trends of modernity can be.

None of those are *my* idols. I have opinions on our nation and its culture. But I don't worship and live for my opinions. My idols bite deeper into my soul.

The most innocuous pursuits of life, hopes and dreams, cherished possessions, things we yearn to possess, vocational and creative aspirations, not to mention more serious personal lusts for money, power, status, and retirement accounts…ambition, envy, resentment, unforgiveness …*anything* can become the "other god" or "idol" of these first two commands. Good desires are as susceptible to the erosion of covenant-righteousness as the obviously destructive. It all depends on where we put them—in a hidden shrine-room, or into God's hands to purify for his purposes.

For years I was a competitive runner. I loved to run. God used running in my development as a young Christian. He *gave* me running as a gift. Then came a time when he made clear that running had become *too* important. From the good thing he had given me, it was in danger of becoming an idol. I knew what was required—I had to lay it down, give up running for a time, until it was no longer another god in my life.

The Lord gives…and the Lord may need to take away.

I have had many such relinquishments through the years. I have had to lay down aspects of my writing, business goals, finances, even relationships. Some relinquishments are permanent and lifelong, others are temporary—until I have turned them over to the Lord to refashion as tools to develop Christlikeness within me. The many substitute idol-gods that have come and gone in my life will be different than yours. But God's command is clear—*No* other gods before the Lord your God.

Recognizing the idols that stand out of sight in our private hidden sanctuaries is no task for the spiritually faint of heart. It takes humility to see them for what they are, and courage to lay them on the altar, then to enduring the pain of watching God either burn or crush them to purify into gold for his use.

Most of the raw material with which we fashion our idols is *God's* raw material he wants to use for his glory.

Gold is good because God made it. Golden calves are not.

God, open my eyes to the false gods and idols I unknowingly substitute for your best in my life. Many have come and gone. I have endured many relinquishments. Most of them are now in my past. But what new golden calves are creeping into my consciousness unseen. Open my eyes to see them before it is too late. Give me courage to put them on your altar so that you do not have to wrest them out of my hands.

33. Do Not Speak God's Name Carelessly

"You shall not take the name of the Lord your God in vain." (Exodus 20:7)

This command is as relevant and timely as a walk through the mall. This is both a national command and a very personal one.

The epidemic of using the words *God* and *Jesus* and *Christ* and *Lord* as throwaway expressions of emphasis or cursing has become so rampant as to be horrifying to anyone who takes the commands of God seriously.

Sadly, it is *not* horrifying to most. We hardly notice.

We should be ashamed of ourselves. For Christians, the words, *Oh my God!* represent the deepest cry of the human heart, the ultimate prayer when words fail, the words of Jesus to his Father on the cross.

For us let it also be a prayer, and *only* a prayer, not a frivolous and thoughtless turn of phrase.

Rise up, people of God. Let us be complicit in this sin no longer. Let us quietly, graciously, courteously, gently, sensitively, and lovingly rebuke this thoughtless scourge of disobedience to one of God's primary and important commands.

His name is precious. Let us behave accordingly, and treat it as a holy name to be honored.

Casting the net of interpretation further into the sea of practicality, it may be that we who may not consider ourselves loose and careless of tongue with God's name, can yet look in the mirror and find ourselves in this command.

Our *tongues* may not disobey this command as thoughtlessly as does the world. But what about our thoughts, our motives, our heart's desires, even our speech in more subtle ways than whether or not we use divine expletives?

Do we take God *himself* "in vain," treat his role in our lives casually and carelessly in more ways than our speech? Calling ourselves his followers, calling ourselves Jesus' disciples, how seriously do we take the command-obedience that discipleship demands?

What vanities and carelessnesses lie at the heart of my claim to be God's man? Perhaps I don't swear using God's name. But in how many other ways do I subtly and invisibly take the person and character of God and Jesus in vain by claiming to follow them, but not doing what they tell me?

Is pretense Christianity and pretense obedience, simply another form of inward disobedience to this command—lifting the hands of worship on Sunday but falling in with the world's values and priorities for the rest of the week, wearing a cross around the neck with no clue what the cross actually *means*, with even less intent of discovering that meaning in order to live in its reality, saying *Jesus is my Savior* with no moment-by-moment dedication to live in the reality of his Saviorhood?

Are not all of these a taking of God's name in vain?

Calling oneself a *Christian*, a believer in *God*, a follower of *Jesus*—these affirmations carry serious, practical, daily, eternal consequences. If I *say* these things, let me be sure I mean them and am not speaking, or even thinking, casually, carelessly, or in vain.

Reading the command from this angle:

- *Honor God.*
- *Honor God's name.*
- *Honor God's character.*
- *Honor God's claim to my obedience.*

Honor what it means to be God's child in every way—in speech, in thought, in behavior, in totality of life orientation.

Lord God, keep me from frivolous speech, empty commitments, and unmeaning proclamations of my faith that have little influence on my daily life. Open my eyes to whatever ways I may be taking you for granted, and thus treating you in vain. When I hear those around me curse with your name, or exclaim "Oh my God," sting my spirit with inner revulsion. Then turn those words into a whispered prayer from my own lips to honor you with my whole being.

34. Observe the Lord's Rest

"Remember the sabbath day, to keep it holy. Six days you shall labor, and do all your work; but on the seventh day is a sabbath to the Lord your God...." (Exodus 20 8-10)

All the difference in the world exists between the many diverse methodologies Judaism and Christianity have brought to their interpretations of this command. They range from the complex and contorted legalisms that grew to infect the Old Testament Sabbath, to the somber and dour Calvinist day of quiet when children had to talk in subdued tones, refrain from frivolity, and read only "religious" books, to the mega-church rock concerts of modern evangelicalism.

We can be certain of only one thing—that God does not endorse 24-7 workaholism that rides roughshod over family relationships, personal health, and creative and spiritual calm. He designed the human constitution such that it *requires* rest. The very fact that sleep exists tells us that we are not supposed to be wired every minute. Rest is not merely commanded by God, it is also commanded by our bodies, our brains, our emotions, and our inner psychological make-up.

But "rest"—bodily, spiritually, emotionally, creatively, and relationally—is achieved individually not by religious legalisms. Some "rest" their bodies for nine hours a night, other for six. Some work in the morning and rest in the evening. Others are energized to work late. What constitutes physical, emotional, and spiritual rest is temperamentally defined. What has the effect of rest for one may be hard work for another. Sitting around all day doing nothing may have fulfilled the Calvinist sabbath but would be torture for some natures, leaving them mentally exhausted at the end of the day. Boredom can be physically as well as emotionally taxing. Some are energized by people and fellowship. Others find constant human interaction fatiguing.

Applying this sabbath command, therefore, is not as easy as saying, "Go to church every Sunday and don't clock in at the office or do any hard work." Nothing is so exhausting to some as a long church service. On the other hand, few things energize my particular mental and physical constitution more than a hard thirty mile bicycle ride.

Nor can we assume that "spiritual" rest—however we achieve it—is only a once-weekly necessity. We also need spiritually recreative seasons of solitude, reflection, and brain-rest throughout the week—even daily.

If we were seeking merely to understand the meaning of sabbath rest in the context of the Old Testament, we could turn to *Leviticus* and find all the answers we need. But we are in quest of deeper scriptural gold than legalisms—whether Jewish or Calvinist, Catholic or Orthodox or evangelical. Therefore, we must look to the deeper intent of God's Sabbath.

Is it merely to set one day a week aside in which to do no work? Though the command of Exodus 20 is specific to a "day" of rest, deeper means and purposes are obviously drawn up into it because *work*, like *rest*, is individual. If a paid pastor's "work" day is Sunday, does being in church every Sunday constitute *his* sabbath? Being *in church* cannot be the only measuring stick for what is meant by God's rest. We are also faced with the reality that Jesus himself did not always "keep the Sabbath" according to Jewish law. We don't know if he attended synagogue services every Saturday. But it seems doubtful.

The question therefore arises: What comprises the essence of this command—*rest* or *church*?

Is God commanding us to take a day a week to remember him for the purpose of resting from work, or to attend church services? It's a question that makes one think. One of my dear lifelong friends, a German farmer, examples to me both the question that arises and also the balance. On my frequent visits to his home over the years, I have been struck with his commitment to rest most days—a mid-day *siesta*, as it were. But during the harvest when the crops have to get in, he is on his tractor in the fields fourteen or sixteen hours a day on Sunday, and every other day as necessary.

No siestas during harvest! Is my friend breaking the sabbath by harvesting on Sunday? Though it might have only been a few grains, the Pharisees made the same accusation against Jesus.

This may not be a legalistic enough interpretation for some. All we can say for certain is that we are told to rest regularly from work, at least a day a week, to remember the Lord and keep our bodies, minds, and spirits holy to him. The example of my friend tells me that the "day of rest" cannot be legalized. *Rest* comes to us in infinitely varied ways—in solitude or in the company of others, on a hike in the country, working in the garden, at the beach, on a bicycle ride, in church or at home, or perhaps, days or weeks later, with a great sigh of satisfaction when the crops are safely in.

The Ten Commandments say nothing about institutional observances. *Rest*, not meetings, is the essence of the sabbath.

Thank you, heavenly Father, for the balance you built into your creation between growth and activity and rest and recreation—from the seasons to the need of my body to sleep every night. You have placed this balance into your universe, into the earth, into the DNA of all growing things, and into me. Give me wisdom and insight to live the balance, not only weekly but daily.

35. Honor Your Father and Mother

"Honor your father and your mother, that your days may be long in the land which the Lord your God gives you." (Exodus 20:12)

The common assumption of our time is that the command to honor one's parents is of temporary duration, and applies only if they deserve it. In other words, modernity changes the command to: "Honor your father and mother only if they are honorable people."

Even if they are honorable, the command is assumed to apply *actively* only during the years of childhood and youth, after which it becomes entirely *passive*, distant, impersonal, and hands-off. The injunction, it is assumed, does not give a parent the right to interfere with a son's or daughter's autonomy as an independent moral and spiritual agent beyond the age of eighteen. After that, no further obligation of deference to parental wisdom or authority is required. Indeed, when a parent crosses that line, the sixteen or eighteen or twenty-five or forty-year old has every right to explode in anger and tell his or her parents where to get off.

Nothing could be a more *inaccurate* reading of this command. The honor-injunction is lifelong. It is meant to be energetically and *actively* practiced by sons and daughters throughout their parents' lives…and beyond.

Repeat—*actively* practiced. Dynamically lived as long as one's parents are alive.

A moment's reflection reveals that it must be so. When does a child even become *capable* of true honor? Not by five, hardly by ten. How many parents of teens would say that the boy or girl of fifteen is capable of true *honor*…or eighteen? Yet modernity would send a defiant boy or girl of eighteen off into adulthood, all parental strings cut, before they have become capable of so much as a first grade level of honor in the full sense of the word.

Our culture has turned the very years when honor should at last be sending down roots into character into years instead when *dishonor* is in full bloom, and when many parent-son and parent-daughter relationships are severed almost completely. Along with divorce, I believe few things grieve God more than youthful rebellion toward parental oversight.

God obviously means something more long-lasting by this command than for it to end before it has begun—before true honor is developed in the child's heart at all. He certainly means more than the command with which modernity has replaced it: *Thou shalt resent thy parents, blaming them for all wrongs in thy life, cherishing thy resentments even after their death.*

While the relationship obviously shifts through the years to the mutuality of mature respect—which wise fathers and mothers are eager to enjoy no less than their sons and daughters—the change that comes with maturity does not alter the intrinsic mentoring role that God built into the fact of parenthood. Mothers and fathers remain *parents*. Nothing makes then unparents. A parent is meant to be a mentor—hopefully a wise one—to his or her children until death separates them. The very words of the command speak of a lifelong injunction—"that your days may be *long*."

True honor toward one's parents, deep honor, the honor God intends, does not even begin extending into the heart until one's own adulthood. It has but faintly begun in the twenties, sends down roots in the thirties, and is starting to bear fruit by the time one's parents are reaching the end of their life's road. Still the deepening of parental honor continues. The death of one's parents is intrinsic to the spreading of its roots. To our regret, we often awaken to lament that the honor we increasingly feel did not flower in our hearts soon enough to be lived and demonstrated more actively and visibly when the dear ones were still with us.

By this continuing process we are engaged in molding, framing, and building the legacies we choose to value. I am passing on a legacy of character, spirituality, and good choices to my sons even though I have also sown weakness, flaws, and mistakes into that legacy. I am no more a perfect father than was my father. Our failed humanity is built into the equation. Upon me is laid the command to choose honor toward *my* father. I cannot control what my sons do. I can only control the honor in which I choose to live.

Through the eyes of my adulthood, I am aware of so many wonderful influences that my father passed on to me that transcend his flaws, or even whether he was what we would call a spiritual man. I have had to *seek* the good seeds he planted into my life. I have had to develop seeing eyes that probe deeply into his character. Then I have chosen to water and nourish those seeds.

He was the father God gave *me*. That fact tells me all I need to know about my father, and makes him precious in my eyes. All legacies must be sought. Honor is chosen. Obeying this command has nothing to do with the honorability of our parents. This command sits squarely on the heads of the sons and daughters of the parent-child equation. It is a command spoken to children, not parents. *Adult children as well as young children.* It is a command every one of us *choose* whether or not to obey.

Honor of parents, grandparents, forebears, and their legacy is found throughout the Old Testament. The fascinating heart of these oft-repeated commands is this: Honor was not commanded because a given man or woman or father or grandfather was necessarily an *honorable* person. Some were; some weren't. Honor was commanded, period.

Honor was commanded toward the good *and* the bad. Honor was commanded not because any of them were perfect, or good people at all, but because they came before. Their blood and legacy flowed into and through their descendants. It was

> the legacy of their *bloodline* that was to be honored, not the virtue of their character. If they happened to have lived virtuous lives, so much the better. But that was not the basis for honor.
>
> My forebears' blood is *in* me and in our nation. I am to honor them for that. I honor them because I am alive.
>
> Honor is not based on virtue but on honor for the past—*because* it is *my* past.
>
> Modernity has turned all this upside-down. Modernity says that we are no longer required to honor anyone whom we consider dishonorable. If we don't like them, we don't have to honor them.
>
> The entire culture shouts at children from the day they are born to *dishonor* their parents. No wonder so many young people enter the teen years full of rebellion and independence. Flexing their teen muscles, they are but living out the lies of unvirtue society has fed into them all their lives. *

My wife Judy and I, now in our seventies, think of our four parents daily with a love that grows stronger every year. The intensity of that love is often tinged with pangs that we were so young and immature when we were young and immature. But the pangs of regret are overshadowed with smiles and memories, and the happy knowledge that we will see them ere long, and, in some miraculous way, be enabled to be their son and daughter again in the full honor with which we will then be capable of loving them.

To you whose mothers and fathers are still living—lose no opportunity to actively and visibly demonstrate, not merely your love, but honor to your own dear ones who gave you life. You may be wise and mature in your own right. You may be keenly aware of their flaws and foibles through the eyes of your adulthood. But they remain the life-mentors God knew it was best to give *you*.

Heavenly Father this is not a command I struggle to obey. I love and honor my father and mother more than I can say. I regret I did not show it more when they were alive, but I know you have this covered. Therefore now again, publicly and for all the world to hear, I say again, as I have told you many times, thank you from the deepest wellsprings of my being—thank you for Denver and Eloise Phillips, whom I honor. Thank you for the myriad traits of character they built into me, even in ways they were unaware and that I have had to probe to discover. Thank you for choosing them to be my father and mother.

36. Do Not Kill

"You shall not kill." (Exodus 20:13)

It is curious that one of the two briefest and most seemingly simple commandments—along with *Do not steal*—is even debated. It seems straightforward enough. What is there to debate?

* Michael Phillips, *Endangered Virtues and the Coming Ideological War,* Fidelis Publishing, 2023, p. 171.

As it turns out, more than we might think. Taking it literally, a school of thought in our time interprets the prohibition as covering *all* forms of animal life. Upon this foundation are based various animal rights and dietary movements that tender-hearted individuals find comforting.

Such interpretations and life-choices are fine if one is led in those directions. But that is clearly not the intent of the command. As translated, this cannot possibly be a universally literal command. The Israelites killed and ate animals, which were also used in their sacrifices. Both forms of killing were ordained, even commanded by God.

The command here is against taking *human* life.

Hence arises another of the debated points—capital punishment. Opposing capital punishment on the basis of this command, however, is dubious alongside the numerous capital punishments instituted in the Levitical Law. That is not to say that capital punishment is good or bad, right or wrong, only that the sixth commandment cannot legitimately be used as an argument against it. Indeed, in the *very next chapter* (Exodus 21), several instances of capital punishment are commanded. (Including the command to put to death anyone who curses his father or mother.)

Based on the meaning of the Hebrew word used here (RASAH), many translations translate the commandment, "You shall not murder." That RASAH is indeed translated "murder" in most of its other uses in the Old Testament, probably indeed makes this the more accurate rendering.

Splitting such interpretive hairs, however, is pointless for Christians. Jesus raises the command to an altogether more personal level by equating mere anger with murder: "You have heard that murder makes you liable to judgment, I tell you that if you are *angry* with your brother you are liable to judgment." (In the Greek text, the word Jesus uses is PHONEUO—also "murder.")

Once we bring Jesus' words into our reading of the Old Testament commands—"You have heard that it was said...but I say to you"—everything changes.

To get intensely personal, then—how else are we supposed to read the Bible?—we should read this command, not even as, "Do not get angry enough to murder," but rather:

Do not get angry at all.

I will never come within miles of *murder*. Does that justify my ignoring this Jesus-translation of the word?

In reflecting on the wider implications of the command, I also realize that there is a form of "killing" we are all guilty of. I intend no splitting of analytical hairs with this interpretation. Rather, I hope to make this, and all the Ten Commandments, intensely and practically real in *my* life.

I have found it is fearfully easy, by word or gesture or expression, to *kill* another's enthusiasm, energy, even their vision for an idea or activity or something else they are excited about. What we might call throwing a wet blanket over what someone has excitedly shared. The deflated expression, the sudden doubts cast over enthusiasm, in how many ways do we "kill" the varied forms of incipient *life* trying to sprout within another's mind and heart by cool disapproval, and by a whole range of subtle unsympathetic, thoughtless, derogatory, judgmental, nit-picking, and critical responses?

If I would treat others as I want to be treated, what does criticism feel like to *me?* It's deadening, deflating, vision killing.

Criticism kills.

Therefore, as far reaching as some might consider my interpretation, I internalize and personalize this command as a reminder to find ways to give *life* by my words and gestures and expressions of response. I may not agree with every idea I hear. My responsibility is not to counter, rebuke, or criticize, but to give life.

The *life* of our common humanity transcends agreement or disagreement about ideas. Everyone around us is hungry for the affirmation of personhood. We have the opportunity to give it every day

I thus read this command through the lens of its opposite: *Give life.*

Lord God, send people my way who need a shot of enthusiasm about themselves. Then remind me of what I have just written. Give me words and expressions and smiles that convey life.

37. Do Not Commit Adultery

"You shall not commit adultery." (Exodus 20:14)

It is remarkable how effortlessly the enemy has infiltrated our culture, and even the church, with the normalization of adultery. It should break our hearts. Shame on the clergy for excusing it, too-easily forgiving it, marrying and re-marrying so-called Christians into new so-called marriages founded in adultery, and for committing adultery themselves.

Shame on the church for tolerating this Jezebel in its midst rather than calling it for what it is—sin!

The command is absolute, unambiguous, black and white, binary. There are no excuses.

No one accidentally commits adultery. It is always a choice, a conscious choice to break God's law, to disobey our Father. I think we may legitimately include sex before marriage in the wider scope of what is meant by adultery—*all* sexual activity *outside* marriage.

It is a choice to sin.

Adultery is not just any sin. It is probably the most serious sin of the flesh. Adultery brings three other commandments in its wake—allowing the beguilement of a *false god* to take the place in one's affection for the Lord (whether it be sex, misplaced love, or mere weakness), *stealing* (the purity, faithfulness, fidelity, trust, and truthfulness that is stolen from another can never be recovered), and *covetousness.*

It is a very, very serious sin. Four commandments are shattered in one fell swoop. What is lost is lost. No one ever forgets. Adultery is *never* undone.

The world's sin cannot be condoned or excused. But neither can it be condemned with the same force as the knowing conscious sin of those who claim to be God's men and women.

The world is lost in sin. What else can be expected of it? But that adultery has become rampant in God's church is a monstrous violation of everything God holds holy in human relationships.

Do NOT commit adultery, commands the Lord.

Adultery is sin.

It is *always* sin.

It is chosen sin.

It is serious sin from which there is no turning back. Once lost, sexual purity is gone forever.

It's not a "Do the best you can," command.

It's a 100% command:

- Be *perfectly* pure sexually…
- *after* marriage…
- toward one, and *only* one…
- *lifetime* marital mate…
- of the *opposite* sex.

God's command is unambiguous.

I have no words to pray, Lord. I don't know whether to pray for your forgiveness on behalf of a church so clueless as to ignore this command, or to pray in my flesh for you to rain down fire on a church lost in its disobedience and on the pastors and priests that encourage it. All I can do is say, Lord, heal your people though it may take Malachi's Furnace to accomplish it.

38. Do Not Steal

"You shall not steal" (Exodus 20:15)

Let us not approach this command, or any of the commands, with the immediate legalizing tendency to find the exception, the escape hatch. I don't know about the Jews in Hitler's Germany, or the beggar stealing a loaf of bread to keep his children from starving. Those are legalizing red herrings. You and I are not likely to need to steal to feed our starving children. If your children *are* starving and you have nowhere to turn, then my heart and prayers are with you.

For the rest of us, however, let us not dissect the commands for the exception, but embrace them for the application. The commandments are stark, unyielding, final. This command, like the command against adultery, is binary, black and white, willful, chosen.

Do NOT steal, commands the Lord.

Stealing is sin.

It is *always* sin.

It is chosen sin.

Need and desire do not remove the sin. The progressive leniency and tacit acceptance of shoplifting does not remove the sin. Poverty does not remove the sin. Wanting to live in the U.S. does not remove the sin of stealing a citizenship that does not belong to you. *All* stealing is sin, and there will be an accounting.

There may perhaps be the one-in-a-thousand cases where one actually does accidentally steal something belonging to another without realizing it. We will later consider what is called unintentional sin in *Leviticus*. But let us not be distracted at the point of *this* command.

If there has been a case of accidental theft, the solution is simple—give back what was taken.

This opens a window into a great truth. There are remedies for sin. Repentance is the remedy. Unlike adultery, stealing is a sin that *can* be undone, repented of, restitution made, and hopefully forgiveness extended.

Zacchaeus from Luke 19 is our wonderful model. It may not lie in our power to make *fourfold* restitution for what has been stolen. But we can make the example of Zacchaeus a universal truth revealing how stealing, and most sin, is undone—by repentance and restitution. They may not remove the consequences. But they allow forgiveness to flow. Interestingly, the Levitical Law added a Zacchaeus-like surcharge, so to speak, on restitution—from an extra twenty percent to double, even four times, exactly as Zacchaeus promised to repay. His promise to repay four times over came straight out of the Law.

Where forgiveness flows, healing can begin, and wholeness flourishes.

In the Old Testament Law, theft nearly always carries punishment as well as restitution. George MacDonald uses the idea of theft somewhat tangentially as his entrée into the larger topic of justice, punishment, forgiveness, and atonement. Though not directly applicable to the injunction against stealing, his treatise adds fascinating interest to the Zacchaeus remedy and the Law and its remedies. MacDonald begins his lengthy sermon *Justice* as follows:

> Suppose my watch has been taken from my pocket. I lay hold of the thief. He is dragged before the magistrate, proved guilty, and sentenced to a just imprisonment. Will I then walk home satisfied with the result? Have I had justice done me?
>
> The thief may have had justice done him—but where is my watch? It is gone, and I remain a man wronged.

Who has done me the wrong? The thief. Who can set right the wrong? The thief, and only the thief—nobody but the man that did the wrong.

God may be able to move the man to right the wrong, but God himself cannot right it without the man.

Suppose my watch is found and restored, is the account settled between me and the thief? I may forgive him, but is the wrong removed? By no means.

But suppose the thief think himself to repent. He has, we shall say, put it out of his power to return the watch, but he comes to me and says he is sorry he stole it and begs me to accept for the present what little he is able to bring, as a beginning of atonement. How should I then regard the matter? Should I not feel that he had gone far to make atonement—done more to make up for the injury he had inflicted upon me than the mere restoration of the watch, even by himself, could reach to?

Would there not lie, in the thief's confession and submission and initial restoration, an appeal to the divinest in me—to the eternal brotherhood? Would it not indeed amount to a sufficing atonement as between man and man?

If he offered to bear what I chose to lay upon him, should I feel it necessary, for the sake of justice, to inflict additional suffering upon him as demanded by righteousness? I should still have a claim upon him for my watch, but should I not be apt to forget it? [*]

Again, Lord, I do not know what to pray personally about theft itself. However, if I have been guilty of any unintentional thefts that I am not aware of—perhaps emotional or psychological, if my insensitivity has stolen another's joy, if my criticism has stolen another's hope or enthusiasm—bring these to my awareness that I may repent to you, and, if possible, to whomever else is involved. If such is not possible by the infinite miracle of your timelessness, receive into your heart my repentance of every tiniest lapse of attentiveness. Make right the hurts I have inflicted through the years by insensitive thefts against the personhood of others. In a way I cannot fathom, miraculously undo my myriad lapses and unkindnesses. Heal, and bring eternal good from my words and deeds that were less than they should have been.

39. Do Not Speak Falsely About Others

"You shall not bear false witness against your neighbor." (Exodus 20:16)

The wording we are familiar with here, "Do not bear false witness," carries the tone of a courtroom—a witness being grilled by an attorney, and lying about what he or she has seen—*bearing false witness.* The intent here, however, is far broader, carrying implications that penetrate into almost every corner of human relationships. I would expand the wording to include even *implied* falsehoods about another. I would go further than that—including speaking critically of others…belittling, condescending, making fun of, to the point even of *implying* any form of negativity.

I therefore paraphrase what I am confident is God's intent in this commandment:

---

[*] George MacDonald, *Unspoken Sermons, Third Series,* "Justice," quoted from *George MacDonald's Transformational Theology of the Christian Faith.*

Do not speak negatively, critically, or falsely about others,
neither infer criticism or judgment, nor by word, gesture, tone,
or implication, convey so much as a hint of denigration or disapproval.

The reason is obvious. My criticism, my negative assessments, my implications *may* be wrong. If so, and I have spoken them, then I have not only broken one of God's holy commandments, I have passed along an untruth to someone else. Who can tell what might be the consequences of my untruth-speaking tongue.

Even if what I speak about another is true, I have no business passing it on. The delight we take in talking about other people is nothing less than a disease. If we know a fact about another, even if we have no idea whether it is true or not, the juicier the better, especially if tinged with weakness, failing, or sin…we can't wait to pass it on!

We turn everyone else's business into *our* business. We assume that any morsel of news is fair game to be broadcast publicly to anyone and everyone.

"You'll never guess what *I* just heard…"

This is simply, unequivocally, categorically *wrong*.

We have *no* business speaking of what we've heard second hand. It does not belong to us. The spicy revelation, the titillating tidbit of hearsay, the racy hint of scandal, the delicious rumor—such scraps of news are the life blood of the gossip-monger.

But such news is not mine to pass on!

When a morsel of evil comes into your hearing, let it fall to the ground. Don't pick it up. Ask no questions. Do not continue the conversation.

If you are not part of the problem, or part of the solution, keep your mouth shut. Thomas Kempis is absolutely ruthless in his pointed admonitions:

- *Do not be too confident in your own opinion.*
- *Do not busy yourself with the words and deeds of others.*
- *Turn your eyes unto yourself.*
- *Do not be idle or spend your time in talk.*
- *Meddle not with curiosities.*
- *Withdraw from speaking vainly and gadding idly.*
- *Do not busy yourself in matters which appertain to others, nor entangle yourself in their affairs.*

Gossip is as epidemic in our time as using the Lord's name in vain. It may be a worse violation for Christians because no one even considers frivolous talk a sin. It's part of normal conversation to talk about others.

Pay careful attention to the conversations you are part of—talk about people who are not present positively dominates most casual chatty conversations! No one thinks of loose talk as a violation of love, or as the sin James makes abundantly clear it is. But in all these ways, loose tongues kill love by starting fires of innuendo, suspicion, and doubt.

It's more than just speaking *falsely.* It is speaking ungenerously, ungraciously, or unkindly. The problem is speaking about other people's business at all!

Kempis' words are pointed: *Meddle not with curiosities.*

Paul points to the truth that should rule our conversations: *Love is not rude...it does not rejoice in wrong but rejoices in goodness and truth.*

Let us speak about others in *love,* our words seasoned with grace, passing on the good report in season. Let us speak of what we find wonderful in others.

It may be an old-fashioned truism, but never a more scriptural principle was spoken than, *If you have nothing good to say, say nothing at all.*

God wants us not only to be witnesses of the truth of his being and character, but to be purveyors and witnesses to the truth and goodness of our neighbors.

Let us spread God's salt and light with our speech, not vinegar.

God, as aware of this tendency as I am, and as much as I hate it, I see myself slipping into it so easily in conversation. I ask you to silence me, convict me, box me on the ears when I begin speaking about others. Send alarm bells into my brain to shut me up. May I spread your salt and light with my speech. And when I talk about others, may I speak of them graciously in ways that build them up to all who may be listening. Keep criticism far from my tongue.

40. Do Not Covet What You Do Not Have

"Do not covet your neighbor's house; you shall not covet your neighbor's wife, or his manservant, or his maidservant, or his ox, or his ass, or anything that is your neighbor's." (Exodus 20:17)

This is a hard command. I wonder if God saved it for last because it is so important, or because it is one of the most difficult. Probably 99% of the people who have ever lived have broken it more times than they can count. It is also one of the most devious of the commands. The wooings of Command #25 ("Do not let sin beguile you") come whispering their covetous subtleties into our ears from morning till night. Eve ate the fruit because she coveted it.

The very meaning of "covet" drips with the serpent's venom: *To yearn to possess.*

Yet how easily we soften it to make excuse for ourselves.

"Wouldn't it be nice if..."

"I'd really like..."

"Life would be so much simpler if..."

And hey…what's wrong with wanting a more dependable car, a little more money in the bank, wanting our wife or husband or children to have nice things?

Covetousness creeps in so effortlessly because there *isn't* anything wrong with trying to better our lives. It sneaks up on us exactly as does idol-worship. When does wanting a legitimately good thing which God might have no objection to cross the line into covetousness?

We gain profound insight by the words of the text, which essentially read, "Don't covet what someone *else* has." It is when I yearn to possess what *another* has but I don't, that I am on dangerous ground. I have crossed the line into envy. Jealously is not far behind.

This tenth commandment offers a wonderful example why it is important not to get distracted by red herrings of literality. As important as it is to take the Bible literally when it is called for, not many of us have to struggle with being covetous of our neighbor's ox. Oxen don't enter much into our daily lives.

But *all* of us struggle with yearning for what we do not have—a nicer home or car, a better job, a little more cushion in the bank account, a trimmer figure, or better health.

One of my dear friends, late in life when he could afford it, bought a brand new Corvette. Proud to show off his new toy, he took me for a ride. I tried to make a show of enjoying it. But all I could think was, "What a waste of money?" It did not move my envy-needle a hair's breadth. If someone gave me a Corvette, the first thing I would do is sell it. Fancy cars hold no interest for me. I've never coveted a car in my life. Neither have I ever coveted another man's wife, or another woman at all. That God specifies sexual covetousness, however, reveals what a dreadful temptation it is for much of humanity. The epidemic of adultery is rooted in covetousness. Neither have I ever coveted anyone else's home

In my case, covetousness sneaks into more private and unseen corners of my mind, then worms its way into my heart, where it becomes more insidious and dangerous.

Some of what I consider my most important books have sold poorly. I wish they had done better. I find myself envying the sales figures of other authors. It's covetousness plain and simple.

All my life I have struggled to keep from coveting the temperament and personality of my more outgoing friends and acquaintances. Covetousness again—not of possession, but of internal make-up and personhood.

I have a radio interview scheduled next week. I am dreading it. I am full of covetousness of certain personalities who are more brilliantly articulate and glib—one of them a close and dear friend. I am not covetous of his ox, but I do covet his golden tongue, keen intellect, and ready wit.

The final words of the command slam the door against trying to weasel out of it with whatever excuses or justifications we devise: "…or *anything* that is your neighbor's." Covetousness is not just money, possessions, or husbands and wives.

That *anything* is sweeping and unconditional.

I am sorry, Lord, for coveting my friend's articulate tongue. If I am more like Moses and slow of speech, then I thank you for his example of obedience, reluctant though it was. And I thank you for creating me as I am. Thank you that I can speak with my fingers if not always as well as I might like with my tongue. Show me all my secret covetousnesses. Expose them to my inner eyes and help me root them out.

Series Five

Obedience

The Levitical Law

Order, community, well-being, nationhood, and compassionate relationships in the human family

Leviticus: Hidden gold in the Old Testament reveals the Divine Fatherhood

From the moment God raised Moses up to lead the Israelites out of Egypt, Aaron was at his side. We must assume that he was also a faithful and righteous man. God chose him to be Moses' mouthpiece and to take his own prophetic place with his brother:

"And the Lord said unto Moses, See, I have made thee a god to Pharaoh: and Aaron thy brother shall be thy prophet…and Aaron thy brother shall speak unto Pharaoh." (Exodus 7:1-2, KJV)

It is easy for readers of the Old Testament to assume that the story of the Hebrew people emerged out of a vacuum, that everything about their story was completely unique, even that the Old Testament itself is a completely unique document. But this is not the case. Other nations and cultures had their own creation accounts and flood stories. They were developing language in similar ways, borrowing from and blending with one another, and thus also producing their own written histories. The Hebrew people were part of an expansive Middle Eastern culture whose nations were moving toward modernity on many cross-pollinating parallel and intersecting tracks.

One particular area of culture in which the world of the Middle East was growing and advancing in the centuries between 2000 B.C. and 1500 B.C. was in the codifying of law.

Reading the Bible apart from its historical context, we presume that the Law given to Moses was completely unheard of, that God dictated to Moses all the precepts of an entirely new system of ordering life, relationships, and society. However, this is an inaccurate perception. At many points the Law of Moses reflects what was taking place throughout the Middle East.

The oldest collection of laws that has been discovered comes from Abraham's home town, the Sumerian city of Ur. It dates from approximately 2050 B.C. The most famous and extensive collection of laws prior to those of the Old Testament originated in Babylon during the reign of Hammurabi in the 18th century B.C. Collections also exist of Hittite and Assyrian laws. Educated and raised as a prince of Egypt, Moses would have been familiar with all these. Interestingly, what survives of these other law codes are written on stone tablets.

Not only do undeniable similarities exist between some of these prior collections and the Law of Moses, the format, too, is similar. The individual precepts of the law often end with curses against any who violate the law or damage the tablets.

The Law of Moses therefore, was not the first such code of law. Neither did the sacrifice, circumcision, the tabernacle, the priesthood, shedding blood to atone for sin, or even the idea of "covenant," originate with the Hebrews. Such means and methods were in widespread use in the Middle East among many peoples, races, and tribal groups.

Whereas most of the prior law codes dealt with property, the Law of Moses *is* unique, however, in its emphasis on *people*. God took the Hebrews where they were, using ideas familiar to them, and imbued those concepts with new meaning and higher purposes—placing into Israelite law notable and distinctive features that indeed set it apart and raised it to a loftier plane than any existing law of the time. Of course the most singular of all was Israel's covenant with one God, *the* God, the God with no name who called himself I AM.

Then YHWH added other distinctive elements of righteousness that indeed set the Levitical law apart. Not only did God command what the Israelites were to *do*, equally emphatic were those practices among the peoples around them that God did *not* want the Israelites to imitate—kingship, idols, shrines to pagan gods, etc. These *don'ts* highlighted important points of disobedience to God's law.

In my *Eyewitness Old Testament* books I paraphrased God's two originating commands to Adam and Eve in the garden regarding the two trees as:

- *Partake of life.*
- *Do not partake of sin.*

In a sense, the Levitical Law codified in detailed and specific form how God's people were to do both. The *do* and the *don't*.

In its completed form, the Law of Moses became the "gold standard" of all Law in the ancient world prior to Greece and Rome.

When we read the Levitical Law, recognizing what God was trying to accomplish through it, we come to see that it is not always as legalistic as it appears. God was gradually revealing himself as a good and loving Father taking care of his children.

As any good parent does, one of the first means of doing so is to establish parameters and boundaries for attitudes and behavior—setting everything in life, human relationships most of all, into perspective…revealing and explaining in gradually expanding and deepening ways how life is to be lived. The first means by which parents accomplish this is through command.

We tend to think of the Old Testament Levitical Law as little more than legalistic do's and don'ts that have little bearing on our lives.

Exploring between the lines of what seems like a morass of regulation and ritual, however, to discover God's purpose and intent, the divine Fatherhood lies as a deep buried vein of gold through the entire account.

To understand the Old Testament, we have to read with the underlying awareness that a millennium later Jesus would personally embody and complete the revelation begun in *Exodus, Leviticus, Numbers,* and

Deuteronomy. Jesus did not change the revelation. He fulfilled and brought it to completion. If we have eyes to see it, the gospel itself is embedded in the earlier writings

The theme of goodness and righteousness holds the Old Testament together. It is fundamentally a Jesus and Fatherhood message. The word *holiness* is used eighty-seven times in *Leviticus.* God wants his children to be *good* children.

Leviticus 19 is an excellent example. its regulations are surprisingly relevant to us today, and indeed relevant for all times throughout history.

- Respect your mother and father.
- When you reap the harvest of your land, do not reap to the very edges of your field or gather the gleanings of your harvest. Do not go over your vineyard a second time or pick up the grapes that have fallen. Leave them for the poor and the foreigner.
- Do not steal.
- Do not lie.
- Do not deceive one another.
- Do not defraud or rob your neighbor.
- Do not hold back the wages of a hired worker.
- Do not curse the deaf or put a stumbling block in front of the blind.
- Do not pervert justice.
- Do not show partiality to the poor or favoritism to the great, but judge your neighbor fairly.
- Do not spread slander among your people.
- Do not do anything that endangers your neighbor's life.
- Do not seek revenge or bear a grudge.
- Love your neighbor as yourself.
- Do not practice divination or seek omens.
- Do not put tattoo marks on yourselves.
- Do not degrade your daughter by making her a prostitute.
- Do not turn to mediums or seek out spiritists, for you will be defiled by them.
- Do not use dishonest standards when measuring length, weight or quantity.
- Use honest scales and honest weights.

One of those I find most fascinating is found in verse 32: *Stand up in the presence of the aged, show respect for the elderly and revere your God.*

This down-to-earth practicality is astonishing to read. In today's culture, youth rules. Our entire society centers around the young. Imagine if today's world took the command seriously—*Rise respectfully when an old man or woman walks into the room.*

Some may be surprised to find Aaron here as a prophetic "type" selected to embody one of the important command-principles of the Old Testament. We tend to associate Aaron with wishy-washiness and disobedience, as the man who allowed the Israelites to make the golden calf as soon as Moses' back was turned. But Aaron's legacy is far more significant than that.

Aaron's life anticipates Series Nine—Judgment and Forgiveness. The principle undergirding the two-part sequence of that series reveals a vital progression in God's dealings with man as exemplified in the history of the nation of Israel. Sin, as it must be, is met with God's *judgment*. God's intent—misunderstood by most Old and New Testament theologians—is not punishment for its own sake, but to produce *repentance*. Repentance leads to God's *forgiveness*, which in turn leads to healing and *restoration* of the relationship between God and the sinner, between Father and his child, which it is hoped will lead to true *righteousness* in the end.

The progression—sin, judgment, repentance, forgiveness, restoration, righteousness—lies at the heart of God's eternal purpose in creation and for his people. This thematic progression weaves its way through the entire Old Testament saga. Genesis 3—evil enters the story. Genesis 4—God warns Cain of sin. Genesis 7—sin is judged. The prophets write of restoration. And finally millennia after Cain and Noah, we read in Malachi 4—"the sun of righteousness will rise with healing in its wings." It is an unfolding chain of purpose that overarches the whole with eternal meaning.

Aaron embodies this progression. He yielded to sin, he repented, was forgiven and restored, and God raised him up as the first prophet-priest to administer the Law.

"And take thou unto thee Aaron thy brother, and his sons with him…that he may minister unto me in the priest's office…and thou shalt make holy garments for Aaron thy brother…to consecrate him, that he may minister unto me in the priest's office." (Exodus 28:1-3, KJV)

As Israel's first high priest, ordained thus by God, Aaron was the man chosen to be the first priestly-type anticipating Christ himself. His was indeed a high and holy prophetic calling.

Aaron thus took his place beside Moses—the two prophet-brothers leading Israel through the exodus and initiating the Levitical Law and the covenant of the Aaronic Priesthood.

As a practical matter, it is clearly impossible for this particular book, to enumerate *all* the commands of the Levitical Law. Such is not my purpose. The same was true when we looked at the book of *Proverbs*. My purpose is not to compile a *Strong's Concordance* of commands, but to prayerfully discover how to practically *do* what God tells his people to do.

The commands that follow in this series, and in all the groupings, have been selected as representing in a general way a range of situations addressed in *Leviticus* in what to our ears is almost ridiculous and often outdated detail. Most of us are not going to face our bull falling into a ditch or goring our neighbor. Nor is leprosy a disease we will often encounter. The dietary and medical regulations, on the other hand, are astoundingly practical and surprisingly relevant all these years later. I find the instructions about mold, mildew, disease, and infection particularly fascinating, important for a primitive people, and full of spiritual relevance as descriptive of how sin infiltrates our lives. But five chapters (10-14) about food, medicinal practices, purity, and protecting against the spread of disease, leprosy, and mold will hopefully be adequately summarized by *Keep your camp pure.*

May God give us eternal eyesight to probe deeply and discover the heart of his Fatherhood in the commands of the Law.

Series Five

Obedience

41. Love your neighbor as yourself.

42. Show kindness to widows, orphans, strangers, and aliens.

43. Help and be kind to the poor.

44. Keep your camp pure.

45. Work hard and rejoice in what you undertake.

46. Respect the property of others.

47. Make restitution for wrong.

48. Bear no grudge, seek no revenge.

49. Lend without interest.

50. Periodically cancel debt.

41. Love Your Neighbor as Yourself

"Love your neighbor as yourself. I am the Lord." (Leviticus 19:18)

The common mistake, both in culture and religion, is to view Old Testament "law" as a negative, demanding, collection of legalistic rites and prohibitions. Sad to say, the ancient Israelites and not-so-ancient Jews are responsible for the beginnings and perpetuation of this myth that has prevented the true *knowing* of God for over 3000 years. This myth and this mistaking of the nature of the Law is still, even in our own time, probably more responsible for myriad false ideas about God—in both the Christian church and the general culture—than any other single factor.

But it is all wrong. We must blast this myth to smithereens before we do anything else. To understand God at all, this myth, and the imaginary tyrant god standing behind it like an evil presence wielding thunderbolts of vengeance, must be demolished.

We should not have had to wait 2000 years since Jesus' time to demolish it. The myth was obliterated in the blinding light of this very command that informs and undergirds the entire Levitical law. Jesus himself encapsulated that Law into two succinct commandments: *Love God...Love Man.*

When Jesus was asked, "What is the greatest commandment?" his familiar answer contained two parts: *Love the Lord your God with all your heart,* and *Love your neighbor as yourself.* Some assume that the second command was added by Jesus as a new covenantal "fulfillment" of Old Testament law. But the second command is as ancient and intrinsic to Judaism as the first. Yet history shows all too clearly that by Jesus' time, love for one's neighbor had indeed been relegated to a near-forgotten Levitical footnote in the lexicon of Pharisaical religiosity practiced by Israel's leadership. When Jesus brought "the second commandment" back into the light, powerfully illuminating its practical reality by the parable of the good Samaritan, he was only reminding his listeners what had been God's intent from the beginning of time, that love for God and love for others are one and the same. They are inseparable. Love for God cannot exist in a vacuum. Love for others, our neighbors, our fellow men and women of humanity, is the oxygen in which Love for God thrives.

The second "great commandment" commonly called the golden rule is so simple it can be expressed in five words: *Love your neighbor as yourself.* It doesn't get much more practical than that. And this, says Jesus, embodies the essence of the Law.

Love, not thunderbolts. Kindness, not vengeance.

Goodness embodies the Law—the goodness of a loving Father desiring the best for his children.

That's why it is important to begin this series of commands of the Levitical Law with the towering command found in Leviticus 19:18. As Jesus said clearly—this verse contains one of the two commands that embodies the *whole* Law, and encompasses and draws up into it all the many other specifics of the Law.

The Levitical Law is incredibly detailed. As I said earlier, it would be impossible and profitless to try to list and comment on every one of those hundreds of commands. Many have little bearing on our lives today (leprosy, the bull in a ditch, how to prepare dozens of types of sacrifices, how the priestly robes should be made, etc.). Thus we look for larger themes that reflect God's overspreading intent and represent the myriad specifics in more general ways. Once we see it from this perspective, the Law begins to look very different. The words that rise to the surface continue to explode the myth of legalism:

- *Love.*
- *Help.*
- *Be kind.*
- *Respect.*
- *Honor.*
- *Don't be angry.*
- *Forgive.*

When we dig deep enough, looking for its high themes, recognizing the Father of Jesus as the Author of the Law rather than an imaginary pagan idol, in the midst of most of the precepts of the Law we discover the caring love of a concerned Father for his immature babes. This is our challenge as we read the Old Testament—to discover the divine Fatherhood.

When you leave your house today, how would you like people to treat you…how would you like them to speak to you…what expression would you like to see on their faces when they look at you…how would you like them to respond to you?

When I look in the mirror and ask myself those questions, I have just outlined my *own* marching orders for the day.

Maybe this isn't a negative or legalistic command. But it is certainly a demanding one.

*Be nice to your neighbor…*of course.

Gracious…kind…thoughtful…generous…considerate…unselfish. All these go without saying. Aren't these nothing more than what good parents try to teach their children?

But even these character qualities are not enough.

Is it possible that I am actually expected to *love* my neighbor…with the same care and attention I give to my own needs and concerns and priorities and thoughts and opinions?

Love my neighbor…*as myself.*

As I love myself…as I want others to love me.

As shocking as it seems, once our eyes are opened to this high truth, it is exactly this neighborly *love* that we find throughout the Old Testament law.

This is such a mighty revelation, God, that in the Old Testament Law you reveal yourself as a good and caring and loving Father. How many of my preconceptions must go! Reveal your Fatherhood more and more as I read. Reveal your Fatherhood in the commands of the Old Testament. Foundational to them, as I do my part, help me to love all the neighbors you send me, love them as my brothers and sisters of your family...love them as I want to be loved myself.

42. Show Kindness to Widows, Orphans, Strangers, and Aliens

"This is my commandment, that you love one another." (Exodus 20:4)
The stranger who sojourns with you shall be to you as the native...
and you shall love him as yourself. (Leviticus 19:34)
The Levite, because he has no portion or inheritance with you, and the sojourner, the fatherless, and the widow, who are within your towns, shall come and eat and be filled. (Deuteronomy 14:29)
When you reap your harvest in your field, and have forgotten a sheaf in the field, you shall not go back to get it; it shall be for the sojourner, the fatherless, and the widow...When you beat your olive trees, you shall not go over the boughs again; it shall be for the sojourner, the fatherless, and the widow. When you gather the grapes of your vineyard, you shall not glean it afterward; it shall be for the sojourner, the fatherless, and the widow. (Deuteronomy 24:19-21)

At first glance, the above passages which are quoted in some length appear to reflect those detailed and specific commands of the Law I said we need to read in the context of its higher themes. But the first four commands of this series wonderfully harmonize the general and the specific—infusing the high theme of a Father' devoted care and love for his children into very specific, practical, daily-do-able commands.

Reflect on the words of the first four commands of this series: *Love...Show kindness...Help and be kind...Keep pure.*

All these attributes and expressions of love proceed directly out of the divine character of Fatherhood. God *is* these things. God *does* these things. Therefore, he commands his children to demonstrate *his* character in these specific ways in their relationships with each other.

This command and the next specifically focus that Father-love toward the weak, the alone, the helpless, the disadvantaged. *Help and be kind to those in need.* It is intrinsic to the entire theme of Christianity and the basis for what is sometimes called a "social gospel." One does not have to look hard to see here too, if such is one's intent, the basis for modernism's progressive agenda. To find it embedded deep in the Old Testament, however, is a little surprising. The Israelites and Jews of the Old Testament, and throughout history, are not remembered for their openness and kindness to strangers and Gentiles.

Yet here it is—Be kind to *all* the disadvantaged.

Widows and orphans, in a sense, typify the essence of the command, and remained a paramount concern through history. The New Testament writers were equally insistent that the church protect and care for "widows and orphans." It is only very recently that women have risen societally in the western world to a position in which widows are not left destitute by the loss of a husband, and that the squalor and horrifying conditions of orphanages is becoming a thing of the past. Say what one may about the politics of liberalism, the social "safety net" of most of the world's advanced nations has brought a reality to the implementation of this command that has been unknown throughout most of history.

While the plight of "widows and orphans" may not be as desperate as in past times, this remains a pointedly detailed command. We mustn't ignore the specifics. When my brother-in-law died, we brought my newly widowed sister into our home to live with us, as we did my mother-in-law after the death of Judy's father.

On the other hand, we have to be equally attentive to the higher thematic command to which these words point:

Show kindness to all the disadvantaged, lonely, alone, and in need.

Both the general and the specific in this command are practical and imperative. The lonely and alone surround us. Their need may not be financial. There are thousands of ways to "show kindness." Several doors from us lives a dear lady in her eighties. She and Judy are "mail slot pen pals" and exchange notes and brief letters several times a week. She often adds little edible treats to her messages, and we reciprocate.

She is alone but not lonely, full of the joy of life, with no obviously visible "needs." She fits none of the above categories. The other day I prepared a small bowl of pudding for her. As I was getting it ready, I noticed the roses blooming out our kitchen window. I plucked a particularly nice white one, laid it on the tray with the bowl, and took it round to our friend.

The next day the little note that came through our mail slot was for me, not Judy. After sharing a poem from a book she had been reading entitled "One Perfect Rose." she wrote, "A gentleman has never brought me 'a perfect rose'—ever!!"

I was moved to smiles and tears. It was such a small thing, such an easy gesture of kindness. I didn't even think of it as a gesture of kindness. It was automatic, the kind of thing one simply *does*.

Yet it touched her.

Such opportunities for kindness are abundant around us, if not every minute certainly every day. I am convicted by my own words that I do not instantly jump at every one of these moments. But I forget. Life is a constant rush of urgencies and distractions that will be forgotten.

The white rose from our yard will *not* be forgotten. Kindness touches hearts. We simply have to slow down enough amid our busy lives to perceive those moments, then pluck the roses of kindness to plant into the hearts of those in our midst.

Urgencies will quickly vanish. But every kindness will pass into eternity and be glorified into the reflection of God's character it expresses.

> "Have you ever noticed how much of Christ's life was spent in doing kind things—in merely doing kind things? Run over it with that in view, and you will find that He spent a great proportion of His time simply in making people happy, in doing good turns to people...
>
> "'The greatest thing,' says someone, 'a man can do for his Heavenly Father is to be kind to some of His other children.' I wonder why it is that we are not all kinder than we are? How much the world needs it. How easily it is done. How instantaneously it acts. How infallibly it is remembered. How super abundantly it pays itself back...
>
> "Where Love is, God is. He that dwelleth in Love dwelleth in God. God is love. Therefore love. Without distinction, without calculation, without procrastination, love. Lavish it upon the poor, where it is very easy; especially upon the rich, who often need it most; most of all upon our equals, where it is very difficult, and for whom perhaps we each do least of all.
>
> "There is a difference between trying to please and giving pleasure. Lose no chance of giving pleasure. For that is the ceaseless and anonymous triumph of a truly loving spirit. 'I shall pass through this world but once. Any good thing therefore that I can do, or any kindness that I can show to any human being, let me do it now. Let me not defer or neglect it, for I shall not pass this way again.'" *

Give me opportunities, Lord, to show kindness to the disadvantaged. Remind me to seize them, not ignore them. The rose I share may represent a singular moment in someone's life, and echo into his or her heart in unexpected ways. The faint strains of eternity may tug at those hearts with a reminder that you love them and care about them. Let me not defer or neglect those moments, for I may not pass that way again.

43. Help and Be Kind to the Poor

When you reap the harvest of your land, you shall not reap your field to its very border, neither shall you gather the gleanings after your harvest...strip your vineyard bare...gather the fallen grapes of your vineyard; you shall leave them for the poor...If your brother becomes poor, and cannot maintain himself with you, you shall maintain him. (Leviticus 19:9-10; 25:35)

This is essentially a continuation from the previous command from Deuteronomy. We might easily have combined them as one. But this is such a central biblical injunction, encompassing Scripture from *Genesis* to *Revelation*, that its emphasis must never be overlooked. Its imperative should remain in the forefront of everything meant by the practical living of faith.

---

* Henry Drummond, *The Greatest Thing in the World.*

Here, too, we see the general and the specific woven into a unified fabric. The above words sound specific, but they also represent a high theme that plunges straight to the heart of God's Fatherhood.

How practical is the specific in which the overspreading general command is contained:

"When you reap the harvest of your land, do not reap to the very edges of your field or gather the gleanings of your harvest. Do not go over your vineyard a second time or pick up the grapes that have fallen. Leave them for the poor and the foreigner. (Leviticus 19:9-10)

Here is a specific passage that we easily see drawn up into the high themes of both Commands #42 and #43—a loving Father taking care of the disadvantaged among his children.

Sadly this command and many like them are taken out of context and regularly cited as basis for various political agendas, social programs, and taxation measures. It is not a question of whether such programs and agendas are bad or good. We can take a stand on either side of such societal debates.

What you and I need to keep in *our* focus is the hypocrisy of misusing, and misrepresenting Scripture. We need to take the Bible's commands seriously, read them accurately, and obey them sincerely and honestly.

All the commands proceed out of the great commands—*Love God, Love your neighbor. Help the poor* cannot be divorced from *Love God.* Helping the poor is but one element in a holistic life-perspective in which love of God and love of man are completely intertwined. There is no separation between them. Those who would help the poor because the Bible says to do so, while at the same time advocating *removing* God from society and culture and schools and the entire public square, are deluded by their own ignorance of the high themes and overarching message of Scripture.

Love of God and love of man are one.

Even understanding this truth, however, this is surely one of the most difficult of scriptural injunctions to know how to obey practically. Does a coin in the beggar's cup outside the Temple in Jesus' day, or a five dollar bill to the homeless man on the street corner in our own time indicate obedience? Probably not. Do welfare programs at the governmental level satisfy the command? They obviously don't accomplish much either.

We are commanded to help the poor. But *how*...practically? The command isn't, *Give money to the poor*, but *Help and be kind to the poor.* What, then, if they don't *want* help but only want money? What if they spurn kindness because that's not what they want either, only money.

Does giving *money* to the poor equal *help* the poor?

It's the age-old question whether it is better to give a poor man a fish that will feed him for one meal, or teach him how to fish. Which is the real source of lasting *help*? Does giving a homeless man money, or giving him a job and teaching him how to do it, provide more lasting help?

Poverty and all the societal questions that come with it have no easy solutions.

I ask these questions seriously and with sadness and confusion in my own heart. I ask God these *How?* questions every time I pass a homeless man or woman with his or her cardboard sign, *Please help, God bless.* Do they want help? What *help* might be in my power to give? Or do they only want money, which, if given, in reality may give them *neither* help *nor* kindness?

I read in the above scriptural passages the simple injunction: *Scatter some of the extra harvest blessings from your life around in the fields where you live as helps to those who have not been so fortunate.*

Several years ago my favorite running route took me through a redwood park. I noticed a young man, probably in his twenties, sitting on one of the park benches, then again, and again. I realized he was homeless and living in the woods among the redwoods with a park bathroom nearby. At the time two of our sons were estranged from us. We had not seen them in a long time. My heart went out to this young man in the park. I could not help thinking of my own sons? What if this were *my* son and a Christian man were somehow put into his life and was able to help him?

It became very personal whenever I saw him. Where were his parents? Did his parents know where he was? If not, I grieved for them just as I grieved for my own sons. I didn't know where one of them was either.

I began taking a break in my run, trying to engage him in conversation. Then I stuck a five dollar bill in my trunks the next time I went out, hoping to sweeten the pot and encourage him to open up to me. I wanted to be able to give the very *help* I was praying for someone, somewhere, to give in reaching out to my own sons. *Do as you would be done by* was very real to me during those runs through the park.

This went on for some time...more five dollar bills, more attempted conversation... what's your name, where are you from, where are your parents?

But I was talking to a brick wall. The eyes staring back at me were blank and empty. I could find no point of contact on which to begin building help or kindness. I eventually was able to coerce out of him his name and home town, but little else. I managed to get a faint lead on how to contact his parents, but the information was sketchy. I wrote to what I thought might have been his home address, but the letter was returned.

All at once the young man disappeared from the park. I went by every day, praying for another opportunity, hoping to see him again. But there was no trace of him.

Months went by. Then unexpectedly, suddenly I saw him walking slowly along the sidewalk in the middle of town three miles away. I approached and did my best to catch his eye. I greeted him and tried to engage him in conversation, hoping he remembered me, still wanting to get a lead on his parents. But the expression staring back at me was just as blank as ever. It was as though he was deaf.

At last he spoke. "Can you gimme ten bucks?" he said.

I wasn't running at the time but was in my street clothes. I knew it was over. I knew it would accomplish neither help nor kindness, but I fished a ten out of my billfold and handed it to him. Then I watched him turn and drift along the sidewalk without a word.

I never saw him again.

I've never forgotten the young man, and have prayed for him through the years. And for his parents.

This is not a particularly hard command to obey superficially, or to *think* we are obeying with money. It is a very hard and conscience-tugging command to know how to obey *effectively*. Welfare doesn't help. Governmental programs don't help. Financial assistance only perpetuates the problem. Trying to help in our day can even be dangerous. The poor of our time are often so mired in drugs and crime that it's not as simple as bringing them into your home for a meal as was the case during the Great Depression, and even as Judy and I used to do in the early days of our bookstore with needy and sometimes traveling customers with no place to go at the end of the day. Doing that now might well put your whole family at risk. Homeless drug addicts and those hiding from the police may not be the "poor" this passage is speaking of. *Leviticus* has other remedies for law-breakers.

Lasting and fruit-bearing *help* is very difficult to get into the hearts who need them the most. Nevertheless, hard and confusing though it may be, we are commanded to help and be kind to the poor. We need God's wisdom.

Give me insight, wisdom, and compassion, Lord God, and practical guidance in knowing how you would have me obey this command, and what specifically you would have me do to help the poor who cross my path.

44. Keep Your Camp Pure

The LORD said to Moses, "Command the Israelites to send away from the camp anyone who has a defiling skin disease…so they will not defile their camp, where I dwell among them." (Numbers 5:1-3, NIV)

The LORD your God walks in the midst of your camp…therefore your camp must be holy. (Deuteronomy 23:14)

In the introduction to this series I noted this as a summarizing command for a wide range of specific commands given by God, most notably in Leviticus 10-14. In another sense, however, if holiness and obedience—foreshadowing Matthew 5-7— are underlying themes in the Levitical Law, this may be one of the most important commands of all—drawing up into it the *whole* Law, not just what to do about mildew, leprosy, and infection.

Holiness *is* purity.

The "camp" thus becomes a metaphor for all of life—everything about us, our bodies, minds, behavior, where we live, who we are, the people with whom we share life, our families, our spiritual practices…all these are incorporated in "the camp" where we live.

Leviticus 19 speaks straight to you and me:

- Keep your food pure.
- Keep your worship pure.
- Keep your behavior pure.
- Keep your responses pure.
- Keep your relationships pure.
- Keep your marriages pure.
- Keep your sexual practices pure.
- Keep your words pure.
- Keep your thoughts pure.
- Keep *yourselves* pure.

God gave the Israelites specific regulations appropriate to their primitive lives. Leviticus 13 concerning leprosy is so specific as to be almost humorous to read. Yet underlying the specificity we continue to discover the Fatherhood of God caring about the well-being of his children.

This is not just for the Israelites. It is for you and me. He cares for us also through this command. We are commanded to keep everything in the camps of our lives pure—especially marriage and sexual practices.

The detailed specifics are surprisingly contemporary. There is so much concern about black mold today that a house cannot be sold where mold is found. Then we read Leviticus 14, detailing the extreme measures laid out to stop and eliminate mold, culminating, if the mold cannot be contained, in the destruction of a house. These mold-instructions were written over 3000 years ago.

Was the Old Testament ahead of its time or what! In some ways, it is not a primitive document at all.

Any heart-mold or mind-fungus or spiritual-mildew or relational-leprosy that I allow to infiltrate my thoughts or behavior will become a creeping, growing, invisible impurity that will take over more and more parts of my heart and mind and relationships if I do not stop them.

Impurity—of the mind, heart, or body—always spreads.

Infection—of the mind, heart, or body—spreads.

Leprosy—of the mind, heart, or body—spreads.

They must be stopped, cut out, and killed or they will continue to infect more and more aspects of personhood with their creeping and pervasive death.

Character mold is lethal. It spreads.

Heavenly Father, give me a scrutinizing eye as I walk through my "camp" to spot hints of spiritual and character mold, mildew, fungus, and leprosy before they gain a foothold, and take steps to rid them from my life-camp. Protect me, protect my family, protect those I love from their pervasive influences.

45. Work Diligently and Cheerfully in What You Undertake

Lazy hands make for poverty, but diligent hands bring wealth. (Proverbs 10:4, NIV)
Do you see a man skilled in his work? he will stand before kings;
he will not stand before obscure men. (Proverbs 22:29)
A glad heart makes a cheerful countenance. (Proverbs 15:13)
A good wife…works with willing hands…she rises while it is yet night
and provides food for her household…
she opens her hand to the poor…strength and dignity are her clothing…she looks well to the ways of her household, and does not eat the bread of idleness. (Proverbs 31:10, 13, 15, 20, 25, 27)
Whatever your hand finds to do, do it with your might. (Ecclesiastes 9: 10)

Loving and serving God with "all your heart, and with…all your might" to my mind implies diligence and cheerfulness. I read this command between the lines everywhere in the Law. The phrasing of this command borrows from *Proverbs*, where hard work, prudence, diligence, and cheerfulness are constant themes. The principles of *Proverbs* run throughout the Bible from beginning to end. They thus weave through all the command groupings.

Working hard in the ancient world went without saying. Life was hard for everyone. If you wanted to eat, you worked hard.

Cheerfulness is the rub. It's especially the rub today when life *isn't* so hard for the majority of people in the civilized world. They *think* it's hard and constantly complain, but life today *isn't* hard by the standards of the past.

People just don't like to work. Leisure has become one of the gods of our time. If they *do* have to work, they will expend as little energy as possible, stopping at quitting time on the dot, then grousing about their bosses all the way to the bank to cash their paychecks. In modern western culture, most people define their lives by leisure activities, weekends, hobbies, sports, clubs, groups, church, and vacations. The "job" is seen as a necessary evil rather than as the defining focus of life.

How different is this from the biblical standard!

Caleb is the Old Testament example of what it means to work hard and with zeal. With Joshua he was one of the two faithful spies who was enthusiastic to go in and take the land of Canaan. Years later, as an old man, he was still at Joshua's side, eager and full of vim and vigor to work hard. After conquering Canaan, he asked to be given a whole mountain, and was ready to tame it.

Retirement…leisure…two weeks on a beach…don't bring such things up to Caleb! He had no thought of taking it easy now that the hard work of conquest was done. *Retirement…*forget it!

"The Lord has kept me alive…these forty-five years," he proclaimed after they had subdued much of the land, "since the time the Lord spoke this word to Moses, while Israel walked in the wilderness; and now, lo, I am this day eighty-five years old. I am still as strong to this day as I was in the day that Moses sent me; my strength now is as my strength was then, for war, and for coming and going. So now give me the hill country of which the Lord spoke on that day." (Joshua 14:10-12)

Little wonder that God said of Caleb, "my servant Caleb…has a different spirit." (Numbers 14:24)

It is this *different spirit* that represents the essence of this command. We are to bring the spirit of Caleb into everything we undertake. Slothfulness, angling to get away with as little as possible, checking the clock for the next break or for quitting time—these are unknown to men and women whose work ethic is modeled after Caleb. They do *more* than expected, not try to get away with *less*.

The totality of this command, carrying through all the way into New Testament times, is so encompassing that even slaves are commanded to give their *best* to their masters.

What few recognize today is that according to Scripture, work *itself* is a virtue.

Hard work builds not just physical and mental strength, but spiritual and *character strength*. Work stands alongside kindness and goodness and forgiveness as among the many complex traits that contribute to the whole man in building righteousness. Work alone cannot accomplish that eternal objective, but it plays a vital role along with other virtues in maturing us toward it.

Work—not leisure and vacations, not sports and entertainment, not travel and retirement—is the grounding foundation of the community of life God established among his people.

God may not be raising an army to conquer a country as was the case with Joshua and Caleb. But he is still engaged in enlisting enthusiastic and zealous men and women to demonstrate and live a *different spirit* in the work he gives them to do. Caleb's zeal and energy was noticed by God, by Moses, and by Joshua…and it reaped its reward. Hard work and cheerful zeal pays itself back many times over.

The most lasting reward is within our own characters.

Reinvigorate my enthusiasm and zeal, Lord, for the work you have given me to do. Give me a Caleb spirit, ready to claim a new mountain at eighty-five, ready to subdue new frontiers. Give me good cheer in my work. Energize my vision. If you have something new to which you would have me devote my time and energy, show me that new mountain.

46. Respect the Property of Others

If a man steals an ox or a sheep…He shall make restitution…When a man causes a field or vineyard to be grazed over, or lets his beast loose and it feeds in another man's field, he shall make restitution…When fire breaks out and catches in thorns so that the stacked grain or the standing grain or the field is consumed, he that kindled the fire shall make full restitution…For every breach of trust…or for any kind of lost thing…he whom God shall condemn shall pay double to his neighbor…If a man borrows anything of his neighbor… he shall make full restitution. (Exodus 22:1, 5-6, 9, 14)

Some of the specifics contained in the Law are so detailed they are almost impossible to untangle. I find myself reading for the sheer interest of it. The fascinating specifics reveal God's care for his people, even if those details have little connection to life today.

I must confess that the endless details about preparing different offerings, and what priests should wear, can put me to sleep. But the relational and practical life instructions shout caring Fatherhood in every line, and are endlessly compelling.

God *loves* his people! Subject to their obedience, he will spare no effort to ensure that their lives are good. When Moses speaks of the blessings that come from following God's precepts, those blessings emerge directly out of the heart of his divine Fatherhood. Therefore it is incumbent upon every serious reader of Scripture to climb high in their reading, to discover the overarching truths inherent in the biblical specifics.

In the case of this particular command, the higher meaning is not difficult to see. God values and respects property. Possessions are one aspect of his provision. Thus he occasionally "blesses" with an increase of possessions. In Moses' time, such was almost the sole indication of God's blessing. We read of the number of cattle and sheep and goats a man owned as indications, not only of wealth and prosperity, but also blessing.

We mustn't make *too* much of possession. *Things* are temporal, we realize that. Possession represents a *passing* form of blessing, to be sure. By the time of Jesus this reality had supplanted goats and cattle in the eternal calculus of blessing: Go and sell all you have…and *then* you will be blessed and have riches in heaven."

Though possession is no longer an indicator of God's blessing, we must yet look higher into the reality that possessions *are* intrinsic to our lives just as they were for the ancient Israelites. Most of us do not measure wealth by the size of our flocks. But there are principles here that apply equally to bank accounts as to oxen and sheep.

It may not be true that God honors and values possession as *eternally* important. But he honors and values possession insofar as possessions are included in the commerce and relational milieu of our temporal lives. We work hard, we build homes and raise families and participate in communities. Possessions, properly understood as passing, are yet intrinsic to that flowing and growing life-experience. *Worshiping* wealth and possessions is lethal. *Using* and *enjoying* and *sharing* the possessions that are the fruit of hard work is bound up in the way God provides for and blesses the fruits of our labor.

In God's economy, therefore, respect for the *property* of others is intrinsic to *love* for our neighbor. Possessions are to be respected as extensions of individuality. Respect of a man or woman draws up into it respect for his family, his home, his work, and his possessions. Respect for the property of others proceeds out of two of the Ten Commandments, the prohibitions against stealing and covetousness.

I love the following passage as revealing this great truth, even in the care God takes to cover every possibility. He wants to leave no doubt how his people are to respect the property of their neighbors. There are many such Fatherhood-care passages in these early books of the Bible. They make fascinating reading, not because of the *specifics*, but because of the love, care, consideration, and respect for others that are woven through them.

> *"If a man delivers to his neighbor money or goods to keep, and it is stolen out of the man's house, then, if the thief is found, he shall pay double. If the thief is not found, the owner of the house shall come near to God, to show whether or not he has put his hand to his neighbor's goods.*
>
> *"For every breach of trust, whether it is for ox, for ass, for sheep, for clothing, or for any kind of lost thing...both parties shall come before God; he whom God shall condemn shall pay double to his neighbor.*
>
> *"If a man delivers to his neighbor an ass or an ox or a sheep or any beast to keep, and it dies or is hurt or is driven away, without any one seeing it, an oath by the Lord shall be between them both to see whether he has not put his hand to his neighbor's property; and the owner shall accept the oath, and he shall not make restitution. But if it is stolen from him, he shall make restitution to its owner. If it is torn by beasts, let him bring it as evidence; he shall not make restitution for what has been torn.*
>
> *"If a man borrows anything of his neighbor, and it is hurt or dies, the owner not being with it, he shall make full restitution.* (Exodus 22:7-14)

It's not only the possessions of others that God cares about. Our own possessions—in balance, understood as temporal, as blessings to be *used* not worshipped—are important. The emphasis now shifts to *stewardship*.

As we shall see in Command #50, at a fundamental level, all property is God's. Yet as God's people, we are given stewardship over possessions. Some have more earthly goods, some have less. *Desiring* to have more, and working hard merely to amass *more*, obviously misses God's intent to use possessions to build both character and selflessness.

When God provides and blesses the fruit of hard work and obedience, however, stewardship and respect for those around us flow in as regulating standards by which we use, care for, and minister to others with the blessings he has given.

Possessions represent one more aspect of that truth that we are to leave our fields of blessing open, building no fences around them to preserve and protect our wealth, but using the abundance of the harvest God has given to help and minister and provide for those whose fields have not yielded so much, or perhaps who have no fields at all.

I don't happen to own an ox, nor do any of my neighbors or friends. But I have lent, borrowed, and given away tools, cars, lumber, books, and that most precious of all commodities, time. What if I borrow a book or a tool and somehow damage it…suddenly there is *Leviticus* staring me in the face with its restitution instructions. The ox has become a book or tool, and the command is upon me.

God, I thank you for your provision, for the possessions you have provided which I enjoy. May I always see them as yours not mine, passing through my hands but for a time as they will one day pass into the hands of others. Give me equal respect for the property and possessions of others, recognizing your work in their lives just as I recognize it in my own. Give me wisdom to wisely steward your provision, and to wisely respect the provision, property, and blessing you have given to others.

47. Make Restitution for Wrong

When a man or woman commits any of the sins that men commit by breaking faith with the Lord…he shall confess his sin…and he shall make full restitution for his wrong, adding a fifth to it. (Numbers 5:6-7)

Emerging directly out of the previous command, when property is *not* shown respect—whether field, ox, wife, slave, home…or book or car or tool—or when a crime against property, or even simple carelessness, has occurred, restitution is required.

Both commands summarize in a general way the many detailed applications instituted by God in the Law for injuries, wrongs, transgressions, and carelessnesses such as are listed throughout *Exodus, Leviticus,* and *Numbers.*

God is a God of fairness and justice. Though some of the examples are repeated from the previous command (though here with the emphasis on restitution), the detail, even the repetition, shows how thoroughly God was trying to drive home to the people that fairness, justice, and respect for others was to imbue *all* facets of human relationship.

"When one man's ox hurts another's, so that it dies, then they shall sell the live ox and divide the price of it; and the dead beast also they shall divide. Or if it is known that the ox has been accustomed to gore in the past, and its owner has not kept it in, he shall pay ox for ox, and the dead beast shall be his. (Exodus 21:35-36)

"If a man steals an ox or a sheep, and kills it or sells it, he shall pay five oxen for an ox, and four sheep for a sheep. He shall make restitution; if he has nothing, then he shall be sold for his theft...If the stolen beast is found alive in his possession, whether it is an ox or an ass or a sheep, he shall pay double...When a man causes a field or vineyard to be grazed over, or lets his beast loose and it feeds in another man's field, he shall make restitution from the best in his own field and in his own vineyard. When fire breaks out and catches in thorns so that the stacked grain or the standing grain or the field is consumed, he that kindled the fire shall make full restitution. (Exodus 22:1, 4-5)

The principle of "an eye for an eye, a tooth for a tooth" (Exodus 21:24) is often cited as confirming the theology of God's vengeance. However, this entirely misses the point. It is not *revenge* God demands, but fairness.

In ancient times, over three thousand years ago, dealing with primitive people, God had to convey and example justice in what were occasionally raw and primitive ways. We cannot misjudge God's intrinsic character on the basis of measures he was forced to implement because the Israelites were at a basic and incomplete level of understanding.

We are supposed to read the Old Testament intelligently, raising these prehistoric precepts up into higher regions which enable us to see their eternal meaning and purposes. If I borrow a book from you and lose it, then I buy you a new book to replace it, it's a pretty simple application. In my case, "an eye for an eye" becomes "a book for a book."

The Old Testament isn't as much rocket science as we think. Once we train our spiritual eyes to see the divine Fatherhood in its precepts, most of its conundrums fall into place. Mysteries remain, of course. But when the high themes emerge, much takes on new clarity.

There is accountability for wrongdoing. That accountability proceeds out of God's heart of justice, not revenge. It is how fathers teach their children accountability. It is how our heavenly Father teaches his children that love is responsible, accountable, kind, and just to our brethren.

Thank you, God, for being such a good and loving Father that you insist on us being good and loving to our brothers and sisters of humanity. Deepen my sense of accountability for every facet of my life. Give me wisdom to live that accountability in all ways, in my use of time, in my work habits, and most of all in every aspect of my relationships with others.

48. Bear No Grudge, Seek No Revenge

You shall not take vengeance or bear any grudge. (Leviticus 19:18)

Here we encounter another command with a very New Testament sound. This command alone should give the lie to the notion of a vengeful and unforgiving almighty Sinai tyrant of a god. God would hardly give a command that contradicts his very nature.

> *You shall not take vengeance or bear any grudge against…your own people, but you shall love your neighbor as yourself: I am the* L*ORD.* (Leviticus 19:18)

God could say it no more clearly: "Because *I* bear no grudge, because *I* seek no revenge for wrongs done me, because *I* forgive…therefore I want *you* to reflect my Fatherhood nature by bearing no grudge, seeking no revenge, and forgiving wrong done to you."

But faithless and unbelieving multitudes throughout history have ignored both the man-directed component of this command, as well as its high God-revealing truth. Hidden between the lines here, as in all the commands, we again discover compassionate Fatherhood!

Holy Spirit, give us eyes to perceive Fatherhood in the Old Testament!

This is an exceedingly important and significant command on many levels—between man and man…between woman and woman…between man and woman…between child and parent…between wife and husband…between business associates… between employers and employees…toward those who have wronged us…toward those who have taken advantage of us…toward those who mistreat us…

You shall bear no grudge!

> *You shall not…deal falsely, nor lie to one another…You shall not oppress your neighbor…You shall do no injustice in judgment…You shall not go…as a slanderer among your people…You shall not hate your brother in your heart…You shall not take vengeance or bear any grudge…but you shall love your neighbor as yourself: I am the Lord.* (Leviticus 19:11, 13, 15-17)

How much within the complex dynamics of human relationship is laced with unseen gripes, grievances, unspoken angers, annoyances, irritations, and unforgivenesses. It's endemic to the human constitution. These sins of attitude lie hidden in us all…sometimes *deep* within us.

The moment I wrote the above words, my mind flitted to what I can only call a grudge against a worker who overcharged us for his work three weeks ago. I have been nursing a profound annoyance ever since.

What am I going to do? I am condemned by my own words I *have* to let it go. But it's not easy. *It's so unfair…it's not right!* shouts my Old Adam.

Lay it down, quietly replies the New Man. It's a trifle, less than a week's gas or groceries. A petty grievance is not worth disobeying one of God's preeminent commands. The loss of money will be forgotten. But if I allow it to grow its mold in the inner corners of my spiritual house, the black stain of offense will remain on my character.

Keep your camp pure. Do not let mold and mildew grow.

But I *want* to listen to my Old Adam! I am justified in listening. It's a daily battle to keep that satan silenced.

As glaringly as this command exposes my soul, the most significant truth here is what this command tells us about God himself. God's vengeance and wrath against sin, the image of an Almighty tyrant intent on punishing in eternity every sinner who does not repent, stands as *the* most grievous historic stumbling block preventing the human species knowing its Creator…preventing God's men and women—his children!—from knowing their Father.

The doctrine of eternal vengeance is a profound falsehood sitting squarely at the heart of much Christian theology. What will those theologians have to answer for who have perpetrated this falsehood through the millennia?

This falsehood is swept away by the unequivocal implications of Leviticus 19:18.

You shall not take vengeance…but you shall love. I am the Lord.

God will have *justice*. But justice informed by love not vengeance. *

God, forgive me for believing the falsehood that you are a tyrant of eternal vengeance. Forgive me too for nursing a grudge against the young painter who charged us more than I thought he should. By forgiving him, I step into the higher forgiveness that is intrinsic to the divine Fatherhood of your character. Bring him back into our lives that I may live out my forgiveness practically. You command me to forgive because you forgive. Purge me from annoyance, grievance, anger, and unforgiveness wherever they lurk within me. Create in me a pure heart—pure and forgiving, as you are pure and forgiving.

49. Lend Without Interest

If your brother becomes poor…take no interest from him or increase…
You shall not lend him your money at interest. (Leviticus 25:35-36)

What a positively fascinating command for our time. Two obvious responses spring immediately to mind.

One, *how impractical!* It just shows, shouts the objection, that you can't take the Bible literally. This was clearly written for another era, for people less sophisticated than we of today who didn't understand modern economics and trade and commerce. No one could live by such an idea!

The second truth we find here is a sobering one—the entire world, rich nations and poor, governments and private business, communism and

* It is interesting that the "vengeance is mine" passage, noting that we should leave vengeance to "the wrath of God," is from Paul not *Leviticus*. (Romans 12:19) Much of the theology of God's vengeance and eternal punishment of sinners originates in apostolic Christianity not the Old Testament Law. This is but one of many misperceptions about God that is traditionally blamed on the Old Testament Law but that actually stems more from Christian teachers and theologians twisting both the Old Testament and Jesus' teachings to validate their Augustinian and Calvinist Jesus-saves-from-the-wrath-of-a-vengeful-God doctrines.

capitalism, millionaires and those on welfare…*everything* in the world economy is based on a blatantly *unscriptural* principle. The whole globe operates in direct *disobedience* to this clear command of God.

We can react in many ways to this fact. Times *have* changed. It *was* different back then. Altogether distinct economics regulated nomadic and rural societies in different ways. Banks and investments didn't exist. Our global system couldn't function without interest. We can parse the command by saying that God was only prohibiting charging interest to the poor.

All well and good. Another dozen reasons could be added to these. I'm not advocating abolishing world trade and banks and commerce. And it is true that the specific wording references the poor.

I simply present this as a command given by God. I don't know how it applies to investments and modern banking and the not-poor. What do we do with it? Do we ignore it because the rest of the world ignores it? Can we blithely conclude that this prohibition against interest (specific though it is) was written for a people in the middle of the desert after the exodus, therefore we are justified in ignoring it?

We have to dig really deep here to see the eye-opening truth that everyone who borrows money, in a sense, is "poor" in comparison to he from whom he needs to borrow. Without quibbling over the investment strategy of leverage, the fact is that those who have *enough* rarely need to borrow. So how broad do we make our interpretation of "poor?" In the end, everyone will find their own level of response to this most intriguing command.

I am not quick to excuse laziness or half-hearted obedience. I'm not in the habit of explaining away the forcefulness of the commands, though I am on a continual quest for deeper meanings that probe the heart and purposes of God. We are *commanded* to obey. Yet I readily admit that the *how* of obedience is not always readily apparent.

This command presents unique difficulties. It *might* be possible to disengage from the world so completely that you had no connection to its reliance on interest whatever—no mortgage, no credit cards, nothing financed, no bank account, no checking…nothing whatever connected to the world's monetary system.

To embark on such a lifestyle, one would probably have to be rich before trying it. In all likelihood one's wealth would have come from the world's interest-based financial systems. So it's a Catch-22—obedience flowing out of prior disobedience.

The fact is, however, for most people today it would be impossible to disengage from the world's finances. Not because of disobedience, but simply *impossible*.

Looking at the command more personally, the command isn't directed at governments or businesses or banks…but to individuals. It does not command, *Abolish interest,* or, *Live without paying interest,* or, *Live debt free so you are not paying interest.* The command is: *Lend to the poor without interest.* Whether or not a world financial agenda is implied, I don't know.

Therefore, I don't read this command economically or globally. I read it to *me.* Most of the borrowing and lending in our lives has been on the borrowing side of the ledger. Debt has been constant all our married lives. We ran a business for thirty-five years that was entirely founded on the system of debt and interest. We have bought and sold several houses, financed a half dozen or more cars. We have bank accounts and credit cards. Debt remains a very real and sometimes very pressing and stressful reality in our lives.

We have *paid* probably more than a hundred thousand dollars in interest, for all I know, maybe much more. But the command is about *lending* not *paying.* Therefore, in the times in which we have had occasion, and have been in a position, to loan others money, we have charged no interest. I don't know that any of those individuals or families were "poor." But they had a need and we took the command against interest as comprehensive not partial.

This is a command where we recognize that we cannot change the world. Obedience can only be personal. The world economy is not my responsibility. My own finances, relationships, stewardship, and obedience are.

God, give me wisdom in my application of this complex command.

50. Exercise Wise Stewardship Over God's Provision

And God blessed them, and God said to them, "Be fruitful and multiply, and fill the earth and subdue it; and have dominion over the fish of the sea and over the birds of the air and over every living thing that moves upon the earth…I have given you every plant…and every tree…you shall have them for food…And God saw everything that he had made, and behold, it was very good. (Genesis 1:28-29, 31)

You shall not thus pollute the land in which you live. (Numbers 35:33)

When you come into the land which I give you, the land shall keep a sabbath to the Lord. Six years you shall sow your field, and six years you shall prune your vineyard, and gather in its fruits; but in the seventh year there shall be a sabbath of solemn rest for the land…
And you shall count seven weeks of years, seven times seven years,
so that the time of the seven weeks of years shall be to you forty-nine years…
And you shall hallow the fiftieth year…in it you shall neither sow, nor reap what grows of itself, nor gather the grapes from the undressed vines. (Leviticus 25:2-4, 8, 11)

Be diligent to know the state of your flocks, and give attention to your herds. (Proverbs 27:23, KJV, RSV)

When I initially began praying about the final command of this series, the focus of my thought was directed toward the Sabbath years of Leviticus 25. During these Sabbath years God commanded that the land be given a year's "day of rest" and lie fallow. These culminated every fifty years with a "jubilee" of "seven Sabbaths of years." During these jubilee years a wide range of provisions were outlined which had the effect of a gigantic "restart" to society. Slaves were set free, land returned to prior owners, certain debts were cancelled, and families were to return to their familial properties.

These Sabbath and jubilee instructions are surely among the most intriguing aspects of the Levitical Law. I was particularly intrigued by God's care for fairness and justice. After setting up the principle of land Sabbaths, the remainder of Leviticus 25 details an enormous range of specific instructions for their implementation—what can and cannot be eaten that the fallow land produces of itself, how provision is made for sustaining the people during and following Sabbath years, how slaves are freed and property returned, how the whole system of ownership and debt is adjusted depending how long land or a slave has been owned (verses 15-16, for example), how the poor are provided for, how property is redeemed, differences in the jubilee provisions for city dwellers and those living on the land.

It makes positively fascinating reading!

Trying to imagine application to modern society, however, is impossible. The world would fall apart if people took this seriously! Imagine how people would take advantage! Mortgages cancelled…property returned to previous owners…the end result would result in some form of communist chaos.

It's obviously unrealistic and impossible to read these passages through a global third millennium economic lens.

Yet my fascination with Leviticus 25 persisted. I continued to ask God, "How does this apply to us *today*?"

Slowly a great truth dawned. As much as any command of those I was considering, I realized a higher principle at work here. The specifics of Leviticus 25 pointed to the high truth of stewardship over *all* God's provision. The land itself was the particular focus. But "land," and all the specifics associated with land use, symbolically point to that higher truth: *Stewardship over God's provision.*

Indeed, the whole earth and everything in it is God's provision. This command is rooted in Genesis 1-2!

From being an ancient anachronistic series of unworkable ideas, suddenly Leviticus 25 explodes with contemporary relevance—taking good care of the earth…stewardship over the planet God designed for us…and everything in it, especially human life.

It's not as simple as saying, "Oil and coal are bad, we must ban them." Or, "Dams kill fish and spoil natural habitats, we must ban them." Maybe we should, maybe we shouldn't. But biblical stewardship can be the basis for neither right nor left wing political agendas. Stewardship also involves *using* God's provision. Arguments can be made on both sides of most political questions. If God has invested the earth with oil, the argument can be made that *using* it does not violate stewardship over the earth. I would not turn this into a political treatise by advocating either use or prohibition. I would only emphasize the point that biblical stewardship is rooted in *wise use*. In our time most of the questions involved are more complex and multi-dimensional than such obvious violations of stewardship as killing buffalo for sport, dumping toxic poisons into water supplies, aborting unwanted babies, or threatening the planet's oxygen supply by destroying forests.

Stewardship extends much further than the earth and human life, to stewardship over money, time, ownership, the possessions God gives me, family ties and legacies, relationships, even slaves. If we can escape legalistic specificity, Leviticus 25 may also contain application in business and employer-employee relations.

The same principles are at work through the entire Law—food and eating regulations (stewardship over physical health), the handling of disputes (stewardship over relationships), family regulations (stewardship over family legacies)...legal stewardship... national and governmental stewardship...stewardship over animals and buildings...and on it goes.

The entire Law is suffused from beginning to end with this theme—taking care of God's provision, undergirded by the principle of compassion and kindness:

> *"You shall not wrong one another...you shall do my statutes, and keep my ordinances and perform them; so you will dwell in the land securely. The land will yield its fruit, and you will eat your fill, and dwell in it securely."*
> —Leviticus 25:17-19

There are of course many reasons for stewardship. The most foundational reason of all is that everything is God's. We don't *really* own anything. Everything we have in life, everything that passes through our hands, is on loan. We take good care of his things so that when our time comes, we may pass them on to whomever he will loan them to next.

> *"The land shall not be sold in perpetuity, for the land is mine; for you are strangers and sojourners with me."*
> —Leviticus 25:23

What a privilege it is, God, to participate with you in stewardship over the earth and in the earth, and over all forms of human life. Give me wisdom to see this principle in all my affairs and relationships. Show me where even the Sabbath rest and jubilee traditions of Leviticus may contain truth you want me to implement. Above all, give me a shepherding and stewarding heart over all the provisions with which you have blessed me.

Series Six

Separation

Be Very Careful

The danger of being lured by the world away from God

A protégé who carried forward his mentor's vision

In a strict Old Testament chronology, we would probably look at the book of *Deuteronomy* here as the bridge between the Levitical Law and Joshua and the conquest of Canaan. Having already considered its Choice and Consequence Code in some detail as, with *Proverbs*, foundational to the entire Old Testament, we need only remind ourselves that the very essence of that Mosaic life-code leads inexorably to the imperative of world-separation. Separation from the world *is* the Choice and Consequence Code.

Probably no other spiritual words are so familiar and have been so oft-quoted throughout the history of western civilization as, "You shall love the Lord your God with all your heart, and with all your soul, and with all your strength." What the Jews call the *Shema Yisrael* appears in Deuteronomy 6:5 in the midst of one of the most powerful and important passages in the Bible.

In many ways, this passage sets forth the anchoring principles, not only of the book of *Deuteronomy*, but also of the entire Old Testament:

> *These are the commands, decrees and laws which the Lord your God directed me to teach you to observe in the land that you are to possess, so that you, your children and their children after them may fear the Lord your God as long as you live by keeping all his decrees and commands and so that you may enjoy long life. Hear, Israel, and be careful to obey so that it may go well with you and that you may increase greatly in a land flowing with milk and honey.*
>
> *Hear, O Israel: The Lord our God, the Lord is one. Love the Lord your God with all your heart and with all your soul and with all your strength.*
>
> (Deuteronomy 6: 1-5, author's paraphrase)

Where in this passage, it might be asked, is "separation from the world?"

Like so many of Scripture's deepest truths, we have to look for it between the lines. Love for God does not exist in a vacuum. It comes with strings attached. Moses is commanding an entire life orientation of practice and belief that is drawn up into what "loving God" means. The words, *with all your heart, and with all your soul, and with all your strength,* are intrinsic to that life perspective—that compass orientation.

He does not say to love God with *some* of your heart, and with a *portion* of your soul, and with a *little* of your strength. In *Deuteronomy* as well as in John 12:32, all means *all*.

Embedded within the *Shema* of verse 5, therefore, is a hidden imperative that is too easily glossed over—the world, the perspective of man, the entire kingdom in which Satan rules, does *not* love God...indeed hates the ways of God. To *love* God with the "all" of the Shema requires *detachment* from everything the world represents.

Thus Moses commanded the Israelites:

- Love God.
- Come out of the world.

The two commands are bound together in the same way that the first and second commandments spoken of by Jesus are bound together.

Separation from the world is not only intrinsic to the greatest commandment of Mark 12:29-30, it is intrinsic to the entire Old Testament message. When Joshua took over the reins of Israel's leadership after the death of Moses, in a sense his clarion call was straightforward:

- We are Israel.
- The nations of Canaan represent the world.
- The two can have *nothing* to do with each other.
- Ever.

Modern Christianity has almost entirely lost the imperative of the *absolute, lifelong, strings-attached, world-separation obedience* meant by "love God." Christendom has reinterpreted Deuteronomy 6:5 with its more comfortable theology of loving God with *some* of your heart, a *portion* of your soul, and a *little* of your strength.

People are taught that to "become a Christian" is as easy as deciding what to have for dinner. Acknowledge a few fundamental beliefs, pray a simple prayer, join a church, come to a Bible study, and hey, you're *in*! So-called "Christians" float in and out of activities, changing churches and groups with the same fleeting commitment with which modern society views marriage. Separation from the world…how often is that unpleasant and old-fashioned message preached from Christendom's pulpits?

Imagine the difference in times past of what it meant to "become" a Jew, to convert body, heart, and soul to Judaism. It was not something you could do halfway. *Everything* would henceforth and forever be altered. You would be leaving behind everything in your past—family, friends, culture, dress, eating habits…literally everything.

World separation *en toto.*

How many grown men would "become Christians" today if one of the first requirements was being publicly circumcised, then changing all your lifelong habits, from the foods you ate to how you dressed, subjecting yourself to criticism and rebuke and possibly persecution from everyone associated with your past life?

It's a very different thing than the lackadaisical dedication exhibited by modern Christendom. The totality of commitment required by Islam more resembles the pattern of Deuteronomy 6 than either today's Judaism or Christianity. Converts to Islam, deceived as they may be, go in for the whole world-separation treatment. It is true that many historic sects within Judaism have "separated from the world" in certain outwardly visible ways as well. But most of this has been informed by legalisms, not because love for God and obedience to the Shema penetrated so deeply into the hearts of those in such communities that the power of transformed Godly lives was visible for all to see. It is possible to separate from the world legalistically, yet still without *all* really meaning ALL.

This command from Moses to *Love God* by separating from the world is total. Love for God means more than singing worship songs or praying with your hands in the air or feeling God's presence. It means a lifelong, heart, soul, mind, and strength commitment to view *everything* through the lens of world separation.

Series Six

Separation

51. Be strong and courageous not to walk in the world's ways.

52. Watch yourself closely so the world does not ensnare you.

53. Do not yield to the world's enticements.

54. Do not associate with worldly people.

55. Make no friends of fools.

56. Do not bring sin into your home.

57. Do not covet or imitate what the world's people have or do.

58. Women do not wear men's clothing, men do not wear women's clothing.

59. Do not be lured into worshiping false gods.

60. Do not follow others into sin.

51. Be Strong and Courageous Not to Walk in the World's Ways

[9]When you enter the land the LORD your God is giving you,
do not…imitate the detestable ways of the nations…
You must be blameless before the LORD your God. (Deuteronomy 18:9, 13, NIV)
Be strong and very courageous, being careful to do according to all the law
which Moses…commanded you;
turn not from it to the right hand or to the left. (Joshua 1:7)

The most deadening spiritual narcotic flowing through the veins of Jesus Christ's church is the lethal assumption that separation from the world doesn't matter. This anesthetizing influence was introduced into the church even while the Apostles were still alive. New daily doses are being peddled every Sunday by the spiritual drug dealers occupying 90% of the pulpits of the world.

It's the drug called *Christianity without sacrifice.* Discipleship without relinquishment. Christianity-and-water as C.S. Lewis so memorably put it. Love of God in a vacuum with no mention of world separation.

Christendom's great lie is simple to state. The lie has two parts:

- Christianity and the world can coexist and live cozily together.
- Christianity can adopt the world's values, methods, perspectives, and habits and still "love God," still pretend to be living the Gospel of Jesus Christ.

This twofold lie at the heart of Christendom is as appealing and mesmerizing as Islam's lie of virgins awaiting jihad martyrs.

The implications of Christendom's acceptance of the lie are far-reaching and deadening to any hope of impacting the world in the way Jesus said his followers are meant to. They may influence the world in other ways. But living by the lie of coexistence and intermingled methods and perspectives renders it impossible to live the Bible's commands and influence the world *in the way Jesus commanded.* That influence can only come by refusing to walk in the world's ways.

I use the word *impossible* intentionally. The two worldviews cannot coexist. When Christians are told otherwise by *tolerance-of-the-world* pastors and priests, they are being fed nothing short of a lie.

This lie has been so thoroughly infused into the worldly Christianity of our time that the command of separation is one of the easiest of biblical commands to ignore, overlook, slough off as meant for another time. It is automatically assumed by the great majority of Christendom that the many commands of separation concerned only the ancient Israelites not mixing and intermarrying with the pagan nations around them.

We live in an enlightened modern era. *What could the conquest of Canaan have to do with us?*

Fast forward a thousand years, the same excuses are used to ignore Paul's words to the Romans, "Do not be conformed to the world." Again they say, *What could Paul's world-phobic words of Romans 1 have to do with us?*

It is not the world's *externals* that are at stake. Many false "separations" of externality have been tried and made into legalistic idols. The Amish do not drive cars or use electricity. They talk and dress and shave differently, wear distinctive hats and bonnets, and band together in exclusive communities. All these, and many other superficial separations have failed to impact the world as Jesus said his followers were to impact the world. Some of these may have spiritual value on their own (as I think they do). I admire the courage even external separations require. But they are not enough.

Refusing to walk in the world's ways bites deeper into personhood. It is the world's methods, outlooks, priorities, perspectives, its *way of seeing* that lies at the heart of separation. Jesus calls his followers to *see* things as he sees them not as the world tells us we should see them, then to *live* his commands on the basis of that alternate eternal eyesight. Doing so requires taking Jesus as our example while rejecting the example of the world. Romans 1 and 12:2 and 2 Corinthians 6:17 are about *how we see and interpret the world and our role in it*...not legalisms.

Would Jesus bring in a light show and rock band to the sermon on the mount in order to appeal to young people? If he were alive today, would he appoint a gay and lesbian among the disciples for the sake of diversity, or attend the wedding of Cana if it were a same-sex wedding? Would he approve of abortion because women have the *right* to do whatever they want with their bodies?

Posing such questions is disgusting. Yet the church's tolerance of a thousand acceptable norms of our post-Christian culture is such an affront to God that it is almost surprising he has not employed the James and John strategy of raining down fire from heaven to wipe out the modern church altogether so that a new true church might start afresh.

But we're not talking about mega-churches, light shows, rock bands, or progressivist-tolerant Christendom. We're talking about you and me. The command isn't to Christendom...it's to us. It's to *me*.

Where do *I* also thoughtlessly fall into lock-step and walk in the world's ways? That's a more sobering question than denigrating the cancer of progressivity that has put the church to sleep.

When Paul paraphrased God's command to ancient Israel as, "Come out from among them and be ye separate," * it wasn't a call to dress differently, but to *think* differently, to see right and wrong and truth and obedience through *God's* eyes. And then, seeing as God sees, to walk a different life path.

Everyone is so fearful of the Cultural Thought Police today that they are terrified of being seen as "exclusive." That's why this command is

* 2 Corinthians 6:17

linked with the oft-repeated words of Moses and Joshua—Be strong and courageous. It takes *courage* not to walk and think in the way the world says you must.

Rightly understood as an internal exclusivity of outlook, not an external exclusivity of judgment—*exclusive* is exactly and precisely what God commands us to be. *Make no covenant with the world and its ways...do not be conformed to this world...come out from among them and be ye separate.*

We are called to *internal* exclusivity.

We are called to be distinctively motivated, separate-seeing, conspicuously detached yet engaged and loving courageous people who walk in the world but not of the world. The footsteps of our life orientation are established and ordered by the commands of Jesus, the prophets, and the apostles. *

George MacDonald wrote:

> "By *the world* I mean all ways of judging, regarding, and thinking, whether political, economical, ecclesiastical, social, or individual, which are not divine, which are not God's ways of thinking and regarding. I mean all ways of thinking which do not take God into account, and do not set his will supreme as the one only law of life. I mean all ways of thinking which do not care for the truth of things, but exalt the customs of society and its practices, which heed not what is right." †

Lord God, give me eyes to see as you see—eternal eyesight to perceive the imperative yet often invisible dividing line between in and of—between seeing through your eyes and seeing through the world's eyes. I am in the world, help me not be of it. Make the world's values so distasteful to me that the world exerts no allure upon my soul.

52. Watch Yourself Closely So the World Does Not Ensnare You

Take heed to yourself, lest you make a covenant with the inhabitants of the land...
lest it become a snare in the midst of you. (Exodus 34:12)
Be careful not to be ensnared by inquiring about their gods, saying..."We will do the same."
You must not worship the Lord your God in their way. (Deuteronomy 12:30-31)

Again we encounter one of Moses' *Be careful* commands, repeated so often by Jesus among his *Alert and watchfulness* commands. This command is not merely to watch and remember *God's* commands, but watchfulness against the *world's* dangerous and cunning methods and snares.

Two pivotal words here personalize the command to world-watchfulness with chilling foreboding.

Yourself...ensnare.

---

* In my book *Endangered Virtues,* I explain this balance with particular reference to the cultural changes inundating Christians in a section entitled, "Disengaged Engagement."

† George MacDonald, *Unspoken Sermons, Second Series,* "Self-Denial."

As the saying goes, this really is *all about you.* This is a very personal warning. The world is out to get *you.* There is a bull's eye on *your* forehead, and Satan has loaded the gun.

The principle is ancient beyond reckoning. God said to Cain, "Sin is crouching at your door. It desires to have you." (Genesis 4:7)

It wasn't a general warning. It was to Cain. Neither is today's command general—it is to *you.* It is to *me.*

This ought to scare the socks off us! We are all Cain. Satan *wants* us!

Satan rarely uses frontal assaults. His methods are sly, subtle, invisible, crafty. They are usually disguised as good. His method is to ensnare by cunning. He sets his snares with temptations tailor made for each of us. He doesn't tempt me to rob or kill, but with far more subtly disguised bait.

It's all about me too. Satan wants *me.*

When I had been writing for some time, after we had started a family, Judy and I were made forcefully aware that our family was an object of attack. We knew we were in the crosshairs. That was fifty years ago. Anyone who speaks out for God now, in *today's* cultural climate, who speaks on behalf of scriptural truth and obedience to the commands, and who speaks against the lies of the age, will be in the crosshairs more than ever.

The bull's eye is on our heads. Satan desires us. The world will use any means to lure God's people into its deviant and evil perspectives.

Not only is the principle ancient, it is as contemporary as the news. Only last week a public announcement was made by an overtly evil group whose agenda is a complete societal reversal of traditional and sexual morality and ethics. Its message to the world, which their spokesperson actually voiced proudly and militantly: "We are coming for your children!"

Nothing has changed since Cain's time. Sin desires to have us.

This blatant frontal assault against Christianity may have some impact culturally. But Satan's subtle tactics to infiltrate the church and the hearts and minds of God's men and women use more devious snares. His objective is not just Christian children, it is hearts and minds and the totality of how Christians *think.*

Satan lays his snares with countless trojan-decoys that seem innocuous but that are filled with the world's outlook and perspectives. He seduces with our favorite foods that seem not only harmless but delicious. But they are laced with poison. That poison is the world's outlook.

They did not destroy the peoples, as the LORD commanded them,
but they mingled with the nations and learned to do as they did.
They served their idols, which became a snare to them.
They sacrificed their sons and their daughters to the demons;
they poured out innocent blood, the blood of their sons and daughters, whom they sacrificed to the idols of Canaan; and the land was polluted with blood.
Thus they became unclean by their acts, and played the harlot in their doings.
Then the anger of the LORD was kindled against his people, and he abhorred his heritage; he gave them into the hand of the nations. (Psalm 106:34-41)

In a thousand ways Satan lures God's people away from the Bible's commands. The commands always point toward the heart of God's intent. Any voice, from whatever quarter, saying that the commands don't matter, however disguised, is a voice originating in the pit of hell. Though the enticements are quiet and soothing, speaking goodness and peace, masquerading as light and truth, offering the very things we crave, Satan's ultimate desire is unchanged.

Sin desires to *have* you.

Judy and I wear battle scars from the past fifty years. We are in a war. The snares are everywhere. God's words to Cain serve not just as a warning, they also give us our daily marching orders:

"Sin is crouching at your door. It desires to have you…*but you must master it.*" (Genesis 4:7)

Obedience to the commands give us the practical tools to watch ourselves closely. The world cannot ensnare one who is walking in the commands.

Help me, Holy Spirit, to recognize Satan's snares before they trap me, to smell the poison even when it is dosed into my favorite food, to watch myself closely, to be wary of everything in the world—how the world thinks, what the world considers acceptable. Open my eyes to see worldliness literally in everything that surrounds me in the hedonistic culture of this age in which I live.

53. Do Not Yield to the World's Enticements

Watch yourselves very carefully, so that you do not become corrupt and make for yourself an idol…do not be enticed into bowing down to them. (Deuteronomy 4:15-16, 19, NIV)

World separation is so pivotal to the Old Testament story, and so deeply embedded in the commands of its prophetic writers, that this command and the previous, on the surface so similar, each bear consideration for the important nuances they illuminate.

First we are commanded to *watch ourselves closely.*

Now the command plunges to the heart of free will itself. When the enticements come…*do not yield!*

It seems that the world and its ways would not be attractive to God's people. And yet how enticing the world is!

This is a great mystery. From the moment of birth, sin exerts its allure. Children are drawn to what they cannot have and know they shouldn't do. They are attracted by the naughtiness of other children and compelled to imitate it. The sin nature of children is obvious and easy to see.

You and I are exactly the same. We never outgrow it.

I really hate it, but I see it in myself all the time. The enticements of the world exert their allure on us every second. It's in the air. We can't escape it. *Why* we are drawn to worldliness is the sixty-four-thousand-dollar question. But we can't deny that it's true.

God's command to Cain, "You must master it," is of course the proper and effective response to the world's enticements. It's as simple as the truism, *Just say no.*

Turn your back.

Walk away.

Don't yield.

Easily said. Not so easily done when those enticements are so cleverly aimed at our own weaknesses. They are intrinsic in Satan's master plan to *have* us. They are tailor made for each of us individually, the invisible traps cunningly set to attract and beguile *me* with my own personal Turkish Delight.

There is that deep within us all that *wants* to give in to those enticements, that wants to be part of what the world offers.

Evil fascinates. Sin draws and lures.

Not only are we Cain, we are all Edmund in *The Lion, the Witch, and the Wardrobe.* Turkish Delight comes in infinite individually beguiling colors and flavors. Eve's came in the form of a "pleasing fruit." Cain's came in angry jealousy of his brother. Saul's came with the allure of "all that was good" of the possessions of the Amalekites.

Satan entices individually. We yield to the world's enticements because we *want* to yield.

I'm always on the lookout for movies that depict personal growth and development. Intrigued by the connection between Julia Roberts and prayer, I recently began previewing *Eat, Pray, Love* on TV. I could not watch for long, but it exercised a profound effect on me. The Julia Roberts character is frustrated with her life, and is ensnared by the independent feminist deception of modernism. That was the bait of her personal Turkish Delight. Though she has a good and loving husband, she decides she doesn't want to be married any longer. She wants to be "free" to do her own thing. She was baited by the allure of progressivist feminism.

At her crisis moment of independence, in very unHollywood fashion, she gets down on her knees and prays a remarkable prayer. I watched positively riveted as a tearful and seemingly broken and sincere Julia Roberts uttered the words:

Hello God. I am sorry I've never spoken directly to you before. I hope I've expressed my ample gratitude for all the blessings you've given me in my life. I'm in serious trouble. I don't know what to do. I need you to answer. Please tell me what to do. Oh God, help me. Tell me what to do and I'll do it.

I was stunned. Telling Judy about it later, I said, "It was the *perfect* prayer. It could have come from a character in one of my books. I have had my characters pray almost those identical, powerful, life-changing, eternally significant words: *Please tell me what to do. Oh God, help me. Tell me what to do and I'll do it.*

At that crossroads moment, the Roberts character had a choice. She had come to that moment lured by the enticement of the world's pull. I realize that it was a movie. But it was based on a woman's life, and illustrates to perfection the crossroads everyone faces every day.

What would she do? The great world was calling, luring, beckoning her to do her own thing, to cast off restraints and expectations, to live a life of independence answerable to no one.

The eternal questions were: Was she *really* seeking to know what God wanted her to do? Did she intend to listen to him? Did she intend to *do* what he wanted her to do? Was the prayer real?

I sat spellbound. But not for long. The answer to those questions came soon enough and I had quickly had enough. For what happened next I depended on detailed reviews of the movie. The character proceeded to divorce her husband then embark on a world tour of hedonism, casting off restraint...India, Bali, Italy...sleeping with men...eating and loving...no responsibilities...even keeping up the façade of spirituality with a visit to a guru's ashram in India, all in a fruitless and self-centered quest for inner peace.

She does everything *except* seek to know what God wants people to do, how he wants us to live. The prayer seemed so emotional, heartfelt, and sincere. Yet it was soon revealed for what it was—a prayer laced with underlying hypocrisy.

The prayer itself was a lie.

She never had any intention of seeking what God wanted her to do, or doing it. She was only seeking a spiritual justification to do what *she* wanted to do—which was divorce her husband and live a hedonistic life of self-gratification.

It's easy to criticize Hollywood. Why would we expect its characterization of prayer to be other than as disingenuous as it was for the self-absorbed author of the book upon which the movie was based? Yet how many of our prayers are equally hypocritical—attempts to coerce the justification of doing our own will out of the pretense of seeking God's will. How much prayer is exactly that—addressing spiritual words to God to delude ourselves into thinking that he sanctions and is leading us to yield to the world's enticements. We can pray "perfect prayers." All the while we may be seeking nothing but our own worldly will. We want to yield, and so we ask God's permission.

We are cunningly skilled at layering over our dishonesties with so many obscuring spiritualisms that we don't recognize them any more than the book's author recognized her hypocrisy as she moved from episode to episode playing games with God. Without the hedonistic lifestyle, how many Christians follow exactly this pattern—moving from church to church, experience to experience, spiritual episode to spiritual episode...playing games with God.

When we pray, *God, show me what you want me to do,* are we prepared to do what he has already shown us he wants us to do?

He has made the answer clear in a multitude of ways. It is his will that we turn from the world's enticements, reject them, push away the world's allure and do not take the first poisonous bite.

Do not yield.

The battle between those three words and the enticements Satan places before us faced the ancient Israelites. It faced the movie's character after the emotion of her prayer was past. It faces you and me every day when we are met head-on by the values, perspectives, and enticements of the world.

Heavenly Father, I pray that same prayer—tell me what to do and I'll do it. Bring that prayer to my remembrance when the world's enticements are in front of me exercising their allure. At that moment, help me not to yield, to turn my back, to refuse to listen, and to do what you have told me to do. When I rise from my knees, I ask for the humility and courage to do what you have made clear is your will.

54. Do Not Associate with Worldly People

You shall not walk in the customs of the nations…I am the LORD your God, who have separated you from the peoples…You shall be holy to me; for I…have separated you from the peoples, that you should be mine. (Leviticus 20:23-24, 26)

Make no treaty with them…Do not intermarry with them…
Break down their altars…and burn their idols
in the fire. For you are a people holy to the LORD your God. (Deuteronomy 7:2-3, 5-6, NIV)

Some of the commands, as I term it, "bite" more deeply than others. They bite deeply because they bite personally. A command that probes with stinging conviction into my heart, may not be the same command that does so into yours. That's why the Bible is such an inexhaustible reservoir of truth. Its commands are so individually practical!

But our enemy is devious and cunning in the same way. Every enticement he serves up is personally prepared. The Bible's truth, as well as the world's enticements, come individually packaged.

Similarly, I find some commands more troublesome and perplexing than others. I don't mean only harder to obey, but more difficult to understand in light of the modern world around us and its complexities, stresses, and relationships.

This is one of those. How do we get to the essence of what God intends here? On the surface of it, judgment, exclusivism, and self-righteousness literally shout off the page as the world's inevitable and angry response to the presumption of this command.

My first response is, "Does this *really* apply now…to me…in my daily relationships and interactions? Isn't this *too* hard. Does this actually still have meaning in these modern times?"

Entering Canaan under Joshua, the line between the Israelites and "the nations" around them was crystal clear. The command was easy to understand: *Have nothing to do with non-Israelites.*

For us three thousand plus years later, however, the lines between Christians and "the world" are hopelessly blurred. How can we possibly see into the hearts of those around us to determine who is "worldly," or even what defines "worldliness?" Aren't we supposed to love everyone?

These are hard questions. Pat answers and formulas won't cut it.

So I will offer none. I don't know *how* this command is to be practically obeyed in all the complex circumstances in which you and I find ourselves. Yet none the less is this a command God intends to be taken seriously.

Jesus mixed with, and apparently enjoyed friendships with sinners and tax-collectors, even some Pharisees. Obviously, then, this command does not imply that we cut off relationships with unbelievers altogether.

That said, one of the great truths of the Old Testament is that worldliness rubs off. Satan's lures and enticements are waiting to ensnare us whenever we turn around. If we intend to interpret this command with latitude, as Jesus did, we had better watch ourselves closely. Worldliness is a lethal virus a thousand times more invisibly contagious than the most deadly strain of Covid 19. [*]

The New Testament adds a fascinating distinction to this same command, emphasized in various ways in the epistles and paraphrased as follows: *Avoid world-minded believers, and the shallow and hypocritical who do not live their faith.* [†]

Is the prohibition, then, not so much against worldliness in general, but against *Christian* worldliness...pretense religiosity which is laced with a worldly outlook and worldly attitudes and behavior? We see Jesus making precisely this distinction—condemning the hypocrisy of the Pharisees, but *not* condemning so called sinners and tax collectors.

Yet myriad difficulties remain in applying this command.

- Who makes the determination of worldliness?
- By what standards do we judge, when we are commanded not to judge?
- Does it apply in the same way to those who are growing and trying to change, like Zacchaeus, and those who are content and self-justified in their worldliness?
- How does it apply to an individual I believe God has put me in contact with to help?

---

[*] I am compelled to repeat George MacDonald's definition of "the world" from his sermon "Self-Denial." So easily does modernism lure us into thinking that worldliness and a serious walk with God are compatible, that we need to remind ourselves often how opposite they truly are. "By *the world,"* MacDonald writes, "I mean all ways of judging, regarding, and thinking, whether political, economical, ecclesiastical, social, or individual...which are not God's ways of thinking and regarding...which do not take God into account, and do not set his will supreme...all ways of thinking which do not care for the truth of things, but exalt the customs of society and its practices."

† This wording is taken from #'s 37 and 56 in *The Commands of the Apostles.*

- On the other hand, might such an individual be one whose influence could draw me into his or her worldliness without my realizing it?

I do not intend to tell anyone how to obey this command other than to reiterate my conviction that we cannot ignore it. Obviously the application will be prayerful and individual.

A friend and I were talking recently about what should be our response to those attending a certain social gathering who were engaged in lifestyle choices in direct conflict with the Bible's clear commands. We were puzzling together about the difficulty of this very command.

Finally my friend said, "Maybe it simply boils down to whether or not they claim to be Christians. If not, there is no prohibition against being with them…so long as their worldliness doesn't rub off, and we do not convey acceptance of their lifestyle. If they *do* claim to be Christians, then for those relationships a worldliness is involved for which there is no excuse and which we should avoid. But in all honesty, I really don't know."

I don't know either. It is indeed one of God's hard commands. *

I know all your commands are important, God. None can be ignored. But the command not to associate with worldly minded people is so hard to know how to live out among my many relationships. Everyone is worldly to some extent, just as I am. Give me wisdom and insight to know when you would have me back away from further relationship from one whose influence is unlikely to challenge and exhort me toward Christlikeness.

55. Make No Friends of Fools

The companion of fools will suffer harm…Stay away from a fool. (Proverbs 13:20; 14:7, NIV)

Again, we hearken back to *Proverbs* where we began. This might be considered a cousin-command to the one we just considered—at once perhaps more straightforward, yet with its own range of complexities.

Foolishness isn't exactly worldliness. But it *is* a character trait that rubs off. Foolishness, like worldliness, is contagious. It is not necessarily a sin. Simple *immaturity* probably most precisely defines foolishness. Yet immaturity, too, is catching. We have to be careful and watchful around foolish immaturity. It's not something to laugh off.

How significant that foolishness is such an underlying topic throughout *Proverbs*, indeed one of its most important themes. God takes foolishness seriously. He would not do so if *only* immaturity was at stake. Jesus chose twelve immature men, yet entrusted his eternal message to the eleven truth-pointed of them who remained. He didn't mind the immaturity, as

* This was a memorable discussion, Len. Thank you for your contribution to my thinking on this thorny dilemma.

long as their hearts were Godward. They were immature, but none of them fools.

Foolishness is a particular kind of immaturity that Solomon makes clear is chosen. It is *willful* immaturity, self-content in its immaturity, uninterested in growth into wisdom and understanding and discernment. *Proverbs* records the life-patterns, attitudes, and behavior habits of the wise man and the fool. Both *choose* their destinies of personhood.

Solomon's words are subtly fascinating. We are not prohibited from associating with fools, told to avoid them, or to have nothing to do with them as is the case with worldly people.

We are told not to make *friends* of them. A curious but significant distinction.

Not only does worldliness rub off, so does character. We are influenced in myriad ways by the people we associate with. Some men and women bring out the best in those they keep close, raising them by their influence into loftier regions of personhood. This is not merely a spiritual force. We have all been influenced by teachers, not necessarily *spiritual* men and women, but yet who challenged and lifted and exhorted and opened doors and windows of knowledge and understanding and character. Theirs was an upward-influence.

We are also aware of those individuals whose impact is just the opposite—friends and associations whose influence on those around them is downward. Observe any group of children or teens and you instantly see the downward-pullers, never satisfied unless they can draw those around them *down*, into frivolity, pranks, mischief, pushing the boundaries and breaking the rules, into loose talk and making fun of their weaker peers, smoking, swearing, cheating, lewd talk, immodest dress and behavior, flirting, covering their tracks with untruth, and, as they grow older, into increasingly reckless behavior. Later in life those seeming innocent patterns become cruelty, untruthfulness, immorality, drinking, drugs, lying, and perhaps illegality.

It is therefore obvious why we shouldn't make friends of fools. They influence us in foolishness...and *worse* than foolishness. Fools constantly skirt the invisible line between foolishness and sin. What fools consider "fun" may be a door on the other side of which sin is lurking. These are dangerous lines to walk in companionship with foolishness.

Spend too much time with such individuals and we may find ourselves walking through those doors, never even realizing the moment the line was crossed. The immature are often drawn to foolishness, as but one more form of worldly enticement. Drawn into its vortex, they become fools themselves. Immaturity often *leads* to foolishness, which can *lead* to sin.

Obviously, then, with character at stake, we should choose to walk through life with *influence-lifters.* There may be many foolish and immature people among our acquaintances. But friendship, mentorhood, and influence should be reserved for a few. Jesus was very selective. He chose twelve, not a crowd. Such men and women are more difficult to find than fools. Wisdom has to be sought, foolishness will surround us without having to look for it.

We also need to alert our spiritual sensitivities to another form of foolishness—equally destructive but more difficult to discern. That is the foolishness of the erudite, intellectual, self-satisfied mocker of truth. Their foolishness is not characterized by mischief, pranks, loose behavior, or immorality but by self-righteous Narcissism. There are many such individuals who are esteemed and admired in our society, famous personalities whom we are all familiar with. They are possessed of what the world would count greatness, but by the standards of God's wisdom of *Proverbs*, their lives exhibit just the opposite. We must beware of making role models of those who are more in love with themselves than intent on walking in God's truth.

Remembering Jesus' injunction in Matthew 5:22, we must be careful about using the word *fool* to characterize either those mired in frivolous or Narcissistic foolishness. There are many of both kinds of people in the world—fools and Narcissists—and we are commanded to keep them at arm's length. Their influence on character and life-direction is toxic. Nothing good comes of friendship with the foolish or admiration of the foolish, no matter how famous a Narcissist may be who lives his foolishness on display before the world, unless it be reaffirming what kind of people we *don't* want to be.

As for you and me, let us be the kind of men and women who bring those around us *higher* into regions of wisdom and maturity. Let us be character-lifters. daily renewing our personal commitment to be men and women of character, integrity, and righteousness. If some of the world's foolish are influenced in positive ways by being around us, we will thank God.

Keep my eyes warily open, Lord, to spot foolishness that has the subtle potential, if I am not careful, to sway me away from your outlook, your thoughts, your perspectives, and pull me downward. Give me wisdom to make mentors of wisdom. Give me strength, courage, and determination to turn away from foolishness, no matter that all around me others may be drawn toward it and even admire it. May I walk a different path.

56. Do Not Bring Sin into Your Home

"And you shall not bring an abominable thing into your house." (Deuteronomy 7:26)

The phrasing of this command prompted much thought and prayer within me. Many elements of the Levitical Law were directed against idol worship, especially images of the foreign gods of the peoples of Canaan. For reasons that are strange to me, images of idols and gods were an enormous snare to the Israelites. Nor were they unique. People in all times have been drawn to external objects they can imbue with supernaturalism—statues, rosaries, crosses around the neck, crucifixes on the wall, St. Christophers on the dashboard. It's basically pagan superstition dressed up in Christian clothes.

The above scripture culminates one of many injunctions from Moses' lips against idols:

> *"The graven images of their gods you shall burn with fire; you shall not covet the silver or the gold that is on them, or take it for yourselves, lest you be ensnared by it; for it is an abomination to the Lord your God. And you shall not bring an abominable thing into your house, and become accursed like it; you shall utterly detest and abhor it; for it is an accursed thing."* (Deuteronomy 7:25-26)

Rather than railing against rosaries, crucifixes, saint-medallions, or the variety of cross-adornments people wear to pretend they are in some mysterious way affiliated with Christianity, I asked God for insight into the larger and more general application by which all of us could internalize this command.

Much in these two verses is of interest. There are the second and tenth of the Ten Commandments. There is the particular Turkish Delight to which the Israelites were susceptible—gold. There is that wonderfully descriptive word that identifies their danger as well as our own—*ensnared. Beware…false idols ensnare.*

Mostly we see God's positive hatred of objects of false worship. He detests and abhors them. They are an abomination.

Strong words.

He hates them because they *ensnare*. He hates them for *our* sake. It is his Fatherhood that hates them, because he loves us and wants the best for us. Idols of false worship do not bring his best into our lives.

On the higher plane of his Fatherhood, God hates *whatever* is capable of drawing us into *any* form of worldliness, or drawing us away from obedience. It gradually came to me that sin is able to creep into our homes, into our hearts, into our families, into our churches in ten thousand unseen ways. Our "homes" are not merely the houses where we live but our entire lives, especially our hearts and brains, our affections and priorities.

It is a frightening reality how easily sin enters the "homes" of our thoughts through the airwaves and internet and phones and television. It does not enter unbidden. We invite it to enter! In how many ways do we allow, encourage, and invite the world's influence into the *homes of our minds*?

No borders and boundaries are left. Satan's ensnarements are swirling in the air we breathe. How can we possibly keep the tidal wave of false gods and worldly snares out of our mental homes when their presence and influence is so pervasive?

Judy and I regulate the movies and television programs we watch. But the ungodliness of the internet has free access straight into our mental homes, and into this very computer on which I am writing. The world's influence is embedded into every chip and program and app in this device I am staring at this very moment. I am attempting to communicate deep and imperative truths about God's commands…on a device designed and programmed to spew anti-God worldliness into me in a thousand unseen ways! I'm not sure how to handle that horrifying dichotomy. I can only pray for protection and God's wisdom as I write.

This is no frivolous issue for me. I pose these conundrums because I am convinced that the one thing we must *not* do is ignore this command.

Sin, worldliness, and a multitude of false gods clamoring to be worshipped are in the air. They are on my phone. They are on my computer. They are in the airwaves inside and outside our home. They are in our culture. They are in the political discourse. Commercials are created to tempt and beguile. Ad campaigns are psychologically designed to penetrate the gaps in our diligence and awareness—chinks in our spiritual armor.

All these worldly influences lure, draw, tempt, and beguile our attention and curiosity and affections toward idols the world says we should worship.

The idols and sin of worldliness is *everywhere*.

And they are still, in our modern day and age, an *abomination* to God.

That is why over and over and over Moses warned:

- *Be careful.*
- *Be watchful.*
- *Take heed to yourselves.*
- *Do not yield to the world's enticements.*
- *Do not be lured by sin.*
- *Keep the camp of your home pure.*
- *Remember God's commands…*
- *…and walk in them.*

Heavenly Father, awaken me to the danger of sin, false gods, and idols seeking entrance into my mental and heart-home, as well as those that would love nothing more than to take up residence in my bedroom or living room, or even on my computer. I ask for your protection, and your wisdom. Keep me diligently, ruthlessly aware of the world's attempt to penetrate gaps in my attentiveness, and in the hedge of protection you have around me when I am living in and by your commands. May I hate sin's false idols as much as you do. May the world's abominations also be as abominable to me as they are to you.

57. Do Not Covet or Imitate What the World's People Have or Do

You shall not do as they do…in the land of Canaan, to which I am bringing you. You shall not walk in their statutes. You shall do my ordinances and keep my statutes and walk in them. I am the LORD your God. (Leviticus 18:3-4)

The images of their gods you are to burn in the fire. Do not covet the silver and gold on them, and do not take it for yourselves, or you will be ensnared by it, for it is detestable to the LORD your God. Do not bring a detestable thing into your house…Regard it as vile and utterly detest it, for it is set apart for destruction. (Deuteronomy 7:25-26, NIV)

The word *imitate* of this command exposes its most chilling danger. It's not just eyeing another's income, house, car, possessions, or sales figures with envy. The real danger is imitating what the world's people *do*. It is this deadly pattern of imitation that draws children and teens to follow their peers into sin. It's what makes the worldliness of Hollywood so corrosive in our culture—people *imitate* what they see.

It's not covetousness alone, it's giving covetousness life by acting on it…*imitating* the ways and habits and behavior and customs and fashions and speech patterns and music of the world.

One of the great cancers that is systematically destroying the church in our day is its compulsion to imitate the world's methods. Thinking that *adopting* the world's ways will cause the world to listen to its message, rather than standing *against* the world's ways as the Bible commands, foolish churches around the world are signing their own death warrants. Imitating the sin of the world's progressivism won't bring salvation to the world. It will only make Satan laugh at the ease of his victory over a spineless church that has lost its way.

The organized church of Christendom is so far gone in its worldliness that I see little hope of a reversal of its course unless God dramatically and miraculously intervenes.

You and I probably won't change this. With grief in our hearts, making sure its cancer does not infect us, there's not much we can do but get out, and allow the organized church to continue in its blindness on the road to hell and make sure it doesn't take us down with it. There perhaps God will be able to purify it according to the prophecy of Malachi 2:1-2 and 3:3. But this is no time for God's people who love the truth and see the foolhardiness of the church's complicity with the world to go down with the ship.

So we have to live this command personally.

The tenth commandment lies at the heart of all these separation commands. We covet the world. At a more foundational level, dreadful as it is to say it…we covet *worldliness* itself. That is precisely why organized Christendom is in its death throes.

The lure of the world is in us all. As God said to Cain, we must master it.

In all the ways we have seen, this means just saying no, turning our backs, walking away, resisting the enticements, refusing the various Turkish Delights Satan serves up specially prepared with our names on them. It's a daily battle of awareness, watchfulness, and attentiveness.

The war against the world will never be easy in this life. The more adept we become at saying no to the world's enticements, Satan's cunning also increases. Unable to lure us with obvious sins, he lays the traps of temptation with good, even seemingly noble and Godly inducements designed very specifically to take advantage of a chink in *my* spiritual armor—subtle blind spots of character I am completely blind to. Satan doesn't mind dressing up his enticements with spiritual clothes. He will use *anything* that lessens commitment to command-obedience and gets me thinking and seeing—in tiny ways at first that he will add to as long as I unknowingly succumb—through the world's eyes rather than God's.

Resisting the lure of the world is never as easy, say, as committing to read a devotional every day or going to church every Sunday. The enticements are invisible, each one personally aimed at the soft underbelly of individual weakness.

I propose a strategy that I believe increases one's gradual immunity to the lure of the world's enticements. As it does, it also lessens natural covetousness toward what the world's people have and do. This strategy is based on Command #20—setting the desires of our hearts Godward.

By setting my internal compass daily, reminding myself, affirming to God and myself, that I *want* to obey the commands, asking God to *remind* me of the commands, asking for *his help daily to see through his eyes*...all these daily affirmations have an impact over time.

God answers those prayers!

But I must diligently keep praying them, continually affirming to myself perhaps most of all, that deep down *I want* to see through God's eyes. My deepest heart's desire is *not* for the things of the world, even though the Old Adam of my nature may continue to cast its eye toward them.

Our friend Jim Durkin called this talking to the soul:

> *Soul, you devious Old Adam, listen and listen good. We are not going the way you want. My heart's desire is Godward. You are fighting a losing battle. So get in line, Soul—you and I are moving the way I have pointed my spiritual compass, toward God's North.*

Thomas Kempis explains this daily pointing of our inner compass Godward in this way:

> Renew your purpose and stir yourself up daily. Diligently search into and set in order both the outward and the inward man. Continually recollect yourself, fix

your good purpose every morning, and every night examine how you have behaved in word, deed, and thought.*

Over years, over a lifetime, this determination, and the accumulated choices of watchfulness that enable us to say *No* to the world, all combine to lessen the allure of its enticements.

Full immunity will never be possible in this life. There is no magic cure for worldliness. But the powerful vaccine of compass orientation *toward* God's North and *away* from the world, followed by daily booster doses of:

- Godward-remembrance,
- Renewal of purpose, and
- Accumulated choices,

—combine to gradually build into spiritual character a determination, perseverance, and single-mindedness that not even Satan will be able to overcome.

God, I point myself this day toward your North, toward the righteousness of Christlikeness that is your goal and desire for me. Remind me through the day to re-set my compass as often as it takes to keep my eyes wide open to the inducements of the world's ways. When worldly values, when what the world's people have and do, when the world's ways and means, cause me to take a second look, wake me up with a dash of ice water in my face. Keep my senses alert.

58. Women Do Not Wear Men's Clothing, Men Do Not Wear Women's Clothing

A woman must not wear men's clothing, nor a man wear women's clothing, for whoever does these things is an abomination to the LORD your God. (Deuteronomy 22:5, RSV, NIV)

Let the controversy explode!

Before anyone launches his or her attack against *me* for the above words, may I slip in the reminder about not shooting the messenger. These are the words of Moses, directly from Deuteronomy 22:5. I would not have included them were they not in the Bible in black and white:

"A woman shall not…neither shall a man…"

Whatever one makes of it, the verse goes on to call women who dress like men and men who dress like women "an abomination to the Lord."

This is not *my* command, it is God's through Moses. I merely report the fact of it. One thing is clear—God takes all matters concerning gender, sexuality, sexual practices, sexual sin, how men and women dress, and

---

* Thomas Kempis, *The Imitation of Christ.*

everything having connection with what might today be called "sexual orientation," *very* seriously. God and the Levitical Law clearly stand on opposite sides from modern progressive culture across an impossibly wide divide. God takes these matters so seriously that he calls transgressions *abominations*. Many sexual practices considered normal today were punishable by death.

It is easy for the modernist simply to say that this command, and all the sexual practice and gender orientation commands, no longer apply and can thus be ignored. Poof—problem solved.

But it's not that simple. If cherry picking the commands is your method, throwing out the ones you don't like, where do you draw the line? People of course are doing that all the time with the commands of Jesus. Foolish people constantly say, "All those gender regulations are in the Old Testament. That doesn't apply anymore. But I believe that Jesus was a great teacher and that people ought to follow his teaching…I just don't go along with everything else about Christianity."

There is no "everything else." The teachings of Jesus are the entire ball game. They come as a package.

Those who say, "I believe what Jesus teaches about love, helping the poor, being kind, feeding the hungry, and clothing the naked," but who ignore the more piercing spiritual commands—*Do what I command you, do not commit adultery, do not divorce, do not swear, be a servant of all, hunger for righteousness, don't judge, glorify God with your life, be perfect as your heavenly Father is perfect*—are fooling no one but themselves. Pretending to honor Jesus but ignoring the large percentage of his commands is nothing but hypocrisy.

All the Bible's commands come as a package. That does not mean they are all to be taken literally. Reading the Bible with intelligence requires interpretive fluidity and common sense. We have to seek God's intent. It is obvious God no longer wants people killing their enemies. It is not so obvious that God no longer wants men and women dressing or behaving interchangeably. Gender that reflects God's creation is built into the unchangeable fabric of life, killing one's enemies is not.

Not only does an intelligent reading of the commands require probing to discover the heart of God's intent, it also requires doing so with an open mind, not simply reading into this or that command what one happens to want to read into it. If I don't like a certain command because it infringes uncomfortably on my selfish independence, will I then excuse myself by interpreting it as a command that no longer represents God's intent? That is how many people read the Bible. Progressives are wonderfully adept at this strategy. But it's hypocrisy. It's playing games with God.

Where God's intent slams against personal desires, biases, and opinions, the question becomes whether or not I'm honest enough to admit it. If I *am* reading the commands honestly, not merely picking and choosing the ones that confirm my biases and opinions and political leanings, then the next question becomes, "What do I intend to do about it?"

"How seriously and personally are you and I going to take the Bible's commands in regulating how we order our lives?"

Open my eyes, Lord, to those commands I may not be taking seriously enough, where I am excusing myself, wriggling out from the imperative of obedience with false interpretations and hypocritical justifications. Purify my motives, heavenly Father. Expose my falsehood when I read your commands through the world's eyes not yours.

59. Do Not Be Lured into Worshipping False Gods

Be careful not to be ensnared by inquiring about their gods, saying…"We will do the same."
You must not worship the Lord your God in their way. (Deuteronomy 12:30-31)
If one…appears among you and announces to you a sign or wonder…
and…says, "Let us follow other gods…
and let us worship them," you must not listen…It is the LORD your God you must follow,
and him you must revere. Keep his commands and obey him; serve him and hold fast to him…
You must purge the evil from among you. (Deuteronomy 13:1-5, NIV)

It may seem that many of these separation commands all say the same thing. In a sense that is true. They are all variations on the theme:

- *Separate yourself from the world.*
- *Do not be lured by the world's enticements.*
- *Do not imitate the people of the world.*
- *Do not walk in the world's ways.*

Yet each one contains significant distinctions. Examining, personalizing, and practicalizing these differences is vital. These are no analytical rabbit trails. These nuances, and the obediences or disobediences that follow, represent life and death, spiritual growth or spiritual stagnation.

The principle of separation from the world, and what are literally hundreds of commands urging the imperative of separation throughout the Old Testament, is one of *the* primary themes of the Bible. That it is so little heeded, preached, and obeyed in our time does not indicate that it is less important now than it once was. It only indicates that Christians feel justified in ignoring this fundamental biblical message.

Notwithstanding this unfortunate reality, those who take command-obedience seriously must prayerfully and introspectively plumb the depths of these gradations of distinction with serious and thoughtful care.

Though a cursory reading might breeze past the words of this command as a mere corollary to several of those we have already considered, I find great interest here—and probing personal conviction. When enjoining this command upon the Israelites, Moses was mostly speaking of physical idols—the golden calf and smaller idol-statues fashioned in gold and silver—as well as the places and temples and sacred "high places" used in worship by the Canaanites and other foreign peoples.

The specifics have changed but not the principle. The world's *things* are still so much a part of our lives that they bring worldliness into our homes and thought-patterns 24/7. What sits in the middle of every living room—a television? What is clutched in the hand of every young person between ten and twenty, and in half the rest of the population? Are smart phones inculcating Godliness into our younger generations? Or has the cell phone become one of many golden calves of our time?

I'm more intrigued, however, by the worship we give to the false gods of our motivations, our ambitions, life goals, our appetites and desires…how we spend our money and time…to what we devote our energies…even to the false gods of our religiosity.

All these are interpenetrated with potential false gods to which we give our attention, allegiance, thought, and energy…and which, it is not too strong to say, our *worship*.

Independence—I will do my own thing, nobody will tell *me* what to do!—is one of the supreme gods of our age, worshipped almost maniacally by the cult of progressivism.

Leisure is a passionate ambition and desire of worship for many.

Politics and cultural change is increasingly a black hole of energetic false worship with many cult-idols vying for attention—liberalism, conservativism, feminism, racial equity, social justice, and a myriad of lifestyle agendas that exist all over the cultural map that has been so thoroughly redrawn in recent decades.

It is hardly necessary to mention *money, sex, power, influence, fame,* or *what-will-people-think* as false idols of worship. They are so overt and visible in the world that they go without saying.

All these are obvious. What about the idol of *orthodox doctrine*, the idol of *denomination*, the idol of the *weekly worship service?*

Let's look even deeper into the mirror. What false gods of worship sit in *my* house, in *my* heart, in *my* brain? Nobody but me can answer that question. But when an answer comes, that's when I need to re-read command #56 and do some spiritual house cleaning. Nobody can tell me, nor can I tell you, what the Holy Spirit may reveal about our own personal idols of worship when each of us looks into that prayer-mirror.

Anything can become an idol of false worship if it detracts from God's primary purpose in our lives—to grow us into his sons and daughters who are walking in his ways not the world's.

As painful as it might be, I ask you, Holy Spirit, to show me the false idols of my worship. Give me courage and humility to face the truth about myself, to recognize my susceptibility to the idols that are of particular allure to me, and to destroy their power to detract me from Christlikeness.

60. Do Not Follow Others into Sin

Do not follow the crowd in doing wrong. (Exodus 23:2, NIV)

We again encounter a separation command with unique and important shades of intent. Though the commands in this series contain this same underlying message, being led into wrong by those around us is a problem all its own. If we are not watching ourselves closely, taking heed to ourselves, and remembering God's commands, the unfocused internal compass of character all too easily wavers, not sure what direction it wants to point. The result is weakness of moral, ethical, and spiritual fiber—a lack of the courage necessary to refuse to go along with the crowd.

When I first read this verse from Exodus 23, I was shocked at what a contemporary command it is:

Do not follow the crowd in doing wrong,

How much of the current sin in the world—from race riots, to mass theft, to the tidal wave of progressive cultural change, is rooted in weak-minded conformity with "the crowd"—going along with the world…following others into sin. The startling relevancy of the Old Testament continues.

Most sin and temptation come through other people. Most of the world's enticements subtly assault us through those we are closest to. Just as we want to dabble in worldliness, we *want* to go along with the crowd. To be seen as different, even in good and virtuous and courageous ways, is to invite criticism and ridicule.

Conformity with the world is the ten-lane super-highway leading straight to sin. Christians as well as atheists disobey Romans 12:1 a dozen times a day for this very reason. Going along with those around us is the easy way—drifting through life…going with the flow…without conviction, without courage, without the courage of individuality.

The world worships what it considers independence. Yet it sacrifices individuality on the altar of conformity. The independence it so worships is nothing but a mirage.

This command highlights the lynch mob mentality we've all seen in movies countless times. The propensity to go along rather than standing courageously for right and truth is as ancient as humanity.

Adam went along.

The Israelites were swept into the mob mentality in building the golden calf. Aaron went along.

The rabble-rousing crowd clamored for the death of Jesus. Pilate went along.

And how many goings-along with the progressive sins of contemporary culture characterize the spineless contemporary church?

Coming in *Exodus*, this command is so ancient it even precedes *Leviticus*. It is one of the earliest biblical commands. It is impossible to misinterpret. It is personal. You and I will encounter its practicality *today*.

We will not be swept into a lynch mob whose ringleaders are holding a rope. You and I will be swept into a lynch mob of *ideas*, whose ringleaders are intent on destroying the influence of Christian truth in our world and culture.

We will encounter it in the mob-mentality of the progressive worldview assaulting us like a cultural tsunami in the political arena, on television, by those around us in school and the workplace. This tidal wave of mob-thought, mob-outlook, mob-opinion, and mob-sin is inundating us from every side. We are the Israelites. Those surrounding us in the world of liberal sin-abominations are cheering the golden calf of progressivism.

What will be our response?

Who will be our mentors of courage—Adam, Aaron, Pilate…or Moses and Joshua?

God's command to his people in the midst of this mob onslaught of evil is unmistakable, pointed, and personal. Obedience and disobedience is binary. We will either *choose* this day to be strong and courageous to obey…or we *choose* to follow the crowd in trampling on the truths of God. Exodus 23:1-2 is such an imperative passage, it is worth reading from several translations:

- Thou shalt not…put thine hand with the wicked…Thou shalt not follow a multitude to do evil. (King James Version)
- You shall not join hands with a wicked man…You shall not follow a multitude to do evil. (Revised Standard Version)
- You shall not make common cause with a wicked man…You shall not be led into wrongdoing by the majority. (New English Bible)
- Do not follow the crowd in doing wrong. (NIV)
- Thou shalt not follow a company to do evil. (Wycliffe Bible)
- Do not follow the crowd when it does what is wrong (Complete Jewish Bible)
- Don't take sides with important people to do wrong. (Common English Bible)
- Don't join mobs intent on evil. (Living Bible)
- You must not follow the masses to do evil. (Modern English Version)

Some of the commands are nebulous, difficult to know how to interpret, culturally and historically ambiguous.

Not this one. While the *how* of application will obviously be personal and situational, the essence of this command is stark, unyielding, and as clear as God could make it.

God, how piercing are these words from Exodus. Give me open and watchful eyes to see the danger. Give me courage to stand firm, to resist the crowd, to incur criticism, and to obey your command.

Series Seven

Watchfulness

Humility of Character

Life's anchoring principles embodied in God's commands

A prophet's faithful life

Two images come to my mind when I think of Samuel. The boy Samuel listening in the night and hearing God's voice, and the man Samuel, in a sense *watching over* Israel during Saul's reign, rebuking Saul's disobedience, and then shepherding David into the kingship. Both are images of attentiveness, a listening heart seeking God's will for Israel, and willingness, as both boy and man, to obey God's voice.

After the period of the Judges which followed Joshua, the nation of Israel floundered in disobedience to the commands laid down by Moses. Though also a judge, Samuel was the nation's first "official" prophet, one of the truly great men of Israel's history, a man who walked in the footsteps of Moses.

David usually steals the limelight of this period in Israel's history. But it is Samuel, not David, who takes his place alongside Moses in stature as one of the preeminent figures of the Old Testament. Of the four men who symbolize Israel's rise as a world power during this crowning climax to its turbulent saga—Samuel, Saul, David, and Solomon—Samuel is surely the one who stands highest in obedience, humility, and Godliness of character.

By any standards, Samuel was a great man, a true prophet of Israel. The nation he inherited was in a freefall of national and religious decline. Eli, his predecessor judge and high priest, likewise a Godly man, had relinquished control of the tabernacle to his immoral sons—the RSV calls them "worthless men." Realizing that his sons had not given their lives in true service and obedience to God, Eli knew that he had failed by allowing them to continue in the priesthood. His tragic life ended with the knowledge that God's judgment would fall on his posterity.

The early chapters of *1 Samuel* set up the context of Samuel's life. From his birth, Samuel's mother Hannah dedicated her son to the Lord's service for life. Almost from infancy, Samuel was prepared for service. As a boy he was taken to live at Shiloh to minister to and serve the aging Eli.

The significant verse 1 Samuel 2:26 (symbolically half of the parallel verse in Luke 2:52) established Samuel's course in life: "And the boy Samuel continued to grow both in stature and in favor with the Lord and with men." Samuel was thus a prophetic forerunner of the Lord himself.

The era of apostasy under Eli's sons into which Samuel was born is poignantly illuminated as the passage is introduced for which the boy Samuel is best known.

> *Now the boy Samuel was ministering to the Lord under Eli. And the word of the Lord was rare in those days; there was no frequent vision…Then the Lord called, "Samuel, Samuel!" and he said, "Here am*

I."...And the Lord called again, "Samuel!"...And the Lord called Samuel again the third time...And the Lord came and stood forth, calling as at other times, "Samuel, Samuel!" And Samuel said, "Speak, for thy servant hears." (1 Samuel 3:1, 4, 8, 10)

In the following chapter—by which time Samuel is recognized as a prophet—the Philistines attacked and defeated Israel, captured the ark of the covenant, and killed both Eli's sons. When the news came to Eli, he fell over backwards, broke his neck, and died. At the time the wife of one of his sons was about to give birth. Hearing that her husband and father-in-law were dead, the text reads, "she bowed and gave birth."

The words that follow from her mouth gave prophetic definition to the final years of the judges into which Samuel was born: "And she named the child Ichabod...And she said, 'The glory has departed from Israel.'" (1 Samuel 4:21, 22)

Yet in the coming years, Samuel gave new spiritual focus and vision to the nation, keeping the flame of faith alive and preparing his people for the season of Israel's glory.

Samuel, like Moses, was one of Israel's towering forerunning shepherd-prophets who anticipated Jesus. He was Israel's watchful shepherd, intent on turning the Ichabod-nation back toward obedience to the commands given by his predecessor Moses.

Series Seven

Watchfulness

61. Keep watchful by knowing God's commands.

62. Read and re-read God's law.

63. Fix God's words in your mind
and store his commands in your heart.

64. Apply your heart to understand God's purposes.

65. Do not help an evil man or woman.

66. Do not let sin become a thorn in your side.

67. Seek counsel, guidance, and advice.

68. Meditate on God's precepts.

69. Listen and humbly heed wisdom, insight,
instruction, and correction.

70. Live by the truth you know.

61. Keep Watchful by Knowing God's Commands

Be careful and watch yourselves closely…watch yourselves very carefully… keep his decrees and commands. (Deuteronomy 4:9, 15, 40, NIV)

This entire series, with Samuel as our mentor of watchfulness, expands on Command #52. It is important to remind ourselves of the command to watchfulness as intrinsic to separation from the world. Here we focus, however, on the higher watchfulness visible in the life of Samuel, not merely to avoid the world's enticements (though obviously that too), but to sustain an entire life-outlook and perspective. This command points toward a *worldview of watchfulness*, as it were, a way of seeing, an attentiveness of character—the overspreading watchfulness that permeates all of life with God's perspective. Most of the Bible's commands can be seen as fruits growing on the tree of a life well-lived in the reality of *this* specific command.

Our introduction to Samuel in Scripture is as an attentive listener, ready even as a child to respond to the Voice. His spirit was awake.

Wakefulness is thus synonymous with alertness and watchfulness. God needs men and women who are spiritually wide awake and attentive to the influences, good and bad, coming at them. They are watchers, listeners…wisely paying attention to right and wrong, good and evil, and all the influences—personal, spiritual, and cultural—that surround them.

It was this wide-awake mentality that enabled Samuel to perceive what Saul did not. The exchange between the two in 1 Samuel 15 when Saul failed to destroy the Amalekites is one of the Bible's memorable confrontations. God's command was clear. But Saul lost his focus. (For the purposes of the principle involved, we will leave aside the conundrum, "But how could a loving God command such atrocities?) Samuel was watchful of God's commands, Saul was not.

It is not germane to the command whether Saul fully understood what God had commanded. He *should* have known and understood. But in the heat of battle and its aftermath, his watchfulness waned. Saul went to sleep. The command was no longer forefront. He had not made it his priority to see through God's eyes.

Not so Samuel. Awake, vigilant, alert, attentive, and watchful…he *knew* God's command. He evidenced his childhood watchfulness by listening. And now as Saul returns from battle, flush with victory, no doubt expecting praise and kudos for his triumph, it is initially again through *hearing* that Samuel detects the disobedience that has followed Saul home.

Pretending to have obeyed perfectly, Saul proclaims, "I have performed the command of the Lord."

But Samuel replies, "What then is this bleating of sheep in my ears?"

The exchange is a pivotal scriptural moment of contrast between spiritual attentiveness and spiritual lethargy. The distinction between these two men highlights the essence of this command before us:

Spiritual watchfulness requires hearing, then knowing, then understanding God's commands.

Samuel heard, knew, and understood. Saul thought he knew best, and thus forgot what *God* had told him to do.

Clearly the *do* of obedience must follow. But to *do* the commands we have to *know* what they are. Know them clearly. Keep them at the forefront of our attention.

This ancient story is laden with practicality for you and me. Spiritual watchfulness requires some brain work, study, reading, thought. To know the commands, we have to *hear* them, *learn* them, take them inside. That takes work and effort. Watchfulness doesn't come by accident. Seeing through God's eyes requires training in a "worldview of watchfulness" over many years.

That's one of the purposes of a book like this—to get to *know* the commands. In the rush and pace and stress of life (Saul's attentiveness drifted in the midst of a great battle), if we don't know the commands, our attentiveness will drift just as Saul's did.

Again Kempis's words reorient the needle of watchfulness:

> Renew your purpose and stir yourself up daily...
> Give no heed to the many whisperings of this world.
> Listen not to the voices sounding without, but for the Truth teaching inwardly.
> Thus prepare yourself for the receiving of heavenly secrets
> Gladly receive the pulses of the Divine whisper.*

Learn God's commands, *listen* to God's commands, *know* God's commands, seek to *understand* God's commands, *do* God's commands.

Like Samuel, we must pay attention and remain attentive to the whispers of the Voice.

As I read and study the Bible, Holy Spirit, energize my brain to recognize your commands, and how to live them. Give me watchful attentiveness to listen and learn them, to know and understand them, and to keep them at the forefront of my thoughts.

* Thomas Kempis, from *The Imitation of Christ.*

62. Read and Re-Read God's Law

And day by day, from the first day to the last, he read from the book of the law of God...
Now on the twenty-fourth day of this month...they stood up in their place
and read from the book of the law of the Lord...
On that day they read from the book of Moses. (Nehemiah 8:18; 9:1, 3; 13:14)

The first four commands of this series are intrinsically linked. Learning to see through God's eyes takes diligence and work. We have to study and think and *learn* what God wants, *how* he wants people to think and behave, *what* he wants his people to do.

The specifics of this particular command jump ahead in the biblical story. The Law and subsequent writings of history (some of the earliest probably written by the watchful Samuel) and poetry and songs (David) and proverbs (Solomon) were set down in writing and transcribed and came into general use in Israel much later than the exodus. The early Levitical Law would not have actually been *read* by the Israelites during the time of Moses and Joshua. It was a preliterate culture. Writing was still in its infancy. Their history and teaching was spoken.

By David's and Solomon's time, writing was common. Books were being produced (more accurately scrolls)—though were still not in circulation for the common man. The application of this injunction has obviously changed through history. Today we *can* read. Most of the ancient Israelites could not. Like many others, this is a command whose obedience-specifics have progressed, developed, and become more personal through time.

Yet from the beginning, notwithstanding the literacy limitations of the populace, this was a command initiated by Moses himself:

"At the end of every seven years...you shall read this law before all Israel in their hearing." (Deuteronomy 31:10-11)

Though generation upon generation forgot Moses' command, Ezra did not forget. Centuries later he sought to reestablish obedience to this important foundation stone of a righteous life:

"And they stood up in their place and read from the book of the law of the Lord..." (Nehemiah 9:3)

To *know* God's commands, to remain watchful, God's written instructions have to remain clearly in focus. The prophets command God's people to *read* his commands, his law. This command is as practical for us as for the ancient Israelites. They did not obey it. They lost their focus. They drifted into disobedience. It's simple cause and effect.

If I do not keep God's instructions in the forefront of *my* thoughts, I will lose my focus just as surely as they did. The practicality here is daily. The implications determine the course of one's life-orientation.

In phrasing this command, I debated what word to use, whether it ought to be generalized and made it more applicable to our lives today:

Read and re-read God's *Word*.

Read and re-read God's *commands*.

Read and re-read God's *instructions*.

All these capture the essence of the command. We can easily substitute them in our minds.

In the end I let the "Law" stand. The word may have negative connotations for some. Yet this is how the original command comes in Scripture. I felt this was how it should remain. It is incumbent upon us to read *Law* in its larger and overarching sense, not merely as indicating the Levitical Law of *Exodus, Leviticus,* and *Numbers* as it would have when Moses first spoke the command. With the hindsight and increasing revelation of history, we are able to read more expansively and personally into the glorified Law, so to speak, the higher Law that was in God's heart when he gave Moses the foreshadowing but passing "law."

We read the Bible, including both Old and New Testaments as God's *Word and Revelation*—seeking to *know* and *remember* and remain *watchful* about his commands, purposes, instructions for our lives…that we might obey them.

It may not be the interpretation others would give, but I read Psalm 119 as a massive outpouring from David's heart representing the fruit of his obedience to this precise command.

He could not have written Psalm 119 had he not been reading and re-reading God's law for most of his life. His love for the precepts, ordinances, commands, and statutes in that psalm reveal a deep and personal awareness of what those precepts, ordinances, commands, and statutes meant. He *knew* God's commands. He did not always obey them, which is sadly also part of his legacy. But he knew them. Over and over he repeats his love for God's Law.

David had obeyed this command.

God, remind me today, even if but for a moment if I have no time for more, to read something from your Word. Deepen my love for your law. Stimulate my heart to echo David's words, and take them into my depths—I will meditate on thy precepts…I will delight in thy statutes…I will not forget thy word…I will never forget thy precepts…Oh, how I love thy law…through thy precepts I get understanding…thy word is a lamp to my feet…I love thy precepts.

63. Fix God's Words in Your Mind and Store His Commands in Your Heart

Fix these words of mine in your hearts and minds; tie them as symbols on your hands and bind them on your foreheads. (Deuteronomy 11:18, NIV)

The progression from the previous command to this is straightforward and obvious. It's not enough simply to legalistically, intellectually, or unthinkingly *read* God's Word. There is a higher purpose involved.

We *do* read, of course, to gain intellectual knowledge. Much legitimate research requires such reading I would not be misunderstood as disparaging the intellectual component of vigorous faith, as I think I've made clear. When the Bible is read *only* intellectually, however, we may be led away from truth as often as toward it.

Then, too, we're all familiar with the tendency for eyes to gloss over the words on a page. When that happens, we probably can't be said to be "reading" at all. My first few attempts to get through *Exodus, Leviticus,* and *Numbers* many years ago were certainly characterized by the glassy-eyes method!

In a technical sense, therefore, it is possible to obey the previous command to *read* and *re-read* God's Word, either for the wrong reasons or with the wrong kind of reading. Effective reading of God's Word has a specific purpose—to implant God's Word *into* us. Not into our brains by rote, like memorizing the multiplication table. That, of course, has certain limited value. But high mathematics moves on from there. So too does the impact of God's Word.

We read and re-read so that God's principles and perspectives become so deeply ingrained in us that they infuse themselves into the DNA of character and personhood.

I view my mental, emotional, and spiritual personhood as composed (simplistically, but usefully) of three parts: *brain, mind, heart.* The comparison is also made between *body, soul, spirit* which corresponds in a general way to the first three. These distinctions of the complex human make-up can also be seen as *physical, mental,* and *spiritual.*

My brain is a computer. It receives, processes, and stores information. It is a physical apparatus made up of "little grey cells" and electrical connections in my head that are capable of amazing things.

My mind is that part of my human consciousness that makes use of the brain's computer. The mind is located *in* the brain but in a sense is separate from the pure physicality of the brain. My mind, or intellect, *thinks,* learns, sets goals, processes information, makes determinations, and draws conclusions. An even more important power contained in the mind is the power of decision. The mind is the seat of *volition,* where choosing and behavior originate. The mind *decides* what to do with the information stored in the brain. Most important of all, it makes choices about patterns and habits of *behavior*.

We might call the brain the computer, the mind the computer programmer. Simplistic again. I'm trying to make a point not write a thesis in behavioral psychology. There are myriad details which need to be omitted for the sake of this specific discussion. Logic and rationality, for example, bridge both brain and mind and are active in both. (Though when the mind is not choosing in harmony with the truths God built into his creation, its logic and rationality often leave the building.)

Then finally we come to the heart, soul, and spirit, by which we identify the non-physical component of our deepest humanity that *feels* and responds to the emotive, spiritual, relational, creative, and imaginative currents of life. An analyst would pull these three apart and dissect them further. I trust that you are able to understand the point I am making.

All these factors of personhood interweave into the tapestry of what it means to be human, and, further, what it means to be made in God's image. Yet it is possible to shut the mind and heart off from the spiritual influences of that image-ness. That is the puzzling yet amazing aspect of volition and the human power of choice. It is possible to reject the very origin of how and why we possess free will in the first place. It is possible to use the mind and the intellect to deny the existence of what gives the mind the power to think. Many do deny that reality, and consider the utter illogic of their conclusion as representing the apex of logic.

We are at last in a position to understand the beauty of this two-command progression. All aspects of our humanity are drawn into it—body, soul, and spirit…brain, mind, and heart.

Read and re-read God's law,
thus store his words in your heart,
so that they will go into the deepest places within you.

Or restated a little differently:

Implant God's Word in your mind by repetition, study,
and thought to help you make choices toward obedience.
Then store his commands in your heart
so they become intrinsic to your deepest being.

When we read God's Word, we are not robots or AI machines. We are thinking, responding, feeling, spiritual beings, responsible to bring his principles into the DNA of our manhood or womanhood. Psalm 119 is one of the clearest windows we have in Scripture revealing what the sequence of these commands (Read God's law…fix his words in your mind…store his commands in your heart) looks like in a single human life.

Increase my hunger for your Word, Lord God. As I read, whether a single verse, a passage, or merely reflect on a principle or truth you have made real to me, lodge that verse or passage or principle deep into my mind. Fix it there to stay. Increase the storehouse of your words and precepts and truths that live in my heart. May they infuse my brain, my mind, my heart, my complete being, with your perspectives. Give me your eyes to see people, the world, and myself as you see them, and as you see me.

64. Apply Your Heart to Understand God's Purposes

If you…store up my commands within you, turning your ear to wisdom and applying your heart to understanding…if you call out for insight and cry aloud for understanding… then you will…find the knowledge of God. (Proverbs 2:1-4, 5, NIV)

The progression continues:

- Be watchful…learn God's commands.
- Read and re-read God's law.
- Fix and store God's commands in your heart.
- Apply yourself to understand God's purposes.

They will culminate later in the final command of this series:

- Live by the truth you know.

Progressivity of *growth* is one of the underlying foundations of the Christian life. The vague "spirituality" many seek, which offers an ethereal sense of the great beyond, some ambiguous eternal *meaning* to the universe, which in practical reality means little, is a spirituality with little or no cause and effect, choice and consequence, progressions. Many take what they want in the nebulous vacuum of their own thoughts and desires (as in the film *Eat, Pray, Love* discussed earlier) and don't worry about implications. They don't have to think about Truth in an absolute or personally-determinative way. Lower case relativistic "truth" (truth for *me*) is all such etherealists seek.

True Christianity, on the other hand, is based on a progressive series of *presuppositions*, fundamental *Truths*, and yes—unpleasant as worldly "spiritualists" may find it—*demands*. Christians are supposed to live and think and behave in certain ways.

Truth is upper case, absolute and binding. The underlying Truth of Christianity, which encompasses those requirements, builds precept upon precept. Christianity comes to mankind as an unfolding revelation—both through history, and in the lives of each individual Christian man and woman.

The fourth command in this particular progression (and there are many such progressions within Christian Truth) points toward one of the highest objectives of that upper case, demanding, Truth—understanding God and his purposes. This progression of commands has been building toward this climax. Samuel *understood God's purposes.* Saul did not. By fixing and storing God's commands in his mind and heart (as his prayer journal of Psalm 119 recounts), David *understood God's purposes.* His life fell apart at command #70. But he was faithful in obeying the first four (#s 61-64) of the progression.

God's purposes were abundantly clear in the Levitical Law. Moses understood them. The majority of Israelites and Jews, however, turned the Law into a series of hopelessly legalistic regulations. Their spiritual focus fell apart at this very command. They tried to obey the legalisms without seeking to *understand* God's purposes. It is here, at command #64, where ancient Israel began to disintegrate spiritually. Not applying themselves to understand God's purposes, how could they possibly obey?

Christians fail as God's people at the same stumbling block. Little has changed in three thousand years. If one command in this book is mostly ignored by the vast majority of Christendom, it is found right here. Christianity has developed its own complex range of legalisms, from church regulations to denomination affiliation to worship tradition to doctrinal correctness, each of which contains its own hundreds of specifics. These legalisms are so embedded into the indoctrination Christians all along the spectrum receive in their church training they are hardly viewed as legalisms at all. Most Christians thus live their lives in stultifying adherence to what they have been taught, rather than following this progression into the high regions of life with God.

They have not applied themselves diligently to *understand* God's purposes. To truly understand God's high purposes, we have to ask a series of pointed, personal, probing, and eternally vital questions.

- What kind of men and women does God want us to be?
- What kind of man and woman does God want *me* to be?
- How will this purpose be achieved?
- What are God's purposes in eternity for *all* his created children?
- How is the Gethsemane prayer to be lived in daily life?
- How infinite are God's love and forgiveness?
- How is God's Fatherhood intended to be the lens through which Christians evaluate his eternal purposes?
- What is meant by Christlikeness?
- Does *my* heart's desire line up with *God's* desire for me?
- How does the goal of becoming like Jesus influence my moment-by-moment choices and decisions?

Sadly, the doctrinally correct teachings of most churches and denominations have so cluttered the brains of their faithful church-going members with formulas and legalisms, that most of these questions, if posed to their congregations on a Sunday morning, would be met with blank stares.

God, give me courage and dedication to apply myself to understand, to call out for insight, to cry aloud for understanding. Lead me, Holy Spirit, into the deep knowledge of God so that I will correctly understand his eternal purposes, then embrace and fall into those purposes in my own daily life.

65. Do Not Help an Evil Man or Woman

Do not help a wicked man. (Deuteronomy 23:1, NIV)

We've encountered variations on this theme several times. The separation commands are similar enough as to be almost interchangeable, though the nuances are vital.

In this case, a distinction exists between not *participating* in wrongdoing or yielding to the world's enticements, and helping *others* to do so. In other words, giving moral support to, perhaps unspoken—aiding and abetting—*their* wrongdoing. This we may do in so many unseen and subtle ways. In our time it might be phrased, "Do not be an enabler. Do not help a man or woman *continue* in their sin."

How many votes are cast for ungodly men and women? How often do we "go along," giving tacit approval by our silence, to behavior and attitudes of friends and loved ones whom we know are thinking and behaving wrongly and contrary to truth? How many known criminals are defended by attorneys who know they are guilty? Of course it is intrinsic to the modern criminal justice that everyone deserves a defense? But what of the *biblical* standard? And do we not do the same on a smaller scale?

How often do we enable those closest to us because we can't say no? We give what is called "moral support" to wrong, knowing inside that it is not *moral* at all. They are wrong, and *we* are wrong for silently condoning it.

Of course saying no is hard. Obedience to this command will be hard. There are *always* extenuating circumstances. God is no legalist and doesn't expect us to be. "Evil" and "wrong" are sometimes not easy to define. Most of us won't be in the position of being faced with helping someone rob a bank. But we may be in a position of enabling one we love to continue in behavior that, while not to be characterized as "evil," may yet be personally destructive to their morality, growth, and character. Moral support is the last thing they need. What they need is *moral accountability.*

How many Christians condone abortion and vote for pro-abortion policies? They silently go along with this national disgrace. How many pastors marry adulterers without a thought? It's now become more blatant than that. How many pastors perform same sex marriages? There will be much to answer for one day for the myriad ways Christians disobey this command every day, justifying their disobedience with hollow excuses of love and tolerance and forgiveness. Even love carries consequences.

It's not just the pastors and priests who are responsible for the contemporary tidal wave of disobedience to this command. It's the millions of Christians who go along…condoning the sin, giving sanction and support by their silence, continuing to fund churches whose programme is in direct violation of this command.

Here is a very specific command staring us in the face. It is being ignored on so many levels all around us that it is fruitless to enumerate them—in politics, in church policies of worldliness that welcome the world's sin through wide open doors of accommodation, by the people all around us who consider taking a stand against sin to be judgmental.

You and I cannot change that. All we can do in the corners of life where we live is obey this command ourselves. Doing so won't be easy. Obeying this command will invite criticism, condemnation, and anger.

If your church and pastor are accommodating sin, even encouraging it and welcoming it with open arms, then the problem is compounded all the more. Leadership-sin is added to the sin of the sinner. Sin piles upon sin, and churches and their leaders are complicit.

If your pastor has let his watchfulness guard down, and is not being a faithful shepherd by keeping sin out of the church home, how long will you stand idly by and pretend there's nothing wrong? Compounded sin accrues ever-increasing sin-interest. The debt is spiritually bankrupting many churches.

Our contemporary culture, and Christendom's weak and cowardly response to its sin, is admittedly a difficult challenge that faces every one of us. Watchfulness doesn't function on auto pilot. It is fearfully easy to go with the world's flow and hope that God has it covered. Unfortunately, in God's economy it doesn't work that way. God can't "cover" our lack of watchfulness.

Samuel wasn't perfect in his watchfulness. It was hard for him too. He might have been too quick to appoint David king. As Samuel later discovered, though David had a heart for God, he did not have the character or good judgment to match. David was not an *evil* man by any means. Indeed, he was a man after God's own heart. But his selfishness and flaws of character led him *into* sin.

Might Samuel have been more careful to mentor him into a higher level of righteousness before proclaiming him king? As it was, Samuel was an enabler of David's immaturity. Not an "evil man," David's disobedience yet led to evil consequences. Samuel was accountable along with David for not keeping the camp pure.

The separation and watchfulness commands are hard commands. They were hard for Samuel and David. Obeying them will be hard for us.

God, give me courage to put my watchfulness on the line for your truth. Sting my awareness when I lapse into justifying, silent, enabling of sin, but am too cowardly to take a stand. Give me courage not to help, accommodate, and justify sin in those I love by pretending to go along with it, giving moral support because I am too weak to stand for moral accountability. Most of all, give me eyes to see when I am in danger of giving aid and comfort to my own sin.

66. Do Not Let Sin Become a Thorn in Your Side

If you do not drive out the inhabitants of the land, then those of them whom you let remain shall be as…thorns in your sides. (Numbers 33:55)

We usually associate the "thorn in the flesh" imagery with Paul's description of his troubles in 2 Corinthians 12. However, it came originally from God's words to Moses in Numbers 33:55. The analogy gives powerful insight to sin that we allow to remain alive within us, sin that we do not deal with, sin to which we give aid and comfort in the hidden shadows of the heart. It may be that *you and I* are the man and woman whom we are helping to accommodate and live comfortably with sin. I may be giving *moral support* to my own sin, not forcing myself to face my own *moral accountability.*

> *If you do not drive out the inhabitants of the land, then those of them whom you let remain shall be as pricks in your eyes and thorns in your sides, and they shall trouble you in the land where you dwell.* (Numbers 33:55)

The distractions, red herrings, intellectualism, and pointless analysis that people bring to their reading of the Old Testament to prevent personal response to its commands are too wearisome even to address. It's hardly worth asking *why* God commanded the Israelites to kill the inhabitants of Canaan. That has not been given to us to understand. To us has been given the responsibility to glean the higher meaning of these events that lead to *Fatherhood* on God's side, and to the *obedience* of sons and daughters on our side.

The land God is leading *us* to fight for and possess today in *our* lives is the land where spiritual sonship and daughterhood dwell, and where Fatherhood is the ruling life-order of an other-worldly kingdom. He has not put Canaanites in our way that we must kill. Our enemy is the sin within us that prevents land-possessing childship that is the lifeblood of that kingdom.

The land God would have us possess and conquer is occupied by the sin nature of the Old Adam. That sin nature, and all the many ways it dwells in the land of our minds and hearts and motivations and desires, must be ruthlessly put to the sword. Sin can be given no quarter. The fullness of sonship and daughterhood cannot flourish or coexist with chosen ongoing sin. The inhabitants of the Old Adam must be killed, trampled...*driven out.* Any sin-inhabitant we allow to remain, hidden away, pampered and fed and kept alive, will come back to haunt us. It will be a thorn in the side of sonship and daughterhood that prevents the kingdom life of Fatherhood and childship from flourishing...until it is removed.

Samuel's spiritually watchful eyesight was keenly attuned to Saul's thorn in the flesh. Saul was greedy for the possessions of the Amalekites. As we read the account, we can see it so clearly.

But are we equally skilled at looking deep in the mirror to detect our *own* Amalekite sin-thorns? This is not an ancient story about a cruel God ordering a bloody massacre. This is a parable whose practicality meets every one of us the minute we walk out the door in the morning. There is a land to be conquered. There is a Fatherhood kingdom to be fought for. There is sonship and daughterhood to be claimed and won. But the Canaanites and Amalekites of my self-motivated weaknesses and sins and selfishnesses will fight ruthlessly against every truth of that kingdom, and kill their power within me if they can. What potential new insight this may give to Paul's thorn in the flesh. Perhaps it came from something he had been unwilling to drive out of his own life.

We are in a war. The Amalekites of sin must be put to the sword. Otherwise they will remain nagging thorns, and will pick and prod and poke and undermine full childship in the land of Fatherhood.

Some thorns in the flesh are not easy to see. I might twist and squirm in front of the mirror and never see a thorn that Satan has cleverly stuck in my back where I cannot see it. The enemy is even more clever than that. Not every sin-thorn is an irritant. Some thorns actually feel good. They give aid and comfort and moral support to our weakness and selfishishness. We *want* to keep them comfortably in place. Most sin is pleasant to live with.

Thorns in the flesh can even be *good* things! Saul's temptation was for good things—the best of sheep and the cattle. After all, he put *most* of the Amalekites to the sword. Like Saul, we flatter ourselves that we have dealt with *most* of our sin. What Saul spared were good things—good and lovable sins. The words of Scripture are illuminating—he spared "all that was good."

The children, the sheep, the pleasant and cuddly sins are the most invisible thorns in the flesh.

The moment-by-moment practicality of this command brings Joshua's invasion of Canaan and Samuel's confrontation with Saul into our lives every day. We are involved in a lifetime battle for the conquest of the land of our new nature in Christ against the inhabitants—even the pleasant and cuddly ones—of the Old Adam.

Oh God, thank you for revealing your Fatherhood in the Old Testament. You are no tyrant against the people of your creation. You are a tyrant against the sin that would prevent me from entering into my sonship in the kingdom of your loving Fatherhood. Keep me from old covenantal distractions about why you commanded things that are hard to understand. Keep me focused on the land you want me to claim and possess. Open my eyes to my sin-thorns that are hard to see. Give me courage to pull them out, that I may enter the land of your Fatherhood with single-minded purpose.

67. Seek Counsel, Guidance, and Advice

A wise man listens to advice. (Proverbs 2:15)
The discerning heart seeks knowledge. (Proverbs 15:14, NIV)
Plans are established by seeking advice…by wise guidance. (Proverbs 20:18, NIV, RSV)
In the multitude of counselors there is safety. (Proverbs 11:14, KJV)

One of the piercing and descriptive phrases used repeatedly through the Old Testament of Israel's kings and its people during seasons of disobedience is found in the final verse of *Judges* just before Samuel arrives on the scene.

Every man did what was right in his own eyes. (Judges 21:25)

The words are few. But worlds of insight into the history of mankind on earth is contained in this verse. Nothing has changed in three thousand years. Such exactly describes the world in which we find ourselves today.

The stark reality of this verse sits squarely in the middle of the tense relationship between Saul and Samuel. Saul did what was right in his own eyes. He wanted to keep the good thorns.

It will be Samuel's "god-grandson" Solomon, if I may characterize the relationship thus, who will articulate this command in many diverse ways throughout *Proverbs*. Solomon brings specificity of circumstance to the development of watchfulness, emphasizing an open-minded and listening mentality that is hungry for counsel, advice, and guidance.

The operative word in this command is *seek*. It's not enough half-heartedly to go along with a few pointers we happen to pick up as we drift through life.

The wise and growing man or woman *wants, seeks,* and *asks for* counsel. Hungry truth seekers are on the constant lookout for spiritual men and women wiser than themselves, whose experiences they can glean from on their progressive roads of growth. They are untiring and vigilant in the quest for wisdom.

In our time, however, true *seekers* are rare. Whatever people learn, however they grow and develop, however they expand their spiritual perceptions, they do it on their own terms. They don't want anyone else's help, especially unsought. My business is *my* business, thank you very much.

I will try to learn…but I'll do it *my* way.

I will try to grow…but I'll do it *my* way.

I will try to be a good Christian…but I'll do it *my* way.

I often say that independence is one of the gods of our age. Its corollary is equally destructive—*self-satisfaction.* The lips of both independence and self-satisfaction constantly repeat—to themselves and to the face they present to the world—the life-mantra: "No one will tell *me* what to do!"

Self-satisfaction is a great mystery to me. Most people like themselves just the way they are, and see no reason to change. They bitterly resent being told what they *ought* to do. This is to be expected from the people of the world. But self-satisfied Christians are one of the most confusing anomalies in life. The fact of self-satisfaction in God's church, especially in its clergy, is utterly baffling. It is so clear that everyone ought to see—a self-satisfied Christian is a man or woman, pastor or priest, destined for stagnation.

We all know the familiar scenario that separates the seeker from the self-satisfied.

As we're approached by a parent, boss, co-worker, teacher, pastor, husband, wife, even a friend, we instantly detect a serious expression. We cringe knowing a lecture is coming. Defensiveness instantly rises to the surface.

Then comes the unsought word of advice: "I'd like to talk to you about something…I've noticed that…I think you ought to…"

It doesn't matter if the counsel is kind or blunt, or how much explanation leads up to it, or how respected the individual may be…what we *hear* is:

You have a blind spot, a weakness…you are thinking and behaving insensitively, immaturely, or self-centeredly…you need to change…therefore, this is what you ought to do.

Whatever the motive of the hopeful counselor, however appropriate might be what is said, the words are received as criticism.

Three normal reactions usually characterize the self-satisfied:

- *Anger*—How dare you! What do you know…you're just as bad…what gives you the right to interfere with my life!
- *Silence* as they sit either pouting or inwardly fuming.
- *Defensiveness*—But you don't understand! Explanations and justifications follow, telling the hopeful counselor (in a wide variety of ways, some angry, some more measured) why they are wrong and have no right to give advice.

In all three cases, tension enters the relationship. Little change results. Life goes on. Self-satisfaction desires no change, sees no reason to change, and rejects all counsel toward change.

The response of the seeker is entirely different A heart of humble gratitude opens toward he or she who has brought the counsel—

appreciation in recognition of the courage it took to speak in what is always a difficult situation.

The word might have been painful to hear. It's never pleasant to be confronted with a blind spot, a weakness, or to be told that I have behaved insensitively, foolishly, untruly, or in an immature way. Those things hurt!

But do I want to grow? Do I want weaknesses and insensitivities and immaturities rooted out? Or do I want them to remain as unseen sin-thorns in my back and side where I can't see them?

The mature response of the growing Christian is therefore:

"Thank you. It's not pleasant to hear, but I hadn't been aware of that. I will think and pray about what you say and see what the Holy Spirit would have me do. Thank you again for having the love and courage to speak honestly to me. If there is more that comes to you in this regard, please bring it to my attention."

I am not for a minute implying that all counsel people give is necessarily *good* or sensitively-given. Unfortunately many people are eager to give opinionated and foolish advice more rooted in their own busy-body immaturity than wisdom proceeding out of the mind of Christ. Advice from such individuals is usually not helpful and often represents but a smokescreen to keep them blind to their own immaturities. The world is full of Job's counselors * eager to tell everyone else what they should do while not taking care of their own spiritual houses.

Therefore, I may not be required to follow every piece of counsel or advice I am given. In the final analysis, God's Spirit is the final arbiter of truth.

That's why the truth seeker must *seek* counsel from wise men and women he trusts, not simply wait for it. My own eyes are self-motivated. That cannot be helped. My eyesight is not always to be trusted when I am looking at myself. The more I choose trusted life-advisors for their *wisdom* (not because they will tell me only what I want to hear), the more I will avoid being at the mercy of Job's counselors who do not necessarily have my best interests at heart.

A watchful and growing heart *desires* guidance, *seeks* advice, *asks* for counsel, and hungers to be more Christlike next year than he or she is today. Keeping on target toward that upward growth requires help from people who love me and see what I cannot see myself.

I do not want to do what is right in my own eyes. I want to do what is right in *God's* eyes. I need the eyes of other wise men and women to see what I cannot.

Give me courage, Lord, to seek advice and counsel from those I trust, and to listen and take to heart their words with humble gratitude.

---

* From the Old Testament book of *Job*, counselors who mingle judgmentalism and condemnation with their opinionated and unsought advice (which in the spiritual realm may also be laced with doctrine and theology). Their counsel is thus not only insensitive and critical, it is void of insight and discernment.

68. *Meditate on God's Precepts*

I will meditate on thy precepts, and fix my eyes on thy ways.
I will delight in thy statutes; I will not forget thy word. (Psalm 119:15-16)

Psalm 119 is nothing short of the loftiest window into David's heart for God. It is a towering poetic symphony of love for God's commands, law, precepts, perspectives, and eternal purposes. We will peer more through this window in the following series of commands.

David was a man of antiquity. He did not see all the way into God's purposes. But his deepest *desire* was to know them and understand them. To do so, it is obvious from his own words that he read and re-read the writings of Moses. Though there is much scholarly debate about when the ancient Hebrew writings were compiled in the form in which we have them today, it is almost certain that the Mosaic Law had been copied and re-copied many times by David's time and was readily available to the upper educated classes. David was an educated and literate man. His own writings attest to his love for writing and the written word.

Psalm 119 illuminates David's private devotional life more majestically than any of the other psalms. He read and studied and meditated on God's Word diligently. He did so because he *loved* it!

David loved God's Law. He loved God's commands.

Think what an extraordinary thing this is. The world positively *hates* the imposition of restrictions—of being told what it can and cannot do—right from the start with Adam, Eve, and Cain. The world puts up with legalities, but under silent protest. Deep down it *hates* Law.

Even more the world *really* hates the notion of command.

How can David then, in so many ways a man of the world, say that he *loves* God's Law and commands? Who does that? Who *loves* command!

Honestly speaking, I can say that I share what David was thinking and feeling. When I read Psalm 119, David's outpouring resonates with my own heart. I feel one with David. My heart is joined with his in mutual love for God's precepts.

Why this is, I cannot say. I can only conjecture that because I have been, in the words of this command, pondering and thinking about and meditating on the Bible's commands for more than fifty years, somehow those "words of God" have gotten so deep into me that I *love* them.

I realize that to the world such a statement will be more than ridiculous. Nevertheless, love for God's commands is *in* me, inseparable from the deepest of who I am as a man.

It began early in my life with 1 Corinthians 13. I realized that it contained specific and practical qualities and attributes that I was meant to live by. From there I realized that the gospels were also full of specific and practical patterns of behavior I was told to *do*…*commanded* by Jesus to do.

From the words of Jesus, that love for its commands spread to encompass the whole Bible. As it did, the Fatherhood of God emerged. The

Father of Jesus was gradually revealed as the loving author and energizing life-giver of the commands, who commanded the commands and established his precepts out of his eternal Fathering *love* for his created family of sons and daughters.

I have been widening my study of the commands of the Bible ever since. The more I ponder and pray and meditate on the commands, the deeper grows my love for them. I know they reveal the character of God. In the commands I know I am discovering, one specific revealed piece at a time, the deepest essence of God's purposes for mankind, indeed for his whole universe in eternity. In this process, I am also discovering God's very nature.

With such eternal mysteries and truths embedded in the Bible's commands, how can I not love them!

This is therefore a very personal command for me. With all my heart I believe in David's example, and am determined to continue following it. Because my life is a testimony to its truth, I know that meditation on the commands leads to love for all God's precepts, which bears fruit in a deep and growing and expanding *knowing* of the heart of God.

I would not be misunderstood. I am as human as was David. The weak self-centered nature of my Old Adam does not like *being commanded* any more than anyone else likes it. While in this life, my fleshly nature will always be more or less at war with my love for God's commands. Obedience is often painful and unpleasant. I am probably no better at it—squirming and squawking with my heels dug in—than anyone.

None of us find obedience to hard commands easy. I make excuses and recite my own litany of defenses and justifications. I try to wriggle out of the demands of obedience, just like Saul did, just like Moses did when God first told him to go to Pharaoh. I too tell God why I shouldn't have to obey such-and-such a command.

But the deeper part of me still loves God's commands. I will continue to meditate on them, do my best to memorize them and ponder them, and ask for God's help to obey them. I must believe, and I am confident that, millimeter by millimeter, the Holy Spirit will continue to gain ground against the futile but persistent objections of my Old Man in the battle that selfish Adam is destined to lose in the end. *

God, I love your commands. Increase my love for them. Most of all help me to live and do them.

---

* For those interested, I have compiled a small booklet for my own use in "meditating on God's precepts." It is private and personal. I use it nearly every day and I make it inexpensively available to others who are on this same personal road and may find it useful. It is called, *A Book of Daily Memory Reminders.*

69. Humbly Listen and Heed Wisdom, Insight, Instruction, and Correction

If you call out for insight…you will find the knowledge of God. (Proverbs 3:3, 5)
Listen to advice and accept instruction, that you may gain wisdom. (Proverbs 19:20)
With humility comes wisdom. (Proverbs 11:2, NIV)
Blessed is one who heeds wisdom's instruction. (Proverbs 29:18, NIV)
Teaching is a light, and correction and instruction are the way to life. (Proverbs 6:23, NIV)

Seeking guidance and advice (#67) is Step One in what for many is a very difficult personal progression, but one which is intrinsic to growth. We move on now to Step Two. Both commands #'s 67 and 69 literally fill the book of *Proverbs*. In the latter of the two we here encounter the imperative *do:*

Humbly *heed* wisdom, *follow* advice…*grow* and *change* from the insight, instruction, and correction you receive.

The progression is twofold. Both halves are imperative.

- *Seek* advice and wisdom. (#67)
- Humbly listen and *heed* advice and wisdom. (#69)

While it is true that the world is full of disingenuous Job's counselors anxious to give everyone their two cents worth, not all unsought counsel is bad counsel. Christians are told to warn one another. Older Christians are told to teach the weak and immature. It may be that a sensitive and Spirit-receptive friend or older more experienced Christian has been led of God to speak a word of counsel to me. If I have a blind spot, I am obviously blind to it. How can I ask for counsel for something I am unaware of? Going to brothers and sisters in the faith with words of counsel is an integral component of the church's function in the New Testament.

My first response should be to assume that wisdom and Spirit-leading has motivated the encounter, and to receive the counsel I am given humbly and gratefully. If I've become the victim of an insensitive Job-counselor, there is plenty of time for God to reveal that later. Initially, my responsibility is to humbly *listen* and *heed*, assuming honest and God-led motives.

I have been in this situation many times as a would-be *counselor*, having approached various individuals with a sense of God's leading for a word I was meant to give them. The responses have been mixed. Though I may be convinced I am speaking on God's behalf, my counsel has been angrily rebuffed as often as it has been graciously accepted. It is probably true that on some of these occasions I have not been as led of the Spirit as I thought I was—God only knows. In my later years such situations are rare. These days I recognize the wisdom, on the other side of the coin, of waiting to be *asked* for counsel, not giving it unsolicited.

This command, however, pinpoints the humble response of the *counselee*. We have to examine our hearts with what is often painful humility. I have been on that side of the fence many times too.

How often have I replied with, "Oh, gosh…I hadn't seen that about myself. I am so grateful for your pointing it out. Thank you so much! I will get to work on it and take it to the Lord in prayer immediately."

It's not easy to respond to unsolicited advice so graciously! Even as I write, I am convicted by how *hard* it is to heed my own words!

Obeying these two commands (#'s 67 & 69) will be among the hardest, most humanly unnatural things we will face in our walks with God. However much we may sincerely want to grow, it is hard to prevent the defensive hackles rising on the backs of our necks when we see that expression and hear those ominous words, "I'd like to talk to you about something…"

Everything changes if I'm the one *seeking* guidance. I have become the initiator. There's an area of my life where I do *not* feel self-satisfied. I know my insight is incomplete. I do not know what to do or how to overcome a certain weakness. I want guidance and counsel and advice…even correction if it is needed.

I *want* to grow! I *want* to become more Christlike.

Therefore I seek out those whose maturity and wisdom in some particular area I respect and trust, whom I know will take my request seriously and prayerfully, who will desire my best, not simply give a knee-jerk response of what *they* might do themselves. I seek guidance from wise counselors who can put themselves in *my* shoes.

The exchange is now completely reversed. I am the initiator. "Could I talk to you seriously…I need your wisdom…I would like to ask for your counsel…"

The wise counselor will usually respond with some version of, "That is an important question. I will pray and ask for God's wisdom before replying." Quick responses invite opinion rather than God's perspective. This is one of the ways to differentiate between *wise counsel* and *opinionated counsel*—a waiting spirit of calm and prayer vs. a quick response of opinion and the Job's counselor's own experience.

Then comes the all-important second phase of the sequence. When wise, thoughtful, and prayerful counsel is given to me, how can I be anything but deeply grateful…then do my best to heed it? If I'm not prepared to heed it, I have no business asking for it.

Seek and *heed* represent the hinge-point connecting these two commands. They work in tandem. The seeker must also be a humble listener and *heeder*.

The questions for me then boil down to:

- Am I an open-minded, non-defensive, growth-desiring, weakness-rooting-out, seeker of change and betterment and maturity in my life?

- Am I humble enough to seek counsel from those wiser than myself?

- Am I humble enough to take whatever counsel I may be given to the Holy Spirit for confirmation, and then heed and follow what confirmation comes?

Commands #'s 67 and 69 are thus intrinsically linked. They form a progression that will lead those who live in their reality into ever-enlarging regions of growth, wisdom, and maturity.

Lord, give me the humility to be a seeker of wisdom from others, honesty to seek counsel only when I mean it, and wisdom within myself to see truth when it is given me and courage, humility, and wisdom act upon it.

70. Live by the Truth You Know

The word…is in your mouth and in your heart, so that you can do it. (Deuteronomy 30:14)

The progression of the first four commands of this series considered earlier now reaches its climax. Here the fruit of righteousness comes alive and bears the fruit of obedience.

I prayed for some time with a variety of commands related to this central imperative, attempting to uncover what seemed to be the composite essence of the idea. Corollaries are phrased in Scripture in many ways, perhaps best summed up in James 1:22, "Be doers of the word, and not hearers only." James was echoing his brother's summation to the Sermon on the Mount in Matthew 7:24, "Every one then who hears these words of mine and does them will be like a wise man…" The two sons of Mary and Joseph always speak with the same practical *do* in their words. This command embodies the heart of Jesus's sermon in Matthew 5-7 and James' entire epistle.

However, this is not merely a New Testament command. Solomon's proverbs are likewise full of this exhortation, worded in dozens of ways to fit specific circumstances. Its origin extends even further back, all the way to Moses.

This command embodies the full scope of the book of *Deuteronomy*. Its significance in our lives, therefore, is enormous.

Moses' farewell address to the Israelites, comes on the eve of his death. That he stood and spoke what we have in the full book of *Deuteronomy en toto* to the nation all at once is doubtful. We are told that Moses spoke it to all Israel (31:1), and later that he wrote down the law (31:9). The impact and purpose of Deuteronomy is not dependent on exactly *how* Moses' final long exhortation was delivered, or how and when it was written down.

No doubt by spoken, and obviously by *written* word, in great detail Moses reminds the people what they already know, or should know. It is a lengthy review of events and truths and commands.

Moses is reminding them of *the truth they know.*

At that time I said to you…
And we set out…
Then we turned…
And I commanded you…
And now give heed to the statutes and ordinances I teach you, and do them…
Know therefore…
You shall therefore lay up these words of mine…
These are the statutes and ordinances which you shall be careful to do…
You have seen all that the Lord did before your eyes…

Then he reaches his climax:

> *You know* (29:16)…*you have seen* (29:17)…*the things that are revealed belong to us…* (29:29)…*the word is…in your mouth and in your heart, so that you can do it. (30:14)*

In other words:

- You know the truth.
- You have seen the truth.
- The truth is in your heart.
- Therefore…*live by the truth you know.*

The thought patterns, fruit-of-the-Spirit behavior, relational attitudes, and habits of selflessness incumbent upon Christians dedicated to a life of practical daily discipleship isn't rocket science.

We mostly know the truth.

We *know* what is required of us.

Even most non-Christians, pretense Christians, and Christians in Name Only *know* the truth.

Moses' two-pronged choice-and-consequence command reverberates through the ages down into our own time. It confronts every man and woman on the planet every day:

> *This commandment which I command you this day is not too hard for you…the word is very near you; it is in your mouth and in your heart, so that you can do it. I set before you this day life and good, death and evil…therefore choose life.*
>
> Deuteronomy 30:14-15, 19

The truth is in our hearts.

We *know.*

There's nothing new and revolutionary in this book about the commands. There's no great mystery here. I'm not telling anyone reading these words anything they don't know.

It's just a question of who's going to do them.

It's more basic than that:

Am *I* going to do them? Am *I* going to live by the truth I know?

I will have to answer that question in the next five minutes…and every five minutes for the rest of my life.

Oh, Lord God, keep me from taking what I know so for granted that I don't pay enough attention to DO *the truth I know. Keep James' words and Jesus' and Moses' exhortations ever before me—Be a doer of the word…he who hears these words of mine and does them…the word is in your mouth and heart so that you can do it. Give me grace, humility, wisdom, and courage to obey these three wonderful mentors, one of them your own Son, of faithful obedience.*

SERIES EIGHT

RIGHTEOUSNESS

BEING A MAN OR WOMAN AFTER GOD'S HEART

Personalizing the Psalm-prayers

A man whose compass was pointed Godward

Today's church is probably more prayer conscious than at any time in its history. Prayer has become the genie-bottle of today's modern version of the Christian faith. The prayer urged upon today's Christian public is a prayer usually laced with blatant self-centeredness. It takes two forms—*special circumstance requests* and *blessings:*

Lord, I have this need, please answer my request.

Lord, pour out your blessings in my life.

The roots of such prayer grow in a shallow soil that contains little of the necessary maturity-additives called patience and self-denial. "What have you done for me lately, God?" is the mentality with which many approach prayer.

We're all well acquainted with the pray-and-God-will-perform-miracles-in-your-life scam. Watch the blessings pour forth. Watch God "work in your life." These are the promises made from a thousand pulpits and in a thousand books across the land.

Some years ago I found myself reflecting on the subject of prayer. If the prayer I heard around me seemed superficial, how deeply did *I* understand the nature of the kind of prayer that makes spirituality vital and dynamic? Is it possible that being a "man of prayer," or a "woman of prayer" may not in itself be as significant as we think. There are thousands of people who pray earnestly or, to use the term associated with prayer, *fervently.* Yet many of these, it must be admitted, also pray ineffectively.

Along with self and blessings centered prayer, there is another kind of prayer that those in church settings are familiar with. We're acquainted with those who pray loudly and at great length, confessing their sins over and over, then with passion and tears interceding for friends and families, for the sick and the unsaved, for cities and churches and nations, for new outpourings and prophetic utterances and revival.

Yet in this over-abundance of seemingly devout words, do we not sense something equally amiss as when listening to popular personalities equate answer to prayer with tangible worldly blessings?

Much prayer is also directed toward a perceived need for change in *others.* We pray for friends and family members, for cities and governments, for husbands and wives and children. We pray for the *whole world* to be changed. But we rarely pray that we *ourselves* will be changed.

What segment of Christendom emphasizes prayer more than Catholicism? Prayer undergirds the entire life of the Catholic. Learned prayers exists for every day, every situation, every possibility life can throw at you. But do rote prayers, memorized prayers, and rosary prayers penetrate eternity's purpose with any more power than the genie-bottle prayers of blessings-satiated evangelicalism? Meanwhile, pastors and priests the world over solemnly intone thousands of pulpit prayers weekly, read out of a prayer book or from a bland script typed up the night before, while their bored listeners struggle to keep from falling asleep.

What is the difference, I began asking myself, between *effective* prayer and *ineffective* prayer? I don't mean merely between prayers that are answered and prayers that aren't. We don't always know. We are not given the capacity to see when and how God answers prayer. But independent of *yes*-answers or *no*-answers or *non*-answers, might *effective prayer* exist on a more eternal level altogether?

Many try to set aside ten minutes or half an hour, or as much as an hour a day in prayer. Others use prayer lists to focus their thoughts and prayers toward people and situations of concern. During my college days, a group of concerned Christian students set up a twenty-four hour prayer vigil in our church so that someone would always be praying for our witness on campus. I've attended men's meetings and study groups, and personally spearheaded a group of men dedicated to the purpose of praying for our church and its leaders. I have participated in early morning men's prayer meetings where the commitment was high to "impact our city for God." Yet eventually the numbers wane. Bloodshot sleepy eyes replace enthusiastic vision.

All commitments and visions, like new year's resolutions, go through cycles of high vision and low vision. When one is young, one assumes vision will last forever. But it seldom does. Not even the vision to pray effectively lasts throughout a lifetime. So how do we tap into *eternal* purposes in our prayer life, so that we are not subject to the ebbs and flows of ever-repeating resolve and discouragement?

Eventually I realized that *time* and *energy* in prayer are no more reliable measuring devices than visible answers for gauging eternal effectiveness. My ultimate conclusion was this: It is not praying *itself* that determines significance. Rather, *it is what kinds of prayers we pray.*

The most effective and eternal prayers are prayers of a certain sort. All prayers are not equal. Being a man or woman of prayer means little if one is praying prayers that point in different directions than does the ultimate compass of God's purpose. Having one's prayers answered means little if one's prayers (and therefore the answers we seek) are temporal. Laboring in prayer means little if that labor is focused only on the immediacy of need, or the immediacy of emotion, rather than permanency of spiritual character.

We pray for prosperity, for healing, for ease, for guidance, for happiness, for insight into the Scriptures. We pray for everything except to be people of a certain sort. That is something no genie bottle of prayer, no rosary, no blessings-cult can accomplish, but only broken alabaster bottles of sacrificial nard. Who is emphasizing deep-cutting surgical prayer for Christlikeness of character within our own hearts?

One man who emphasized it was the ancient king of Israel.

How can we penetrate the veil of effective and eternal prayer like David did? How can we insure that the quiet and invisible breathings from our lips to him who lives within us and gives us life contain power to carry into eternity?

We don't know a great deal about the specifics of how the Lord prayed other than that his whole life exemplified the phrase Paul later used to reveal how prayer was to undergird the life of faith when he said, *Pray without ceasing*. In the three towering examples of the Lord's prayer, the John 17 prayer, and the Gethsemane prayer, perhaps we find all we need to know about how to put into practice Paul's *unceasing* command.

However, in my quest to understand prayer more deeply I have wanted to know how men who walked with God prayed. As I scanned the biblical gallery of faith, one individual rose above the rest. That man was David. He was an individual that the Bible describes as "a man after God's own heart."

What a remarkable thing to say of a mortal being! God truly *loved* David.

In many ways, David's heart, both toward himself and toward God, offers one of the clearest scriptural windows into the mystery of prayer. David recorded hundreds of his own deeply personal and intimate prayers. We know *exactly* what he said to God, and often what God said to him in return. We know about the varied moods of his heart that stirred him to prayer. We know how he prayed when he was spiritually high. We know how he prayed when he was discouraged and despondent. We know of his immature and selfish prayers. We know of his frantic and desperate prayers. We know of his all too-frequent prayers that God would rain down vengeance on his enemies—the unfortunate dark side of his prayer life that is also intrinsic to David's story. We know of his humble and sacrificial prayers. We know how he prayed when he was afraid. We know of his keen awareness of his own sin and weakness. We know of the guilt he felt. We know of his joys, his despairs, his triumphs in prayer. We can all quote his soaring hymns of prayer. We are comforted by his peaceful idylls of quiet happy prayer.

We know how he prayed in *all* these different states of mind. We know because he wrote his prayers down.

We know *how* David prayed, *what* he prayed for, and what he was *thinking* and *feeling* as he prayed. If we can look beyond the *avenge-me-God* prayers, in David's prayer-walk we discover a model for effective prayer that probes the purposes of eternity.

Thus I found myself praying that God would give me a heart like his.*

---

* The life of David, including his prayer life, is explored in more depth in Volume 2 of *The Eyewitness Old Testament.*

David's Major Psalm Prayers

I hope this list may be fruitful to some. Obviously I have not included all these as separate commands. I have tried to find their unifying themes and phrase the commands of this series in ways that draw David's entire prayer life up into them.

Psalm 5
Lead me in your righteousness.

Psalm 17
Hide me in the shadow of your wings.

Psalm 19
Let the words of my mouth and the meditations of my heart be acceptable in your sight.

Psalm 25
Make me know your ways, teach me your paths. Lead me in your truth and teach me.
Turn to me and be gracious.
Relieve the troubles of my heart.
Forgive my sins.
Guard my life.
May integrity and uprightness preserve me.

Psalm 26
Prove me and try me, test my heart and mind.

Psalm 27
Teach me your ways and lead me on a level path

Psalm 43
Send out your light and truth, let them lead me.

Psalm 51
Wash me thoroughly, cleanse me from my sin.
Teach me wisdom in my secret heart.
Purge me.
Fill me with joy and gladness.
Create in me a clean heart, and put a new and right spirit within me.
Restore to me the joy of your salvation.

Psalm 61
Let me dwell in your tent forever.

Psalm 71
Be to me a rock of refuge, a strong fortress.

Psalm 86
Teach me your way that I may walk in truth.
Unite my heart.

Psalm 90
Teach us to number our days that we may get a heart of wisdom.
Let your work be manifest.

Psalm 119
May my way be steadfast in keeping your statutes.
Do not let me wander from your commandments.
Teach me your statutes.
Open my eyes that I may behold wondrous things in your law.
Teach me your statutes.
Make me understand the way of your precepts.
Strengthen me according to your word.
Put false ways far from me.
Graciously teach me your law.
Enlarge my understanding.
Teach me the way of your statutes.
Give me understanding that I may keep your law and observe it with my whole heart.
Lead me in the path of your commandments.
Incline my heart to your testimonies.
Turn my eyes from vanities.
Teach me your statutes.
Teach me good judgment and knowledge.
Teach me your statutes.
May my heart be blameless in your statutes.
Teach me your ordinances.
Uphold me according to your promises.
Teach me your statutes.
Give me understanding that I may learn your testimonies.
Keep my steps steady according to your promise.
Let no iniquity get dominion over me.
Give me understanding that I may live.
Give me understanding according to your word.

Psalm 139
Search my heart and know my thoughts.
See if there be any wicked way in me.
Lead me in the way everlasting.

Psalm 143
Teach me the way I should go.
Teach me to do your will.

Series Eight

Righteousness

71. *Pray with David:* Search me, O God, and know my heart.
Try me and know my thoughts. See if there be any wicked way in me,
and lead me in the way everlasting. (139:23-24).

72. Incline my heart to your commands (119:36).

73. Teach me your ways (25:4-5, 86:11, 119:12).

74. Give me understanding and wisdom in my secret heart (51:6, 119:34).

75. Help me not to stray from your commands (119:10).

76. Give me wise judgment and knowledge (119:66).

77. Protect me from falsehood, keep my steps steady,
let no sin get dominion over me (119:29, 119:133).

78. Create in me a clean heart and put a right spirit within me (51:10).

79. Guard my life—may integrity and uprightness preserve me (25:20-21).

80. Guide me, lead me, and help me walk in truth (25:5, 86 11).

71. *Pray with David:*

Search me, O God, and know my heart. Try me and know my thoughts. See if there be any wicked way in me, and lead me in the way everlasting.

Search me, O God, and know my heart. Try me and know my thoughts.
And see if there be any wicked way in me, and lead me in the way everlasting.
(Psalm 139:23-24)

Psalm 139, by any standards, ranks as one of the seminal mountain top passages of Scripture, taking its place with Genesis 1-2, Exodus 20:3-17, Deuteronomy 6-8, Psalm 23, Proverbs 3:1-18, 1 Corinthians 13, Philippians 4:8, and of course Matthew 5-7, John 13-17, the parables of the Prodigal Son and Good Samaritan and much in the gospels.

Climaxing this incomparably beautiful anthem of praise to God's all-knowing love for his expansive universe, and for every tiniest part of each of our created beings, David was clearly swept into the loftiest regions of inspiration when he set down for all time the ultimate prayer of humanity.

It is the prayer God created every man, woman, and child who ever lived and who will ever live to be made capable of praying. It is the prayer that embodies the eternal purpose of life. It is the prayer of God's North. It is the prayer onto which the Godward compass of personhood locks whenever one prays, "God, make me your man or woman."

It is *the* prayer of all prayers.

Notwithstanding David's unfortunate tangential rant in verses 19-22, Psalm 139 is rich beyond measure. Even these four parenthetical verses remind us that David was human after all. In a way it makes the towering prayer that follows the brief diatribe all the more precious in that it was prayed in the midst of a very active and often conflicted sin-nature.

I love the Lord's Gethsemane prayer and try to be fed by it daily. But David was just like me! He was a weak and frail man. This outpouring from the deepest regions of his heart after he has vented his venom against his enemies brings this ultimate prayer close into the reality of life…into the reality of *my* life.

This entire psalm could provide food for many days of rich devotional contemplation. I admit to a certain envy of artists and songwriters and musicians whose gifts in the creative arts are beyond my imagining. I've only written one song in my life. It was simply entitled "Psalm 139." Earlier I called Psalm 119 "the loftiest window into David's heart for God." Alongside it sits the equally translucent portal into eternity of Psalm 139. The only line from that song I now even remember clearly was, "This is too glorious, too wonderful to believe—I can never be lost to your Spirit."

This central truth captures the essence of David's insight as is so creatively and passionately conveyed in this psalm:

God is everywhere! He knew us before we were born. He knit us together in our mothers' wombs. He is with us when we are awake, when we sleep, in light, in darkness. He is in heaven, he is in hell. He has been with us in our spiritual journeys toward him from their inception. He birthed those journeys himself! Of course he is with us and beside us and in us all the way through them.

> He sees us when we take our first steps toward Him, and notes the very beginnings of our heart's longings for Him. In the parable, the father was watching and saw the prodigal as he came painfully and wearily homeward, and when he saw him he ran to meet him. [31]

God *knows* us more intimately than we know ourselves. There are no secrets. Far from finding this a fearsome thing, David rejoices in it. He *loves* the fact that God knows his innermost heart.

How precious to me are thy thoughts, O God! (Psalm 139:17).

Then David takes an unprecedented step into regions we have no record of any man having gone before. He *invites* his all-knowing, all-seeing, eternal creator-Father *all* the way inside, and asks him, almost pleads with him, to give him, David, the same intimate self-knowledge of himself that God has. He asks for God's eyes into himself.

He does not resist the secret knowledge of himself. He courts it, hungers for it. With all his heart he begs God to scour his innermost self, shining in the light of righteousness, illuminating, revealing, healing, cleansing, perfecting.

It is simply the most remarkable righteousness-hungering prayer of a mortal man in Scripture. These words poured out of the heart of David as a single prayer. It remains for us to pray David's words as we follow his footsteps into these hallowed regions of intimacy.

I am not alone in deriving inspiration from Psalm 139. The lyrics of many songs have used it. The words of one of my favorite hymns by J. Edwin Orr, I find almost as powerful a prayer as those by David's own hand. Combining hints of Gethsemane and John 15 with a haunting old Maori melody from New Zealand, it brings prayerful chills every time I quietly sing it.

Cleanse me, O God, and know my heart today.
Try me, O Savior, know my thoughts I pray.
See if there be some wicked way in me,
Cleanse me from every sin and set me free.

Lord, take my life and make it wholly thine;
Fill my poor heart with thy great love divine.
Take all my will, my passion, self, and pride;
I now surrender, Lord—in me abide.

[31] J.R. Miller, *Help for the Day,* London, Andrew Melrose, date unknown, p. 141.

With David, Lord, I pray: Search me, O God, and know my heart. Try me and know my thoughts. See if there be any wicked way in me, and lead me in the way everlasting.

72. *Pray with David:*

Incline My Heart to Your Commands

Direct me in the path of your commands. (Psalm 119:35, NIV)
Incline my heart to thy testimonies. (119:36, RSV)
Turn my heart toward your statutes. (119:36, NIV)

The selections of this series are not technically phrased as commands, but prayers. This was one of the many conundrums in my completing this final installment of the commands trilogy. I knew the prayers of David were vitally important. However, they were not directly enjoined upon us as were the commands of Moses (*Choose life*) or Solomon (*Get wisdom*). David's prayers emerged out of his private outpourings to God. The *Psalms* represent his prayer diary.

As I prayerfully worked on this book, gradually the great truth came alive that God's principles, even his commands, are not only revealed by direct "command," as important as that is. They are also quickened into our lives by *example*, especially by the examples of our Godly forebears.

Thus, when we read, "Noah walked with God," we take the example of his life as challenging us also with the incumbency, which I take as a command, to "walk with God." Neither are we commanded in so many words, "Model your lives after Jesus' example," but I take that as a given. I thus treat it as one of the Bible's most fundamental commands.

I have often reflected on what it would be like had Jesus kept a prayer journal. David did. David's prayer life has been preserved for us, not only so that songs can be written about it, but so that we can *follow* his example. We are *meant* to follow his example. We are *expected* to follow his example. What a gift from God to illuminate the life of intimate prayer. In the psalms we have David's spiritual autobiography.

This is therefore the doorway into understanding David himself, and the prayers he prayed. It is not merely the starting point for understanding David, it is the starting point for understanding ourselves. We cannot idealize David. Nor can we idealize ourselves. We come to prayer as imperfect, weak, frail, selfish creatures. We come to prayer to be made *better* creatures, asking God to make of us what we, in our weakness, cannot make of ourselves. We come as products of sin, asking to be made righteous.

The recognition of who and what we are is the soil in which effective, eternal prayer sends down its roots both into our own personhood and into the heart of God. In praying to have hearts like David's, we recognize the changeableness and frailty of his humanity, and our own. We recognize that even in prayer, we will by our very natures be vacillating, changeable men and women of mixed and self-centered motives. We cannot prevent sin intruding, even into the most holy thing in life that we do.

All his life David was torn, as are we, in two directions—toward righteousness, and toward the weakness of his own manhood. In that weakness, he gave himself to his maker. Thus, we recognize the high gift David gave to God in prayer. It is our opportunity to give it also. We have that opportunity every day.

David is Everyman and Every Woman. He is you and me. In David we see the exact image Paul spoke of in Romans 7, a man constantly wrestling with the two sides of his nature. Paul's words pinpoint David's character with precision: "In my inner being I delight in God's law; but I see another law at work in the members of my body…making me a prisoner of the law of sin." (Romans 7:22-23, NIV) These words might have been written by David himself.

We all understand. It is the plight of our humanity. Even after entering into relationship with God, we continue to vacillate between the two directionalities of the inner human compass—toward the bright Sun of righteousness and toward the black hole of sin.

In these revelations, I saw that David's prayers had indeed become *commands* upon my life. All that remained was to find an appropriate phrasing consistent with that imperative, then to distill and combine his *many* wonderful prayers in ways that convey the overspreading themes that informed David's prayer life with such exampling power.

This second "prayer-command" is one David wrote and expressed throughout his psalms in many ways.

The terms *precepts, statutes,* and *ordinances* are used literally hundreds of times by David in the psalms. I often treat them as essentially synonymous with "law" and "command." Taken together, if we can escape the preconceptions of their old-fashioned flavor, they widen and expand those ideas in enriching ways.

As I peruse Psalm 119, for example, I derive from these words more than mere "law." David is asking not merely to be reminded of the *law,* the Ten Commandments, the do's and don'ts of *Leviticus.* He is not merely asking God to *remind* him at all. This prayer is far larger in scope.

David is asking and inviting God to instruct him, fill him, enlighten and deepen and teach him in *all* his ways. He is praying to be filled with God's perspectives, priorities, purposes. He wants to see through God's eyes.

More than that—he wants to see into God himself! He wants to know God's heart! He wants to know everything about God!

I love these David prayers! I want exactly the same thing. I want to know everything about God!

David is insightful and wise enough to know that all these priorities, perspectives, purposes, and insights into God's character and being, revelations into the very heart of our Creator-Father, are revealed, if we probe them to their origin, in the statutes, precepts, ordinances, and commands God has given.

I am fond of alliterative links between words as occasionally representing more than gimmicks of syntax. In the word "precept," I discern more than rules and commands. I find God's *precepts* offering a window into the higher realms of his *perspectives, priorities,* and eternal *purposes.* Likewise, his *ordinances* are not mere regulatory rules and laws, they are defining *objectives* that reveal the whole scope of God's eternal intent for his universe.

The word *incline,* too, is full of meaning. It is a hugely important foundational idea in prayer—the image of a child leaning against his father. It represents the request for the Spirit of God to turn our mind and thoughts and heart and attention to him. We are so constantly and completely distractible away from the deep and important priorities in life. It is one of my greatest frustrations. I simply *forget* God, *forget* the commands, *forget* to pray. I *want* to focus my thoughts on God, prayer, and the commands...but I forget.

This wonderful prayer is a request to God to help with forgetfulness.

I know, Lord, that I will get caught up in today's events, urgencies, thoughts, conversations, and frustrations. I want to think of you, but I know my own humanity. I know I will forget. So I ask you to do what I cannot seem to do on my own. Prick my brain and heart. Spark my remembrance toward you and what you would have me think and do. Help me remember to pray with David: Turn my thoughts toward you, toward the commands, toward the prayers of David. Incline my heart toward you. Lean my heart toward you. Give me eternal vision through your precepts to see your high perspectives, priorities, and purposes. Give me vision to see into your heart, and to know you as my loving Father. Incline my heart with remembrance toward your Fatherhood. Incline my entire life direction toward you.

73. *Pray with David:*

Teach me your ways

Make me to know thy ways, O Lord; teach me thy paths.
Lead me in thy truth, and teach me. (Psalm 25:4-5)
Teach me thy way, O Lord, that I may walk in thy truth. (Psalm 86:11)

In isolating the prayers David prayed in *Psalms,* I am struck with one phrase he uses over and over: *Teach me your ways.* Psalm 119 is full of this prayer. The dual nature of the prayer is not immediately apparent but grows in importance the more we reflect on it.

Asking to be taught has consequence. It implies something from us. Teaching is not passive. It implies study and learning on *my* part. I cannot expect God to teach me by osmosis. *Learning,* the flip side of *teaching,* is hard work.

Delving beneath the surface, we uncover a fascinating insight. From the parallel expression through Psalm 119 and elsewhere—*I love your law...I love your statutes and precepts*—it is clear that David not only possessed the law, he was intimately familiar with it. David *knew* the law. He had done his homework. He had *learned* the law.

He was not praying merely to be taught the law. His prayer reached higher. This prayer stretched toward eternity. It is the word 'ways" that reveal the heart of this prayer.

I love your law…now teach me your *ways,* your *purposes,* your *methods…*teach me what you want to accomplish…*in me.*

David is praying what few people pray—for God to reveal *how* he works, what are his ways and means, his methods and objectives in human life…in the human heart. Where is God taking his created universe, and his created men and women? What is he trying to accomplish in them?

All too often prayer reveals what *we* think God should do, or what we *want* God to do. We impose the purposes *we* want onto God, then pray accordingly. We are praying according to *our* ways and means and desires and objectives, with requests like:

Bless this enterprise and make it prosper.
Help my friend come to know you.
Make provision for my need.
Help me get a better job.
I pray for an opportunity to witness to my neighbor.
I pray for the peace of Jerusalem.
I pray for your Church.
I pray that abortion will be abolished.
I pray for the conservative candidate to win.
I pray for the liberal candidate to win.
I pray for healing for my son's illness.
I pray for revival in our church, city, and nation.
I pray for the soon return of Jesus.
I pray for healing.

But do all these dovetail with *God's* ways and means and purposes? Some probably do, but our perceptions of *how* and *when* we want God to answer these prayers also may not always dovetail with his ultimate purposes. David, too, prayed many *David*-motivated-prayers.

Take vengeance on my enemies.
Bring down those who seek to do me harm.
Vindicate me.

He was occasionally no better at discerning God's eternal purposes than we are. Yet in the midst of his self-motivated prayers, he continued to pray, *Teach me your ways…*not my ways but *your* ways.

Teach me *your* ways. Teach me what *you* want me to pray for above all the temporal and selfish things *I* want to pray for.

And God *did* teach David his eternal purpose, that we become his sons and daughters who are conformed to the image of Christ.

The high prayer that coincides with God's purpose, therefore, is:

Humble me, break me, and work within me the selfless heart of an obedient child.

As we have seen, in his better moments, *this* was the deep prayer of David's heart. This prayer empowers all other prayer.

David was not a paragon of virtue. He cannot be considered a role model of behavior, or even of wisdom and maturity of character. He was, however, the prototypical biblical *role model of prayer.* He continually set and reset his internal spiritual compass by praying over and over, "Teach me *your* ways."

A deeper theme runs through the *Psalms* which not even David's rants of vengeance can drown out—that is the music of the divine Fatherhood. For all his ups and downs and human flaws, this music David heard.

In his quieter moments, when the fiery tempest within him stilled, when he was alone perhaps strumming his harp, hearkening back to his youth as a shepherd boy on the hillside with the sheep, the divine Fatherhood found entrance into his heart and mind and soul. It was a different image of God than the Israelites had known. Something new in the divine revelation was coming to life.

To put it into today's vernacular, in those quiet moments of solitude, David was discovering what it meant to have a "personal relationship" with his Father-God.

When one reads history through the spiritual lens of God's eons-long unfolding attempt to infuse his Fatherhood into his creation, and to progressively reveal himself as *Father* to the men and women who are his highest creation, David stands at a unique and pivotal crossroads. He has one foot firmly planted in man's primitive and tribal past, even as with the other he is striving to become an eternal son.

He is a man in the process of *becoming*.

It is toward *this* purpose that David's heart drove him when he turned to God.

He did not know of Jesus as we do. The term "Christlikeness of character" was unfamiliar to him. Yet none the less was righteousness David's heart's desire. He wanted to be an obedient son.

God's answer to his prayer, *Teach me your ways*, informed and breathed life into David's perspective about everything—most of all about himself and the man he was. He knew that it was *inside his own being* where God's most significant ways and means in the universe were being wrought.

God's purpose was sonship. As he prayed and listened, as he stumbled and then rose again and again from his prayer-knees, David was slowly in the process of discovering it.

With David, Lord, I pray: Make me to know thy ways, O Lord; teach me thy paths. Lead me in thy truth, and teach me. Teach me thy ways, O Lord, that I may walk in thy truth.

74. *Pray with David:*

Give Me Understanding and Wisdom in My Secret Heart

"Teach me wisdom in my secret heart." (Psalms 51:6)

This prayer has perplexed me. Why pray for wisdom in secret…in his *secret* heart?

It seems that wisdom ought to be made public. Everyone certainly needs it. The lasting legacy David's son Solomon has left the world is a practical and public exposition of how wisdom is lived in life—what are the attributes of wisdom, what are the fruits of wisdom.

What, then, is the reason David worded his prayer thus?

As I pondered it, I began to see that this prayer is not as much about wisdom, as for what it reveals about David himself.

David was a very public man—in the national spotlight all through his tumultuous life. He is the biblical character about which we know more than anyone but Jesus. In some ways we know even more about David's inner thoughts and the events of his life than we do those of Jesus. David is the last person about whom we would use the phrase, "a private man."

Yet David nurtures a secret in his heart.

It is a good secret, a precious secret. It is a *secret* because he knows that few others—if any—would be capable of understanding it.

In hindsight as God's revelation has increased, *we* understand about that inner chamber within the heart where David cherishes his secret. But as noted in the previous command, something new was being birthed in David's life that primitive humankind had not known before. As public as was his life, in this one thing David stood alone.

The secret was that he shared the innermost places of his being with Another. He lived in secret intimacy with the very One the Israelites worshiped as "the Lord" (YHWH) or "God" (Elohim). But David was learning to live with him in the secret places of his heart as a *Father*, and even perhaps in faintly foreshadowing ways, as a *friend*.

This secret region in David's heart was shared only with his Father-God. When David prayed, he was praying both *out of* his secret place but also to the one who dwelt *in* that place with him. David's life foreshadows the Spirit-life of the Christian who lives with the Spirit of Christ dwelling alive in his or her heart.

Therefore David prays to be given wisdom, knowing that God's revelation *to him*—into his deepest heart—can only be known in secret because no one else dwells there with him but God.

In discussing the new name of Revelation 2:1, George MacDonald probes this same truth. "The true name," he writes, "is one which expresses the character, the nature, the being, the *meaning* of the person who bears it…Who can give a man this, his own name? God alone. For no one but God sees what the man is, or even, seeing what he is, could express in a name-word the sum and harmony of what he sees…It is the blossom, the perfection, the completion, that determines the name."

MacDonald is probing deep into the relationship God desires with each man, woman, and child of his creation—a completely unique relationship between Father and child shared by no one else. It is thus, in a sense, a "secret" relationship—characterized by that same secret place in the heart David knew so well. The secrets of that relationship are so unique that God is able to reveal aspects of his infinite divine nature to each one of us that are known to none other.

MacDonald continues:

> With every man he has a secret…In every man there is…an inner chamber of peculiar life into which God only can enter…
>
> Each of us is a distinct flower or tree in the spiritual garden of God,—precious, each for his own sake, in the eyes of him who is even now making us,—each of us watered and shone upon and filled with life, for the sake of his flower, his completed being, which will blossom out of him at last to the glory and pleasure of the great gardener. For each has within him a secret of the Divinity; each is growing towards the revelation of that secret to himself…Every moment that he is true to his true self, some new shine of the white stone breaks on his inward eye, some fresh channel is opened upward for the coming glory of the flower, the conscious offering of his whole being in beauty to the Maker. [32]

It is this *new shine* breaking on his inward eye, some new *secret of the Divinity,* that David is praying for when he prays, *Teach me wisdom in my secret heart.*

That same inner private chamber exists within us all, a secret place where you and I each dwell alone together with God. As we await the revelation of the white stones upon which our own new names will be written, we can thus pray David's prayer with him.

With David, Lord, I pray: Teach me wisdom in my secret heart.

75. *Pray with David:*

Help Me Not to Stray from Your Commands

With my whole heart I seek thee; let me not wander from thy commandments. (Psalm 119:10)

I have extolled David's prayer life in glowing terms. However, I would not have us read David's life more than Paul's or anyone's through rose-colored glasses of idealism. Paul and David were both very human men whose weaknesses and immaturities are as glaring in the pages of Scripture as is their wisdom. That's what makes them such wonderful vehicles for God's truth—they are just like us. Yet they are also *more* than us! In their humanity

[32] George MacDonald, *Unspoken Sermons, First Series,* "The New Name."

they rose above their humanity to touch the fringes of God's garment, and write about the high truths of eternity.

We now come to one of David's prayers that, to my thinking, exposes his human weakness as much as it illuminates God's purposes. David's prayer here—*Let me not wander from your commandments*—is misdirected. He is praying for God to do for him what only he can do for himself. In a sense, he is praying to be excused from the hard work and personal decision of obedience.

It is an example of the *sanctification-by-fiat* false doctrine 2,500 years before Calvin and others popularized it into the lexicon of evangelical orthodoxy. It is a disingenuous prayer. David's inner waffling is revealed in Psalm 119:11: *I do not stray from thy precepts.* Yet his whole life is an example of oscillating back and forth between obedience and disobedience. Exactly the same thing could be said about you and me. I'm not condemning David, only saying, let's be honest when we pray, not make grandiose proclamations of our obedience when our lives don't measure up.

In praying *Let me not...* David is asking for God to do it *for* him, in the same way that millions of wrongly-taught Christians think that Jesus accomplishes salvation *for* them and that they don't have to do much of anything in the bargain.

The Spirit of God draws, helps, energizes, goads, strengthens, illuminates, and empowers. But righteousness is not something the Spirit can accomplish *for* me, *for* you, or *for* David, no matter how much we pray for it. Obedience to God's commands is not the result of prayer, it is the result of obedience to God's commands.

The idea contained within David's prayer of Psalm 119:10, and my slight rewording of it here, is a worthy prayer. Asking for God's help—*Help me not to stray*—is much different from *Let me not stray.* But if we pray correctly by asking for God's help, let us not forget whose court the ball is in. Once we rise from prayer, even with God's help...the ball is in my court not his.

God cannot, in his very nature, make us do anything, nor does it align with his eternal purposes, to *make* us, by fiat, obey his commands. Doing what God has told us is not a matter of prayer, but of doing what God has told us. We ask for his help to obey. Then we obey.

As David has phrased his prayer, it is not a prayer God can answer. He has prayed, *Teach me your ways,* but in his *let-me-not* prayer from Psalm 119:10, David reveals that his understanding of God's ways, and his understanding of the prayers God can answer—though not as glaring as when praying for vengeance on his enemies—is still flawed. What would a prayer, *Let me obey your commands* even mean?

We can legitimately pray:

Help me obey your commands.
Help me remember your commands.
Help me not to stray from your commands.
Remind me not to stray from your commands.
Help me not to want to stray from your commands.
Give me strength and courage not to stray from your commands.

Sting my conscience when I am about to stray from your commands. Humble me by circumstances so that I won't stray from your commands.

But if we're not prepared to do our part, God can't answer, "Let me not…make it so that I won't…"

Prayer is a two-way street. Obedience is the other half of the equation.

With David, Lord, I pray: With my whole heart I seek thee; let me not wander from thy commandments. And now, Lord, help me do my obedient part not to stray from your commands, but to obey them.

76. *Pray with David:*

Give Me Wise Judgment and Knowledge

Teach me good judgment and knowledge. (Psalm 119:66)

This like the previous is a complicated prayer. It is a good and right prayer to pray. It is a prayer God can and does answer. It is a prayer God *wants* us to pray. James tells us to pray for wisdom. In praying this prayer, we are following David's and Solomon's examples, and also obeying the very wise counsel of the Lord's brother. And truly, only God gives the highest wisdom. So this is a doubly prudent prayer to continue praying all our lives. God can and does give wisdom, wise judgment, and knowledge to those who hunger for them. He is the *only* source from which they come.

But neither does this prayer contain a magic formula. Solomon and David both prayed it, and meant it sincerely. To an extent God answered their prayers. We see knowledge and wisdom evidenced in their lives. Equally glaring, however, are the examples of horrendously *bad* judgment.

Like everything in God's economy, we have to hold up our end. If we pray for wisdom, and God gives it, we have to live and obey and walk in that wisdom, or it will count for naught…and may be taken away in the end. The lasting legacy from David's deathbed is not of a saint of God who has absorbed God's loving and forgiving nature into the secret place of his heart, but of a still vengeful man. As he was dying, he summoned Solomon and gave him a summary of the Deuteronomic charge:

"Be strong and show yourself a man, and keep the charge of the Lord your God, walking in his ways and keeping his statutes, his commandments, his ordinances, and his testimonies, as it is written in the law of Moses, that you may prosper in all that you do…"

A wonderful farewell to give a son.

But then David goes on to recite a litany of grievances against his enemies, finally telling Solomon to kill the Benjamite Shimei for cursing him. (1 Kings 2) Then David dies, with revenge on his lips.

We have to internalize and pray these wonderful prayers with perspective, learning from both sides of David's example. If I pray for wise judgment, I need to exercise wise judgment when God gives it. What a mightier example of the Christ whom he foreshadowed would he have left the world had David said to Solomon, "Go to the Benjamite Shimei and tell him I have forgiven him for cursing me." That would not have been merely wise judgment, but Christlike judgment. We extoll Solomon's "wise judgment" in the matter of the two women claiming the same baby. But where was his wise judgment when he took a second wife…then a tenth…then a hundredth, and allowed them to bring their idols and customs into the palace?

Wise judgment and knowledge are still subject to the Choice and Consequence Code.

The knowledge half of the prayer is equally intriguing. I'm not sure pure "knowledge," as such, is something we can pray for and expect God to give us. He won't implant facts into our brain surgically. Knowledge is something we have to seek and study to acquire. Gaining pure *knowledge* (history, mathematics, science, etc.) is hard work.

I think David means something else here. To my ears, this is another phrasing of his desire to know *God*. That's the *knowledge* he wants most of all. It's not facts he wants. The doctrines and opinions and ideas of men's religions are full of purported *facts* about God—many of them wrong. David's prayers were pointed in another direction—toward God…not just to know *about* him, but to know God *himself*.

To *know God* was the passion of his heart. When he prayed, *Give me knowledge,* I believe he was praying, *Open to me your heart, your being, your nature, your character, your purposes.*

Without even knowing it, the cry of David's heart was, *May I know you as Father. Give me knowledge of your Fatherhood.*

When we speak of the Spirit praying for us what we do not even know to pray, I think we see marvelous examples of it in David's life. It may be that his judgment did not always line up with his prayers. He was a man stepping but falteringly into his sonship.

But the deepest cry of David's heart never wavered. That deep heart's cry was to *know God.*

With David, Lord, I pray: Teach me good judgment and knowledge. And when you give them, give me courage, insight, humility, and wisdom to walk obediently in them.

77. *Pray with David:*

Protect Me *from* Falsehood, Keep My Steps Steady, Let No Sin Get Dominion Over Me

Put false ways far from me…Keep steady my steps according to thy promise, and let no iniquity get dominion over me. (Psalm 119:29, 133)

Prayers for God's protection have long perplexed me. The more we prayed for protection over our family, the more relentless became the enemy's attacks. In my doubting moments, I almost felt like praying for protection was a self-fulfilling prophecy that *invited* the attacks. Many times I wondered if it would have been better not to pray for protection at all. I know that is not the way God works, but it is the way Satan works. I admit that the confusion remains.

Yet all God's notable men and women in the Bible prayed for protection. That God will watch over and protect his people is one of his most persistent promises. That I have not seen some of the visible evidence of it that in my humanity I expected to see obviously does not invalidate the prayer. I know it only reveals how poor is my eternal eyesight, and that I am not yet capable, in this particularly confusing area in life, of seeing through God's eyes.

But though I do not fully understand how the prayer and God's promise of protection (Psalm 91) are interlinked, or what, if any, is the cause and effect between them, I am yet convinced that we are to pray. Whether we see results or not, we are to continue praying for protection, and clinging to the promise that God protects his own.

This threefold prayer, combining two verses from Psalm 119 as I have phrased it, is an intricately multi-layered combination of prayer-ideas.

Does God keep sin, temptation, falsehood, and evil *out*? Does he build a fence around us so that Satan cannot touch us?

He didn't with Job. Nor has that ever seemed God's way. So what kind of protection does God give? It's a complex question, for which no pat answers help.

In this prayer, as in many of his prayers, David's focus is internal, not external. His first prayer is not that God would keep falsehood at bay. He is not praying for a hedge of protection *around* him. Rather, he is praying that he *himself* would not be false.

Protect *me* from falsehood. Help me not to embrace falsehood, succumb to falsehood, and thus to *become* false. It is a wonderful prayer balancing God's part and David's:

Protect me and give me strength and wisdom not to be false. Keep falsehood from getting inside me and taking hold within me.

This takes the prayer for protection to a higher level.

The second phase of the prayer is an acknowledgment of David's weakness. This is one of David's supreme character strengths, one of many things that make him an example to us—his recognition of his weakness. His *strength* was his awareness of his *weakness*, exactly as Paul articulated in 2 Corinthians 12:9.

So David now prays:

Lord, I want to be kept from falsehood. Protect me from falsehood. But I am weak. My steps may falter. I know I will stumble. I need your help. Therefore, steady my steps. Be with me. Walk with me. Let me hold to you at my side when the path is rocky and uneven and treacherous.

Finally, the two prayers lead yet deeper into the depths of David's heart. David desperately wants to walk in the reality of the first of the three prayers. He hates his sin nature. He wants so badly to be God's man. Out of that deep reservoir of hungry longing for righteousness, the powerful prayer bursts from his lips:

Let no sin get dominion over me.

I find this an incredibly poignant prayer. It represents David's deepest heart-yearning. However, the simple yet suggestive word *Let* has crept back in, subtly shifting to God's shoulders whether sin will or will not get dominion over him.

It's that same ambivalent escape hatch that reveals David's conflicted nature we observe sprinkled through *Psalms* in the midst of the most probing prayers of the Bible. Even David's prayers are conflicted and occasionally indecisive. Whether it's blaming his enemies, succumbing to his weakness, or praying an equivocal prayer, too often he leaves himself a back door out of the imperative of obedience.

God cannot prevent sin getting inside. He couldn't prevent it with Adam. He couldn't prevent it with Cain. He couldn't prevent it with Saul. He couldn't prevent it with David.

Sin gets inside when we let it inside. Sin is kept out when *we* keep it out.

There is no back door out of the imperative of obedience.

With David, Lord, I pray: Put false ways far from me…Keep steady my steps according to thy promise, and let no iniquity get dominion over me. May I be strong not to let it, nor expect you to do it for me.

78. *Pray with David:*

Create in Me a Clean Heart and Put a Right Spirit Within Me

Create in me a clean heart, O God, and put a new and right spirit within me. (Psalm 51:10)

We circle back around to one of David's seminal prayers. Psalms 51 and 139 resound with a single heart-cry. Both open us deep into David's innermost being. For all his faults, and they are well documented, the legacy of transparency David has left the world is truly extraordinary.

Worldly manhood shields and hides. To expose the innermost self is the hardest thing for men to do.

Yet David *reveals*. He opens himself.

Let the world in! Let the world see what a weak and sinful man I am! Let the world behold my faults in all their ugliness!

Oh, but God…cleanse me of them, purge me, wash me, forgive me! Create in me a clean heart, O God…put a right spirit, your own Spirit, within me.

This prayer like that of Psalm 139:23-24, takes my breath away!

David's humanity remains. He is an example of transparency…yet he constantly struggles with it. In spite of the beauty of his prayer here in Psalm 51, the disingenuous echoes of Psalm 17 cannot have been forgotten by God either: "If you try my heart…if you test me you will find no wickedness in me." (Psalm 17:3. paraphrase)

The prayer of transparency will always be more difficult for men. We want desperately to maintain the illusion of strength and self-reliance. Why are John Wayne and Clint Eastwood such film icons? Because we want to be like them. We give easy lip service to humility, sensitivity, and tenderness. Inside, however, we are not quite prepared to give up the illusion of tough independence. We think we can preserve the machismo persona, but do so humbly and compassionately. We want to channel the Psalm 17 David not that of Psalm 51.

A sensitive and *caring* John Wayne.

Who wouldn't rather be seen as the perfection of manhood represented by Michelangelo's seventeen foot high mighty marble David? What man wants to emulate the emaciated, bloody form…vulnerable, nearly naked, at the mercy of a cruel world, hanging on a cross?

The statue of David…the cross of Jesus. Strength and power…weakness and frailty.

If our masculine egos could pick but one role model, which would it be? Let us lay aside for a moment this game we play of praying for a John Wayne version of macho Christlikeness. There is no such thing as Christlikeness with a macho twist. Though many men make such the object of their vision of "manly Christianity," sitting around casually talking about spiritual things with a drink in one hand and a cigar in the other, it is an illusion.

The level of transparency of the 51st and 139th psalms are virtually unknown in today's world. They are painful, humbling, mortifying, tormenting. Do we *really* want to know what God will find in our innermost depths? How many even of serious Christians pray the prayers of these two psalms and *mean* them?

Outward and external prayers are easier. It doesn't hurt to pray externally. It costs nothing. Indeed, there is often a fleshly payoff. Spiritual dividends accrue in the accounts of the Old Adam when we pray for others, when we pray for blessing and provision, when we intercede mightily and prophetically. No requirement comes with such prayers to admit weakness, to admit sin, to admit bankruptcy of strength. The Old Adam loves to pray self-aggrandizing prayers. It feels good to pray prayers that prop up the demon-Self.

In Scotland where we have occasionally attended church, an entire litany of needs is raised every Sunday that becomes the focus for the public prayers from the pulpit. These begin with intercessions for those in the congregation and work their way up in the end to the queen herself, and now the king.

When David prays, if he can take his eyes off his enemies, the focus is in the opposite direction, *inward* instead of outward. It is just David and God in that secret heart-place they share.

Alone, open, vulnerable, exposed, humble, honest.

In the weakness of his frail humanity, in his recognition of it, and in his struggle to overcome it—we discover the transparent heart of prayer which made David God's man.

"What do you see in me, Lord…what is down there in the dark places that you would get rid of…what would you have me do about it…search me, cleanse me, try me, know my heart, know my thoughts…create purity within me."

Then silence. Let God speak. Let the searchlight probe.

David's prayer life was eternal. His prayers were eternal because he prayed for the one thing that will last throughout all eternity—childness of heart toward God his Father.

I love Michelangelo's David. As magnificent as the statue is, however, it does not represent David's true heart. I cannot but wonder what the impact might have been had the great Florentine sculptor bent his seventeen foot man to the ground, and portrayed him instead on his knees.

With David, Lord, I pray: Create in me a clean heart, O God, and put a new and right spirit within me.

79. *Pray with David:*

Guard My Life—May Integrity and Uprightness Preserve Me

Guard my life…May integrity and uprightness preserve me (Psalm 25:20, 21)

I remained hesitant for some time about how to comment on this prayer. I skipped it several times and moved on. Yet I returned over and over to what I felt was the importance of integrity and uprightness in David's prayer life. The two terms are used more than thirty times in the psalms. I knew we could not take this prayer lightly.

As David prayed in Psalm 25:21, however, I continued to stumble over the *May* for the same reason I did over the *Let me not* of #75. Both expressions carried that subtle shifting of responsibility from David to God to accomplish what only David's own obedience could accomplish. It may not be that all readers will interpret these phrasings as I do. You may find them legitimate expressions of prayer. My thoughts are intended to stimulate your *own* conversations with God. Many will derive insights surpassing my own.

As I continued to return to this prayer, staring at the words and asking the Holy Spirit for illumination, at length I backed up and read the preceding words. I quickly saw that I had failed to read the *whole* prayer. Verses 20 and 21 go together. It is a composite prayer of two parts. The instant I read the words—

Guard my life…

—a lightbulb exploded.

Of course, I thought. *Integrity* and *uprightness* are among the qualities of character (and obedience!) by which God *guards* our life and *preserves* us in his will.

The unity of the complete prayer suddenly resonated with a beauty I had not beheld until that moment. It was a prayer for the very thing loving fathers do—guard, protect, and preserve their children.

This was a prayer from a son to his Father!

A yielding prayer, yet the prayer of a mature son who knows he takes his own share in its outcome.

I love the enveloping thought of God guarding me, wrapping his arms of love around me, preserving me…yet growing me into the maturity of sonship evidenced by my own chosen life of integrity and uprightness.

Walking in those qualities of character—that is up to *me*. Yet as I pray to be taught his ways and as I learn his ways and as I mature in integrity and uprightness to walk in his ways, *he* remains my overseeing guarding, protecting, preserving, Father, doing all he can to inform, animate, strengthen, and empower my small obedience unto the developing of my sonship.

The partnership of *his* overspreading and guarding Fatherhood, and *my* weak but sincere childship is breathtaking.

The simple words, *Guard my life,* have become for me a prayer that brings quiet peace. I will continue to pray it, and from this day on the words have new meaning. Perhaps the most profound revelation is that God has been answering that prayer all along, since before I was even born. (139:5, 13) In the same way that I will be watching over my sons until the day I die, God has been watching over me every day of my life.

It is what fathers do.

God is a good Father, a loving Father, a watching Father, to whom we can pray, *Guard my life,* knowing that he does, he has, he will…and he always has been.

With David, Lord, I pray: Guard my life…May integrity and uprightness preserve me.

80. *Pray with David:*

Guide Me, Lead Me, and Help Me Walk in Truth

Lead me in thy truth, and teach me…Teach me thy way, O Lord, that I may walk in thy truth. (Psalms 25:5; 86:11)

I love bookends, both literal and figurative. Whenever I am writing a novel, the first and last chapters act as bookends to the whole. The Bible is bookended by the beginning and the end—creation and eternity. Alpha and omega.

This final prayer of David's is the bookend to where we began. Commands #71 and #80 enclose David's life of prayer.

We began with the foundation of David's prayer life—Psalm 139: *Search me and know my heart.* This is the essence of prayer. Then the final words of that psalm's prayer now bookend all the prayers and send us forth to live in the reality of David's prayers: *Lead me in the way everlasting.* (139:24)

This present prayer amplifies and gives further specificity to that originating prayer from Psalm 51, amplified in my own words:

Search me, know me, teach me your ways and lead me in your ways…
and now with the rest of my life before me, guide me, lead me,
and help me walk in your truth.

As we've seen, David struggled with this last bookend. But the takeaway from this sojourn through his prayers is to personalize and absorb his prayer foundations, and then, continuing to ask for God's help, to walk in the reality of those foundations.

In command #53, I referenced the prayer I had seen in a movie. In many ways it was exactly this very prayer of David's: *Please tell me what to do. Oh God, help me. Tell me what to do and I'll do it.* It was a prayer asking for God's help.

But the foundation of transparent honesty in the heart of the woman praying the prayer was missing. There was no intention of obedience. It was not a prayer God could answer.

Transparency with God, and the intention of obedience, bind these prayer-bookends together. Upon their interconnected strengths are woven the life-tapestry in which God *can*, and *does*, and *will* guide and lead and help his sons and daughters to walk in the way everlasting, the high truths of eternity.

Whenever David lays down his self-justification, silences the outburst that God will slay his enemies, and finally drops to his knees, his prayer focus always turns, in complete transparency, toward God's inner searchlight.

He prayed to be *known*, and that God would help him *become.*

We often pray for circumstantial specifics. David prayed for *righteousness.*

The prayers of the 51st and 139th psalms give the Spirit of God willing invitation for divine examination and remaking from the inside out—to weave the tapestry of our personhood on the strands of *transparency* and *obedience.*

- *Purge me, wash me…*(Psalm 51:7)
- *Create in me a clean heart…* (Psalm 51:10)
- *Search me, O God, and know my heart…* (Psalm 139: 23)
- *Lead me in the way everlasting.* (Psalm 139: 24)

The root of David's prayer life probes to the depths of the God-man relationship: He had no secrets with God. Transparency characterizes David's personhood as a man. He came to God naked of soul—exposed, vulnerable, empty.

Adam's blood runs through David's veins too. David has his own fig leaves, behind which he attempts to hide his sin. As often as he came to God naked and vulnerable, he also came to him full of excuse, defense, and self-justification. He usually tries this first, thinking that he can stand mighty and independent in the power of his manhood, exactly as Michelangelo characterized him.

Like David, we have our private mental statue-images of ourselves—as tall and powerful and self-reliant as the immortal marble masterpiece standing in Florence.

But in the end David always realized it was hopeless. Again and again he stripped his soul bare to the divine gaze. Eventually he always ends up back on his knees—naked again, exposed, vulnerable, praying to God, "Search me and cleanse and create a pure heart within me."

When confronted with their sin, in their initial reactions Adam and David are not so very different. But when Adam is found out, he passes the buck, blames Eve, and makes excuses. When David is found out, after a brief struggle, he recognizes that in God exists his only refuge from the terrible thing within him.

Adam tried to run *from* God. David runs *to* God. It may take him some time to come to his senses, but God is always his refuge.

David *wanted* to be clean…*wanted* to be pure…*wanted* to be righteous…wanted to *obey*. It cannot be said of many that they *want* to be free from sin and be righteous. We would like to be *somewhat* righteous…if only it doesn't cost too much. We want to give God permission to go only so far in answering our inner prayers. A little righteousness will do us just fine.

But David: "Search me…try me…see if there be any wicked way in me."

Any wicked way.

The David-prayers are total. No private cellars where darkness is allowed to remain. The secret place of the heart David shared with God was a secret place of light.

There is a cost to taking up the challenge to pray the David prayers.

When God begins answering them, past perceptions are turned upside-down. With the David-prayers we embark on a road that leads not to a marble statue of worldly greatness, but to a broken naked form on a cross.

With David, Lord, I pray: Lead me in thy truth, and teach me…Teach me thy way, O Lord, that I may walk in thy truth.

Series Nine

Judgment and Forgiveness

Life's Eternal Consequences

God's faithfulness in the midst of sin

God's Judgment and Forgiveness Illuminated in the Writings of Isaiah and the Major Prophets

The Scriptural progression always leads to restoration

The thematic umbrella of the following series of commands departs from the wording of those that have come before. The other eleven series—loosely sequenced progressively through the Old Testament—are titled to highlight areas of obedience intrinsic to spiritual growth. The title of this series, on the other hand, highlights *God's* side of that equation.

Here we will focus on the thematic unity evident through the prophecies of Isaiah and the other prophets. We will attempt to discover commands incumbent upon *us* that emerge out of *God's* judgment and forgiveness that were so intrinsic to his relationship to Israel during the tumultuous years of the mid-first-century B.C. If God forgives, obviously we must also forgive. Likewise, if God judges sin, we must repent of *our* sin. Every command in the Bible emerges out of the character and eternal purposes of God. Our obedience to the commands represents the daily and practical means that *we* live according to *his* purpose, and model *our* lives after *his* character and being.

The writings of the prophets, originating during Israel's downfall at the end of Solomon's reign (c. 931 B.C.) and throughout the dispersions and captivities of both Israel and Judah that followed, are characterized—as the prophets speak on Gods behalf—by prophetic denunciations of judgment against Israel's unfaithfulness. A parallel thread continually runs through them, however, of God's ultimate promised forgiveness and the restoration that will follow. This includes, especially in *Isaiah*, beautiful prophecies foretelling the coming of Israel's Messiah.

I use the thematic title of Judgment and Forgiveness for the purpose of recognizing these important themes in the unfolding scriptural story, interspersed—as we have done throughout—with ongoing "life coaching" practicalities from the book of *Proverbs*.

The thematic title of Series 9 is therefore in some ways more about God than you and me. If we allow ourselves to plunge to the depths of those two words—*judgment* and *forgiveness*—with truth-seeking open minds, laying aside doctrinal preconceptions, approaching the flow of the Bible with an eye toward the overarching unity of God's eternal purposes, the sequence of those words may lead us into unexpected realms of new understanding of the Bible's High Logos.

Solomon's searchlight for the discovery of truth remains imperative: *Though it cost you all you have…get understanding*. We will need to appropriate that command more than ever to get to the bottom of what the major and minor prophets have to reveal about the sequence of judgment which is followed by forgiveness.

Zeroing in on specifics, with a proof-textual, myopic perspective—examining the Bible's details with a microscope rather than looking to God's eternal purposes through a telescope pointed to the heavens—usually produces a truncated, incomplete, and in some cases *false* interpretation of those details.

The Bible's specifics can *only* be understood through the lens of God's eternal purposes, never through the microscope (or even backward-held telescope) of doctrinal detail. The proof-texts of tradition and indoctrination will never yield God's highest truths. Some truth gets in of course. But many falsehoods also sneak in through the back door of tradition-bound teaching. God's *highest* truths will never be revealed by the methodology of doctrinal correctness.

- First comes judgment.

God judges sin. The judgment of God's wrath will fall on sin. The fire of God will consume sin. In ways we cannot see into completely, God's judgment will also fall on unrepentant *sinners* for their sin. God will judge both sin *and* sinners.

- Then comes forgiveness.

In the Bible, *forgiveness* always follows *judgment*. Always. This is the scriptural sequence.

Judgement...
then...
forgiveness.

When I read the Bible from cover to cover for the first time many years ago, looking for the big picture, asking God for insight into its high themes not its details, trying to read through a telescope rather than the doctrinal microscope of teaching I had received, gradually my eyes were opened to a startling truth that would rock the world of my theologic preconception. It was exactly the above progression:

In the Bible, forgiveness always follows judgment.

The message was so loud and clear I could not imagine why it was the best-kept secret in Christendom. God's final and ultimate purposes are *never* characterized by judgment.

The *final* word is always forgiveness, reconciliation, healing, and unity.

In God's eternal plan, judgment always represents a means to an end. It is a necessary aid to the healing process along God's progressive road toward reconciliation and the unity of his universe.

The message of the prophets—looking through the telescope the right way round, not looking backward at the Old Testament but forward to eternity—is that judgment is not itself the end.

Forgiveness always follows.

Reading with insight, the progression in the prophetic books is clear:

Repent, Israel…judgment is coming.
Repent!
God will judge.
He will destroy.
He will wipe Israel from the earth
Israel will be remembered no more.

And when judgment and punishment have done their work, then…

He will forgive…
heal…
restore…
and remember Israel's sins no more.

The Old Testament prophets are infused with this eternal perspective of Israel's restoration—of the redemption of all mankind, which is *all* Israel. Even the prophets themselves were unable to grasp the fullness of eternal power with which God would imbue their words.

Once we behold the sequence with eternal eyesight, the prophets fairly explode with the eternal symphony of the universal reconciliation of all things.

> *Thus says the Lord God: Behold, I will take the people of Israel… and will gather them from all sides, and bring them to their own land; and I will make them one nation in the land, upon the mountains of Israel; and one king shall be king over them all… and they shall be my people, and I will be their God.* (Ezekiel 37:21-23)

For you shall go out in joy,
and be led forth in peace;
the mountains and the hills before you
shall break forth into singing,
and all the trees of the field shall clap their hands.
Instead of the thorn shall come up the cypress;
instead of the brier shall come up the myrtle;
and it shall be to the Lord for a memorial,
for an everlasting sign which shall not be cut off. (Isaiah 55:12-13) [33]

To thoroughly "get understanding" of the commands, and why they are so important in the life of the Christian, we have to understand God himself. We have to understand his purposes. We have to understand *how* he works. We have to understand *why* he does what he does, and what he is trying to accomplish in his universe and in our own lives.

[33] For a more thorough perspective into the role each of the prophets play in conveying these unfolding themes, see *The Eyewitness Old Testament, Volume 2.*

Understanding the judgment-forgiveness sequence is intrinsic to understanding God's eternal purposes. It opens one more doorway, among the many we have explored, into the imperative of the Bible's commands.

Series Nine

Judgment and Forgiveness

81. Confess sin.

82. Forgive when you have been wronged.

83. Judge others fairly

84. Overlook offenses and weaknesses in others.

85. Repent of unintentional sin.

86. Be honest and truthful in dealings and relationships.

87. Turn away anger with gentle speech.

88. Wear a cheerful countenance.

89. Spread peace.

90. Keep your Word.

81. Confess Sin

When a man is guilty…he shall confess the sin he has committed. (Leviticus 5:5)
I acknowledged my sin to thee, and I did not hide iniquity…
I will confess my transgressions to the Lord. (Psalm 32:5)

Surprising as it may be to say, sin is not the worst of it. Sin is built into the equation of human life. *Why* God allowed this consequence of free will seemingly to ruin humanity will remain a mystery. But that is the reality. We are all sinners. We sin.

Good people sin.

Bad people sin.

You and I will probably sin today, hopefully in small ways, but it's unavoidable.

The worst of it is…trying to hide it. *Pretending that we haven't sinned.* Making excuses and defending ourselves. Or just keeping quiet about it.

The *secret* sin.

This was the worst of Adam's original sin—not the sin itself, but trying to hide it, trying to hide it from God, and even from himself with excuses. Had he rushed to the open arms of his Father immediately with confession on his lips, who knows how it might have changed human history and the relationship between God and man.

This is the essence of hypocrisy—pretending to be better, more upstanding, more spiritual, than we really are. Hiding our innermost selves from view. Wearing a mask of virtue and respectability. Pretending that we're *not* sinners.

That's why we're commanded to confess sin. Confession opens the door to the secret places and lets in the light. Hypocrisy lives in the darkness of pretense. Confession explodes pretense. Confession obliterates hypocrisy.

I'm a sinner!

I know it. God knows it. Other people know it. No games. It's who I am. I won't try to hide it.

Obviously this doesn't mean telling everyone we meet all our hidden sins. We've all met Christians who do this regularly as an attention-seeking device. The general public confession of *what-a-terrible-person-I-am-will-you-all-pray-for-me* usually leads to little personal growth in the conquest of sin. It's a selfish and unhealthy exercise often with no purpose other than to shine the light and keep attention focused on oneself.

Confession to others is the least important kind of confession. What others-confession may be appropriate is mostly limited to personal and private exchanges between *sin-er* and *sin-ee*.

The truly important components of confession are clearly:

- Confession to God.
- Confession to myself.

Those are the two we can't try to hide from. Adam tried to hide from both—he tried to hide from God and he tried to hide from himself.

No one else may ever need to know of either the sin or the confession. If I have sinned against another or caused hurt to another, that must be dealt with relationally. But most inner sins of the heart and mind are private, no one else has been injured, they involve no one else, require no restitution or healing of relationship, nor demand accountability other than to God. Nothing is accomplished by making them public. Those areas of concern in my life are between me and God.

Confession is a two-step process. It's meant to *lead* somewhere. Confession alone is healthy—it helps prevent the illusion of righteousness and is thus the primary antidote against the cancer of hypocrisy. But if it doesn't accomplish what it is meant to accomplish, then it has been worthless. Hypocrisy may be somewhat forestalled—at least we're not pretending to be better than we are. But we haven't done anything about it. There's been no change.

That's the purpose of confession—change, growth, improvement. Whatever we've done, we're not supposed to do it anymore. Otherwise the confession means nothing. Repentance without the commitment to change behavior and thought patterns will succeed only in introducing a new form of pretense and hypocrisy—pretending to be repentant and sorry when we're not sorry enough to change.

It's the weekly confessional ritual. Beneath the regular confession sits an even more devious form of hypocrisy.

The pattern is all too familiar to every one of us, Catholics and Protestants alike. If long term life-impact growth and change does not result from confession, then the confession is a sham.

Confession is not a *Get-out-of-jail-free* card that makes sin go away—giving license to keep repeating it, and keep confessing it. When Jesus said, "Neither do I condemn you, go and sin no more," he meant it. Confessing to adultery, lying, gossip, stealing, sex outside marriage, swearing, unresolved anger, disrespect of parents, sexual perversion, or cheating, *and then continuing to do them,* is the worst kind of spiritual hypocrisy.

Confession of sin is an important aspect of, the *conquest of sin.* There are many weapons God gives us to fight that war of victories and failings, major battles and minor skirmishes. It is a process of growth that lasts a lifetime. Confession alone won't win the war. But if taken seriously and leading to change, it helps us take a little more ground against sin every day.

The entire Old Testament sacrificial Law was an elaborate ritualistic mechanism to convey the related truths of judgment and forgiveness, and the importance of confession in the conquest, not the tolerance, of sin.

God, give me an open, transparent heart, willing to confess my sin—eager to confess to you. Show me where I need to confess to others. Keep me from pretense confessions. Bring to my remembrance any unfinished business I have with anyone, and with you. With every confession I make, strengthen my resolve not to fall into the same sin again. May my confessions be stepping stones into higher realms of obedience to your commands. Stand with me, Jesus, and make me bold in warfare against my sin.

82. Forgive When You Have Been Wronged

You shall not take vengeance or bear any grudge…but you shall love your neighbor. (Leviticus 19:18)

For thou, O Lord, art good and forgiving. (Psalm 86:5)

He who forgives an offense seeks love, but he who repeats a matter alienates a friend. (Proverbs 17:9)

We now put ourselves on God's side of the confession equation.

When I have been sinned against, it then becomes my opportunity to follow Jesus' *neither-do-I-condemn-you* example and step into the *forgiveness* half of the judgment-forgiveness progression.

As hard as it may be to forgive when we have been wronged, just think what it means. In a small way, I am given the opportunity to take God's part—in the tiny world of *my* relationships—and share in what he is doing every day. I have the privilege of stepping into and participating in what God is constantly doing in his universe, and will continue doing to all eternity—bringing healing, forgiveness, reconciliation, and the unity of love to his creation.

Whenever I forgive, I am foreshadowing the great Forgiveness that will bring all things into oneness in eternity!

This command, therefore, reveals a priceless honor. The commands are not burdensome legalisms. They are invitations to share God's life!

In this case, the confession matters nothing. There may or may not be a confession at all. If so, if I have been confessed to and forgiveness flows from my heart out to meet it, then the brotherhood of universal humanity has flowered as a result of my small obedience. If there has been no confession, even if there has been no repentance by one who has wronged me, I still am privileged with the opportunity to forgive anyway.

I can go so far as to forgive *even when another thinks me in the wrong.*

This is the highest forgiveness of all—the forgiveness of Jesus on the cross.

Unlike Jesus, however, confession and forgiveness may flow from my heart simultaneously as one. I may legitimately pray, "Father, forgive what wrong I may have done, or what wrong I am unaware of. Show me *my* sin so I can repent more knowledgeably of it. But if I have *not* sinned against my brother or sister, I forgive them for misjudging me, as you forgive the multitudes who sin against you."

The fly in the ointment of forgiveness is the lurking well-disguised self-righteousness that imputes wrong on the part of others toward me whose origins contain more of my own wrong attitudes than I want to admit. Feeling aggrieved by inflicted wrong—whether real or perceived—is one of the clearest hallmarks of the Old Adam. The more tenaciously I cling to the sense of undeserved injury, the more clearly this command is pointed toward *me* than someone else.

Some truisms are painfully on the mark. They are truisms because they are true. The old adage that we are most critical of others when they mirror our *own* faults and besetting sins is so accurate it hurts. It's also said with precision that when I point my finger at someone else's fault, three fingers are pointing back at me. It's the speck and log, and most of us are guilty of it every day.

If ever we need to be looking in the mirror and then sinking to our knees, it is when reading these two commands: *Confess* and *forgive*.

Holy Spirit, I invite you to clean out the basement where I am storing old resentments, grudges, grievances, or unforgivenesses. Open the closed rooms of my memory. Shine in your spotlight. Reveal where I have not yet forgiven. Give me humility to do so no matter how justified I consider the reasons I have been withholding it. Deepen within me your heart of eternal forgiveness. Make confession and forgiveness ongoing realities of my life with you, daily expressions of my prayer-liftings to you and my outflowing love toward others.

83. Judge Others Fairly

You shall do no injustice in judgment…But you shall judge your neighbor fairly.
(Leviticus 19:15, RSV, NIV)

As do most aspects of the spiritual life, the previous command reduces at its essence to an undergirding component of the Levitical Law. If one hundred people, however, were asked, "What is the essence of the Old Testament message?" would even one in a hundred cite Leviticus 19:18: *Love your neighbor as yourself.*

It is but the golden rule stated differently. Love your neighbor as you want to be loved…treat your neighbor as you want to be treated…think about others as you want them to think about you…do for others as you want others to do for you…forgive others as you want them to forgive you.

Jesus says that the golden rule sums up the entire law and prophets. He says that all these commands of the prophets, which are the subject of this book, are all drawn up into a single command:

So whatever you wish that men would do to you, do so to them;
for this is the law and the prophets. (Matthew 7:12)

When I wrong or hurt another person, hopefully not intentionally but in any case, I want him or her to forgive me. When the situation is reversed, how can I expect a difference in my response toward them?

The expansive scope of the Levitical law, the foundation of the biblical perspective on all human relationships emerges out of the principle of the golden rule—reasonableness, selflessness, equality, truthfulness, and fairness.

Treat others *fairly.*

I hesitated to use the word "judge" because of its negative connotation. Yet Jesus commands us, *Judge not,* so the word cannot be avoided.

Jesus' full statement circles back, as do most relational truths, to the golden rule and Leviticus 19:18.

"Judge not, that you be not judged. For with the judgment by which you judge will you yourself be judged, and the measure you give will be the measure you receive." (Matthew 7:1-2, paraphrase)

In other words…fairness. You *and* your neighbor will be treated fairly, equally, equitably, reasonably.

The word *judge* in this command, therefore, highlights a wider principle. Judgment *does* exist in the economy of God's kingdom, just as sin exists and will be dealt with. Unto us, however, has not been given *God's eternal eyesight to judge* all things from hearts of eternal reconciliatory love in the way that God judges.

Not able to see completely with God's eyes, therefore, we have been given a different standard than his by which to judge. The measuring stick of judgment God has given *us* to use, in our limited human capacity for fairness, is the golden rule—judgment based on how I want to be judged myself. This is the blueprint we have been given by which to exercise judgment as human beings.

Leviticus 19:18: *Love your neighbor*—judge your neighbor—*as yourself.*

Before you think a judgmental or critical thought about your neighbor, reverse the roles. Put *yourself* where you have placed your neighbor in your mind. If *you* had done, said, or thought what he or she has done, said, or thought, how would you want him or her to respond to *you*?

- *Judge your neighbor as yourself.*

Other words might have been equally illuminating to use for this command:

- *Evaluate* others fairly.
- *Think about* others fairly.
- *Treat* others fairly.
- *Weigh circumstances* involving others fairly
- *Speak* about others fairly.
- *Do unto others fairly.*

George MacDonald raises the somewhat commonplace idea of "fairness" into the realm of the kingdom of God, saying that the truth contained in this command embodies and will embody the eternal judgment and justice of God. When we are simply *fair* toward others, we are stepping up to the high plane by which God will judge them and judge us—with infinite, eternal, loving, forgiving *fairness.*

If you ask any ordinary Sunday congregation in England, what is meant by the justice of God, would not nineteen out of twenty answer, that it means his punishing of sin? Think for a moment what degree of justice it would indicate in a man—that he punished every wrong. A Roman emperor, a Turkish cadi, might do that, and be the most unjust both of men and judges…

The justice of God is this, that—to use a boyish phrase, the best the language will now afford me because of misuse—he gives every man, woman, child, and beast, everything that has being, fair play. He renders to every man according to his work. And therein lies his perfect mercy. For nothing else could be merciful to the man, and nothing but mercy could be fair to him.

God does nothing of which any just man, the thing set fairly and fully before him so that he understood, would not say, "That is fair." …

A just man is one who cares, and tries, and always tries, to give fair play to everyone in every thing. [34]

God, give me your eternal eyesight to see everyone I meet through your eyes. Fill me with grace to give them the same true and right judgment of fair play that you will give us all, and that you are always giving me. Remind me always to give people the benefit of the doubt. I thank you for being infinitely fair with me, and giving me the benefit of the doubt when I slip and forget the power, and the command, of the golden rule. Help me remember.

84. Overlook Offenses and Weaknesses in Others

Good sense makes a man slow to anger, and it is his glory to overlook an offense. (Proverbs 19:11)

The first four interrelated commands in this series flow and weave together so fluidly it is almost impossible to separate them. Here we face in some ways an even loftier challenge than to forgive. That is to *overlook* offense altogether, as if it never happened at all.

Or, as George MacDonald hints at in the words of this brief exchange, the forgiveness that is in the heart before it is even asked for:

"Will you forgive me?"…
"My heart is open to you…take what forgiveness you think you need." [35]

When we feel the need to forgive, we have already internalized it, made an issue of it that requires forgiveness. What if, however, forgiveness was never even needed? What if I never allowed a potential offense to reach that level? What if I never took it in? What if I never so much as noticed? Or, if I did notice, I did not allow it to settle into my mind or heart as an offense but let it wash over me and fall to the ground?

What if forgiveness was so automatic, so unthinking, so unnecessary, that it was as "the perfume the violet leaves on the heel that has crushed it?"

Think what it would be like to live in such an atmosphere of peace, contentment, and harmony with one's brothers and sisters of humanity that

---

34 George MacDonald, *Unspoken Sermons, Third Series,* "Justice."

35 George MacDonald, *Thomas Wingfold, Curate,* "Helen Awake."

we were *unable* to be hurt or offended. Think what *life* would be spread by the perfume of sweet forgivenesses lavished upon the myriad potential grievances that swirl in the air, yet pass unnoticed and fall to the ground and die. What perfume would imbue the universal human spirit by offenses and grievances overlooked.

> It is a wonderful thing that here and there in this hard, uncharitable world there should still be left a few rare souls who think no evil. This is the great unworldliness. Love "thinketh no evil.," imputes no motive, sees the bright side, puts the best construction on every action. What a delightful state of mind to live in! What a stimulus and benediction even to meet with it for a day! [36]

What informs this other-worldly outlook of relational serenity is the grace to give everyone the benefit of the doubt—another seemingly commonplace phrase that plunges to the depths of the eternal truth of forgiveness.

Again we find this principle anchored in Leviticus 19:18 and Matthew 7:12. Is this not exactly how I want others to respond to *me*—giving *me* the benefit of the doubt, overlooking *my* weaknesses and foibles and immaturities, paying no attention, not even noticing? When *my* grievances swirl in the air, am I not soothed and quieted when the perfume of sweet forgiveness flows over me? How, then, can I give that same "stimulus and benediction" to others?

Along with Drummond and MacDonald, again Thomas Kempis orients our priorities when navigating the challenging interconnected commands of this series:

- Endeavor to be patient in bearing with the defects and infirmities of others…for you also have many which must be borne with by others.
- We would willingly have others perfect, and yet we amend not our own faults.
- We will have others severely corrected, and will not be corrected ourselves.
- How seldom we weigh our neighbor in the same balance with ourselves. [37]

To look beyond the weaknesses of others, overlooking immaturities and unkind words and offenses, going so far as to overlook sin itself, is to take our share alongside God in the eternal making of every individual man, woman, and child as he sees them in their eventual perfection. Our universal heavenly Father is engaged in the ages-long eternal process of growing, luring, developing, challenging, goading, forgiving, and loving each one of us up into the perfected sonship and daughterhood of our new names.

> *He who has an ear, let him hear what the Spirit says…To him who conquers…I will give him a white stone, with a new name written on the stone which no one knows except him who receives it.* (Revelation 2:17)

Let us look into the hearts of our fellow pilgrims on that journey, most of whom do not even know they are on it, our brothers and sisters of humanity

---

36 Henry Drummond, *The Greatest Thing in the World.*

37 Thomas Kempis, *The Imitation of Christ.*

who have never heard of the white stone though they are on the road to receiving the one God is preparing them to receive. Some of these will be ahead of us on the eternal road, others behind. May God give us true vision to see them all as he sees them—in the perfection of their eventual childship, reflecting the names on the white stone that he has at last made them capable of receiving.

This is such a hard command, Lord. In my flesh I do not want to overlook offence in others, only myself. I harbor offenses that I perceive have been inflicted against me, never pausing to think how many offenses others have for hurts I have caused and judgments I have made against them. Forgive me for the offenses I have caused. Reveal them to me so that I can ask forgiveness. Then help me do unto others as I would have them do unto me. Give me grace to spread the perfume of forgiveness into the lives of all those around me. All humanity needs the perfume of offenses overlooked, so let me spread it today into one or two whose paths cross mine.

85. Repent of Unintentional Sin

When a person…sins unintentionally…he must make restitution…and make atonement…
and he will be forgiven. (Leviticus 5:15-16)

This is a most intriguing command! I did not know it was in the Levitical Law until going through the commands of the Old Testament for this book. I have thought and prayed long and hard about the fascinating dynamics of it. In this unexpected command I find one more wonderful example of God's Fathering care revealed in the Law. He cares so much that his children learn to be clean and whole and righteous that he even wants attention paid to *accidental* sin.

Before encountering this command, if asked whether I believed that such a thing as accidental, unintentional sin even existed, I probably would have answered *No.* Reflecting on this command has been a true learning experience.

I always considered sin a matter of motive and volition—*choice.* Sin, as I viewed it was willful disobedience. Chosen wrong. Knowing full well what we are doing, we *choose* to do what we know is wrong.

What, then, is *unintentional* sin?

I began to see that it is possible to do wrong without careful thought about the consequences of our actions and words. Perhaps we *should* have been thinking about them. But we may have been more *careless* than *willful.*

It is true that we are commanded to "Be careful and watchful." So even *carelessness* might represent disobedience to the commands. But does it rise to the level of *sin*? Maybe in some cases *yes*…but also maybe in some cases *no.*

The question then follows—Is all *wrong* to be considered *sin*?

If I speak a word that hurts a friend, even if I did not *intend* it, did not *mean* it, the hurt is still there. There have been consequences and repercussions to my words. Unknowingly, perhaps carelessly, I have *wronged* my friend. I need to apologize and ask forgiveness for my insensitivity.

Whether or not this qualifies as having *sinned* against my friend, not seeing fully through God's eyes, I cannot say. But I have *wronged* my friend.

It doesn't matter what we call it—*sin* or *wrong*. The important point is that I must treat even carelessness and thoughtlessness as serious matters that may require my repentance.

If *wrong* resulted, I need to repent and make it right.

This command is a game changer. This raises the imperative of self-examination to a more exacting level. We are not only responsible to be attentive to our thoughts and motives and actions…now the mirror of self-examination probes into those regions where we consider our thoughts and motives innocent…but where *wrong* has resulted nevertheless.

Wrong can even result from *innocent*, though perhaps careless, motives.

God's searchlight shines even deeper than that—into regions where we aren't aware that wrong has been done at all. Are we still responsible?

It's not that our introspection should reach such accentuated levels that we burden ourselves with imaginary guilt for every word whether injurious or not. I do suggest, however, that there are deeper levels of accountability than we may have previously considered.

In one of my novels I put the following prayer into the mouth of one of my characters. The process of writing it convicted me to take with greater seriousness my own accountability for the unintended consequences of my words and actions through the years, even consequences I may have been unaware of.

These are sobering realizations.

Oh, God, eternal Father, by the infinite miracle of your timelessness, receive into your heart my desire to repent of every tiniest lapse of attentiveness. Make right the hurts I have inflicted through the years. Soothe, heal, and bring eternal good from the insensitivities of my responses and words.

As your infinite Mind holds the history of the universe and every human exchange as an eternal present—every word spoken, every thought thought—may my prayer dwell in that timeless realm to set flowing an infinity of forgivenesses in myself and in others. May my repentance stimulate a flowering of healing with every individual my path of life has crossed.

Within your infinite Presence where they also dwell, I ask forgiveness from every person to whom I was less than I should have been, for the thousands of such moments I cannot remember. Accomplish the work that my forgetful humanity cannot. Glorify every exchange into a transformed eternal Now of reconciliation.

Work wholeness beyond my capacity to apprehend it, Father. In the timelessness of your Love, take the exchanges of my life into your eternal being. Imbue every heart with healing. May we be made one in your eternal heart beyond what was possible in our humanity.

Bring brotherhood alive. In the imperfection of my prayer, accomplish the finished result of the reconciliation that is in your heart to glorify within and between every man and woman of your universal human family.[38]

38 An excerpt from Stirling Marshall's end of life prayer, adapted from *The Invisible War*.

86. Be Honest and Truthful in All Dealings and Relationships

An honest witness tells the truth…Truthful lips endure forever …
Be honest and…speak the truth. (Proverbs 12:17, 19; 22:2, NIV)

The more we reflect on the practical daily-life sections of *Leviticus* and *Proverbs*, the more overlap and similarity emerge between them. Once we get beyond the sacrifices, priestly robes, and extensive instructions about offerings, we see that Moses and Solomon are singing the same tune. This is hardly surprising since God inspired the content of both books. That "song" is wisdom, goodness, selflessness, compassion, honesty, responsibility, accountability, prudence, common sense…in a word *righteousness*.

Fairness, as considered in our response to the weaknesses of others, now widens in scope to include "*all* dealings and relationships." The character quality of exhibiting fairness to all imbues the Proverbs-virtues—wisdom and its seven pillars: understanding, knowledge, discretion, insight, prudence, integrity, righteousness—with common attributes.

Honesty and truthfulness take their place among those seven as preeminent among the Proverbs-virtues. The wise, fair, righteous man or woman of integrity—the man or woman alive to the deepening of the Proverbs-virtues in his or her life—would rather a business deal fell through than bring an iota of dishonesty into the presentation of the facts, would rather lose an election than present himself better than he is or his opponent worse, would never hide his true motives from a friend, would rather lose everything than lie, would sooner see one less qualified and without the same knowledge advance ahead of him and he himself be misjudged rather than present himself other than he is.

Honesty and truthfulness, in the full sense of their meanings—describing the depth of character of the wise and righteous man or woman who walks with God—are so absent in our modern culture, no one needs me to make that point. Of course we see smatterings of honesty and truthfulness here and there like small sprinklings of surface virtue sprinkled over disingenuous motives to create the illusion of integrity.

But *full and complete* honesty and truthfulness, in *all* dealings and relationships—such a level of attentiveness to the commands of character are not merely missing in politics, business, academia, entertainment, and the media, they are missing *everywhere*.

Our culture has become so deadened to virtue, integrity, and the full range of character-virtues that Christians have been infected with the virus like everybody else. They go along with loose interpretations of honesty and truthfulness too, not even noticing the slippage of Proverbs-truth in their own lives.

I am as guilty as anyone. I catch myself making excuses for tiny violations. How often do I think to myself that they aren't *really* such a big deal—pointing fingers at the worldliness of the world rather than looking in the mirror. Just last night we watched a movie on television whose rating we felt made it safe. About halfway through, however, lines of language began to be crossed that we were uncomfortable with. But by then we were caught. We wanted to know how the story ended. I said to myself, "Why do they fill movies with such garbage!" I blamed Hollywood rather than simply turning off the TV. It was a classic example of passing the buck instead of obeying what I knew to be right.

The commands aren't about politics, corporate greed, or Hollywood…they are about you and me. Upon *us* is the command to be people of a different sort—people who walk in the honesty, truthfulness, integrity, and purity to which we have been called.

Therefore I determine this day not to make excuses or justify slippages around the edges. I will not change Washington D.C. or Hollywood today. They are not mine to change. The person standing in front of the mirror is the only one I have been given to change.

Bring to my heart and mind today, Holy Spirit, my own potential moments of slippage before I lapse into them. Give me humble and prayerful courage, integrity of purpose and motive, to be honest, truthful, pure, and righteous in all decisions, interactions, dealings, and relationships I encounter this day.

87. Turn Away Anger with Gentle Speech

A soft answer turns away wrath, but a harsh word stirs up anger. (Proverbs 15:1)

This familiar proverb may appear to have little connection to the theme of this series. This is probably one of the most well-known of the proverbs, most practical and insightful, most ingeniously clever in how magically and instantaneously it works.

And yet—unbelievably—how *little* it is practiced!

Everyone is searching for magic pills that will solve their problems without having to change themselves. Here Solomon has indeed given us a magic pill. This prescription is magical. It may not work *every* time…but pretty close.

Anger stimulates anger. An angry retort to an angry outburst creates yet *more* anger.

The chain reaction of anger reveals one of the most amazing processes in human relationship. Anger *never* works, *never* solves a problem, *never* soothes or calms, and almost never leads to increase of truth or understanding.

Yet defensiveness, blame, and anger remain the standard M.O. in human exchange to meet serious differences of almost every kind. Not all anger is revealed in tempestuous verbal tirades. Silent anger is no less destructive to solutions, common ground, constructive dialog, and mutual understanding as a shouting match. Outbursts of temper are obvious sin for all the world to see, but silent resentment is equally toxic.

As we dig deeper, we find ourselves probing to the heart of this series of commands. Anger produces *judgment* of and against our brothers and sisters.

We all want those of differing perspectives to understand *our* viewpoints, and then to graciously come over to *our* side and embrace *our* perspectives.

Let's be honest with ourselves—this is *exactly* what we want. And what we *expect*. My viewpoints are obviously the most reasonable and true—how can everyone not embrace them? If everyone would only listen logically and with common sense, they would see how right I am. After all…I am *always* right.

That others *don't* listen and understand and embrace our viewpoints rouses anger. Anger is met with anger from the other side. Nothing is accomplished. No one is convinced. Both sides walk away more entrenched in their opposing views than ever.

How can we be so blind to this obvious truth? Anger *never* persuades.

That anger is guaranteed *not* to work must surely make it as one of the most foolish and immature of human responses.

Yet a soft or gentle word, a smile, a response of kindness is almost *guaranteed* to dissolve another's anger instantly.

The sincere smile and gentle word are Solomon's magic pill to diffuse anger! It's so magical we ought to be eager to see anger rearing its head for the opportunity to watch the magic pill work its wonders.

In my book *Endangered Virtues,* I called anger an "unvirtue," an opposite of virtue. It is an unvirtue that is toxic to the universal brotherhood of humanity.

> One of the glaring and unfortunate results of the cultural and political divide in which our nation finds itself is a divisive spirit of hostility between those of differing perspective. Anger toward those with whom we disagree, while not new, has taken over as the new normal. The entire relational chemistry has become toxic. We justify such hostility because each of us is convinced with every grey cell in our brains that our idea-adversaries…are so blatantly and stubbornly wrong. The clash of ideas on both sides thus takes on the harsh timbre of a holy war…of righteous anger, justified anger, necessary anger…
>
> What we're witnessing doesn't advance anyone's point of view, nor does it advance truth. What it actually achieves is to entrench those of differing perspectives yet deeper into them. To say it diplomatically, argumentation is counterproductive. To say it more bluntly, it is stupid to argue…
>
> Many scriptures are of universal application whether or not one subscribes to the entirety of the Christian message…[One] is found in Romans 12:18: "If possible, so far as it depends on you, live peaceably with all." The simplicity of this injunction is formidable in its utter practicality. Every one of us faces the opportunity to live by this straightforward rule of life a dozen times a day.

Christians and atheists alike are supposed to live peaceably with others…Living peaceably with others is a good thing…It costs nothing to be polite, amiable, diplomatic, gracious, and soft-spoken…

Civility is not only virtuous, it's the only approach by which others might be encouraged to listen to what you have to say…

George MacDonald spoke powerfully of the universal humanity in two sermons entitled Love Thy Neighbour and Love Thine Enemy. The titles alone point us far higher than mere civility, as important as that is. They lead us into the rarified air of the second of the greatest commandments: Love your neighbor as yourself. MacDonald wrote, "Lies there not within the man and the woman a divine element of brotherhood, of sisterhood, a something lovely and lovable…Shall that divine something…have no recognition from us?" [39]…

We are all humans together, bound up in the complex dance of alternating self-glorification and self-relinquishment that characterizes our slow pilgrimage toward eternity. [40]

God, keep me from anger when confronted by anger in others. Let such exchanges be opportunities to watch the marvel of anger dissolving when met with gentle speech, kindness, and graciousness. Keep me from defensiveness. May kindness rise in its place. Thus help me be an instrument in my small corner of the world to still the world's anger which is so endemic to our time.

88. Wear a Cheerful Countenance

A glad heart makes a cheerful countenance…A cheerful heart is a good medicine, but a downcast spirit dries up the bones. (Proverbs 12:13; 17:22)

The proverbs of Solomon are so practical and do-able. Here we have another of Solomon's tidbits of wisdom that is as practical and as magical as turning away anger with kindness, civility, and gentle speech.

A cheerful countenance brings light. A cheerful countenance infects those around it, lifts them, raises them into the rarified air of heart-meeting-heart and stimulates a like response. As anger stimulates anger, cheerfulness stimulates cheerfulness.

Try this experiment. Catch the eye of a stranger and flash a bright smile. Ninety-nine times out of a hundred, he or she will smile back. It's an automatic knee-jerk response. They can't help it. It comes involuntarily as the unexpected smile from you hits them between the eyes.

Maybe it's because it is so unexpected in today's world for a stranger to smile at you. I'm not sure why it works, but it nearly always does.

It's amazing to watch. Yesterday on a bike ride, I approached a lady stopped on the path resting and wearing what I can only call a grumpy expression. I turned and looked straight into her face and smiled. The next instant her face exploded radiantly. I laughed to myself as I continued on. It almost never fails.

---

[39] George MacDonald, "Love Thy Neighbour," from *Unspoken Sermons, First Series*.

[40] Michael Phillips, *Endangered Virtues and the Coming Ideological War,* Fidelis Publishing, chapter 10, "Civility."

My wife Judy has one of the loveliest smiles imaginable. Her hospital work takes her daily among the hurting, suffering, and dying. Most of the patients she encounters are in pain, some suffering unimaginably. She also plays her harp in a chemo center where every man and woman present is quite literally trying to keep death at bay. There is enormous physical and emotional suffering all around her.

Yet over and over her smile and cheerfulness and upbeat countenance lift those aching hearts. Her goal when she goes to work is to be a bright spot in someone's day, to ease the pain, lower stress, and bring peace. The quiet gentle music of her harp helps, of course. But I am convinced that the smile always ready on her lips is the secret (and magical!) ingredient.

When our youngest son was four or five, he and Judy were in a restaurant together for breakfast. Their waitress was so grumpy her behavior bordered on rudeness. Judy whispered to him, "The next time she comes, give her a big smile. She seems to be having a hard day." So when she again approached their table, he looked up at her with his big brown eyes and gave her a big smile. Instantly her whole countenance changed. Our son glanced at Judy with even bigger eyes as if to say, "Wow…magic!"

All around us we can't help encountering the frowning faces of the world's incessant grumblers. They are everywhere. God help us not to let their dismal, downcast spirits infect us. God help me not be one of them!

Our call as God's light and salt is to bring what Jesus called "good cheer" into a grumbling, discontented, frustrated, angry world. With Judy, we have the opportunity every day to be the bright spot in someone's corner of that hostile world laced with so much negativity. It may be a friend, it may be a stranger we pass in a store or on the street or on a bike ride. We can bring light as many times a day as we like. It costs nothing but the flash of teeth and a kind word.

When we get in the habit of *wearing* a cheerful countenance among the adornments we put on every day—how much better than make-up, jewelry, or expensive clothes!—the light becomes part of us.

Jesus said, "You are the light of the world."

It's more personal than that: You can be a light in *your* world today.

Let me be light today, Lord, for someone whose day may have begun in pain, darkness., sadness, anger, or frustration. Use me to lift that one out of whatever weight of discouragement is pressing upon him or her, even if only briefly, by the good cheer you are preparing me to give. Keep my smile and kind word ready for the moment you send that man, woman, or child across my path.

89. Spread Peace

Blessed are those who find wisdom…Her ways are pleasant ways, and all her paths are peace… Those who promote peace have joy. (Proverbs 3:13, 17; 12:20, NIV)

This command epitomizes exactly what Judy does when she walks with her harp into a hospital room. She *spreads peace* into the heart of suffering souls. We all have countless opportunities to participate with God in that eternal work of peace-spreading.

Today's world is producing more strife, anxiety, anger, fear, uncertainty, frustration, discouragement, annoyance, weariness, hopelessness, and worry than people know how to cope with. People are desperately hungry to feel the soothing waters of peace flowing over them. But they have no idea where it can be found.

We won't bring peace to either Jerusalem or the world. Praying for world peace is a meaningless exercise. Pray instead to bring peace into *your* world.

How easily we can assist God in answering that personal and down-to-earth prayer. Peace can be spread into an individual heart with a smile, a cheerful countenance, and a kind and encouraging word.

That may sound like a syrupy cliché. But it's not. In a way, it touches the very heart of the gospel. It really is true how easily the principles of *Proverbs* can be practiced every day...if we really want to *live* these principles of character virtues.

In one of his memorable passages, George MacDonald contrasts *peacemakers* with *dividers* who sow division and disunity. Though the latter is not our emphasis here, his perceptive description of *how* peacemakers spread peace—often invisibly, unconsciously, interweaving threads of unity—gives us a beautiful image of the challenge and opportunity before us each day to be God's peacemakers in an angry world.

> Those that are on their way to see God...are peace-makers in the travelling company...who make peace with and among the rest. The true idea of the universe is the whole family in heaven and earth...Now the primary necessity to the very existence of a family is peace ...peace alone makes it possible for the binding grass-roots of life—love, namely, and justice—to spread...The peace-makers quiet the winds of the world ever ready to be up and blowing; they tend and cherish the interlacing roots of the ministering grass; they spin and twist many uniting cords, and they weave many supporting bands; they are the servants, for the truth's sake, of the individual, of the family, of the world, of the great universal family of heaven and earth...the allies and ministers of every clasping and consolidating force in it; fellow-workers they are with God in the creation of the family; they help him to get it to his mind, to perfect his Father-idea...
>
> On the other hand, those whose influence is to divide and separate, causing the hearts of men to lean away from each other, make themselves the children of the evil one...ever obstructing the one prayer of the first-born—that the children may be one with him in the Father. Against the heart-end of creation. .the sowers of strife, the fomenters of discord, contend ceaseless. They do their part with all the other powers of evil to make the world...one heaving mass of dissolution. But they labour in vain. Through the mass...this way and that, guided in dance inexplicable of prophetic harmony, move the children of God, the lights of the world, the lovers of men, the fellow-workers with God, the peace-makers...Blessed are the peace-makers, for they shall be called the children of God—*the* children because they set the Father on the throne of the Family.[41]

41 George MacDonald, *The Hope of the Gospel*, "God's Family."

We scarcely realize how easily, invisibly, and thoughtlessly a careless word may cause division, disunity, or discord…a seed of strife planted that bears malicious fruit.

What this tells us, besides the need to watch our words, is how easily also seeds of *peace* are planted…with the kind, uplifting, gentle, unifying, encouraging word or expression. The peacemakers are, as MacDonald says, fellow workers with God in the development of his eternal and universal family.

God, give me insight how I can weave strands of peace between your children today! Send my footsteps across the path of one who needs peace spread into his or her life. Keep me watchful and ready to seize the opportunity to be peacemaker and peace spreader.

90. Keep Your Word

Whatever your lips utter you must be sure to do. (Deuteronomy 23:23)
It is better not to make a vow than to make one and not fulfill it. (Ecclesiastes 5:5 NIV)

This command can be stated in any number of ways:

- *Say what you mean.*
- *Do what you say you will do.*
- *Let your yes be yes and your no be no.*
- *Don't speak frivolously.*
- *Be a man or woman of your word.*

These all boil down to a corollary of command # 86—truthfulness and honesty:

Be honest and truthful in what you say. Don't promise what you can't deliver.

As simple as the words seem, the principle of being faithful to what you say, being responsible to follow through, is woven as a subtle undercurrent through the entire book of *Proverbs*. Reading between the lines, the accountability of integrity, honesty, and truthfulness informs and gives life to Solomon's entire vision of a life of wisdom.

Truthful speech exemplifies wisdom.

The opposite of truthful speech is frivolously grandiose and optimistic speech with no reality to back it up. Over promising is another form of using words carelessly—pretending that you intend more than you do, pretending what you have no *intention* of devoting your full attention to, making empty promises and commitments, even pretending to be more than you are.

It's what we call happy talk. It's the car salesman style of communication. At root it's deceptive and dishonest.

Frivolous happy talk is so common we think nothing of it. You hear the words, "I promise," over and over on television and in movies. It's become a throwaway expression of hopeful intentions with nothing to back them up. Promise is a *huge* word. It should never be used frivolously.

However, enough railing against a culture that thinks nothing of disingenuous talk. We don't need to belabor the problem. I would have us re-examine our *own* speech patterns in obedience to this command. Have I allowed the world's carelessness of commitment to infect *me*?

This is about far more than *promises*. It's about the full scope of commitment—from marriage vows to being on time.

If, "I'll be there at ten," really means, "I'll *try* to be there by ten…if it's convenient," then the world's carelessness virus has corrupted your word.

If, "I'll have it done by Tuesday," means, "I'll *aim* for Tuesday…and hope for the best," we've been infected. We are speaking the world's language of meaningless commitments, hollow promises, and empty words.

There are no insignificant words, no insignificant promises, no insignificant commitments. Being consistently late may not be so glaring a violation against keeping one's word as divorce. But neither is it insignificant. When Jesus said in Matthew 12:36 that we will give account for every idle word, he was speaking of the entire fabric of speech patterns—in large things and small. *Every* is also a huge word, with implications that may come back on our heads whenever we open our mouths.

Idle promises and commitments are indicators of character flaws that make the life of wisdom outlined in *Proverbs* very difficult if not impossible. The proverbs are lived in the small things. Wisdom cannot co-exist with careless speech. An individual who does not do what he says, whose word cannot be counted on, is not a wise, integritous, and dependable man or woman.

The old expression, *A man's word is his bond*, is rooted in the book of *Proverbs*. Imagine how different might be the world's impression of Christianity if the expression instead was:

A Christian's word is as good as gold. If they say it, you can count on it. When two Christians marry, it's forever. If a Christian says he'll be there at ten, you can count on him walking in at 9:59.

Lord God, keep my lips true. May I always mean what I say, and do what I say I will do. Keep me from laziness about time commitments, and all commitments. Keep me from shallow assurances, empty promises, groundless predictions, and resume enhancements. May I be a person about whom it is said, You can count on him. His word is gold.

Series Ten

Renewal and Restoration

Repenting of Waywardness

Continually renew the covenant of the Book

The boy king who became a Scriptural mentor of faithfulness

This book might have been called "The Commands of the Judges, Prophets, Priests, and Kings"—David, Solomon, Josiah were kings, Samuel was a judge, and Aaron and Ezra were priests. Adam, Noah, and Joshua were none of the above. Only Isaiah and Malachi in our group of twelve men were technically *prophets*. Yet they are all "prophetic" messengers of God.

One of the least known but in my view most important men of the Old Testament is the boy-king Josiah, cousin of the prophet Zephaniah. Josiah reigned as king of Judah between 640 and 608 B.C.

The story of his life reveals why I hold Josiah in high esteem along with Moses, Samuel, David, and Ezra as among the significant "prophets" of this compilation.

Prior to Josiah's reign, the Law of Moses was not only being ignored, the apostasy of the nation and the kings that had immediately preceded him was so great that the Law had been lost altogether. His father and grandfather were among the many kings "who did evil in the eyes of the Lord." There was no reason to suppose that Josiah would not follow in their footsteps. [42]

A turning point came in Judah's history, however, eight years into Josiah's reign. The young sixteen-year-old king experienced a spiritual awakening. Had he been listening to Zephaniah's preaching? Had his prophet-cousin sought the king in private and urged him to do his duty before God?

> *Josiah was eight years old when he began to reign, and he reigned thirty-one years in Jerusalem. He did what was right in the eyes of the Lord, and walked in the ways of David his father; and he did not turn aside to the right or to the left. For in the eighth year of his reign, while he was yet a boy, he began to seek the God of David...and in the twelfth year he began to purge Judah and Jerusalem of the high places.* (2 Chronicles 34:1-3)

Whatever prompted the awakening, the young king proceeded to change the entire course of Judah's history with what are called "Josiah's reforms." Josiah epitomizes the essence of command #20—at a turning point in his life he set his internal compass Godward. For the rest of his life he was obedient to God's commands.

> *Before him there was no king like him, who turned to the Lord with all his heart and with all his soul and with all his might, according to all the law of Moses; nor did any like him arise after him.* (2 Kings 23:25)

---

[42] Josiah's *great*-grandfather Hezekiah, contemporary of Isaiah, was one of Judah's greatest and most Godly and obedient kings. Josiah is a wonderful example of the truth that we all have legacies of righteousness in our genealogies.

What an amazing thing to be said of any man, echoing Genesis 6:9-10: "Noah was a righteous man…he walked with God." Josiah was, in his day, just like Noah had been in his—a man set apart in the midst of a corrupt and wicked world.

The back story of Josiah's reforms tells one of the Bible's great dramas—worthy of a major movie!

Over two generations, led by the evil and apostasy of its two previous kings, the temple in Jerusalem deteriorated into serious disrepair. The Book of the Law was completely lost under what amounted to rubble and ruins. One of the reforms on Josiah's agenda, therefore, was the repair and renovation of the temple.

What followed is one of the remarkable accounts in the Bible, a true mystery story—the unearthing of a buried treasure!

> *And in the twelfth year he began to purge Judah and Jerusalem of the high places…*
>
> *Now in the eighteenth year of his reign, when he had purged the land and the house, he sent Shaphan… to repair the house of the Lord his God. They came to Hilkiah the high priest and… Hilkiah the priest found the book of the law of the Lord given through Moses… Shaphan brought the book to the king, and… read it before the king….* (2 Chronicles 34:3, 8-9, 14, 16, 18, 29-33)

After the Book of the Law was discovered, Josiah did exactly as Moses had commanded in Deuteronomy 31. He led the people in repentance for their waywardness, then read the Law and renewed the covenant as Moses had commanded.

Josiah obeyed!

> *Then the king sent, and all the elders of Judah and Jerusalem were gathered to him. And the king went up to the house of the Lord, and with him all the men of Judah and all the inhabitants of Jerusalem, and the priests and the prophets, all the people, both small and great; and he read in their hearing all the words of the book of the covenant which had been found in the house of the Lord. And the king stood by the pillar and made a covenant before the Lord, to walk after the Lord and to keep his commandments and his testimonies and his statutes, with all his heart and all his soul, to perform the words of this covenant that were written in this book; and all the people joined in the covenant.* (2 Kings 23:1-3)

The account of Josiah's reign is one of the pivotal accounts of obedience in the Bible, making Josiah not only one of Judah's and Israel's greatest kings, but a true prophet of renewal and restoration.

The discovery of the Book of the Law will be echoed again, with much the same result, centuries later under the leadership of Ezra the priest.

SERIES TEN

RENEWAL AND RESTORATION

91. Be still and know God.
92. Consecrate yourself.
93. Circumcise your heart.
94. Continually renew covenant with God.
95. Destroy potential idols.
96. Make no rash decisions.
97. Do not chase fantasies.
98. Avoid people who talk too much.
99. Keep knowledge to yourself.
100. Do not engage in meaningless worship.

91. Be Still and Know God

"Be still and know that I am God." (Psalm 46:10)."

In the list of David's prayers, one of the most powerful verses in the Bible is not present. The reason is because it does not come to us in the form of a prayer, but of a *command.* Most of the commands come to us spoken through God's men. We interpret them as from God, and as incumbent upon our lives because we believe God spoke to mankind through these men.

This particular command stands unique with only a handful of others. Though written down by David, it comes directly from God. It is one we all know well:

Be still and know that I am God.

The quietly thunderous power of these words is so enormous that I have none of my own to add. My fingers can only rest…I lean my head back…close my eyes…rest… absorb…listen…and wait…

Be still…and know.

How often in the frenetic pace of life, among the endless urgencies that call out to be done, and done *now,* do I take time to quiet my senses…breathing deep…eyes closed…and do nothing but wait… listening to the silence?

Truly *still.*

Quiet.

Calm.

Mentally at rest.

Strange as it sounds, one of the hardest things in the world is to consciously slow down, allowing the noise of the world to recede…letting it rush on without me…retreating into the quiet center…and *still* myself.

> Deep within us all there is an amazing inner sanctuary of the soul, a holy place, a Divine Center, a speaking Voice, to which we may continuously return. Eternity is at our hearts, pressing upon our time-torn lives…calling us home unto Itself…It is a dynamic center, a creative Life that presses to birth within us. It is a Light Within which illuminates the face of God and casts new shadows and new glories upon the face of men…a…Silence which is the source of sound…a holy Center where the breath and stillness of Eternity are heavy upon us… [43]

Amazingly and counterintuitively, God says that it is out of the stillness and silence that we will *know* him. We won't know him from analysis, activity, doctrine, sermons, books, church, or theology. These may play important roles in the process of coming to know him. But they are informed and given life out of the stillness of the Center.

---

[43] Thomas Kelly, *A Testament of Devotion*, pp. 29, 74, 115.

God reveals himself in silence.

I may be reading more into the account than is there. But I envision the reality of this command at work in Samuel's early life when he heard the still small voice of God, and also in the experience of Josiah when he "began to seek God" at sixteen.

- The call…
  Samuel…Samuel…
- The quiet Voice…
  Josiah…this is your God. I am your Father. I want you to walk with me as your great-grandfather did…as David did…as Moses did…as Noah did.
- The tumult followed by the silence…
  The Lord was not in the wind…the Lord was not in the earthquake… the Lord was not in the fire; and after the fire a still small voice. (1 Kings 19:11-12)

God speaks that same home-calling summons and invitation of divine Fatherhood into every human heart. But few hear. Few have trained themselves in the stillness to perceive the Voice in the silence as Samuel did, as Elijah did, and as I believe Josiah did.

Be still and know…
Center down into the stillness…and I will speak…I will reveal myself…Be still and you will know me, for I am your God and your Father.
Come to me in the stillness.
I am waiting to meet you…awaiting you in the stillness of the Center.

Thank you, Father, for the example of your men like Samuel and Josiah. Draw me into the quietude of the Center where your still small voice is waiting to speak to me out of the silence. May the quietude of life's divine Center, where you dwell within me, be the regulating energy of my days, and where I return to be held in your care as I sleep.

92. Consecrate Yourself

"Consecrate yourselves, for tomorrow the Lord will do amazing things among you."
(Joshua 3:5, NIV)

One of the significant stumbling blocks that inhibits the people of the world from accurately understanding the truths of Christianity, causing them not even to give those truths a fair hearing, is our use of off-putting terms.

Too easily Christians lapse into their own private "religious" language. The jargon and nomenclature of this language sound ridiculous in the ears of modernism—old-fashioned, out of touch, and judgmentally elitist.

This response is our own fault. We reduce high truths (salvation, prayer, being born again, hell, etc.) to formulas, then dish out cliché-speak to hard questions. Circular reasoning does not help our cause (*The Bible is true because the Bible says it is true*). Such inside baseball communication methods make it difficult to transmit to a skeptical world the deep logic, historical veracity, and intellectual integrity that undergird the Christian message. They make it virtually impossible to believably convey the authenticity, reliability, and truthfulness of the Bible. In delivering truths of God to the world, we are our own worst enemies.

In my writings I intentionally avoid formularistic explanations of theological conundrums and cliché-speak for exactly this reason. Because of this I am regularly taken to task by a few readers for not spelling out salvation, for instance, and other such truths, by the tried-and-true traditional formula-clichés they find comforting.

This said, within the brotherhood of faith, as we try to understand the deep truths of the Bible, many terms and phrases combine to establish the theologic underpinings of Christianity. These do indeed point to important truths that we take very seriously. While we must listen to ourselves through the world's ears, at the same time neither can the world's skepticism dissuade us from appropriating the truths of those ideas, whether the world likes or understands the terms or not. There *are* spiritual truths that sometimes go by hard words we can't ignore.

In this and the next two commands we encounter three consecutive "C" truths that the world may scoff at. Their deep import, however, is woven through the fabric of the Old Testament on nearly every page Indeed, they are *so* embedded in the Old Testament that they may even seem old-fashioned, outdated, and of little importance to many Christians as well as to the world. But they are meant for us, today just as surely as they were for the Israelites of old.

Those truths are: *Consecration, Circumcision,* and *Covenant.*

The first may be the most unfamiliar. But there is no great mystery to *consecration.* It simply means to dedicate, promise, pledge, or set apart. A marriage is a mutual dedication, a *commitment,* of two people to one another—promising and pledging themselves to lifetime love and fidelity and care, each setting the other apart from all others as their lifetime husband or wife. Wedding vows are a form of *consecration.*

Consecration is a particularly *spiritual* form of commitment or dedication—the act or decision of pledging, promising, and dedicating oneself, or even another, to *the service of and obedience to God.*

When priests enter the priesthood and ministers enter the ministry, they take solemn vows that formalized their pledge, their *self-consecration* to the service of God and the church.

From the very beginning, Aaron and his sons and the tribe of Levites were "consecrated" by the heritage of their birth into the priesthood. In Samuel 1, we are told that Hannah prayed a vow to the Lord, promising that if he gave her a son she would dedicate him in the service of God. It was a pledge she made and she was faithful to it. Her son, of course, was Samuel, who was thus "consecrated." As soon as he was old enough, he went to live with Eli the priest, and grew up faithful to the calling to which his mother had pledged him.

Moses and the prophets who followed took consecration far beyond this priestly meaning. They commanded *all* God's men and women—not because of birth, parental vow, priestly calling, or ordination—to consecrate *themselves* to God. Permanently. Irrevocably.

Moses commanded *self*-consecration. He commands us to pledge *ourselves*.

The *word* "consecration" is not only unfamiliar to worldly ears. The whole idea is foreign to contemporary Christianity as well. Pray a certain prayer, believe certain things, go through a catechism class, join a church, recite a statement of belief...and voila, you are "a Christian," a "church member" in good standing.

The prophets intended something altogether different than this easy-come, easy-go, church-and-fluff affiliation that erroneously and hypocritically goes by the name of Christianity. They had in mind—and they commanded—that God's people choose to make themselves Samuels and Josiahs by placing *themselves* under holy orders.

The command is unambiguous:

- *Consecrate yourselves.*
- *Set yourselves apart for the service of God.*

The command carries the same import as if you and I were joining the priesthood. No turning back. A vow lasting a lifetime.

- Have I utterly committed myself to the world-separated life of a disciple of Jesus?
- Have I placed myself under holy orders, as permanently and irrevocably as if I had joined a monastery or convent?
- Am I consecrated and set apart by an irreversible yet moment-by-moment life-decision to follow Jesus in every way I know how?

These questions identify what it means to "be a Christian." I cannot help but wonder what the numbers would be in today's mega-churches if these questions were put before prospective members.

I hardly know fully what it means, God, so foreign is the word to our times and the teaching I have received as a Christian. But to the limited extent of my awareness, it is my desire to be wholly yours for life. I therefore take this moment to dedicate and consecrate myself to you. Take me where I am, for your service, and reveal to me what you want me to do.

93. Circumcise Your Heart

Circumcise yourselves to the Lord, remove the foreskin of your hearts. (Jeremiah 4:4)

The second of the C-words Introduced in #92 is one everyone knows. It is not so old-fashioned and "religious" as consecration. Circumcision is not technically a spiritually-connotive word at all, but one which describes a simple surgical procedure performed on tens of thousands of infant males every day around the world.

In the ancient Levitical law, circumcision was the outward physical symbol to identify the nation of the Hebrews—the symbol of *national* consecration. When God set Israel apart he commanded that all males be circumcised as an outward sign that they were henceforth a people dedicated to him. Circumcision gave visible and down-to-earth reality to the pledge.

If a non-native-born man wanted to join the nation of Israel, he had to be circumcised. Obviously this was not a decision a grown man would make lightly. How different this was to the ease with which people today are told they can "become" Christians. Circumcision was binding and permanent. There was truly no turning back!

How many of today's country club "Christians" would keep their church membership if something this drastic was required to test their commitment, to see if they really meant business or were just playing with the externals of religious ideas like spiritual toys?

We usually associate *heart* circumcision with Paul, one of the most profound wordsmiths ever to set quill to papyrus, and a literary mentor to all who aspire to be writers. But in fact circumcision of the heart is one of the great truths and commands of the Old Testament.

- It originated first with Moses: "Circumcise therefore the foreskin of your heart, and be no longer stubborn." (Deuteronomy 10:16)
- Later the prophet Jeremiah echoed Moses: "Circumcise yourselves to the Lord." (Jeremiah 4:4)
- Paul took up the truth, and amplified its spiritual intent: "Nor is true circumcision something external and physical…real circumcision is a matter of the heart, spiritual and not literal." (Romans 2:28-29)

Moses and Jeremiah saw the higher meaning in the symbolism—that God was calling a people apart who would not just *look* different physically, but that would *be* different spiritually. The two great prophets call God's people up to the higher plane of obedient *self-consecration*, using the powerful imagery of circumcision of the heart to convey it.

"Circumcision of the heart" takes the pledge, the consecration, to a whole new level. The imagery is graphic. Almost chilling.

Remove the foreskin of your hearts.

Most Christians know the term. The idea of a "spiritual circumcision" is woven throughout the New Testament. Yet this is a very difficult command to know *how* to obey in the here and now. I speak of the practicality of the commands—that they are usually truths we can *live*...that we can walk out the door and *do*. That is the beauty of the commands—their daily practicality. Even consecration can be practical and real when it leads us to commit ourselves in prayer to follow Jesus, and to renew the dedication daily to set ourselves apart as his disciples.

Yet circumcision of the heart is so deeply and entirely *spiritual*—an inner transaction between ourselves and God that no one else can see. Plunging to the core of personhood, it is a truth not easy to thoroughly translate into practical obedience in the next five minutes. Circumcision of the heart is ethereal and indefinable. Which is simply to say it is entirely internal and *personal*.

What are the mechanics of yielding, relinquishing, submitting the deepest self to God, saying, "I am yours as irrevocably as if I were to slice off a portion of the deepest part of my being as represented by the heart?"

Who can tell another what is involved in that holy exchange between the Father and his son or daughter?

Then what will be the daily-life practical effect of such a holy relinquishment?

The world may not see the visible evidence or reality of obedience to this command. There are no outward signs or proofs of heart-circumcision as there are for physical circumcision. Perhaps that is why Moses and Jeremiah used such a bizarre term to convey this deeply personal surrender to our Father-Creator.

However we respond to this command, our obedience will never be seen by anyone but God alone.

As I prayed earlier, heart-circumcision is so new, so strange, so beyond what anyone at church talks or thinks about. I hardly know what to pray except, as I prayed before, I desire with all my heart to be completely yours, my Father. I give myself to you anew. I lay myself bare before you and ask you to circumcise my heart with your loving scalpel, and make me one, heart, soul, mind, and strength, with you.

94. Continually Renew Covenant with God

And the king stood...and made covenant before the Lord and to keep his commandments... and all the people joined in the covenant. (2 Kings 23:3)

And the Israelites separated themselves... and read from the book of the law...they made confession...we make a firm covenant and write it. (Nehemiah 9:2-3, 38)

We now come to the third command in this progression—*Covenant*. The three truths of consecration, circumcision, and covenant are inextricably interwoven as one. They represent three sides of a prism, each shining light upon the same truth from different angles.

That truth is:

Yielding heart, soul, and mind in childship to God the Father.

A covenant is simply a contract, a binding agreement between two parties. In the Bible, God established a covenant first with Noah and Abraham and then with the Israelite people as an entire race. That covenant ultimately spread to the whole world.

The covenant was *always* with every man, woman, and child. It was never an exclusive covenant only with the Hebrews, Israelites, and Jews. God established the covenant to be revealed in progressive stages for obscure reasons, but from the beginning it was a *universal* covenant.

In a sense, by the very fact of creation, the covenant began with Adam, though that word was not used. If original sin was passed into the human race by Adam, so too is the covenant with humanity's Father-Creator. If man has not been faithful to keep his side of the covenant, God *keeps* his promises. The Adam-covenant will thus eventually come full circle, drawing all the created universe back into its originating Life, in eternity.

The covenant or contract was mutual. Like all contracts, it stipulated certain commitments to which both parties agreed. The terms God specified in brief were:

- *On God's part:* I am your God and Creator and Father. I will be to you a good and faithful Father. I will bless you, your families, your crops, and give you long and prosperous lives. If you live your lives as my children, I will make life a good thing for you.
- *On man's part:* You will obey my commands, precepts, and ordinances, and thus be my faithful people and obedient sons and daughters. This agreement on your part will insure your receiving the full blessings and benefits of my Fatherhood and this covenant I make with you.

This is obviously greatly simplified. The book of *Deuteronomy* can be seen as a detailed review of the covenant. There, and elsewhere during times of renewal and faithfulness—in particular as we have seen instituted by Josiah and as we will see in the next series under Ezra, exampled in the two above scriptures—the people enthusiastically agreed to the covenant. They agreed to keep their half of the bargain.

The covenant renewal under Josiah:

> *And the king stood in his place and made a covenant before the Lord, to walk after the Lord and to keep his commandments and his testimonies and his statutes, with all his heart and all his soul, to perform the words of the covenant that were written in this book. Then he made all who were present in Jerusalem and in Benjamin stand to it. And the inhabitants of Jerusalem did according to the covenant of God, the God of their fathers. And Josiah took away all the abominations from all the territory that belonged to the*

people of Israel, and made all who were in Israel serve the Lord their God. All his days they did not turn away from following the Lord the God of their fathers. (2 Chronicles 34:21-33)

As the Old Testament shows, however, the Israelites were better at making promises than keeping them.

Jumping ahead 150 years to Ezra's time, again led by a faithful prophet priest, the nation renewed and promised fidelity to the covenant, though neither was it kept by those who followed him.

The covenant renewal under Ezra:

> *While Ezra prayed and made confession, weeping and casting himself down before the house of God, a very great assembly of men, women, and children, gathered to him out of Israel..."We have broken faith with our God...Therefore let us make a covenant with our God...*(Ezra 10:1-3)

> *The rest of the people...and all who have separated themselves from the peoples of the lands to the law of God, their wives, their sons, their daughters, all who have knowledge and understanding, join with their brethren, their nobles, and enter into a curse and an oath to walk in God's law which was given by Moses the servant of God, and to observe and do all the commandments of the Lord our Lord and his ordinances and his statutes.* (Nehemiah 10:28-29)

God's covenant was and is distinct from man's contracts and covenants. It is a permanent and ongoing covenant. It can never be broken. Even should those on man's side not keep the covenant and renege on their promise, God will never tear up the contract.

It is an *eternal* covenant. The prophets are full of this eternal perspective as seen through God's eyes. He promises to be faithful, to keep his Fatherhood side of the covenant, which will ultimately result in the universal heart-consecration of the people to whom he will never cease pouring out his love.

In other words, God continually *renews* his side of the covenant too. It is an ever-expanding eternal covenant:

> *Behold, the days are coming, says the Lord, when I will make a new covenant with the house of Israel and the house of Judah...this is the covenant which I will make...after those days, says the Lord: I will put my law within them, and I will write it upon their hearts; and I will be their God, and they shall be my people.* (Jeremiah 31:31, 33)

Glimpsing this ongoing and permanent nature of the covenant, Israel's righteous prophets and kings, so wonderfully exampled by Josiah, called the people to remember and renew the covenant. Josiah's life gives testimony to this unique aspect of God's covenant with man—that it is an unbreakable and renewable agreement.

The covenant is always there. God's faithfulness to his side of the bargain is 24/7/365—unrelenting, unwavering. His loving divine Fatherhood is over all and in all, actively pouring out his covenant love to all humankind in spite of its waywardness. He is waiting for one here, one there, to remember the covenant, to remember man's side of the eternal equation. He is waiting for hearts to awaken one at a time. He is waiting for men and women to come to him to renew the pledge, to consecrate themselves anew, to circumcise their hearts, and step again as sons and daughters into mutual covenant with their Father.

He is not waiting to *give* his love…he is waiting for hearts to *receive* his love.

God did not just make covenant with Abraham and the Israelites. That mutual covenant is one he has made with you and me. Josiah's example is ours to follow.

Signing on the dotted line means, "I hereby agree to your terms, God. I will continually renew the covenant to obey your commands, precepts, and ordinances. You will be my God, and I will be your faithful son or daughter."

I commit myself to your terms, God. I renew my covenant with you. You are my God. I desire to be your faithful son. Continually reveal to my understanding increasing depths in your commands, precepts, and ordinances that I might obey them, and that I might live ever more completely in the full scope of the mutual covenant you have established with me.

95. Destroy Potential Idols

Destroy completely all the places…where the nations…worship their gods. Break down their altars, smash their sacred stones…cut down the idols of their gods. (Deuteronomy 12:2-3, NIV)

We continue to gaze retrospectively back to the era of Moses, in this case to the second of the Ten Commandments which was, "Make no idols." Here, however, we approach the problem of idol worship from another side—not just after the fact, when it is too late, *after* the golden calf has been forged. Now we must anticipate, looking ahead before the *potential* idol is allowed to become an idol that destroys us.

This is pro-active idol destruction.

Don't wait until the idol has come into your home, your mind, your heart. Exorcise even the *possibility* that it will take hold of you and eventually possess you. That is why Moses' instructions about the altars and idols of the nations was so drastic—destroy them *utterly* so they do not become idols for *you* as they were to the nations of the world. Don't merely eradicate the idol-reminder of sin…destroy the *possibility* of sin.

This command is foundational to the previous three. Three primary causes are at root in the failure to keep God's covenant of consecration and heart-circumcision.

- Forgetfulness:
  Take heed not to forget God's commands.
- Disobedience:
  Walk in obedience to God's commands.
- Idol Worship:
  Make no idols.

Josiah's reforms, therefore, were threefold at exactly these points:

- Remembering and renewing the covenant
- A call to obedience.
- Destruction of idols.

Josiah was positively ruthless against the idols:

> *...and in the twelfth year he began to purge Judah and Jerusalem of the high places, the Ashe'rim, and the graven and the molten images. And they broke down the altars of the Ba'als in his presence; and he hewed down the incense altars which stood above them; and he broke in pieces the Ashe'rim and the graven and the molten images, and he made dust of them and strewed it over the graves of those who had sacrificed to them. He also burned the bones of the priests on their altars, and purged Judah and Jerusalem. And in the cities of Manas'seh, E'phraim, and Simeon, and as far as Naph'tali, in their ruins round about, he broke down the altars, and beat the Ashe'rim and the images into powder, and hewed down all the incense altars throughout all the land of Israel. Then he returned to Jerusalem.* (2 Chronicles 34:3-7)

In my life, I view the first two elements of renewal above as reaffirmation of my childship and God's Fatherhood. I have to *renew* my remembrance that God's covenant emerges out of his Fatherhood. He is a good Father. The imperative of obedience that rests on *my* child-side of the covenant is birthed in *his* Fatherhood-goodness. What else would I want to do as his child than obey him?

The greater challenge lies in the third component of renewal—recognizing potential idols that would detract from my moment-by-moment awareness of this *Fatherhood-childship* foundation of my life.

Using the word *idol* may seem over the top for modern Christians. Yet idols come in many pleasing sizes and shapes and wearing very acceptable clothes. They invariably masquerade as *good* things. That's what makes idols such a tricky business. Looking so respectable, they infiltrate with ingenious guile.

Even Christian doctrines of tradition can be potential idols. The theology which portrays God as a vengeful tyrant rather than as the Father of Jesus is deeply embedded in the psyche of most Christians from years of indoctrination. It is a pervasive virus in my spiritual DNA too. It is so deep inside me that I have to constantly squelch that anti-Fatherhood doctrine from regaining a foothold. Though I am in no danger of "worshipping" this doctrine-idol of a false god, its influence is hard to escape.

That doctrine is just one of my false "sacred altars" I have to smash. I have others. You will have your own.

George MacDonald writes: "How have we learned Christ? It ought to be a startling thought, that we may have learned him wrong. That must be far worse than not to have learned him at all: his place is occupied by a false Christ, hard to exorcise! The point is, whether we have learned Christ as he taught himself, or as men have taught him who thought they understood, but did not understand him." [44]

We all have our private personal potential substitutes for obedient childship. It is these subtle substitutes, not murder or bank robbery, that the enemy deviously uses to lure us away from the bull's eye. He will use as many good and respectable distractions as it takes to undermine the singlemindedness of our discipleship.

Knowing the enemy's tactics, to lure our worship away from God's best, we have to continually follow Josiah, each in our own way, into the innermost regions of our hearts and minds.

That is the battleground where war is waged against the enemy's untruths. We must root out and destroy *whatever* Satan would use as substitutes of our attention, commitment, and affection, and pursue that war with the same holy vengeance Josiah exhibited when he set out to purge Judah.

Reveal to me my own personal potential idols, Lord. Give me the courage of Josiah to destroy them.

96. Make No Rash Decisions

Guard your steps…be not rash…nor let your heart be hasty. (Ecclesiastes 5:1-2)
He who makes haste…misses his way. (Proverbs 19:2)
Do you see a man who is hasty in his words? There is more hope for a fool than for him. (Proverbs 29:20)

Returning to Solomon's practicalities from *Proverbs*, I am reminded yet again how wonderfully the seemingly "spiritual" commands (consecration, heart-circumcision, covenant) translate into down-to-earth realities. Both Old and New Testaments exquisitely balance these two equal components of life as God's children (high spiritual truth and daily life-practicality). That's why we have the books of *Deuteronomy* and *Proverbs*, the Sermon on the Mount and Paul's letters.

High truth and daily practicality are fused as one.

44 George MacDonald, *Unspoken Sermons Third Series*, "The Truth in Jesus."

We might read the progression of this series as:

"You have consecrated yourself to God, you have prayed a prayer of heart-circumcision…wonderful! Now make no rash decisions, don't chase fantasies, and avoid people who talk too much."

In other words—practice high truth in life's trenches.

No one expresses this balance better than the Lord's brother James:

> *Religion that is pure and undefiled before God and the Father is this: to visit orphans and widows…and to keep oneself unstained from the world.* (James 1:27)

It doesn't get more practical than that—servanthood and separation from the world.

Throughout *Proverbs*, loose talk and hasty actions are regularly equated with foolishness. Jesus says to call no one a fool, yet Solomon freely uses the image of the "fool" as the contrast to one seeking wisdom. He identifies the hallmarks of a fool with piercing force. Who can read *Proverbs* without wincing?

When he gives advice about wisdom and foolishness Solomon is not just shooting from the hip. He is God's man speaking truth into the practicalities of life where wisdom and foolishness coexist around us…and *in* us. More than that, when probed deeply, most of his proverbs in some way emerge out of and reflect the character of God. That's why Solomon's wisdom is so important. Through his proverbs, he is telling us who God is.

Why should we not make rash decisions? Obviously because haste leads to *bad* decisions that will get us into hot water. But there is a more important reason—haste does not reflect the character of God.

God is never in a hurry. God takes his time. We are commanded not to be rash and hurried because *God* is not rash and hurried. His processes are slow, from the development of the cosmos, to growing things upon and in the earth, to the gradual unfolding of truth throughout mankind's history.

God does few things all at once. The *process*—a slowly unfolding process—is integral to the final outcome of God's eternal intent. George MacDonald colorfully says that God works toward his ultimate purposes with "infinitudes of tender gradation and delicate mystery."

A seemingly simple command from *Proverbs* such as, *Make no rash decisions,* is thus more profound than it looks. It forces us to examine the decisions we face through the prism of *God's* methods rather than the false-urgencies of life's busyness. We might reword it:

Make decisions by following God's M.O. Take your time, do not be hasty. Allow the process of patience to reveal truth, and bring well-ordered results according to God's timetable.

Speaking of the main character in one of his novels, George MacDonald wrote: "He believed in a holy, unhasting growth, in which God's ways had God's time to be sacredly wrought out." [45]

And of the miracles, he wrote:

---

45 *Donal Grant,* chapter 36, "Explaining the Lost Room."

The miracles are surely less than those mighty goings on of nature with God beheld at their heart. In the name of him who delighted to say "My Father is greater than I," I will say that his miracles in bread and in wine were far less grand and less beautiful than the works of the Father they represented, in making the corn to grow in the valleys, and the grapes to drink the sunlight on the hill-sides of the world, with all their infinitudes of tender gradation and delicate mystery of birth. But the Son of the Father be praised, who, as it were, condensed these mysteries before us, and let us see the precious gifts coming at once from gracious hands—hands that love could kiss and nails could wound. [46]

Keep me from haste when facing decisions, Lord. Remind me, when I go slow, when I take my time, when I refuse to succumb to the urgencies pressing upon me, that I am reflecting your nature. Preserving a countenance of quiet calm, I step into your method for carrying out your will and purposes in the world. Keep me walking with you, not in the ways of a rushing, hasty, urgent world.

97. Do Not Chase Fantasies

Those who chase fantasies have no sense. (Proverbs 12:11, NIV)

Chasing fantasies might be seen as a corollary to rash decision making. We've all known fantasy-chasers—always with a great new idea or scheme…grandiose plans and dreams just around the corner…yet for whom life never seems to change that much.

Certainly we all have personal dreams, goals, visions, and bucket lists. Many of these are realistic and worthy goals we *should* set ourselves to reach. It is because of this command, and the principle at its foundation woven through *Proverbs* in myriad ways, that I rarely tell people about books I am *going* to write, or *want* to write, or am *planning* to write, or *hope* to write. I prefer to speak about books I *have* written, lest my visions of grandeur never materialize. This is one of my own personal ways to heed both this command and the related principle of *Proverbs* not to talk too much.

Yet I am as susceptible to grandiose visions as, to some extent, everyone is. We like to think big. It's the winning-the-lottery scenario…pie-in-the-sky…castle building from which little is likely to come. We may not sucker for the get-rich-quick scheme of a telemarketer. But in a sense all advertising is based on the hope that people will *disobey* this command—get your clothes *cleaner*…lose weight *faster*…receive *more* for your used car…get a *better* deal on your phone…earn a *higher* rate of return. Advertising is based on fantasy, and we all take the bait every day.

Setting realistic goals is intrinsic to a productive life. When I began writing almost fifty years ago, I didn't set out to write a hundred books. I set out to write one. And I didn't talk about that one except to my wife Judy. I didn't broadcast it. I just worked to get it done. In one sense, I suppose at the time, it was a fantasy. I doubted I would ever get a book published. But I

[46] *The Miracles of Our Lord,* "Introduction."

continued to work methodically toward the goal. I never dreamed of much beyond that. Diligent work and planning are where things happen and create the conditions out of which dreams are fulfilled.

The fantasy-chasing principle from *Proverbs* is bound up with many attributes of foolishness—gullibility, frivolity, following the crowd, listening to deceivers, and not heeding wise counsel. A form of laziness is almost synonymous with the fantasy-chaser who hopes that his grandiose dreams will fall into his lap, often expecting other people to put up the money and do the hard work. Meanwhile he or she does little to make it happen.

In praying about these pointed words of Solomon's, it has occurred to me to ponder a spiritual component of this command. For how many individuals is what they call their "Christian faith" little more than a get-out-of-jail-free card rather than a lifestyle of righteousness, obedience, and discipleship? How many are exhorted to pray a salvation prayer to be "saved" from hell rather than be transformed into the image of Jesus?

The experience past, the prayer prayed, the doctrine securely in place…no more worries. Hey, I'm *in*. Saved…eternal security…nothing more to it.

Might this get-out-of-jail-free doctrine be the most serious Christian fantasy of all. How many will learn after the fact that there was more to the story, and far deeper truths involved?

Keep my heart and mind focused on your eternal realities, Lord, your Truth, your purposes, not fanciful unrealities. May I do what you put before me to do faithfully, one step of obedience and hard work at a time, and not be distracted with grandiose dreams and wishful thinking mirages.

98. Avoid People Who Talk Too Much

A gossip betrays a confidence; so avoid anyone who talks too much. (Proverbs 20:19, NIV)
Do not associate with one who speaks foolishly. (Proverbs 20:19, RSV)
Let your words be few. (Ecclesiastes 5:2)

In command #7, we addressed the problem of thoughtless speech, gossip, and passing on other people's business that is not ours to spread. These are seriously destructive habits of loose careless speech.

The problem is greater even than these examples of unguarded speech. It's not just saying what we shouldn't. It's talking too much at all. Talking too much about *anything*.

The scriptural principles violated by talkativeness are many—discretion, prudence, self-control, reticence, even selflessness and the golden rule. None of us like to have our ears talked off by someone so insensitive and wrapped up in himself or herself that he or she thinks the whole world wants to hear every detail of their lives. If that's how *I* feel, the golden rule demands that I examine my own speech patterns too. No one wants to hear *me* talk *their* ears off either.

Talking too much is such a simple vice. Should it even be called a vice at all? What's the big deal? A little too much talk—it's part of life, everyone does it. We love the sound of our own voices. Isn't it going too far to call it a *sin*!

The big deal is that unrestrained talkativeness reveals immaturity of character, self-centeredness, and lack of self-control. According to Solomon, talkativeness is one of the hallmarks of a fool. Sin or not…it's obviously serious business.

> *The prudent hold their tongues.* (Proverbs 10:19, NIV)
> *A man of understanding remains silent.* (Proverbs, 11:12, RSV)
> *Even fools are thought wise if they keep silent.* (Proverbs 17:28, NIV)
> *He who keeps his mouth and his tongue keeps himself out of trouble.* (Proverbs 21:23, RSV)

Digging deeper, as we always do, we observe God's character at the heart of the command. God doesn't talk too much. From time immemorial, man has sought, beseeched, prayed, and begged God to speak more clearly, to reveal himself, to explain what everything means. For reasons we do not understand, however, God has been very cryptic in explaining himself to humanity.

Francis Schaeffer wrote a book entitled, *He is There and He is Not Silent.* I've read the book and I know what Schaeffer was getting at. But the truth is, for most people…God *is* silent.

This obviously raises enormous theological conundrums. Those theological mysteries are not the point we are addressing here, but simply the fact of it. God is a sparse, reticent communicator. He has communicated through his created world, of course. But in what we mean by direct verbal and *clearly understandable* communication…God simply doesn't talk very much. Haven't we all wondered why he doesn't give some clear hint, some direct link to the afterlife so that we would *know* it's true.

But concerning what happens after death, about what lies on the other side of the veil between our lives and the supernatural, between me and God…we are met with resounding silence.

Neither did Jesus talk too much. He spoke when he needed to speak. He was silent when he needed to be silent. But he never talked *too* much. From the records we have, Jesus was not a chatty man. Like his heavenly Father, some of his responses to straightforward questions were frustratingly vague.

This command, therefore, has two sides. Talking too much ourselves, and being around *others* who talk too much. The heart of Solomon's command is blunt and shocking: *Avoid anyone who talks too much.* Surround yourself with people who are attentive to God's commands, and whose lives reflect God's character, and who *don't* talk too much.

The reason is simple: Speech unreflective of God's principles draws us *away* from God's principles.

The most sobering side of the command, however, comes when we turn the coin over. What if *I* am the object of someone else realizing that *I* am one *they* should avoid! Suddenly the command reads: *Don't be such a person yourself.*

Both halves of the command therefore compel me to get very serious with myself on several fronts.

- Do I want to reflect Jesus and God in *my* speech habits?
- Do I want to associate with others who reflect Jesus and God in *their* speech habits?
- Will it call me higher in righteousness to associate with those who *don't* reflect God in their speech.

> *Let every man be quick to hear, slow to speak…If any one thinks he is religious, and does not bridle his tongue…this man's religion is vain.*
> *The tongue is a little member and boasts of great things. How great a forest is set ablaze by a small fire! And the tongue is a fire. The tongue is an unrighteous world among our members, staining the whole body.* (James 1:19, 26; 3:5-6)

Prune and purify my tongue, heavenly Father, that I may not talk too much myself or associate more than I should with others whose loose tongues betray uncircumcised hearts. I ask you to circumcise my tongue as well as my heart.

99. Keep Knowledge to Yourself

A prudent man conceals his knowledge, but fools proclaim their folly. (Proverbs 12:23)

You've no doubt noticed by now that many of the Bible's commands come with a twist, with unexpected applications bombarding us from different angles. The commands are multi-dimensioned. The more layers you peel off, each meaningful at its level of application, the deeper into the core of God's character and purposes you find yourself. That's why I love the commands—they are not as simple as they look. They probe to the heart of God's purposes.

My emphasis on the practicality of command-obedience throughout the years of my writing occasionally raises the critique that such a focus is *too* practical, *too* down-to-earth. What can commands such as *Lend without interest, Use honest weights, Don't talk so much,* and *Don't chase fantasies* possibly have to do with high doctrines like sanctification, salvation, justification, consecration, and faith?

Christians love to sidestep practicality with highfalutin lingo. Thus Calvinism is founded in what to the world is as full of gobbledygook as it is riddled with falsehoods: *total depravity, unconditional election, limited atonement, irresistible grace, and perseverance of the saints.* Christians love jargon like that! Talking about *unconditional election* and *limited atonement* keeps one from having to think of such things as *Don't talk so much* and *Don't chase fantasies* as the more accurate measure of spirituality.

The very question about practicality of the commands exposes the Achilles heel and hypocrisy at the foundation of all religions, Christianity included—the disconnect between theology and real life.

What do the practicalities have to do with the doctrines, what does *Proverbs* have to do with *Romans*?

I answer: *Everything!*

The high doctrines of spirituality are raised into the loftiest realm of their true meanings *only* through the practicality of moment-by-moment command-obedience. Their eternal import is revealed in the commands...and *only* in the commands. No doctrinal or theologic reality exists apart from the commands.

Those who ask what practical commands have to do with high theology have not probed deeply enough into the commands to discover the essence of spirituality, the treasure hid in a field they reveal. Peeling off layer upon layer, digging deeper, always deeper, the commands of the Bible embody the entirety of its message and purpose. That revelation, however, only comes to those who set themselves to obey those commands. For the theologically obsessive, the hidden depths of the commands cannot reveal themselves.

Full revelation comes through obedience to the commands There is no other door.

A command such as, *Keep knowledge to yourself,* on its surface, read one-dimensionally, is confusing. Does this mean we go silent and *never* share our knowledge? What about the function of the teacher, whose sole purpose, some might say, both in the world and in the church, is to share and give forth of their knowledge?

How does a teacher approach this command? Does this command invalidate the entire premise of witnessing?

Then there is the example of Jesus, who clearly came to earth precisely to give the knowledge of his Father to the world. He obviously did not keep his knowledge of God to himself. He left his disciples with the clear imperative, "Go into all the world and make disciples...teaching..." The rest of the New Testament, largely from Paul, would seem to be in direct violation of this command. Paul sought to proclaim his "knowledge" to the whole world. And through his writings he has accomplished exactly that.

We find ourselves having to peel off another layer of the command-onion. Looking deeper, we discover multiple principles at work. We move beyond one-dimensionality in our understanding. We discover the principle that all the commands function as a unity, in harmony, in balance. We discover that we cannot make an idol of single focus from any particular command. We discover that the Bible's commands illuminate an expansive and multi-faceted tapestry of life, the threads of which cannot be legalistically analyzed microscopically. That full-life tapestry can only be revealed in its glory with an eternal perspective.

Peeling down yet further, we look again at the life of Jesus. There we find balance, harmony, unity of purpose because everything he did was informed by God's *eternal* purposes. Jesus saw everything through the lens of eternity.

Sometimes he taught openly, sometimes he was silent. He knew when to speak and when not to. He was largely silent for thirty years. Then he spoke for three. His entire life, seen as a balanced whole, exactly reflects this command. He chose his words and the occasions for speaking and silence with care.

To the hungry, he opened his heart. To those without ears to hear, he did not cast the pearls of his knowledge before the swine of their closed hearts.

He understood that spiritual hunger, openness, and humility must precede reception of the seeds of divine knowledge. He would not scatter those seeds at random. They were too precious to be cast frivolously among thorns.

Peeling still deeper, we perceive the great truth that all Jesus did came from and reflected God his Father. Neither does *God* spread the seeds of his eternal being and purpose randomly throughout his universe. His revelation is purposeful.

It would seem that God inspired these words to be written because he is *himself* the ultimate example of this very principle. We would like God to divulge more of his knowledge in ways our small humanity can understand. But he keeps much of his knowledge to himself. He places the onus on us to hunger after that knowledge enough that we will dig for it, and spare no effort to find it.

In the end we are left with a command from *Proverbs* which may be interpreted on many levels, and in balance and harmony with all the commands.

I ask you, Holy Spirit to reveal how and when to follow Jesus' example to speak in season, and how and when in other seasons to keep knowledge to myself. The desire to avail everyone in the world of my great knowledge is Satan's trap to keep me focused on myself, feeding both pride and self-centeredness in one easy stroke. When the fever begins to infect me thinking that everyone needs to hear what I have to share, help me say with Jesus, "Get behind me, satan." Remind me that most people don't care about what I know, and that it is wisdom and reflective of God himself to keep knowledge to myself.

100. Do Not Engage in Meaningless Worship

"What to me is the multitude of your sacrifices? says the Lord;
I have had enough of burnt offerings…
This people…honor me with their lips, while their hearts are far from me." (Isaiah 1:11; 29:13)

Though the Law handed down by Moses contained enormous and painstaking ritualistic detail about how the Israelites were to "worship" God, later prophets roundly condemned those same rituals for having become…well, *too* ritualistic. This shift is puzzling on the face of it. God *commanded* those rituals in the Levitical Law. Now the later prophets *condemn* them.

On further examination, however, this conundrum reflects precisely the progressively deepening understanding of what those rituals, and worship itself, were supposed to *mean.* That meaning was embodied in consecration, heart-circumcision, and *living* the covenant...being a people of *righteousness* set apart from the world.

Nor was this new. Moses understood. He did his best to communicate that reality. The rituals were not the point, but consecration of heart.

By the time of the later prophets, however, the deep meaning of personal obedience and righteousness, intended to inform the life-blood of worship, had largely disappeared.

Jeremiah well understood that the heart of the Law was never about the rituals and sacrifices. Like Moses, he recognized the source of the true meaning of the Law. He says clearly that the offerings and sacrifices were not the point, and were *never* the point.

> *"For in the day that I brought them out of the land of Egypt, I did not speak to your fathers or command them concerning burnt offerings and sacrifices. But this command I gave them, 'Obey my voice, and I will be your God, and you shall be my people; and walk in all the way that I command you, that it may be well with you.' But they did not obey or incline their ear, but walked in their own counsels and the stubbornness of their evil hearts.* (Jeremiah 7:22-23)

He was not the only prophet to rail against the empty, meaningless worship of ritual void of obedience, righteousness, and heart-consecration.

> *"Has the Lord as great delight in burnt offerings and sacrifices, as in obeying the voice of the Lord? Behold, to obey is better than sacrifice."* (1 Samuel 15:22)

> *Thou hast no delight in sacrifice.* (Psalm 51:16)

> *What to me is the multitude of your sacrifices? says the Lord; I have had enough of burnt offerings...When you come to appear before me, who requires of you this trampling of my courts?* (Isaiah 1:11-12)

> *For I desire steadfast love and not sacrifice, the knowledge of God, rather than burnt offerings.* (Hosea 6:6)

The minor prophet Micah frames the pivotal question succinctly:

> *With what shall I come before the Lord, and bow myself before God on high? Shall I come before him with burnt offerings...Will the Lord be pleased...* (Micah 6:6-7)

Then, in one of the Bible's most powerful sentences, Micah answers his own question:

He has showed you, O man, what is good; and what does the Lord require of you but to do justice, and to love kindness, and to walk humbly with your God? (Micah 6:8)

Well and good so far. Few will be squirming in the pews. Had I quoted the above passages in their full context, we would have read about bulls and rams, altars and blood and grain offerings. All these are remote from our contemporary lives. It's easy to keep this injunction at arm's length. Most Christians agree: "Yes, those ancient Israelites sure were stupid not to see the true meaning of worship."

But the Bible's commands are not only universal, they are multi-dimensional. This command is not merely historically directed at Old Testament Israelites and Jews. It is directed to us today...to the Christian church of the twenty-first century. You and I live in the middle of this command too. Therefore, let us reflect prayerfully on the worship of our *own* day.

Much of what is called "worship" throughout modern Christendom is focused on the traditional Saturday or Sunday service. It is not by accident that in Protestantism it generally goes by the name, "Worship Service."

Most people dress up. Everyone is on their best behavior. Problems, divisions, strife, and hypocrisies are shoved in the closet for a couple of hours. The sanctuary is clean, inviting, and often lavishly decorated. Nobody walks in holding a cage with chickens squawking, or leading a goat or an ox down the aisle. Our worship services are respectable in every way.

But because we don't bring bulls and rams into our church buildings and slaughter them on an altar in front of the sanctuary, are we justified in dismissing the universal intent of this command?

The shocking truth is that Christendom has followed exactly the same progression as did the Old Testament Hebrews. The so-called "worship" of Christendom is filled with the substitution of *new* forms of empty sacrifice. No bulls or goats, but rituals most respectable in their place.

The Protestant worship service, and the Catholic and Orthodox mass, have become infested with idols of a new kind, each with its own ceremonies and sacraments, formalities and rites and traditions.

The worship service and mass have *themselves* become idols of Christendom.

In free-flowing charismatic evangelicalism, the rituals are no less prevalent than in ritual-laden Catholicism. The very practice of raising one's hands in praise has become a ritual of its own as if turned on and off by remote control from the pulpit. It is equally orchestrated and learned by conditioning as are the chanted prayers and ceremony-steeped Catholic eucharist engaged in by millions every week. The specifics have changed since Old Testament times, but not the underlying shell of superficiality.

Is it not time Catholics and Orthodox believers took this command seriously, and asked what God thinks of their rites, robes, icons, and incense:

> *Bring no more vain offerings; incense is an abomination to me. Wash yourselves; make yourselves clean…cease to do evil, learn to do good.* (Isaiah 1:13, 16-17)

Is it not time that evangelicals took this command seriously, and asked what God thinks of their raised hands and praising prayers that are disconnected from the reality of *living* by the Bible's commands:

> *When you spread forth your hands, I will hide my eyes from you; even though you make many prayers, I will not listen…Wash yourselves; make yourselves clean…cease to do evil, learn to do good.* (Isaiah 1:15-17)

Keep me, God, from every form of false and empty worship, public and private. Open my eyes to the legalisms I make idols of, and from every superficiality in my walk with you. Turn me from rote observances to the reality of worshiping you in my heart.

Series Eleven

Legacy

Living as God's People Through Time

Inherit the legacy of the promise

Carrying God's legacy into the future

A hundred and fifty years went by after Josiah and his reforms. By then Judah had been overrun by the Persians and sent into exile. Again God's people slipped into waywardness, forgetful of Moses, the Law, and their history.

The ten northern tribes of Israel were lost in exile to the Assyrian empire in the 700s B.C. Now the two remaining tribes exiled in Persia—Judah and Benjamin—seemed in danger of suffering the same fate. There are two ways for a people to be lost to history—*externally* by being conquered, and *internally* by allowing their core values, traditions, and roots to be lost by waywardness and inattentiveness. The once mighty Israel of David and Solomon was being lost in both ways.

In the mid-400s B.C., however, in an extraordinary gesture of goodwill toward the people his predecessors had conquered, the Persian king commissioned Ezra, a priest of Judah who occupied a high position in the king's administration, to return to Jerusalem with 5,000 Jews to reinstitute Jewish customs and practices in the temple, and to begin rebuilding the city. This inaugurated what is called the "Restoration" period in Jewish history.[47]

Linked intrinsically to the era of renewal and restoration that had been instituted by Josiah, I have grouped the commands of this series together under the theme of "legacy," bringing the saga of the nation of Israel full circle back to the legacy of Moses. Who more fitting to symbolize this legacy than the prophet-priest Ezra, a descendent of Aaron in the direct legacy-line of the original priesthood established in *Leviticus*?

Ezra symbolizes more than a recapturing of the former legacy that God's people had inherited from their forebears—both historical and spiritual—as important as that is. He is also a fit prophet-mentor of the legacy that stretches into the *future*. It is a legacy whose continuation rests on the shoulders of the present generation, and *every* successive present generation.

Thus in this moment of time—*our* moment of time—that legacy stretches *back* in time to Moses and Aaron and Noah, and even Adam…and stretches *forward* in time to those who come after us. It is a legacy, as it did for Josiah and Ezra in their day, that now rests on your shoulders and mine. We stand at that eternally present crossroads between the past and the future—exactly as did Josiah and Ezra.

This dual nature of the legacy explains why legacy-commands always point in two directions.

---

47 The entire sweep of Old Testament history is fascinating. Among the most fascinating eras of all—with yet a mystery at the bottom of it surrounding Ezra—is this period of the Restoration. Once again, therefore, I recommend to those interested in a deeper dive into these events, Volume 2 of my *Eyewitness Old Testament*.

- *The past:* Look back with reverence and respect…honor your parents…do not forget…respect the aged…read the Law every seven years…remember the blessings and curses.
- *The future:* Look forward with sobriety and a sense of accountability, read the Law every seven years…teach your children God's commands…and their children after them…exhort them not to forget…to the third and fourth generation…for this shall be an everlasting sign which shall not be cut off.

The legacy of God's people, and the legacy of the revelation of God's plan and purposes, is a permanent and *continuously* unfolding, growing, expanding legacy of ever-increasing truth that will culminate in eternity. Remembering commands is the link between past and future. *Every* generation of God's people—absorbing and growing strong from, sending roots down into the soil of their heritage from the *past*— is responsible to carry that legacy *forward* to the next generation, one generation at a time, generation after generation, from Aaron and Moses…to Samuel and David and Solomon…to Josiah…to Ezra and Nehemiah…to Jesus' disciples…to James and Paul…and to you and me and those that follow us.

It is a legacy that will carry us all—those who have come before, and those who come after—into eternity.

The historical context out of which the Ezra-Nehemiah era of legacy-renewal emerged is not only fascinating for its own sake, it gives a powerful reminder that, though the continuation of God's legacy is anchored in commands that God's people must obey for the legacy to continue, God himself takes an active share in that continuation as well. God will not let his legacy die. Even when at certain times in history all seems lost, God always raises up a remnant to keep his legacy alive. And often to send it yet again into the future with renewed revelation and forcefulness.

Josiah woke a remnant. Ezra and Nehemiah woke a remnant.

And so it will continue through time. We may be approaching a period of history when all that is left to keep the legacy alive is a remnant that "remembers" what the commands mean—a lifestyle of righteousness, obedience, and world-separated discipleship. If so, God will surely bring that remnant to life. [48]

The series of events represented by the books of *Ezra* and *Nehemiah* is remarkable in that the impetus for the reforms led by Ezra did not come from within Judah but was commanded by the Persian king. God is even able to use unbelieving secular people—even governments!—to enliven the remnant and send his legacy into the future!

The letter Artaxerxes gave Ezra authorizing him, by the king's authority, to rebuild Israel's spiritual heritage must be one of the most astonishing turns of fortune recorded in the Bible.

---

[48] This is the underlying thematic foundation of my futuristic fiction series, *The Tribulation Cult.*

This is a copy of the letter which King Artaxerxes gave to Ezra the priest, the scribe... "Artaxerxes, king of kings, to Ezra the priest, the scribe of the law of the God of heaven. And now I make a decree that any one of the people of Israel or their priests or Levites in my kingdom, who freely offers to go to Jerusalem, may go with you. For you are sent by the king and his seven counselors to make inquiries about Judah and Jerusalem according to the law of your God, which is in your hand, and also to convey the silver and gold which the king and his counselors have freely offered to the God of Israel, whose dwelling is in Jerusalem...Whatever seems good to you and your brethren to do with the rest of the silver and gold, you may do, according to the will of your God.

What a remarkable document! As Ezra himself realized. After quoting the letter above, he wrote:

> *Blessed be the LORD, the God of our fathers, who put such a thing as this into the heart of the king, to beautify the house of the LORD which is in Jerusalem, and who extended to me his steadfast love before the king and his counselors, and before all the king's mighty officers. I took courage, for the hand of the LORD my God was upon me, and I gathered leading men from Israel to go up with me.* (Ezra 7:27-28)

Ezra was not only a devout priest, he was also a scribe and knowledgeable student of the history of his people. He is thought by most scholars to be the author of *1 & 2 Chronicles*, and also conjectured to have had a hand in gathering, editing, writing, collating, and compiling other parts of the Old Testament. He understood obedience to the Law and apostasy, and what were the consequences of both. Ezra knew the Choice and Consequence Code! He witnessed it first hand, and as one of Israel's preeminent historians, he wrote Israel's history from that foundation.

Arriving in Palestine, he found that yet again the people who had been able to remain during the captivity had relapsed into many sinful practices. He was determined that God's people did not repeat their failures of the past. Ezra's mission in life was to establish the preeminence of the Law of Moses as the one and only source of Judah's national identity and ethnic and spiritual heritage.

The book of *Nehemiah*, sequel to *Ezra*, or as it was initially known, *2 Ezra*, recounts the next phase of restoration. Both Ezra (priest) and Nehemiah (governor) had served in high positions for Artaxerxes. It was Nehemiah who took charge of rebuilding the city wall of Jerusalem.

When the work was complete, following Josiah's example and in obedience to Moses, the Law was read. Four chapters of *Nehemiah* are devoted to the public reading of the Law, a celebration of the Feast of Tabernacles, a great national public day of confession, a reaffirmation and sealing of the Covenant, and finally to the dedication of the wall with a great procession about the city, Nehemiah leading one group and Ezra leading the other.

It is all here: the public remembrance, confession, and renewal of the covenant. Ezra's public reading of the Law in Nehemiah 8 and mighty prayer in Chapter 9 are reminiscent of Moses himself. Ezra goes on in the following chapter to reprise Israel's history in brief, exactly as Moses did (though Moses did *not* do so in brief!) in *Deuteronomy.*

> *And all the people gathered as one man into the square before the Water Gate; and they told Ezra the scribe to bring the book of the law of Moses which the Lord had given to Israel. And Ezra the priest brought the law before the assembly, both men and women and all who could hear with understanding... And he read from it facing the square before the Water Gate from early morning until midday, in the presence of the men and the women and those who could understand; and the ears of all the people were attentive to the book of the law. And Ezra the scribe stood on a wooden pulpit which they had made for the purpose... And Ezra opened the book in the sight of all the people, for he was above all the people; and when he opened it all the people stood. And Ezra blessed the Lord, the great God; and all the people answered, "Amen, Amen," lifting up their hands...And they read from the book, from the law of God, clearly; and they gave the sense, so that the people understood the reading.*
>
> *And Nehemiah, who was the governor, and Ezra the priest and scribe, and the Levites who taught the people said to all the people, "This day is holy to the Lord your God; do not mourn or weep." For all the people wept when they heard the words of the law. Then he said to them, "Go your way, eat the fat and drink sweet wine and send portions to him for whom nothing is prepared; for this day is holy to our Lord; and do not be grieved, for the joy of the Lord is your strength..."*
>
> *On the second day the heads of fathers' houses of all the people, with the priests and the Levites, came together to Ezra the scribe in order to study the words of the law...*
>
> *Because of all this we make a firm covenant and write it, and our princes, our Levites, and our priests set their seal to it.* (Nehemiah 8: 1-6, 8-10, 13; 9: 38)

Series Eleven

Legacy

101. Live a peaceable, responsible, domestic, and upright life.

102. Speak truth.

103. Claim and pass on your inheritance in God.

104. Instruct your children in God's commands.

105. Show respect to the elderly.

106. Succeed by planning.

107. Walk in patience.

108. Cultivate love for the Lord's statutes and commands.

109. Walk in integrity.

110. Act justly, love mercy, and walk humbly with your God.

101. Live a Peaceable, Responsible, Domestic, Upright Life

The Lord your God is bringing you into a good land—a land with brooks, streams, and deep springs gushing out into the valleys and hills; a land with wheat and barley, vines and fig trees, pomegranates, olive oil and honey; a land where you will lack nothing. When you have eaten and are satisfied…when you build fine houses and settle down, and when your herds and flocks grow large and your silver and gold increase and all you have is multiplied…praise the Lord your God for the good land he has given you. (Selections from Deuteronomy 8 & 11)

The image of God commanding Joshua and Saul to slaughter their enemies badly miscolors the message of the Old Testament as a whole. Those periods of history are important to understand in context, but do not tell the entire story. They represent, in fact, a miniscule part of that whole. They might even be seen as an aberration in God's eternal plan. Destruction of evil is part of that plan, but we have to look at the bigger picture.

Digging deeper into the sweeping scope of the Old Testament story, I find an intriguing picture emerging of the lifestyle God intended, and still intends, for his people to enjoy which will preserve and sustain his legacy through history. I have no clear insight where prehistoric humanity fits into this picture—cave men and hunter-gatherers who roamed the earth in a constant struggle against the elements and against the wild beasts of the animal world. Those untold generations of our ancestors lived before the ideas of families and dwellings and generations and written language existed. Where did they fit into God's eternal scheme of things? Where even did the nomadic tribal culture of early *Genesis* fit? These are some of the questions I am most anxious to ask when I step into the eternal sunrise.

Here, however, we are focusing on the Old Testament era that begins coming into focus roughly during the years from 1200 to 1000 B.C. Between the lines of conquests, wars, killing, and captivities, I am convinced that God's intent was for his people to spread the salt and light of his covenant with mankind, and to gradually expand the legacy of that covenant throughout the earth and through time, by living peaceable and upright lives of responsibility and domesticity as families and extended families.

Family was the cornerstone of everything.

As we listen to Moses describe the land and the life that God intends and has planned for them, it is a peaceful life of agrarian simplicity, with God blessing their lives as they follow his commands.

The Lord your God is bringing you into a good land—a land with brooks, streams, and deep springs gushing out into the valleys and hills; a land with wheat and barley, vines and fig trees, pomegranates, olive oil and honey; a land where you will lack nothing.

When you have eaten and are satisfied, praise the Lord your God for the good land he has given you. Be careful that you do not forget the Lord your God, failing to observe his commands, his laws and his decrees. Otherwise, when you eat and are satisfied, when you build fine houses and settle down, and when your herds and flocks grow large and your silver and gold increase and all you have is multiplied, then your heart will become proud and you will forget the Lord your God. (Deuteronomy 8:7-8, 12-14—author paraphrase)

If you faithfully obey the commands I am giving you today—to love the Lord your God and to serve him with all your heart and with all your soul—then he will send rain on your land in its season, both autumn and spring rains, so that you may gather in your grain, new wine and olive oil. He will give grass in your fields for your cattle and you shall eat your fill. (Deuteronomy 11:13-15—author paraphrase)

At first I found it jarring to my preconceptions even to read about Israelites living in houses. It is so foreign to the Charlton Heston and "Ten Commandments" image embedded in my brain. Yet Moses speaks of "building fine houses and settling down." These overlooked details of *Leviticus* and *Deuteronomy* speak of quiet and peaceable, or what we might call normal and domestic, lives not so much different in some ways than ours today—houses, families, crops, buying, selling, borrowing, lending money, community life, consideration for others in those communities, helping friends, taking care of the elderly. These are not the primary concerns of a nomadic people or a nation continually at war.

True, there are exceptions to this lifestyle. Moses was happy living such a life, raising his family and tending the flocks of his father-in-law Jethro. But at the age of eighty, God called him away from that domestic life to something much different. In the New Testament, Paul was likewise called to a life much different than quiet domesticity.

The lives of such men, however, are exceptions. Proverbs 31, the portrait of the Godly woman, when read carefully, gives a wonderful picture of exactly this life that I believe reflects God's intent for the majority of his people—not in the specifics (selecting wool and flax and making bed coverings!) but in the underlying concerns, daily work, and perspectives of family life.

A wife of noble character who can find...She selects wool and flax and works with eager hands...She gets up while it is still night; she provides food for her family...She considers a field and buys it; out of her earnings she plants a vineyard...She sets about her work vigorously...She sees that her trading is profitable, and her lamp does not go out at night....She opens her arms to the poor and extends her hands to the needy...She makes coverings for her bed...She makes linen garments and sells them, and supplies the merchants with sashes...She watches over the affairs of her household and does not eat the bread of idleness...Honor her for all that her hands have done, and let her works bring her praise at the city gate. (Proverbs 31: 10, 13, 15-178, 20, 22, 24, 27, 31, NIV)

Here is the noble wife of Proverbs 31 making investments, buying and selling, helping the poor, cooking and sewing and providing fine things for her family.

It's remarkably contemporary. I see this same perspective woven between the lines—with distinctive aspects of peaceable domestic living for men and women, with family at the heart of both—throughout *Proverbs* and the whole Old Testament.

As I read this command, Lord, the word that comes to my mind is contentment—living life and doing one's work diligently and responsibly, where God has placed us, with gratitude and contentment to be part of God's family and his plan. I thank you for my life, Father, for my family, for my vocation, for my work. Deepen contentment within me. May I fall in even more with your purposes for my life—living life as your child with uprightness, diligence, good cheer, and contentment.

102. Speak Truth

Who shall dwell on thy holy hill? He who walks blamelessly, and does what is right, and speaks truth. (Psalm 15:2)

Though this book comprises commands given by kings and priests and others, here we encounter a command singularly exampled, often at great personal cost, by those who were considered actual *prophets*.

Most of them did not seek to be prophets. They wanted God to leave them alone. Moses wanted to remain a shepherd. Most of the biblical prophets, like Moses, wanted to live quiet and peaceable lives. They did not want to speak. Some did everything they could to avoid speaking. As did Moses, many of them tried to say *No* to God. Jonah tried to run away.

> *Then Moses answered, "But behold, they will not believe me or listen to my voice..." Moses said to the Lord, "Oh, my Lord, I am not eloquent...I am slow of speech and of tongue...Oh, my Lord, send, I pray, some other person."* (Exodus 4:4, 10, 13)

> *"Ah, Lord God! Behold, I do not know how to speak, for I am only a youth." But the Lord said to me, "Do not say, 'I am only a youth'; for to all to whom I send you you shall go, and whatever I command you you shall speak. Be not afraid...Then the Lord put forth his hand and touched my mouth; and the Lord said to me, "Behold, I have put my words in your mouth...gird up your loins; arise, and say to them everything that I command you."* (Jeremiah 1:6-9)

But they were compelled, impelled, driven, and commanded...to *speak*. And speak they did. Their writings come down to us in the 14-17 books of the "prophets," depending on how one categorizes them and defines "prophet." Few of the specifics addressed by the prophets apply to us. They are often prophecies against the nations of the middle east and against Israel's apostasy.

Looking beyond those specifics, however, the underlying lesson they leave us, as vital for us today as it was for them, is a straightforward one:

Truth must be spoken.

That doesn't necessarily mean *publicly* speaking out as the prophets did. That calling will come to few. For most, obedience to this command will be quiet and personal. The impulsion to preach and proclaim and "shout it from the housetops" is probably more self-motivated than God-motivated in our day, driven by the flesh not the Spirit. This has never been more true than in the current divisive political climate in the world. Most of the loudest voices in the cultural debate are doing more harm than good toward the furtherance of truth.

Rather than the *public* soapbox—which in our day has become the blog-box and social-media-box—there are two far more eternally important, though hard to discern, ways in which we are called to obey this command. It is relatively easy to stand on a street corner and shout. It is much more difficult to detect the imperative of this command in the quiet personal moments and unseen corners where we live our lives in relationship with those around us. Those are:

- Speak truthfully.
- Defend truth.

The first *speak truth* imperative is one we have touched on many times. *Speak truthfully.*

Do not lie, gossip, spread false reports, share other people's information, exaggerate, fib, engage in "little white lies," or pretend to be what you're not. All these are violations of truth. When you open your mouth, speak with integrity, wholeness, truthfulness...your *Yes* yes and your *No* no.

Truth is operative even when our mouths are closed. "Silent speech" reflects the truthfulness of one's entire character. A man or woman of integrity is a "truthful" man or woman. His or her integrity of character speaks powerfully, though not always with words.

The second truth imperative comes when truth is violated in our presence, and we feel that we must *defend truth* against untruth. This occasional imperative cannot be interpreted solely in the context of the public platform. Truth is most powerfully defended with the quiet dignity of integrity. Doing so may require hard choices, reassessing how we choose, and whom we choose, for friendships, and how we respond to our work environments.

Truth in our time is endangered. But truth is rarely advanced by argument and debate. Character speaks louder than words. [49]

That said, times come in life when we may have no alternative but to speak up—quietly, respectfully, and with dignity, yet none the less boldly.

---

[49] Part 2 of my *Endangered Virtues and the Coming Ideological War* is devoted to practical strategies for defending truth and virtue.

Occasionally God calls his men and women to follow in the footsteps of Jeremiah. When such times come, let us do so with courage yet also with great care that we are hearing *his* voice not our own flesh.

> *Then the Lord reached out his hand and touched my mouth and said to me, "Now, I have put my words in your mouth…I am watching to see that my word is fulfilled…Get yourself ready. Stand up and say to them whatever I command you. Do not be terrified…They will fight against you but will not overcome you, for I am with you…Go and proclaim…"* (Jeremiah 1:9, 12, 17, 19; 2:1, NIV)

May my lips speak nothing but truth. Again I pray, Lord God, that you would circumcise my tongue. Give me courage and a quiet spirit to be silent when you would have me speak truth through silence, and to speak when you would have me speak truth in words. When and if you call me to defend truth, may I do so in the spirit of Jesus—quietly, confidently, never angrily or argumentatively, allowing truth to defend itself without my getting in the way.

103. Claim and Pass on Your Inheritance in God

Give heed to the statutes and ordinances which I teach you…make them known to your children and your children's children…in the land to which you are going over, to possess it; that you may fear the Lord your God, you and your son and your son's son…all the days of your life…that it may go well with you, and that you may multiply greatly…in a land flowing with milk and honey. (Deuteronomy 4: 1, 9; 1-3)

The point bears re-emphasis that legacies extend in two directions, forward and back. As much as I grew to revere my father, it was not until I became a father myself that the import and power of this principle began sending down roots deep within me. It eventually became one of the most powerful spiritual driving forces in my life influencing nearly everything I have written. I saw myself standing between two worlds, looking in opposite directions, gazing into my own sons' faces with a love that cannot be described as I held them in my arms, and at the same time aware of my father's face, over and above and behind me, the man who had once held *me* in his arms looking into *my* infant and unknowing face.

That feeling of my father behind me and my sons before me is always with me, literally every moment. I have framed photographs in our bedroom symbolizing this truth that I gaze on many times a day. These reminders prompt feelings so deep in my heart that tears are never far away, feelings of the deepest love that God has put within humanity to feel. In many ways it may be even more primeval than the love between a man and a woman—the love of a parent for his or her child.

My father has now been gone for twenty-five years, but he is always with me…*in* me. Our sons are scattered across the western hemisphere over thousands of miles, but they are always with me…*in* me.

I believe this is the nature of God's legacy. It is rooted in this primeval, instinctive, anchoring love extending in both directions through the generations, a love he placed in the human heart as a reflection of the love that exists within the Godhead. We love…because God loves.

A legacy pointing in only one direction cannot fulfill itself. We all live our lives at specific places on the legacy-flow of God's history. For a legacy to go forward, it must be fueled and energized from what pours through it from the past.

You and I are *flow-through* points not *genesis* points in the sequential flow of humanity's spiritual history. Many in our time think the solution to their issues is to sever the legacy-hose, slice the flow at their backs, cut themselves off from their parents. Thus they will be free, they think, to start afresh. They live in the illusion, fed into them by the world, that it is possible to generate the flow of the water of personhood and character in and of themselves. They believe they can *originate* love's legacy moving forward while ignoring, disparaging, and cutting off the legacy that has flowed into them from behind.

But it's a fool's game fed by myriad lies of independence-worshipping modernism. It doesn't work that way.

Whether we have had good parents or bad parents has nothing to do with it. We are intrinsically linked to *God's* legacy-flow even more than we are to that of our parents. God's water of life flows from past generations into us—good influences, bad influences, and everything between—and cannot be severed. To neglect this ongoing flow is not merely to deny our parents the honor God commands, it is to deny God himself.

Whether we have children or not, or whether our children have received the legacy we have passed into them or not…neither is that a factor influencing this command. There is a flow to God's purposes. We are part of it. It has been given us to pass on in whatever ways he gives opportunity to do so.

When our sons were young, I wanted nothing in life so much than to transmit all I was as a spiritual man into them—by teaching, by example, by shared life experience. They are all now grown men. There is still nothing I want more in life. But the daily opportunities to build actively into their lives are long behind us. I wish I could still be doing so daily on the level relational ground of man to man. But that is something few fathers are fortunate enough to enjoy, and that few sons and daughters want.

But there remains one vital component to the legacy-flow that I *can* continue to absorb, thank God for, and glean and grow from. That is the flow of God's living-legacy-water into *me* from those that have come before. Naturally my own father and mother loom large as the human faces standing closest behind me. Their photographs and those of my grandparents and aunts and uncles and other relatives in our house remind me that I am not an island, remind me of more than a century of influences that continue to contribute to the man I am.

But the legacy flow is more expansive than only coming through them. My father never spoke a word about God or anything spiritual to me in his life. Yet he represents the most important human link in the eternal legacy flow that has built into my life. For that I honor him and continue to recognize those aspects of his character that may have built spiritual principles into me far beyond his perception of it. My mother, on the other hand, was more direct in her training, and taught and instilled within me the imperative of Deuteronomy 6:18.

My responsibility is to see my father and my mother as occupying more expansive roles than merely as my human parents, to see them as doorways through which I am given the great opportunity of allowing *all* the influences that have been part of my life to flow into me and nurture me and teach me and example to me the truths and wisdom of God. Only by allowing those waters to nourish and feed and strengthen the roots of my character and personhood, will I be able then to pass on those waters to nourish and feed and strengthen others.

This represents the starting point of laying claim to our legacy-inheritance from God.

Without that wide-open human doorway open to teach us what God has to teach us through our parents (not necessarily *from* them…but *through* them), the connection to God's eternally flowing water will produce only a trickle.

Likewise the legacy carrying on after me is much more expansive than only as embodied by our three sons and our grandchildren and perhaps those that will come after them. God's legacy flows into *all* those whom we influence in myriad and often invisible ways. We have little idea in how many thousands of ways we pass on the living and flowing inheritance of God's life-water as it flows through humanity from the eternal beginnings where those waters originated in the heart of God, to eternity itself where they will continue flowing and expanding forever.

The reason for this familial anchoring-point to the legacy is obvious when you open to nearly any page of the Old Testament. That entire biblical saga is based on *family.* The genealogies found throughout the Old Testament are pivotal. They are included for a reason. It is how Ezra was known to be a descendant of Aaron. The genealogies give physical reality to the functional process of God's legacy-flow. The inheritance is passed through time by *people.*

It became one of the popular sayings to arise out of the Four Spiritual Laws and Jesus Movement evangelicalism of the 1960s and 1970s that "God has no grandchildren." In one sense this points to an important truth. But in another sense the belief that spirituality starts anew with every generation is a false representation of the message of the Bible. It's another version of slicing off the hose behind us and thinking we can originate the living waters of inheritance and legacy from within ourselves.

Spirituality *doesn't* start from scratch with every new generation. God's legacy of truth is ongoing, historical, generational. It represents an eternal flow throughout humanity and throughout history. God *does* have grandchildren because God works through humanity. Our human forebears are not only intrinsic to that flow, they are one of the most important parts of it. Even bad actors on God's stage act out their ordained roles with no idea how God is using them to keep his legacy surging through history.

I thank you again, Lord God, for the inheritance and legacy you have passed on to me from those who have come before—both physical and spiritual forebears. May I be faithful to the legacy you have infused into all men and women to pass on your life, not only to my sons and grandchildren, but also to the spiritual sons and daughters and brothers and sisters you have given me, and to all those whose lives in some way my life touches. Remind me often that I am but one man living within the flow of your truth through time. May I receive that flow of your truth, and pass it on through my life into others.

104. Instruct Your Children in God's Commands

And these words which I command you this day shall be upon your heart;
and you shall teach them diligently to your children,
and shall talk of them when you sit in your house,
and when you walk by the way, and when you lie down, and when you rise. (Deuteronomy 6:6-7)
He commanded our fathers to teach to their children; that the next generation might know them,
the children yet unborn, and arise and tell them to their children, so that they should…
not forget the works of God, but keep his commandments. (Psalm 78:5-7)

Claiming and passing on our inheritance in God may seem like a lofty goal. But for few other high truths are we given such down-to-earth, practical instructions how to implement the high truth—how to *do* what needs to be done to move daily toward it.

How do we pass on God's inheritance and legacy? By building the truths of that inheritance into our sons and daughters—instructing them about God, the Bible, what are God's purposes, and how he commands his people to live. This command and the last are intrinsically linked. When my mother typed out Deuteronomy 6:18 and scotch-taped it to the refrigerator in our kitchen, she was *obeying* these words of Moses from over three thousand years before.

Hers has been a profound lifetime example to me of legacy transmission over hundreds of generations!

Whole books could be written about how to carry out this command of instructing our children in the ways of God. Early in my writing career I wrote three such books myself! They are long out of print, and, by way of full disclosure, as they grew our sons did not appreciate being made test cases of family living. My sensitivity to their future feelings was probably somewhat lacking during the early years of my fatherhood, which I deeply regret. But knowing that those years are well behind us, and that no one will now read the book, the title of the last of those three may yet be instructive in pointing parents specifically in the direction I believe this command points. The book was called: *Building Respect, Responsibility, and Spiritual Values in Your Child.*

That is exactly the calling of parents who are serious about passing on God's inheritance. It is exactly what Moses commands parents to do.

But it is a double-sided command and responsibility. It contains both a *teaching* component and an *example* component. Teaching without the example may be worthless. But the *example*, even without the teaching, may yet accomplish the same in the end. The example half of this command is by *far* the most important.

A parent builds God's principles into the generations that follow primarily by observation—as children and grandchildren witness those principles lived by their elders. Verbal instruction—teaching about God's principles—emerges out of, and *only* out of, those principles *lived* and *practiced* daily in the home, in the relationship between father and mother, in responses, attitudes, expressions, behavior, forgiveness, patience, gentleness. As the fruits of the Spirit and the principles of *Proverbs* are exampled, the more specific "instructions" will bear fruit.

There are many bad parents in the world. That fact must grieve God's heart above nearly all other sins. The children of bad parents have to work uniquely, in a difficult and complex relational and memory-milieu, to discover the Father heart of God in their response to these commands. Finding healing without bitterness, keeping the legacy hose between themselves and their parents intact in spite of less than Godly parental examples, is an enormous challenge. From every side the world shouts, "Slice off the hose, cut yourself off from the destructive influences of your parents, you are independent, you can start anew, you can put their influences to death."

All that's a lie. Josiah's father and grandfather were terrible men. They are still listed in the genealogy. There is no attempt by the Old Testament writers to pretend the past doesn't exist and that we can cut ourselves off from it.

But I'm not writing to parents like Manasseh and Amon, Josiah's grandfather and father. But to Christian parents who are in earnest about loving their children as God would have them. Not perfect parents, but sincerely humble parents, equally aware of their flaws as they are serious about building respect, responsibility, and spiritual values in their sons and daughters.

The parental process of building into the lives of sons and daughters, however, doesn't always go as planned, as hoped, or as prayed for. Sons and daughters in our time don't want to be instructed by anyone, least of all parents. Parents aren't perfect examples. Modernism loves to use this universal fact of humanity to bolster the justification—fed to young people the minute they start school—of rejecting their instruction, breaking free from parental constraints, and slicing off the flow of the legacy hose.

Parents are not told anything about results. Results are out of their hands. They are only commanded to faithfully instruct their children in God's principles, reinforcing that teaching and training by their own example. Sad to say, however, even Godly examples are not always followed by those observing their lives. That's the way life works. The saga of the Israelites in the Old Testament demonstrates it clearly enough. Good, faithful, and obedient parents still have to watch with breaking hearts as their sons and daughters reject their training and example.

Blended families, ex-husbands and wives, step-children—these do not exist in the biblical pattern of passing on God's legacy. They are not included in God's model. These are a sad reality in our time. God works in and through them, and will continue his legacy as best he can through leaky hoses. God uses them and honor still applies, but they are not the model he established to pass on the legacy of Godhead-oneness which the family represents.

In its effort to redefine personhood, marriage, and family, modern progressivism is seeking to dismantle and eliminate the fabric that holds God's truth and his revelation together. Christians who go along with its redefinitions are helping destroy the sacred institution that originated in the Godhead itself—the *family*. When traditional marriage and family are lost, the power of the Bible is weakened.

There is no Bible without family.

God's legacy is *family*.

The ongoing fabric holding the entire structure of the Old Testament together is *family*.

- One husband.
- One wife.
- Sons and daughters of one set of parents.

None of us perfectly live our role in this holy three-way relational dynamic. In our charge to reflect God both as parents and children, we are all broken mirrors. In the midst of our flawed humanity, however, this command is given repeatedly and persistently: Pass on God's principles to your children and grandchildren. This command represents the core, foundation, and permanency of what it means to pass God's legacy down through time.

I have done my best to obey this command, Lord. All I can do now is pray to continue being a good son myself. For all my human failings, I ask that the training of their early years will bear fruit in the lives of Judy's and my sons unto Christlikeness, and that our teaching and example will extend into the generations, both spiritual and physical that follow, unto the third and fourth generation, and for all time.

105. Show Respect to the Elderly

"Stand up in the presence of the aged, show respect for the elderly and revere your God."
(Leviticus 19:32)

When I was writing the book *Endangered Virtues*, I used the example of Leviticus 19 to illustrate the powerful idea of national virtue—that the virtues of that chapter were written into the national law of the Israelite *nation*. One of the most stunning of those laws was found in Leviticus 19:32: Stand up in the presence of the aged, show respect for the elderly and revere your God."

Just think of it, a national law mandating that everyone stand when an old man or old woman walks into the room!

It is yet another example of the importance God places on the generations that have come before—not family only, but *all* who have come before. In that book I wrote:

> In Old Testament times, this injunction from Leviticus 19:32 was more than only an unwritten code, it was a national law. The idea is beyond comprehension—what if the U.S. Congress passed a law, upheld by the Supreme Court, that all elderly men and women were to be shown deference and honor wherever they went, their words listened to respectfully whenever they spoke? It is hardly even necessary to mention how differently our culture functions.
>
> Honor of parents, grandparents, forebears, and their legacy is found throughout the Old Testament. The fascinating heart of these oft-repeated commands is this: Honor was not commanded because a given man or woman or father or grandfather was necessarily an honorable person. Some were, some weren't Honor was commanded, period.
>
> Honor was commanded toward the good and the bad. Honor was commanded not because any of them were perfect, or good people at all, but because they came before. Their blood and legacy flowed into and through their descendants. It was the legacy of their bloodline that was to be honored, not the virtue of their character. If they happened to have lived virtuous lives, so much the better. But that was not the basis for honor.
>
> My forebears' blood is in me, and in our nation. I am to honor them for that. I honor them because I am alive.
>
> Honor is not based on virtue but on honor for the past…because it is my past.
>
> Modernity has turned all this upside-down. Modernity says that we are no longer required to honor anyone whom we consider dishonorable. If we don't like them, we don't have to honor them.
>
> The entire culture shouts at children from the day they are born to dishonor their parents. No wonder so many young people enter the teen years full of rebellion and independence. Flexing their teen muscles, they are but living out the lies of unvirtue society has fed into them all their lives. [50]

This is precisely the point I make over and over in my writings. I talk with so many individuals harboring festering parental resentments. I know of many instances of estrangement in Christian families. Children of good parents are equally likely to be bitter and resentful. The world's poison has so thoroughly infiltrated our lives and culture that even children of Godly, upright parents of virtue and character harbor resentments rather than deep gratitude.

But there are bad parents too. Why shouldn't children of bad parents resent them, and cut off their influence?

Because in God's economy, having bad parents does not erase this command. It may make it harder to obey. But the command stands. Festering resentment is a sin, and it lies on the heads of disobedient sons and

---

[50] Michael Phillips, *Endangered Virtues and the Coming Ideological War*, Fidelis Publishing, 2023, p. 171.

daughters not on their parents. It would be nice if all parents were virtuous and perfect in every way. But that's not reality. Parental virtue is not a prerequisite for honor and respect.

The divine Fatherhood can only be fully apprehended through the legacy-door of the past. Honor of the elderly is not anchored in virtue. It is anchored in the legacy of God's Father heart working in and through imperfect humanity.

Give me opportunities to rise in the presence of those of more advanced years than myself. Continue to deepen my honor, too, for those who have come before me to whom I am grateful for the soil of my spiritual root system.

106. Succeed by Planning

Commit to the Lord whatever you do, and he will establish your plans. (Proverbs 16:3, NIV)

Many of the proverbs are so well-known in western culture that most people hardly realize they originate in the Bible. Building a tower and not counting the cost is one of them. It sounds like a "proverb" but was actually spoken by Jesus in Luke 14:28. The principle, however, is straight from *Proverbs*.

Plans are established by seeking advice. (Proverbs 20:18, NIV)
Plans fail for lack of counsel, but with many advisers they succeed. (Proverbs 15:22 NIV)
The plans of the diligent lead to profit as surely as haste leads to poverty. (Proverbs 21:5 NIV)

The fool, on the other hand, plans nothing and succeeds in nothing. Solomon's proverbs are so graphic and pithy because he minces no words about foolishness. There are two main characters in the book of *Proverbs*: the wise man and the fool.

The folly of fools yields folly. (Proverbs 14:24, NIV)

Indeed, planning, seeking guidance before embarking on important enterprises, is not only embedded in Solomon's prescriptions for wisdom, it is a thread running through the entire Old Testament. The sending out of the twelve spies in Numbers 13 is a perfect example. The invasion of Canaan was not haphazard. It was a well-planned military enterprise.

The biblical principle of planning is personified by Nehemiah, who, with Ezra, led the Restoration period of Jewish history in the mid-400s B.C. Numerous management books have been based on Nehemiah's example of strategic planning in rebuilding the walls of Jerusalem. He was a brilliant supervisor, and manager of people, setting a standard for planning, organization, implementation, and delegation that remains a leadership model today. He provided the world a literal textbook in how to succeed by planning.

After his arrival in Jerusalem, Nehemiah secretly made a detailed survey of the city and its walls so that opposing forces would not immediately know what he intended to do.

He is making plans! They are not hastily devised—they are shrewd, almost cunning plans. Even secrecy was intrinsic to his plan.

> *I went out by night…I inspected the walls of Jerusalem which were broken down and its gates which had been destroyed by fire. Then I went on to the Fountain Gate and to the King's Pool…Then I went up in the night by the valley and inspected the wall; and I turned back and entered by the Valley Gate, and so returned.* (Nehemiah 2:13-15)

With his plans established, Nehemiah at last went public, encouraging and exhorting, first the leaders and then the people to join in his bold plan: *Come, let us build the wall of Jerusalem.* (Nehemiah 2:17)

The people responded with enthusiasm: *And they said, "Let us rise up and build." So they strengthened their hands for the good work.* (Nehemiah 2:18) Nehemiah was not just a planner, he was a motivator.

They embarked on the massive project under Nehemiah's leadership, and the wall was completed in an astonishing fifty-two days. The final half of *Nehemiah* is an account of the completion and culmination of Israel's physical and spiritual Restoration.

In my experience, no better motivator exists in the spiritual life than godly mentors who *example* what it means to walk with God. Jesus, of course, stands at the apex of my mentor gallery. But there are many others whom I seek to emulate in various aspects of my life. Josiah, Ezra, and Nehemiah are among them, each for their own reasons, all three together demonstrating that God's legacy has continued through time through men who understood and lived the principle of wise planning. Even long dead mentors are included in the "multitude of counselors" whose wisdom we can seek.

God's legacy in the world moves forward through obedient planning, just as it did through Nehemiah. When we follow the example and wisdom of *all* those through whom God has built into our lives, seeking their wise counsel, planning out what God gives us to do, implementing our plans with diligence and patience, God allows good things to happen.

The model of your servant Nehemiah is timeless, Lord. Thank you for him, and that his example is preserved for us. Give me opportunities to practice his astute M.O. of planning in my living out of your legacy, and in how I pass it into the future.

107. Walk in Patience

Wisdom yields patience. (Proverbs 19:11, NIV)

Patience, like planning, is not merely a foundational principle of *Proverbs*, we see examples of it throughout the Old Testament. Moreover, patience is a scriptural and character virtue, perhaps more than any other, that reflects the nature of God himself. God's legacy throughout human history, throughout the creation and development of the universe, and throughout eternity, is founded as much as any other single principle, on *patience*.

God is *infinitely* patient in bringing his eternal will and purposes to fulfillment.

When I sit fretting having to wait an extra minute or two at a red light, or drive a little too fast to reach my destination three or four minutes sooner, I need to reflect that God's eternal purposes have already been millions of years in the making, and may not reach their conclusion for *billions* more years.

And I am impatient over the loss of a few seconds! I can imagine God looking on and saying, *Mike...really! Sixty seconds at a traffic light! Has my example penetrated no deeper into you all these years? Haven't you been paying attention! Do you not yet understand?*

I have to remind myself over and over that my myriad tiny habits either reflect or go against God's intrinsic nature. Even a simple matter like driving too fast is a slap in God's face. God is patient. If I am *not* being patient, I am behaving contrary to God's example.

If I would be God's man, I am called to reflect God in how I live. I am commanded to model my life by his principles. What am I saying to God and to the world if I persist in habits, behavior, and attitudes that display the *opposite* of how God works, and who God is?

How will the world know him if those who call themselves his people do not live as God lives, do not think as God thinks?

Patience is more easily visible as exemplifying God's method and character, in some ways, even than love. God is infinitely patient. He created the cosmos and allowed it to develop slowly until it became capable of supporting life. Whether one defines the age of the universe in thousands, millions, or billions of years, everyone can agree that it did not develop all at once.

Then God worked slowly through time and history and human intellect and consciousness to grow a people capable of knowing him, understanding him, and obeying him. Neither did humanity become able to respond personally to God as a loving Father all at once. In this too, God was patient.

It is a great mystery, but God takes *time* to reveal himself.

In a world full of so much pain and suffering, God's love is more difficult to see than his patience. His patience is in front of us every day. God's slow-developing processes are easy to see. The stars in the sky speak of it, as does our own humanity.

As obvious as it is, however, God's patience is frustrating to my small human understandings. I want him to hurry it up a little faster, to answer my prayers quickly, to mature me without taking so long about it, to rectify the injustices in the world, to reward the righteous and punish the wicked.

Why did God allow Hitler to do what he did? Why did he not intervene? When is he going to set the world right? How patient is he going to be! The list of my patience-questions for God is a long list.

Again Nehemiah is an example of patience, working through a plan exactly as God does. But while Nehemiah's plan was brought to fruition in two months, God's plan will take aeons to work its way infinitesimally through time, through people, and through the depths of every individual human soul, to its appointed and eternal end. Despite what may be appearances to the contrary, he has eternal purposes for his creation, and for every one of his people. He is infinitely patient in bringing those purposes to fruition. Nor will we fully apprehend those purposes until we enter into eternity ourselves.

Impatience, therefore, in the fast and turbulent world of our daily lives, is a direct rebuff of God's own example. Impatience denies God's own methods. My impatience toward one who is a constant source of irritation demonstrates my rejection of the way God deals with stubborn people. My impatience reveals that one of those stubborn people God has to deal with is me!

We are not merely exhorted to *be* patient, though that is part of it. We are to walk *in patience*…exuding a spirit of calm, unhurried peace within an overspreading life-carriage of serenity.

Patience is the sap flowing in God's tree that allows the fruits of his Spirit to grow. Sap flows slowly. Thus fruit grows *slowly*.

Patience may be the simplest and most outwardly visible of all the character virtues. Many times a day—every day, every hour!—we have the opportunity to exhibit the character of God to a watching world.

It takes slowing down…then gently, quietly, and with unflustered but focused calm, falling into harmony with the still small whispered breath of God's overspreading sovereignty throughout a world he is not finished with yet.

Oh, Lord, this is such a hard command to practice in the fast-moving, stress-filled, urgent life that pulls at me and sidetracks me all day long. Again comes the imperative staring me in the face simply to slow down. I am so full of plans! It is excruciatingly difficult not to want to get them done now! Help me, Father, not merely to be patient occasionally and sporadically. Help me learn to walk in patience. Deepen patience within me. May patience characterize my demeanor and carriage as it does your very being. But patience is not in my nature. I need your help!

108. Cultivate Love for the Lord's Statutes and Commands

I set thy ordinances before me. Teach me, O Lord, the way of thy statutes.
I revere thy commandments, which I love, I will meditate on thy statutes.
Oh, how I love thy law! (Psalm 119:30, 33, 48, 97)

By nature, we *don't* love the idea of command.

Independence, going our own way, "doing our own thing," rebelling against authority, are all built into the human DNA.

Love for authority and command, therefore, must be learned and developed. It cannot be transmitted from one person to another informationally, as knowledge and facts are taught. Even another's example can only take us so far.

Eventually it's up to me and no one else. Ultimately love for command can only come from within. It is *self*-learned, *self*-taught, *self*-developed. It is a quality, a virtue, an outlook on life that we cultivate and nurture and grow of ourselves. No one can do it for us.

As nonsensical as such a statement will sound to the world—I have to *want* to love God's commands. I have to *seek* authority, not despise it.

Coming to the idea of loving command for the first time, many will say:

"Huh—you've got to be kidding! Why would I *want* to love authority or command?"

That's how 99% of people will respond to the idea. But the 1% recognize the idea of command, not as an oppressive constraint to independence, but as the doorway into a deeper understanding of God. As they take their first steps through the unexpected door of command, God's character and methods gradually come into focus. They see that God reveals himself most practically through authority and command.

From the first hunger-seed of desire, the commands slowly take root. The hunger grows because I *want* to understand God.

So I set myself to *know* the commands. They begin emerging off the pages of the Bible with practicality and purpose. As I reflect on them, they reveal ever-deeper aspects of God's eternal methods and designs. It becomes obvious, too, that to know God's high purposes, I must obey the commands that lead to and illuminate those high purposes.

From these beginnings, roots continue down into deeper places within me. The fruit of obedience ripens as I nurture and cultivate the soil. Invisibly and imperceptibly I find a new and unexpected seed sprouting in the soil of hunger to know God. It is the seed of *love*...love for the statutes and commands set forth by God's men—prophets and apostles and Jesus himself, in the Old and New Testaments.

Amazing as it seems, I find that I have come to *love* the idea of command in the Bible! I can attest to this progression. My use of the personal pronoun here is intentional. This has been *my* story.

It was also another man's story. Psalm 119 is the chronicle of one man's cultivation of his own personal hunger and love for the Lord's statutes, commands, and ordinances. This window into David's soul is a scriptural roadmap. It has provided us a model for the cultivation of love for his commands.

By any standard, Psalm 119 is not merely its longest, it is one of the Bible's most remarkable chapters. I consider it so significant that I have included selections from it in my personal memory book. [51] David's example is no

---

51 *A Book of Daily Memory Reminders.*

mere historical chronicle of a man's thoughts. I believe the written record of David's love for God's authority, his statutes, and his ordinances, has deep spiritual energy and potency to strengthen, inform, and focus our own cultivation of love for God's commands.

If we can put aside questions about the darker side of David's nature, overlooking his occasional drift into complaints about his persecutors, Psalm 119 illuminates God through David's eyes. We see and feel *why* he so loved God's commands. Praying with David, we are drawn *into* his life of prayer...and thus drawn into his love for God's commands. [52]

For me, Psalm 119 is a biblical treasure map. I have the singular opportunity to follow David, holding the map he has given us, as he leads along a path—hidden to the eyes of the world—into the high mountains of life with God.

I love your commands, Lord. Deepen my love for them. Expand my love for them. Without obedience, it means nothing to love your commands. Most of all, then, translate my love into obedience to your commands.

109. Walk in Integrity

The integrity of the upright guides them. (Proverbs 11:3)

Many words might be used to encapsulate the full scope of what comprises a life of virtue and righteousness. The most forceful to my mind is the familiar word *integrity*. It is not a word whose meaning is laden with heavy spiritual overtones such as *righteousness*, or watered down to uselessness such as *good*. Integrity is a word rich with power to draw all the diverse wisdom-virtues of *Proverbs* up into it.

The meaning of integrity is straightforward and clear. It is derived from the word integer, the mathematical term for a single whole number. The first and primary integer is the number 1. That defines integrity—*wholeness...oneness*.

In its simplest terms integrity means *strong, whole, and sound*—the *integer* of character, without blemishes or imperfections. In mathematics—no fractions, no fragments, nothing left-over. A piece of wood with a crack is not sound. It will split under pressure. It has no "structural *integrity*" but is structurally *weak*.

This basic meaning of structural integrity is a condition of physicality. But when transferred to the world of morals and personal character, integrity takes on its most powerful import. In that context it rises to express the composite structural *oneness* of all the wisdom virtues Solomon urges throughout *Proverbs*—soundness of character, without cracks or splits,

52 I have since this writing drawn many of these same thoughts, based largely on this book, into a small devotional entitled *Praying with David*.

fragments or weaknesses. No "cracks" undermine the integral fabric and strength and spiritual fiber of the complete man or woman of *integrity.*

Integrity goes beyond mere wisdom, though both are intrinsic to the other. Wisdom can be intellectual, as we see in the life of Solomon. Even wisdom may not regulate how one lives, the choices one makes. Though Solomon was a wise man, he was not whole, of a single piece. There were cracks in his moral character that his wisdom was unable to overcome. Wisdom is still capable of making bad choices.

Integrity extends deeper into character. It encompasses and regulates the deepest regions of life itself. That's why the command is *Walk* in integrity. One might *have* or *possess* wisdom, as Solomon did. But integrity is not an attribute of character that can be *possessed.* It is not static.

Integrity is a moving target. We don't *have* integrity. We are called to live by, make choices that reflect, treat people with, and respond to life with integrity. God's men and women *walk in integrity.*

The spiritual implications are enormous, yet not always obvious. Our inner selves are more split, unwhole, and fragmented than we care to admit. We are *fractional* numbers not *whole* numbers. Not just because we are weak and imperfect human beings, though that is an obvious part of it. More worrisome is that we intentionally choose fragmentation over the complete unity and soundness of a whole and integrated self. We *choose* to compartmentalize our spiritual selves into a fractional collection of different selves that live inconsistently with one another.

Solomon is the prototypical scriptural example of fragmentation. The fissures beneath the wisdom of his mind were fractures in the full integrity of his personhood. His wisdom didn't go deep enough. The cracks and fissures in the sub-strata of his foundations remained. Thus the concrete of his character was structurally unsound.

We allow invisible cracks to form in the composition of our characters, imperfections in the concrete of our foundations, exactly as Solomon did. It's the secret sin, the hidden obsession, the silently nurtured vice, the mixed motives, the fluctuating life-compass that create cracks in the foundation that produce fragmentation of personhood. These distinct "selves" are not merely inconsistent, they are often in direct conflict. We accommodate ourselves to these compromises of virtue and wisdom, living with them because we choose them.

Thomas Kelly wrote, "The outer distractions of our interests," he writes, "reflect an inner lack of integration of our own lives. We are trying to be several selves at once, without all our selves being organized by a single, mastering Life within us. Each of us tends to be, not a single self, but a whole committee of selves." [53]

The forces splitting our foundations are daily and persistent. Integrity never emerges from drift, placing our spiritual lives on auto pilot. We make the choice toward integrity or fragmentation a dozen times a day.

---

[53] Thomas Kelly, *A Testament of Devotion,* Harper and Row, 1941, p. 114.

Walking in integrity requires alertness to the courage of difficult daily choices. Integrity—wholeness of purpose, singleness of eye, constancy of motive—is a hard-won virtue. It is a virtue of strength, valor, moral uprightness, and ethical fiber that is won in the trenches where decisions of life direction and eternal purpose are made.

Walking in integrity won't happen next month, or next year. It happens today. Then when next month and next year come, we will still be walking in integrity in those *todays*.

Lord God, my heavenly Father, develop and mature me into your man, your whole man, a man with no hidden cracks in my character. Reveal what cracks exist in the substructure of my foundations. Show me how to eliminate them that I may be structurally sound in every way. Make of me a man of integrity of whom you can be proud. Lord Jesus, walk beside me, hold my hand, and show me more and more every day how to live in your example and walk in the integrity of Christlikeness.

110. Act Justly, Love Mercy, and Walk Humbly with Your God

He has showed you, O man, what is good; and what does the Lord require of you but to do justice, and to love kindness [*mercy*, KJV], and to walk humbly with your God. (Micah 6:8)

This beautiful verse from Micah is so often quoted that its resounding but quiet power can be lost as our brains race on to keep up with the pace of life. I would urge us to still ourselves into quietness, and let Micah's timeless words above wash over us.

Is this not integrity defined?

- What is *justice* but treating every individual we meet in the way God would treat them, giving fair-play…and as *we* would be treated ourselves in the same circumstances? What is justice but the personification of the golden rule?
- What are *kindness* and *mercy* but an outgrowth of love? We will never go wrong in relationships, in responses, in speech, by giving others the benefit of the doubt, when we lead with mercy. What is mercy but kindness, understanding, and love?
- What is *humility* but recognizing our childness in God, walking in the awareness that we have a Father to whom we are accountable, aware of our flaws and weaknesses, aware in all circumstances that there but for the grace of God go I?

There are profound hidden depths in this verse. The first bonus insight Micah gives is identifying justice, kindness, and humility as *good*. This is more significant than it may seem. Goodness in our day has fallen on hard times. The word is so overused and misused that it has lost its meaning. Goodness is whatever anyone wants it to mean.

Certain Christian theologies err on the opposite side with the silly idea, based on Isaiah 64:6, that goodness isn't really good at all, that goodness won't get you into heaven, that being saved has nothing to do with goodness.

Whatever Isaiah meant, it wasn't that. Goodness is a good thing. God wants *good* people spreading salt and light in the world. All the commands we have considered reveal distinct facets of Godly *goodness*.

For both these reasons, we need to reclaim the value and meaning of *goodness* as intrinsic to Christlikeness. Micah helps us do so with his succinct picture of three components (among many) of goodness. It is *good* to "do justice, love mercy, and walk humbly."

Notice, too, that we have no excuse for not knowing what goodness is. Micah anticipates Paul's words to the Romans, that man is without excuse for not knowing God. God has shown us what is good, God has revealed himself. We *know* that God exists, we *know* what is good, we *know* what God requires. This powerful implication within Micah's words is a game-changer—Man *knows* truth, and man *knows* what God requires.

What God requires is nothing less than obedience. The words Micah uses before the virtues are all verbs—*do* justice, *love* kindness, and *walk* in humility. Micah is laying down a formidable, threefold, *active-verb* challenge of command.

- *Do.*
- *Love.*
- *Walk.*

Finally, the climaxing three words of the verse give power to that *do*, raising the virtues of justice, kindness, mercy, and humility to a lofty spiritual plane. It's not just abstract worldly justice. It's not the mercy of progressivism that turns a blind eye to sin. It's not the humility and goodness of being a "nice person." It's not the Scripture-twisting motto of a well-known Christian liberal arts college, misusing Micah's high prophetic challenge to highlight their cultural emphasis of tolerance and diversity while relegating God to second place behind what it calls "intercultural and global engagement." [54]

God cannot be left out of Micah's command!

We are commanded to *walk with God* in these virtues. We are commanded to walk in God-informed justice, God-informed kindness, and God-informed humility. The goodness Micah is speaking of is the *goodness of God*.

Let us, then, read this muscular verse with insightful eyes to see the depth and wisdom it contains as we walk out into our corners of the world to live its multi-dimensioned truth:

---

[54] Westmont College, Santa Barbara, California, once a "Christian" college, now one bowing to the idols of progressivism and pretending that capitulation is based on the Bible.

He has SHOWED you, O man, what is GOOD; and what does the Lord *require* of you but to *do* JUSTICE, and to *love* KINDNESS, and to *walk* HUMBLY *with your God.*

What a high and beautiful prayer to make the anchoring focus of life. In the years I have left, heavenly Father, draw me ever more fully and practically into the reality of Micah's words. Give me an obedient heart, such that it might to some small degree be said of me when at last I enter your presence, that I loved good and did what you required of me, that I was just, that I loved kindness, and that in my earthly humanity I sought to walk with you. I thank you for the privilege of being your child.

SERIES TWELVE

PURITY

God's Furnace of Purification

Preparing for holiness

Malachi Ushers in the New Covenant in Christ

Though it takes a view of the overspreading thematic story to see it, the tone and message of the Old Testament had gradually shifted since Solomon's time. The exiles and captivities had changed Israel's perspective, widening its worldview to encompass new realities of having to live in foreign cultures. The Israelites were no longer a conquering people killing everyone who stood in their way. They were having to find ways to live the call to separation as a minority people. And, too, along with judgment for its unfaithfulness, gradually a faint melody began to weave through the minor prophets, as it did through *Isaiah*, of a future of forgiveness and healing.

These strains culminate in *Malachi*.

It will come as no surprise by now that many of the passages and personalities of Scripture I view as significant come from obscure and occasionally overlooked places in the Bible. I am constantly on the search for its hidden veins of gold. As we reach the end of the Old Testament, one of those significant veins of eternal import comes to us in the small and often neglected final book. It is not merely the twelfth series of this book about the Old Testament commands, *Malachi* is twelfth and last in the line of "minor" prophets whose names and messages few remember and many consider the least important section of the Bible.

Twelve is the number of Israel. Malachi is the symbolic culmination of Israel's prophetic voices.

The minor prophets are in fact hugely significant in completing the unfolding and progressive bookends of a comprehensive *Genesis* to *Malachi* vision. The prophet Malachi brings this overview to a dramatic climax, complete with Moses-like warnings and an unexpected vision of eternity, thus setting the stage for the coming of Israel's Messiah.

After the high hopes of the Restoration and the rebuilding of the temple in 516 B.C. expectation ran high that Israel would rise again to its former glory as in the days of Solomon. Most of the prophets pointed to such a time. The glories they envisioned were often utopian and extravagant, but the ideal age which seemed to conclude most of the prophetic writings ("In that day…") had not materialized.

These hopes were heightened with Nehemiah's building of the city wall and Ezra's reading of the Book of the Law in approximately 445 B.C. Yet within a generation or two, once again spiritual decline set in. Malachi's words—probably written around 400 B.C. or in the late 300s—speak against apostasy, failure to keep the Sabbath and other aspects of the Law. Even more strongly, he condemns the all-important thorn in Israel's national flesh—intermarriage with foreigners. This was no racism but a preventative to keep them from adopting their customs, beliefs, and worldliness. Moreover, he speaks to the deeper problem of spiritual lethargy and discontent. Simply put—the people had lost their vision. Malachi lays much of the blame for this on the Levites and Israel's priesthood. In other words with the church and its clergy!

The pivotal passage in *Malachi* describes what I call "Malachi's Furnace." It is found in Malachi 3:2-3.

The Spirit inspiring the biblical writers intended for the Old and New Testament messages to be harmonized into a single unity. In that unity, the nature of fire (refinement and purification), and the disciplinary progression evident throughout the Word of God (*destruction* and *correction* leading to *restoration*), paves the way for a triumphant and complete portrait of God's ultimate victory.

Zechariah, immediately preceding *Malachi*, lays out the purpose for Malachi's Furnace.

> *And I will put this third into the fire,*
> *and refine them as one refines silver,*
> *and test them as gold is tested.*
> *They will call on my name…*
> *I will set your captives free from the…pit…* (Zechariah 13:9; 9:11)

It is often assumed that fire in Scripture is a symbol of destruction and judgment only. But like so many misunderstood aspects of old paradigm interpretations, this is an incomplete perspective. Fire throughout Scripture is primarily an image of purification.

In the same way that judgment precedes forgiveness, destruction precedes restoration. Fire is God's means of achieving a twofold purpose. Fire both destroys and purifies. Forgiveness and purification are the *ultimate* purposes. We see this obvious progression in the use of fire to burn impurities out of gold and silver so that nothing is left but pure alloy. There must be destruction of impurity. But it always leads to final purity.

George MacDonald writes:

> For love loves unto purity. Love has ever in view the absolute loveliness of that which it beholds. Where loveliness is incomplete, and love cannot love its fill of loving, it spends itself to make more lovely, that it may love more; it strives for perfection…Therefore all that is not beautiful in the beloved… must be destroyed.[55]

Fire is an expression of God's love, and therefore also of his wrath *against sin.* Fire chastens, cleanses, and purifies the heart of the sinner until the radiant alloy of a Christlike character shines forth. When at last the dross, the impurities, the parasites of sin are burned away, only pure radiant childness will remain!

This progression throughout the minor prophets is absolutely essential to understanding God's purposes. The sequence is given radiant clarity by observing the scriptural distinction between *forever* and *until* as the prophets use the words.

---

[55] George MacDonald, *Unspoken Sermons First Series,* "The Consuming Fire," 1867.

We find the clearest scriptural perspective of fire in the Old Testament prophets. This image rises to a climax in *Malachi* where we note the high truth that the fire of purification is not merely for sinners, but is also intended for the purification of God's people and their Levite-priests.

> *"I will thoroughly purge away your dross and remove all your impurities. I have refined you… I have tested you in the furnace of affliction."* (Isaiah 1:25; 48:10)
>
> *For he is like a refiner's fire… and he will purify the sons of Levi and refine them like gold and silver, till they present right offerings to the Lord… For behold, the day comes, burning like an oven… the day that comes shall burn.* (Malachi 3:2-3; 4:1)

God's purpose is to *eradicate* sin from his creation, to burn out the impurity from his universe. The Hebrews of old were the object lesson of an eternal purifying progression that is still in process. This prophetic theme inherent in the minor prophets completes the judgment-forgiveness sequence from earlier.

There must be a judgment between the impure and the pure. The fire probes to the essence of distinction, dividing bone from marrow, and judges it rightly and swiftly. Then the fire destroys all that is *impure*…but preserves and purifies what God is in the process of making *pure*.

The fire burns only *until* that dual purpose is achieved. The fire does not burn *forever*. Malachi's purifying fire burns *until* the sons of Levi present right offerings to the Lord…after which the sun of righteousness shall rise with healing in its wings. (Malachi 4:2)

This is the misunderstood *until vs. forever* paradox of Scripture.

The crucial word *till* or *until* in Malachi 3:3 is the imperative hinge upon which the meaning of these prophecies turns. The "so that" rendering of the KJV is even more illuminating

> *He will purify the sons of Levi, and refine them like gold and silver, till* [*so that*—KJV] *they present right offerings to the Lord.*

Healing and purification *always* follow the fire.

In the prophetic writings, the word "forever" is often followed by a description of what will happen *after* that forever. "I will punish my people Israel forever… *until* they repent of their sin and I restore them in the land I gave their fathers."

This is how the prophets wrote. Duration of time carries multiple meanings. Healing always follows judgment. When the prophets speak of judgment, "forever" doesn't literally mean *forever*. Purification and restoration *always* follow.

In most of the minor prophets, then, we discover a shift from judgment to healing. In Malachi 3, after asking "who can endure the day of the Lord's coming," Malachi goes on, with that oft-used word that signals the shift from judgment and punishment to restoration, "*Then* the Lord will have men who will bring offerings in righteousness."

Keep your eyes on the two words *until* and *then* throughout the prophets. They always signal a major shift in God's purposes through time—telling the perceptive reader:

"Pay attention, we are shifting now to an eternal not a temporal view."

In Zephaniah 3, we observe first judgment:

> *I have decided to assemble the nations... to pour out my wrath upon them—all my fierce anger. The whole world will be consumed by the fire of my jealous anger.* (Zephaniah 3:8)

But everything is *not* consumed. For the punishment is followed by healing:

> *Then I will purify the lips of the peoples that all of them may call on the name of the Lord.* (Zephaniah 3:9)

Another example of this "forever...until" progression comes in Amos 9:8:

> *I will destroy it from the surface of the ground; except that I will not utterly destroy the house of Jacob.*

The prophets are interwoven from beginning to end with this progression. It is imperative and foundational to all scriptural interpretation.

I will bring judgment... then I will bring healing.

The ninth and final chapter of *Amos* is wonderfully illustrative. For ten verses Amos prophesies the destruction of Israel. Suddenly in chapter 10 he shifts to healing and restoration:

> *In that day I will restore... I will repair... and build... I will bring back my exiled people Israel... never again to be uprooted from the land I have given them.* (Amos 9: 11, 14, NIV)

God is speaking through the prophets of the restoration not of temporal Israel, but of his entire creation!

As Ezekiel wrote, God's eternal purpose is to bring his children home. Nothing will satisfy and fulfill his love but to see them pure and perfect as he is pure and perfect. Malachi's Furnace of fire is the agent of that eternal, purifying, healing redemption.

The Old Testament thus culminates in Malachi's message of preparation and

purification of God's people, unto the universal salvation of all Israel, and thus all mankind.

Malachi is the introduction to the New Testament. *Malachi ushers in the redemption of Christ!* It is fitting that this final book of the Old Testament plays a prominent role in one of the most majestic and triumphant pieces of music ever composed, Handel's *Messiah.*

The books of *Malachi* and *Revelation* hold equal importance. Both Testaments climax with a prophetic view of evil being *destroyed* by the furnace of purification (Malachi 3) and the lake of fire (Revelation 20).

To be understood accurately, the vision of *Revelation* must be seen as the New Testament fulfillment of its Old Testament counterpart. The *hell* which New Testament writers attempted to explain was none other than the cleansing and purifying fire of *Zechariah* and furnace of fire prophesied by Malachi.

Malachi calls it the day of the Lord's coming, obviously a significant term given what follows. For Malachi is not only prophesying the eternal cleansing of the universe of sin, he is also setting the stage, preparing the way, for what will be the next and most important phase of God's unfolding revelation to mankind—the coming of Jesus—*the day of the Lord's coming.*

His chapter 3 opens: "Behold, I send my messenger to prepare the way before me." These are almost the precise words *Mark* uses to open his gospel:

> *"Behold, I send my messenger before thy face,*
> *who shall prepare thy way;*
> *the voice of one crying in the wilderness:*
> *Prepare the way of the Lord, make his paths straight—"* (Mark 1:2-3)

Malachi 3 represents a wonderful climax to the Old Testament! Here is the bridge into the New Covenant.

If only Malachi's book had ended with this promise from the third chapter rather than the disheartening, *lest I come and smite the land with a curse.*

However, let us imagine for a moment. Let us transpose Malachi 3:1-2 to the end of Malachi 4. We thus culminate the Old Testament with:

> *Behold, I will send you Elijah the prophet before the great... day of the Lord comes. And he will turn the hearts of the fathers to their children and the hearts of the children to their fathers...*
>
> *Behold, I send my messenger to prepare the way before me, and the Lord whom you seek will suddenly come to his temple; the messenger of the covenant in whom you delight, behold, he is coming, says the Lord of hosts.* (Malachi 4:5-6; 3:1)

What a sequence this slight change brings! The progression as the old covenant climaxes and gives way seamlessly to the new sends tingles up the spine.

Then turning to the first gospel written in the New Testament, we read:

> *The beginning of the gospel of Jesus Christ, the Son of God.*
> *As it is written in the prophets,*
> *"Behold, I send my messenger before thy face,*
> *who shall prepare thy way;*
> *the voice of one crying in the wilderness:*
> *Prepare the way of the Lord, make his paths straight..."*

In those days Jesus came from Nazareth of Galilee… saying,
"The time is fulfilled, and the kingdom of God is at hand;
repent, and believe in the gospel."

(Mark 1:1-3, 9, 15)

Series Twelve

Purity

111. Be pure in thought and behavior.

112. Do not be the cause of allowing sin to spread.

113. Engage in no sexual relations outside marriage.

114. Hate falsehood and do not circulate potential falsehoods.

115. Examine and test your ways and return to the Lord.

116. Purge temper, anger, bitterness and resentment.

117. Use honest weights.

118. Turn from all hint of impurity and impropriety.

119. Purge evil from your life.

120. Welcome God's furnace of purification.

111. Be Pure in Thought and Behavior

He will sit as a refiner and purifier…he will purify the sons of Levi…like gold. (Malachi 3:3).

Purity is the underlying theme of *Malachi.* The undiscerning reader may miss the music of this quieter strain amid the loud kettledrums of fire and judgment. But stilling heart and brain, dismissing preconceptions of hell and God's judgment, and listening for the melody of eternity God has woven through the occasionally brash writings of the prophets, we hear echoes of a symphony that make our hearts glad:

> *"I have loved you," says the Lord…*
> *"Behold, I send my messenger to prepare the way before me…the messenger of the covenant…For he is like a refiner's fire and like fullers' soap; he will sit as a refiner and purifier of silver, and he will purify the sons of Levi and refine them like gold and silver, till they present right offerings to the Lord…*
> *"Then I will draw near to you…For I the Lord do not change…Return to me, and I will return to you, says the Lord of hosts…Bring the full tithes into the storehouse, that there may be food in my house…I will…open the windows of heaven for you and pour down for you an overflowing blessing…*
> *"For behold, the day comes, burning like an oven…But for you who fear my name the sun of righteousness shall rise, with healing in its wings.*
> (Malachi 1:1; 3:1-3, 5-7, 10; 4:1-2)

It is true, these prophetic warnings of judgment can be read to confirm God's eternal and unending punishment of sinners. I happen to see a higher theme at work through the minor prophets. That theme is the resounding and eternal truth that the fire of purification is for *all*…and the healing is for *all.*

That *all* includes saints *and* sinners.

- The *fire* is for saints as well as sinners.
- The *healing* is for sinners as well as saints.
- The *unity* with the Father in eternity is for saints as well as sinners.

There is indeed a warning here—Malachi's Furnace awaits even God's people, to purify out of them what they refused to submit to his pruning hand in this life. God will have his people pure, to "present right offerings" to him.

It is not by accident that *Malachi* contains the monstrously politically incorrect proclamation: *"For I hate divorce," says the Lord the God of Israel.* (2:16) This verse can be spiritualized as applying to God's "marriage" to Israel and Israel's infidelity. This is certainly a true interpretation. But it is more than coincidental that Malachi uses divorce to illustrate the impurity of God's people and their need for the furnace of repentance, cleansing, and purification. Marital and sexual infidelity and impurity represent the primary examples of personal impurity of behavior and lifestyle which, if Malachi is right, God *hates*.

What are we to do with a piercing word like this? What are Christians who have adopted the fluid morals of the world to think? Does it mean nothing to them that God *hates* sexual and marital impurity?

If Christians are engaged in behavior that God hates, excusing and justifying it and thinking nothing of violating God's purpose, what but Malachi's Furnace can await them? How else can God purify the sons of Levi?

God takes sexual purity so seriously that almost every potential act of impure sexual activity is specifically mentioned in Leviticus 18-20. God *hates* sexual impurity. He uses the strongest possible language to characterize sexual sin—disobedience, perversion, defilement, and wickedness. Those are powerful words of condemnation for what our culture considers perfectly acceptable. A number of the violations listed were punishable by death. Among these was the practice of homosexuality which God calls an abomination. God hates sexual perversion of *all* kinds.

Purity is unique among the virtue commands in an important way. Rooted in premeditated choice, it is possible to be *perfectly* virtuous—to be 100% sexually pure over a lifetime. This can be said about very few virtues. Moral slippage is never accidental. It is chosen. The biblical injunction toward sexual purity, whether from Leviticus or the Sermon on the Mount, is one that can be obeyed perfectly. [56]

Yet in our time, many of the sins of Leviticus 18-20 are on full display among Christians before a watching world. Half of them may secretly exist in the pews in most churches on any given Sunday morning. (Sadly, some of them not even so secretly.) Is it any wonder the world has not been won to Christ and is in a virtue crisis when Christians care so little about obeying the straightforward biblical command toward sexual, moral, and ethical purity.

Thus, Malachi's Furnace awaits. God *will* have his people pure in both thought and behavior, whatever he must do to achieve it.

I fall so short of the complete purity you would have in the hearts and minds of your people, heavenly Father. I desire to be completely pure, in thought and motive as much as in behavior. I can only pray that you will purify me, and prepare me for the purity I long for, and that you will make a reality in the next life.

112. Do Not Be the Cause of Allowing Sin to Spread

Do not let infection spread. (Spiritually implied throughout Leviticus 13)

[56] Obviously there are exceptions. Rape and abuse clearly change this dynamic. Those are terrible scourges which no one takes lightly.

Do not enter the path of the wicked…for they cannot sleep unless they have done wrong…
unless they have made someone stumble. (Proverbs 4:14, 16)
You have turned aside from the way; you have caused many to stumble…
you have corrupted the covenant. (Malachi 2:8)

Judy and I watched an engaging though disturbing television movie last evening, one of many "pandemic" stories making the rounds, though this one was filmed more than a decade before the Covid outbreak of 2020. It is remarkable how well the spread of viruses was understood, and yet how completely porous were every nation's security measures when Covid hit.

The film centered around an outbreak on an airplane which was discovered in flight. The plane landed and was kept in quarantine. All the protocols were followed perfectly and containment should have been complete.

Except…

One disgruntled man saw no need why *his* rights should be curtailed. Grousing and complaining, he angrily resisted being kept in quarantine. Seizing a moment during the chaos, he slipped away, hid in an airport van, made his way into the terminal. As he began coughing, he shoved his way through the crowd, then to his office where he embraced all his coworkers. You can imagine the result. Within minutes he had brushed up against hundreds, who spread the invisible contact to thousands, and within forty-eight hours the entire Los Angeles area was exposed.

I sat thinking, "How could one man be so stupid and insensitive!"

Yet what a chilling object lesson!

Sin, too, is a virus. It spreads exactly the same way, by personal contact. A tiny bad habit (whether it's gossip, loose language, immodest dress, or a rude word or expression) can take root in a brief, even accidental, encounter and be spread. The gossip is repeated…and repeated again. The rude word spoken results in an angry response from the recipient, who then turns rudely on the next person *he* encounters.

It is exactly the Covid scenario that brings Leviticus 13 almost shockingly alive, and why I summarized its detailed regulations as I did above. It is God's object lesson about the invisible spreading of sin!

Sin never exists in a vacuum. Tiny insensitivities, rudenesses, and unkindnesses spread like the droplets of a sneeze.

How much more devastating are the large sins of the flesh. Sexual sin, affairs, divorce, and the many perversions of identity being normalized by the world—these all influence countless lives no less than one man starting a pandemic from selfish carelessness.

Teen girls see others or Hollywood girls dressed scantily and flirting and flaunting themselves, and imitate what they see.

The virus spreads.

An unhappy wife hears about a coworker having an affair.

The virus spreads.

Teen boys in the locker room pick up loose language, swearing, and lewd talk and laughter about sexual behavior.

The virus spreads.

Christian parents watch movies with crude language and sexual content with their children.

The virus spreads into the next generation.

Every tiniest sin has the potential to start an invisible sin pandemic.

If we *saw* our tiny indiscretions against purity and against obedience, *saw* whom they hit with the miniscule droplets of our carelessness, and then *saw* the ripple effect into the lives of thousands, I'm sure we would fall on our knees weeping in shame.

On the other hand, how might God be able to use tiny words and expressions of love, kindness, sympathy, and encouragement in those we encounter all day long.

How widely might virtue also spread in the lives of those we brush past all day long!

Oh God…open my eyes to see what I am spreading into the world around me! Let no careless germs of disease or spiritual-infection or sin pass from my hands, my words, my actions, my expressions, even my thoughts, to others. May I pass to those around me invisible scatterings of light, truth, kindness, and love.

113. Engage in No Sexual Relations Outside Marriage

"You shall not covet your neighbor's wife." (Exodus 20:17)

"If a man commits adultery…both the adulterer and the adulteress shall be put to death." (Deuteronomy 20:10)

This will not be a popular command in the ears of the world. Everyone realizes that marriage is on the rocks. The most serious threat to marriage and the family today, however, does not come from the world, but from within Christendom. The institutions of family and marriage would be as strong as ever if Christendom took the purity commands of the Bible seriously. But Christians have so thoroughly adopted the world's values, standards, and sexual practices that there is little discernable difference. Thus marriage, family, gender reality, and sexual purity are crumbling before our eyes within God's church. Christian leaders, pastors, priests, denominations, and the people in the pews are universally to blame.

Malachi's words are unbelievably contemporary. In the Old Testament the Levites (the "sons of Levi") were the clergy. Malachi is not speaking about the world, but of the need for purification *within* God's church:

> *You priests, who despise my name…I have no pleasure in you, says the Lord of hosts, and I will not accept an offering from your hand…the lips of a priest should guard knowledge, and men should seek instruction from his mouth…But you have turned aside from the way; you have caused many to stumble by your instruction; you have corrupted the covenant…abomination has been committed…So take heed to yourselves, and let none be faithless to the wife of his youth. "For I hate divorce," says the Lord the God of Israel…*

"Behold...he is like a refiner's fire...and he will purify the sons of Levi...till they present right offerings to the Lord." (*Malachi* excerpts)

It is a strong word to Christian leaders of today who have gone along with the world's abominations and brought the full spate of the world's repugnant sexual and marital abominations into their churches.

Do we want spiritual milk or the truth? Nothing has changed since Malachi's day.

You have wearied the Lord with your words...saying, "Every one who does evil is good in the sight of the Lord, and he delights in them..."

Malachi was indeed a prophet. Throughout the world, Christians are saying exactly this!

"Hey, world—God doesn't condemn you! Everyone who does evil is forgiven. Everyone is good in the sight of the Lord. He not only forgives, he *delights* in everyone no matter what their lifestyle. There are no more sins. God is a God of love."

This is Satan's lie. The church has absorbed the lie into its bloodstream hook, line, and sinker with its near complete tolerance of the world's sexual and moral perversity. Modernity tells us not only to be "color blind," but to be *sin blind.*

Thus, Malachi's Furnace awaits. God *will* have his people pure in both thought and behavior, whatever he must do to achieve it.

Keep us pure, Lord, before a watching world. Sting the consciousness of your church awake to the great sin of its disobedience to this imperative command.

114. Hate Falsehood and Do Not Circulate Potential Falsehoods

You shall not utter a false report. (Exodus 23:1)
The Lord hates...a lying tongue...and a man who sows discord. (Proverbs 6:16-17, 19)
Seek good, and not evil...hate evil and love good. (Amos 5:14, 15)

Hate is a strong word. We cringe at the sound of it. Yet there are things we are supposed to hate. Proverbs 6:16-19 lists seven things God hates:

- Haughty eyes.
- Lying tongues.
- Shedding innocent blood.
- Wicked schemes.

- Rushing toward evil.
- Spreading falsehood.
- Sowing discord.

To these can be added from other passages where the strong word *hate* is used:

- Deceptive business dealings. (Proverbs 11:1)
- False idols. (Deuteronomy 23:18)
- Prostitution. (Deuteronomy 23:18)
- Injustice. (Deuteronomy 25:16)
- Hypocritical worship. (Isaiah 1:13-14)
- Feast days. (Amos 5:21)
- Evil schemes. (Zechariah 8:17)
- Perjury and false promises. (Zechariah 8:17)
- Divorce. (Malachi 2:16)

The underlying thread uniting all these is *falsehood*—being false in word and deed, being false to God, to others, to customers, to spouses, to the accused, and to ourselves.

However, most of the above are excused by our culture. We don't call taking advantage an "evil scheme" now. It's just being shrewd. We don't call exaggerated advertising "deceptive," it's just good marketing. Such a simple practice in our culture as the "little white lie" isn't considered wrong. After all, *nobody* is truthful all the time, right?

I hear this over and over in television dramas, "Everyone lies." It is repeated so persistently that it spreads the virus of untruth into the culture.

Anger rises up in me every time I hear it. Everyone *doesn't* lie! We're not supposed to lie. I hate this statement, and God hates it too.

God hates falsehood in *all* its forms.

If sin spreads like a virus, one of its most rapidly proliferating strains is falsehood. Few would knowingly walk up close, breathe in deeply, and fill their lungs with what was known to be a deadly virus. Yet hungry ears greedily gobble up falsehoods with delight, never realizing they are doing exactly the same thing! Invisible germs of falsehood widen and expand as deadly viruses of untruth. Those who pass on falsehoods… *become* the falsehood.

How much stronger can it be said—God *hates* all this! He hates falsehood.

Therefore we are to *hate* falsehood. The very idea of *passing on* a falsehood should be abhorrent to everything within us. The command hits us from both directions—hating the possibility of *receiving* falsehoods that come at us, and the more hateful idea of *giving the virus to anyone else.*

Trite though it may be, we are called to hate the sin not the sinner. Falsehood *itself* is the virus. Sadly in our time, almost *everyone* is a carrier.

God's people must not be! We must hate it so much that we absolutely *refuse* to circulate even so much as a *potential* falsehood. It must be as a hideous thing to us, grotesque, so evil we refuse to touch it, refuse to have anything to do with falsehood.

Yet the virus is insidious and invisible. However mature in faith I may think myself, the mental ground to receive falsehoods remains fertile. The virus enters and sticks to my brain so easily! We *love* juicy tidbits of gossip and scandal! Such invisible seeds are swirling in the air. We breathe them in all day long and never know it.

Satan will use any tactic to lodge a falsehood-spore in some corner of the brain. Those spores multiply, proliferate, and kill truth.

We have to work hard to keep our hands and ears and all our senses clean, alert, awake to falsehood, refusing to give the invisible virus spores an opening, refusing to pick them up, think about them, analyze them, or dwell on them

I do hate falsehood, Lord. But how subtly I may be guilty of embracing or passing on seemingly insignificant whispers of untruth without being aware of it. I beseech you to sting my conscience when the tiniest hint of falsehood circles around my thoughts trying to ensnare me and gain entrance. Give me eyes of awareness to recognize these swirling spores of falsehood for the deadly evil they represent. Keep me watchful and careful, however small and from whatever quarter they come, against all enemies of truth.

115. Examine and Test Your Ways and Return to the Lord

Let us test and examine our ways, and return to the Lord. (Lamentations 3:40)

David's moving prayer of Psalm 139 reverberates down through history:

Search me, O God…know my heart. Try me…know my thoughts…
see if there be any wicked way in me, and lead me in the way everlasting.

Over three hundred years later, with Israel and Judah facing ruin and destruction, Jeremiah echoed David's words with a heartfelt lamentation over the nation he loved. He turned David's inward prayer, using David's very words, into a national exhortation:

Let us test and examine our ways, and return to the Lord.

Over two hundred more years went by. Then Malachi stepped onto the prophetic stage repeating the same message again…and with the same words (*test* and *return*). Now Malachi puts them into God's mouth:

"*Return* to me...put me to the *test*...if I will not open the windows of heaven for you and pour down for you an overflowing blessing."
(Malachi 3:7, 10)

David invites God to test him. Here is God inviting us to test *him* to prove his faithfulness.

Purity begins with self-examination. It is exampled by David, then exhorted by Jeremiah, and finally even demonstrated by God himself.

Without self-examination, purity drifts. The compass wobbles from true North. Human nature will always coast, slow down, get lazy, grow inattentive to virtue. People drift downhill, *away* from righteousness not *toward* it. Purity cannot flourish on auto-pilot.

That's why David's prayer and Jeremiah's exhortation contain two components—*test* and *return*. Together they reset the compass. This command might read:

Frequently get your bearings, examine the direction you are pointing, then reset your inner compass.

A barometer or altimeter offer even better examples. Compasses don't need regulating. Their needles only wobble when false magnetic forces lure their needles off true North. But barometers and altimeters change. Circumstances, climate, pressure, and location all influence their readings. Therefore, they have to be recalibrated.

Both parallels are easy to see. My inner attentiveness, not only to purity, but to *all* the commands, invisibly ebbs and flows. My attention to the commands is not only affected by pulls on my compass from forces not lined up with God's North, but also on my inner personal weather, pressures I am facing, and my location and circumstances. These inner "barometers" have to be recalibrated often.

In George MacDonald's words, "I have to mind what I am about."

How different is my concentration on the commands when in busy traffic, when alone on a Scottish seashore, when facing time pressure in the middle of the day, when facing personal heartache or financial pressure in the middle of the night, when assaulted by criticism, when surrounded by the worldliness of my peers, when absorbed in a television program, when immersed in reading the Upper Room Discourse, or when in a crowded and hectic airport.

I respond differently in all these circumstances. My personal weather is constantly in flux.

Storm approaching...barometer dropping.

Clear skies...barometer stable.

My inner barometer fluctuates all over the place! That's why I need to reset and recalibrate. It's why I try to read the Bible or the commands regularly. It's why I remind myself of Thomas Kempis's exhortations when he echoes Jeremiah:

> Renew your purpose and stir yourself up daily. Diligently search into and set in order both the outward and the inward man. Continually recollect yourself, fix your

good purpose every morning, and every night examine how you have behaved in word, deed, and thought. [57]

Self-examination and recalibration—a simple prescription for discipleship, the antidote to drift, the preventative to command-wobble: *Test and return.*

- When temptation lurks unseen…*test and return.*
- When I feel the allure of the world's values …*test and return.*
- When worldliness tries to squeeze me into its mold [58]…*test and return.*
- When I feel sympathy for what I know is wrong…*test and return.*
- When falsehoods try to gain entry…*test and return.*

Examine…test your ways…and return to the Lord.

Once again, Lord God, I pray the timeless prayer: Search me and know my heart. Try me and know my thoughts. See if there be any wicked way in me, and lead me in the way everlasting. To David's prayer I add Jeremiah's words—Test and examine me, and give me courage to test and examine myself, and return always to you. Remind me daily to keep my spiritual compass calibrated toward your North.

116. Purge Temper, Anger, Bitterness, Resentment

Resentment kills a fool (Job 5:2)
Anger lodges in the bosom of fools. (Ecclesiastes 7:9)

I originally wrote this as "Control Anger." That wording seemed a reasonable summary of Solomon's many differently-worded proverbs about the perversity of anger. Its opposite—self-control—fit perfectly with the terminology, and dovetailed with Paul's, "Let not the sun go down on your anger." (Ephesians 4:26)

Yet the phrasing was missing something. Merely *controlling* anger seemed to avoid the bull's eye, almost providing an excuse not even to aim for the bull's eye. If all we're doing is squelching annoyance, swallowing anger, while the anger *remains*, where do we find the virtue of Christlikeness?

Controlling a bad habit is good. But *conquering* the bad habit has to be the ultimate goal. It is a good thing to *swallow* anger, but *replacing* anger altogether with the virtues of graciousness and forgiveness probe far deeper into the people we are praying to become.

I reflected again on Paul's words from *Ephesians*. Their misuse has led to the erroneous notion that anger is okay…just don't let it go on too long. It's fine to blow your stack, just make sure you've calmed down by sunset. It's

[57] Thomas Kempis, *The Imitation of Christ.*
[58] J.B. Phillips translation, Romans 12:2: "Don't let the world around you squeeze you into its own mould."

another example of Paul's words being distorted, and occasionally doing more harm than good. In this case, they can be used to excuse anger not deal with it.

To drive the testing of ourselves deeper, we need go to the words of Jesus in Matthew 5:22. It is clear that Jesus regards anger as nothing more nor less than sin. Keeping anger smoldering until sunset has no place in the Sermon on the Mount.

It's not a pleasant reality to face, but anger is sin. It doesn't merely need to be *controlled*. It needs to be *purged*.

If what we're concerned with is shoving anger down where no one sees it—holding the tongue, but keeping anger alive—we might as well say, "Control theft, control lying, control adultery, control swearing." Controlling it doesn't get rid of anything. The idea is to eradicate it.

The simple word *lodge* from Ecclesiastes 7:9 highlights precisely why anger is so nefarious. It lodges in the cracks. It sticks. It stays. It sends out roots and suckers that grow invisibly through the hidden regions of our innermost selves.

Even "controlled" anger is but the tip of an iceberg. Seven more demons lie in wait beneath the surface—temper, bitterness, resentment unforgiveness, perhaps violence, jealousy, and vengeance. Anger does not merely cause the compass needle to wobble a millimeter or two. Anger spins it around 180 degrees until we are not looking in God's direction at all.

Anger is endemic to the human constitution. It's a greater problem for some than others simply by personality. The most important starting point is getting rid of the false notion that because it's "natural" it's okay. It's *not* okay.

Anger is so misunderstood that it is not even unusual to hear someone bragging about having a temper since they assume it excuses occasional blow-ups. One loved one dear to my heart, was proud to say that she "just had to get it off her chest." After angrily venting her annoyances, she was equally proud of being able to "move on." Thus the outbursts were justified. However, she could never move on without the explosion. Curiously, many of those bubbling and brewing resentments she had to get off her chest continued to fuel the inner volcano until they came back around again…and again. She had to *keep* getting them off her chest. Never recognized as sin, the justified outbursts (laced with accusations) continued.

This highlights one of the many fictions associated with anger—that after the storm subsides it's over.

It's *not* usually over. Those who blow their stack invariably *don't* move on. Temper smolders.

Anger, bitterness, and resentment are not purged by getting them off the chest if their roots remain lodged inside. They are *sins* to be repented of, their poisonous roots and suckers pulled out and burned.

Test…return…repent…and purge.

Oh, Lord, what an insidious evil is anger nursed and fed and coddled in the heart. Purge me from any bitterness I may be unaware of, lurking unforgivenesses I have allowed to lodge in the cracks of my heart. An explosive temper may not be my personal besetting sin. But it is hard to let go of my invisible and justifiable resentments. Forgive me for letting many suns go down on my silent annoyances and irritations. Reveal them to me that I may put them on your altar to be consumed in your purifying fire.

117. Use Honest Weights

Do not use dishonest standards…Use honest scales and honest weights. (Leviticus 19:35-36, NIV)
Diverse weights are an abomination to the Lord. (Proverbs 20:23)

I love the simplicity of this command. I'm sure I don't need to explain the imagery—weighing out another's purchase with counterbalancing weights on a scale to determine its exact weight. Obviously if the scale is rigged, or the counterweights are intentionally inaccurate to produce a heavier weight for the customer than is the true weight, the unwary man or woman may receive four pounds of grain and pay for five. It was a classic form of deception in the ancient world. Yet in our world, lawyers and advertisers use it all the time.

We don't buy and sell using such weighted scales these days. But how many subtle forms of rigging the weights are considered perfectly normal…if you can get away with it.

A lawyer bills an hour for fifty-five minutes of consultation…a worker leaves at 4:55 when he is being paid for a day ending at 5:00…Amazon charges $6.50 for shipping that costs the company $3.75…a car company places a mileage estimate of 45 mph on the window that everyone knows is pure fiction. Even such a minor violation of truth as Starbucks calling its "small" cup of coffee "Tall" is its version of a subtle, almost subliminal deception.

Using clever jargon to mask an untruth doesn't change the fact—it's not true. The consultation *didn't* last an hour, the shipping *didn't* cost $6.50, the car *won't* get 45 m.p.g., the small cup *isn't* tall. They're all tiny acceptable lies.

White lies, dishonest weights, exaggerations of untruth… invisibly greasing the wheels that keep commerce humming along, so insidious that we imbibe the same habits ourselves. If we're not careful we no longer *hate falsehood.* We are humming along in the deception of untrue weights along with everyone else.

How many miniscule dishonesties creep into daily life that we take for granted? Dishonest weights are intrinsic to the whole ethos of capitalism and the advertising that floods our lives with untruths and dishonest claims every day. We don't hate it. We accept it. We embrace it.

I can't change Amazon's or Starbucks' or Ford's subtly deceptive culture of gimmickry. But I can make sure no dishonest weights pollute *my* dealings.

It's not as easy as it sounds. Such a simple thing as exaggeration that conveys a subtle deviation from 100% accuracy, represents a verbal dishonest weight.

We might reword the command: *Do not exaggerate.* That's exactly what it means.

Keep me scrupulously honest and accurate in my words, Lord, in all my dealings, in all finances, in relationships. Do not let me give in to the temptation of resume enhancement, trying to make myself look better than I am with exaggeration. Be it far from me, Lord. May I give honest work, honest time, honest responses, honest estimates, and may honest weights characterize my dealings with every person I meet.

118. Turn from All Hint of Impurity and Impropriety

"Sin is crouching at the door…you must master it." (Genesis 4:7)
Keep away from everything impure. (Deuteronomy 23:9)
Turn from evil. (Psalm 34:14, NIV)
Take heed to yourselves. (Malachi 2:16)

Again we encounter the result of self-examination and recalibration—to *turn* from impurity. *Test* and *turn* from command #115.

This is a challenging command for everyone. Even *hints* of impropriety…keep away from *everything* impure. Is this an impossibly high bar to hold ourselves to? I cannot be alone in realizing that I have not always been as attentive as I should have been. My confidence in my spiritual awareness can be an Achilles heel of pride. Knowing my heart, my thoughts, my motives, it becomes easy to trust myself *too* much, and overlook the subtleties of the commands. That's why we cannot gloss over the stringency of the *everything* of Deuteronomy 23:9.

Once we modify the command to read, "Turn from *most* hints of impurity," and change Moses' words to, "Keep away from the *majority* of impure things…"—lowering the bar to a more reasonable level—we've begun adjusting the force of the commands to fit comfortably with our unwillingness to face their demands. We may even be modifying them to excuse our personal disobedience.

It's not pleasant to recognize pride as the flip-side of self-confidence, allowing us to justify these downward "adjustments" and "modifications" to the stringency of the commands. Self-righteousness always lurks in the shadows as the dark side of self-confidence. Though motives may be pure, Satan will lose no opportunity to hijack pride in such a cunning way as to give "the appearance of evil" to one watching on the sidelines wondering how much the commands we claim to value so highly really matter.

Good motives may not be enough to prevent hints of compromise, adjustments, excuses, and bar-lowering modifications to the commands worming their way into our thoughts and justifications.

George MacDonald puts a wonderful line in the mouth of his memorable character Curdie: "I must mind what I am about."

This perfectly reflects the message I try to remind myself of often—that no one is immune from the infiltration and subtleties of excuse-making and bar-lowering. Even simple carelessness can be the enemy of Moses' *everything*. When I am heading out the front door brimming with confident enthusiasm, it's almost impossible to notice pride slipping in the back door and taking up comfortable residence in my house.

This is seriously upper-division command discipleship. We're not talking about obvious and flagrant "sins." It's in the little things where Satan attacks the spiritually mature man or woman. Avoid all *hint* of wrong. The small things in life *matter*. The "hints" come in small doses. Yet the more lethal the poison the less of it is required.

Christians are on display before an attentive world. We are reflections of Jesus. Those with whom we mix every day are judging the veracity of the gospel message by what they observe in us. When Christians lower the command-bar, people notice.

I first wrote this command as, "*Avoid* any hint…" I realized, however, that wording to be too passive. This is a command that requires a forceful and vigorous level of avoidance. When potential impropriety looms in your path, it's time to take action, spin on your heels and *turn* away. Go in a different direction… quickly, instantly. Set the bar of command-attentiveness back on the top rung where it belongs.

Test…mind what you're about…and turn.

> He had read stories about thieves and honest boys, and had never seen any difficulty in the matter. Nor had he yet a notion of how difficult it is not to be a thief…Clare did not know that many…a man who passes for respectable in this disreputable world, is counted far meaner than a thief in the next…he began to see that it is not enough to mean well; that he must be sharp, and mind what he was about; else, with hunger worrying inside him, he might be a thief before he knew. He was on the way to discover that to think rightly—to be on the side of what is honourable…is a very different thing from doing right, and being honourable, when the temptation is upon us. Many a boy when he reads this will say, "Of course it is!" and when the time comes, will be a sneak. [59]

I have to repent to you, Lord, for sometimes allowing my self-confidence to pass over into pride. Keep me mentally and spiritually awake so that I do not cross lines that appear to others different than I intend. Bring healing to whatever lives my carelessness may have injured. Keep me from making command-adjustments that excuse me from the high bar of their demands. Keep me wakeful to turn from any hint and everything impure, especially in my own motives. Remind me to keep the bar of command-obedience where it needs to be.

---

[59] Previous brief quote from George MacDonald's *The Princess and Curdie*, ch. 8; this from *A Rough Shaking*, ch. 16.

119. Purge Evil from Your Life

Thou desirest truth in the inward being; therefore…Purge me…and I shall be clean. (Psalm 51:6-7)
Purge the altar and purify it; and they shall consecrate themselves. (Ezekiel 43:26, KJV)

Understanding the word *purge* is one of the fundamental necessities of discipleship. It's why we *test* and *return*—in order to *purge* evil from our lives.

The word "evil" may raise a barrier keeping us from penetrating to the heart of this command that is so essential to purity. *Evil* is such a nasty word. Few think of themselves as *evil*.

That is exactly our problem with sin. It's hard to look sin squarely in the eye. We'd rather pretend it isn't all *that* bad. A little slippage now and then—hey, no big deal. But *sin…evil?* Ugh!

The downward adjustments and modifications raise themselves in our thoughts all day long with excuses to ignore Moses' *everything*, and pretend that something not quite so horrible resides inside us than actual *evil*. A kinder gentler kind of sin.

"I never claimed to be a saint," is used in pretended humility to deflect the stark reality. "Nobody expects us to be perfect."

But that's not true. There *is* someone who does. Jesus not only expects us to be perfect, he said, "You *must* be perfect…"

Obviously he doesn't mean all at once. But perfection *is* and *must* be the goal of every Christian. It is what we are growing toward. If that isn't the goal, one must ask what kind of Christian he or she is. What does being a Christian mean if not that?

Perfection being the goal, then, there are no little sins, no excusable sins, no slippages that we overlook with the absurd statement, "Hey no big deal…I never claimed to be a saint." If you don't claim to be a saint, what are you doing claiming to be a Christian?

That's what Christians are—saints in training, apprentice-saints.

Looking sin square in the eye, the word *evil* shouldn't frighten us, make us bristle, or cause us to look the other way with defensive excuses. The commands of the Bible are serious business. Sin is intrinsic to understanding how the commands work. Sin will always exert pressure against the commands, pressure toward impurity, pressure toward excuse, pressure toward the appearance of evil.

Sin and obedience to the commands are in constant strife and opposition.

But sin and evil are unpleasant, ugly, personal. So the world changes this command to make it more palatable. The world changes *sin* to "issues." It's less threatening that way.

"If it's not too much trouble," says the world, "work on some of your issues, *if* you have time…*if* it's not too hard, of course. Don't stress about it. Don't put guilt trips on yourself. You're a good person, you're forgiven. The most important thing is that you feel good about yourself."

Not only is *sin* eliminated from the personal growth-equation by changing it to *issues*. The *purging* of sin is also eliminated by changing it to *working on* your issues. You don't have to put issues to *death*. You only have to *work* on them, or go to a support group and *share* them. And it goes without saying that you should work on your issues in the world's way, not God's way.

Couched in spiritual jargon, this is also the message from 95% of the world's pulpits. Words like *evil* and *sin* aren't used much even in Christendom. We can't have people feeling judged, convicted, or burdened by guilt. So the church has adopted the world's methodology too. Issues, not sin, have become the focus of the church.

That's not the way Jesus approached sin. "Get behind me, Satan!" was his stinging, harsh, purging word to his best friend. "Go and sin no more," to the adulteress.

There are big sins and little sins, huge evils and tiny evils. They *all* stand between us and the ultimate goal of Matthew 5:48. Even the tiniest will *eventually* prevent God's being able to complete the transformation unto Christlikeness within us.

Is this too hard a word? It is exactly what C.S. Lewis says with equal boldness at the end of *Mere Christianity*. It's just that these days few are paying much attention to that aspect of his message. There are so many more fun and intellectually pleasing things in his writings to focus on.

Small evils, or "sins" if you prefer, small "issues," are like thorn pricks of the rose—tiny, unseen, perhaps only a microscopic speck lodged under the skin. They're easy to ignore, because who's going to call a *rose* evil!

Tiny specks of rose thorn, however, infected and festering and not removed, can lead to sepsis, gangrene, even death. Sin-thorns allowed to dig deeper and deeper into the soul follow the same progression.

As unpleasant as this command may seem, it is really very down-to-earth and practical:

"Pluck out sin-thorns before they fester."

I don't like the thought of evil residing inside me, Lord. Reveal to me the specks, seeds, and thorns of evil, even potential evil that may be hardly noticeable pricks in the skin. Help me get them out. Purge me. Cleanse me. Purify me, whatever it takes. Do not let even the tiniest sin lodge undealt-with in my heart or mind.

120. Welcome God's Furnace of Purification

"Everything that can stand the fire, you shall pass through the fire, and it shall be clean." (Numbers 31:23)

For he is like a refiner's fire…and he will purify…and refine. (Malachi 3:2, 3)

For behold, the day comes, burning like an oven…
so that…the sun of righteousness shall rise, with healing in its wings. (Malachi 4: 1, 2)

About the time I wrote the somewhat controversial book *Hell and Beyond,* I engaged in a fascinating exchange with a reader. We were discussing the nearly unthinkable idea of *choosing* God's purifying fire. The question wasn't a matter of heaven or hell, being saved or not saved, of judgment or forgiveness. Those questions were long behind us. We were pondering together the enormity of the potentiality of being made clean, whole…perfect as Jesus spoke of in Matthew 5:47—utterly and completely *pure* from sin…choosing to take the final step beyond what our growth in this life had been able to accomplish.

What if, we wondered together, we had to take our *own* hand in that final sanctification? What if it took Malachi's Furnace, the fires of purification, to accomplish the ultimate cleansing…and what if God placed the choice of whether to allow the fire to carry out that final work in our hands, and would never force it upon us against our will? Would we *want* the purity of Christlikeness enough to *choose* the fire?

My friend's response was sober, quiet, thoughtful. "Yes…I want it," he said. "I *want* to be pure whatever it takes. As terrifying as it might be, I would welcome the fire."

I've never forgotten his statement. It sums up why it seems fitting to close this discussion of the commands of the prophets with an exhortation, in one sense less practical than many, with no immediate or daily *do* associated with it. This is a deeply spiritual word that challenges us to the core of our belief system. It challenges who we think God is, and what we think his purposes have been with his people throughout the Old Testament…and what we think his purposes are for all mankind in eternity.

> *For he is like a refiner's fire…and he will purify the sons of Levi and refine them like gold and silver, till they present right offerings to the Lord… For behold, the day comes, burning like an oven…the day that comes shall burn.* (Malachi 3:2-3; 4:1)
>
> *"I will thoroughly purge away your dross and remove all your impurities. I have refined you…I have tested you in the furnace…"* (Isaiah 1:25; 48:10)

What are God's *ultimate* purposes, not merely for mankind…but for *me*?

How does God want to make me ready to receive the white stone containing my new name?

How is he preparing me *now* to receive that new name?

What purification might lie ahead?

These are far-reaching questions that plunge to the core of who the Father is to us.

Though Jesus did not need purging from sin, in his will he faced the same terrifying choice. He had to choose his own fire, which was the cross. Just as Malachi prepared the way for his earthly coming, Jesus has likewise prepared the way for our final purification by walking the same road before us.

The final question becomes: Do I trust the Father enough to choose Malachi's Furnace as the ultimate tool in his loving hands to burn me clean? Will I, in Zechariah's words, *rejoice greatly* to be purified? Can I trust myself into the hands of the Father as Jesus did on the cross?

Facing this question brings our journey through the Old Testament to its natural and fitting climax as we prepare for the coming of God's Messiah.

For where else has our journey been leading us but to the heart of the Father, to make us ready to yield all to him?

How much do I want to be made into God's perfectly obedient and radiant child? Will I welcome whatever purifying it takes?

> Ahead I saw a precipice disappearing over a vast chasm…My brain flooded with images from Dante's vision of hell…
>
> Knowing what I was thinking, a voice spoke from behind…
>
> "Do you want to be whole?"
>
> "Yes, with all my heart…But who could ever choose…?"
>
> I shuddered.
>
> "The fire of Malachi's Furnace is at hand," he continued. "It will be more painful than anything you have ever known. As it burns, you will feel the pain in your innermost soul. For the sin it must burn away is inside you."
>
> "How deep is it?" I said in a trembling voice as I peered over the cliff.
>
> "As deep as is required. Have you not yet realized that all things here are eternal? The fire is endless in all directions. Its depths are inside you."
>
> "Are… are the old stories true—that there is no coming out?"
>
> "The fire is meant to accomplish God's purpose," he replied. "The only coming out is by yielding to the refining and purifying of Malachi's Furnace, being burned clean, and coming through it without spot or blemish."
>
> "What lies at the bottom?"
>
> "The All-Consuming Fire where every remnant of sin is destroyed forever."
>
> "What is the… all consuming fire?"
>
> "What else but what the ancients told us—the heart of the Father."
>
> "You don't mean… that God is… down there?" I said in astonishment.
>
> "Of course. He is everywhere. The psalmist stated as clearly as can be said, If I make my bed in hell, you are there. The fire of God, which is his essential being, his love, his creative power, is a fire unlike its earthly symbol in that it is only at a distance that it burns. The farther from him we are, the worse it burns. When we approach close to him, the burning changes to comfort. Old King David, bless him, he knew about the heart of God…All is God's…Heaven is God's home. Hell is his workshop. Why else do you think he invented the fire than to cleanse his creation from sin?"…
>
> I stood for an aion… alone with my own free will…
>
> What did I want? What did I want to become? Did I truly want to be whole? Was I prepared to undergo the suffering it would require to burn the burrowing worms and parasites of sin from out of the innermost depths of my being? Did I want to be pure, clean, perfect, and incapable of sin again?
>
> Did I want to become capable of seeing God?
>
> Did I want to be a child… a repentant and obedient son? No one in all the universe could answer the questions for me…
>
> The thought of throwing myself into the fire was terrifying, too utterly horrifying to contemplate. Yet I recalled what the Scotsman had

said…The farther from him we are, the worse it burns. When we approach close to him, the burning changes to comfort.

The answer was yes… at last I wanted to be God's child.

I drew in a breath, then plunged headlong into the infinite chasm. [60]

And I will put this third into the fire, and refine them as one refines silver, and test them as gold is tested…

They will call on my name, and I will answer them. I will say, 'They are my people;' and they will say, 'The Lord is my God.'

(Zechariah 13:9)

For you shall go out in joy, and be led forth in peace;
the mountains and the hills before you shall break forth into singing.

(Isaiah 55:12)

60 Michael Phillips, *Hell and Beyond*, Sunrise Books, 2012, chs. 19, 22.

EPILOGUE

And thus ends the book of *Malachi* and the Old Testament.

> *Behold, I will send you Elijah the prophet before the great... day of the Lord comes. And he will turn the hearts of the fathers to their children and the hearts of the children to their fathers...*
> *Behold, I send my messenger to prepare the way before me, and the Lord whom you seek will suddenly come to his temple; the messenger of the covenant in whom you delight, behold, he is coming, says the Lord of hosts.* (Malachi 4:5-6; 3:1)

The story of God's revelation, however, is far from over. For as we turn in the Bible to *Mark*, the first gospel written, continuing Malachi's promise of preparation, the most important chapter of that revelation begins as if there has been no break in the story at all:

> *The beginning of the gospel of Jesus Christ, the Son of God.*
> *As it is written in the prophets,*
> *"Behold, I send my messenger before thy face,*
> *who shall prepare thy way;*
> *the voice of one crying in the wilderness:*
> *Prepare the way of the Lord, make his paths straight..."*
>
> *In those days Jesus came from Nazareth of Galilee... saying,*
> *"The time is fulfilled, and the kingdom of God is at hand;*
> *repent, and believe in the gospel."*
> (Mark 1:1-3, 9, 15)

The next book of "The Commands" series follows:

The Commands of Jesus

The three volumes of *The Commands* and the five volumes of *The Eyewitness Bible* present a unity of vision and outlook on God's work and purposes through history and in the individual lives of his people. Their themes and messages form a single tapestry-perspective of the Bible as God's revelation. They are most profitably read in conjunction with each other, and with that overarching unity in mind.

The Commands of the Prophets
The Commands of Jesus
The Commands of the Apostles

The Eyewitness Old Testament, Volume 1
The Eyewitness Old Testament, Volume 2
The Eyewitness New Testament, Volume 1
The Eyewitness New Testament, Volume 2
The Eyewitness New Testament, Volume 3

Special Editions:
The Commands of the Prophets Extra Large Print Edition
The Commands of Jesus Extra Large Print Edition
The Commands of the Apostles Extra Large Print Edition
The Commands of Jesus Journal Edition
The Prayers of the Commands
The Commands of Jesus Pocket Edition
The Commands of the Apostles Pocket Edition

The listings of commands from *The Commands of Jesus* and *The Commands of the Apostles* follow

The Commands of Jesus

1. ANDREW—*Love*

1 Obey my Commands.
2 Love.
3 Love God.
4 Love man.
5 Love the brethren.
6 Pray.
7 Be careful and watchful.
8 Remain alert and on guard.
9 Take heart, take courage.
10 Don't be afraid.

2. JAMES —*Purity*

11 Be pure.
12 Guard against ambition.
13 Commit no sexual sins.
14 Be patient, enduring, persevering.
15 Repent
16 Listen.
17 Listen carefully.
18 Be clear-minded, thoughtful, mentally diligent.
19 Apply yourself to think, learn, understand.
20 Think no impure thought.

3. PETER —*Humility*

21 Be humble.
22 Give when asked and do more than required.
23 Follow me.
24 Care for the suffering.
25 Give to the poor.
26 Believe.
27 Believe in God.
28 Believe in me.
29 Don't be anxious.
30 Believe that you will receive what you pray for.

4. MATTHEW —*Righteousness*

31 Be righteous.
32 If part of your body sins, get rid of it.
33 Be at peace, reconciled, and united with others.
34 Deny yourself.
35 Lose your life.
36 Be a servant.
37 De not defraud.
38 Be a son or daughter of God.
39 Pray, fast, give, and do good in secret.
40 Beware of practicing piety to be noticed.

5. PHILIP —*Forgiveness*

41 Forgive.
42 Forgive 70 x 7 times.
43 Do good, be good.
44 Seek first God's kingdom.
45 Store up treasure in heaven.
46 Be kind.
47 Love and pray for your adversaries.
48 Do good to those who hate you.
49 Do not exalt yourself.
50 Honor your father and mother.

6. JUDAS—*Hypocrisy*

51 Guard against hypocrisy.
52 Let your light shine before men.
53 If someone takes from you, do not demand back what you have given.
54 Seek no spiritual signs.
55 Be born again.
56 Do not justify or worry how to defend yourself.
57 Learn of me.
58 Receive the kingdom of God like a child.
59 Have salt in yourselves.
60 Be a good steward over what God has given you.

7. BARTHOLOMEW—*Trust*

61 Trust and have faith in God.
62 Do not be called teacher or leader.
63 Do not be diverted by externals, traditions, and doctrines, but look to the heart.
64 Don't fret about trifles.
65 Do not show goodness and hospitality only to those who are kind to you.
66 Worship the Lord and serve him only.
67 Do not desire more than God gives you.
68 Do not pray ostentatiously and with empty phrases.
69 Remain gratefully aware of you spiritual need.
70 Take up your cross.

8. JAMES SON OF ALPHAEUS—*The Golden Rule*

71 Do and think toward others as you would have them behave toward you.
72 Don't judge.
73 Deal with your own faults before thinking of the faults of others.
74 Ask, seek, knock.
75 Enter through the narrow gate.
76 Come to me with your burdens and find rest.
77 Take my yoke upon you.
78 Don't swear.
79 Judge rightly not by appearances.
80 Give the world its due and give God the things that are his.

9. THOMAS—*Truthfulness*

81 Love truth, speak truth, do truth.
82 Do not speak carelessly.
83 Acknowledge your discipleship.
84 Let your yes be yes and your no be no.
85 Do not doubt.
86 Speak graciously with words of peace.
87 Let people injure you without retaliating.
88 Show mercy.
89 Proclaim the kingdom of God.
90 Don't insult or call anyone a fool.

10. THADDAEUS—*Obedience*

91 Rule your life by the will of God.
92 Settle disputes promptly and privately.
93 Ask the Lord of the harvest to send workers.
94 Partake of the symbols of my body and blood.
95 Do for the least of humanity as you would for me.
96 Do not give way to anger.
97 Do not close your eyes to the Holy Spirit's work.
98 Give generously and not merely from your abundance.
99 Don't heed false prophets.
100 Obey the commandments.

11. SIMON THE ZEALOT—*Gladness*

101 Be glad in all circumstances.
102 Give up everything.
103 Don't resist evil men.
104 Do not lead others into sin.
105 Teach the nations to obey what I have commanded.
106 Do not follow the example of those who preach but do not practice.
107 Don't cast your pearls before swine.
108 Do not test the Lord.
109 Wash one another's feet.
110 Be wise as snakes and innocent as doves.

12. JOHN—*The Abiding Life*

111 Abide in me by obeying my Commands.
112 Don't separate what God has joined.
113 Love me by having my Commands and words and keeping them.
114 Count the cost of single-minded devotion to God.
115 Don't look back on your past life.
116 Don't call me Lord and not do what I tell you.
117 Do as I do and become like me.
118 Bear fruit as my disciples.
119 Practice my words.
120 This is my Command: Love one another.

The Apostolic Commands

1. JERUSALEM—*Pursue Godliness*

1 Yield yourself to God.
2 Present yourself as a daily living sacrifice to God.
3 Choose to be transformed by the renewal of mind.
4 Seek to grow in righteousness.
5 Train yourself in Godliness.
6 Be constant in prayer.
7 Abide in Jesus.
8 Lead a virtuous life.
9 Set your thoughts on high things.
10 Serve God and live for his glory.

2. ANTIOCH—*Nurture Personal Spirituality*

11 Obey the Lord's commands.
12 Be a doer of the word, not a hearer only.
13 Take your faith seriously.
14 Take heed to yourself.
15 Do not envy.
16 Do not be afraid or lose heart.
17 Keep watchful and alert.
18 Stand firm and courageous in God.
19 Be thankful in all circumstances.
20 Don't worry.

3. GALATIA—*Grow the Fruits of the Spirit*

21 Walk by the Spirit.
22 Make love your aim.
23 Rejoice in all circumstances, especially in your trials.
24 Walk in peace.
25 Respond with patience.
26 Be kind.
27 Do good, love good, be good.
28 Walk faithfully by faith, not by sight.
29 Be a gentle person.
30 Exercise self-control.

4. CORINTH—*Turn from Sin*

31 Repent.
32 Do not be conformed to the world.
33 Hate evil.
34 Sin no more—do not yield to sin.
35 Do not participate in the sins of others.
36 Do not associate with immorality.
37 Avoid worldly-minded believers.
38 Revere no idols.
39 Confess your sins.
40 Keep your conscience clear.

5. THESSALONICA—*Live God's Priorities at Home*

41 Christian leaders, live exemplary lives.
42 Honor marriage.
43 Husbands, love, honor and serve your wives.
44 Wives, respect and submit to your husbands.
45 Children, obey and honor your parents.
46 Practice hospitality.
47 Manage your households well.
48 Raise your children in the wisdom of the Lord.
49 Train young men to be self-controlled, young women to be chaste and domestic.
50 Care for widows and orphans.

6. LAODICEA—*Show Respect in Relationships*

51 Show honor and respect to all.
52 Seek the good of others.
53 Put others first.
54 Be merciful and full of sympathy.
55 Harbor no grievances or animosities.
56 Avoid the shallow and hypocritical who do not live their faith.
57 Control anger.
58 Don't judge.
59 Associate with the lowly. Show no partiality to the rich and powerful.
60 Place no stumbling blocks in the way of another's faith.

7. ATHENS—*Develop Wise and Gracious Habits*

61 Conduct yourself becomingly.
62 Be courteous and full of grace toward all.
63 Do not insist on your own way.
64 Don't be suspicious. (Don't yield to or allow suspicions to fester)
65 Live without guile.
66 Do not be irritable or resentful.
67 Do not be foolish.
68 Mind your own business.
69 Give generously.
70 Owe no one anything.

8. CAESAREA—*Speak with Grace*

71 Speak graciously.
72 Control your tongue.
73 Be quick to listen, slow to speak.
74 Say what you mean.
75 Do not grumble, complain, or speak against others.
76 Do not gossip, slander, or lie.
77 Do not swear.
78 Do not quarrel.
79 Speak to edify, encourage, and bless one another.
80 Speak not to flatter, impress, or please men.

9. PHILIPPI—*Reflect Christlikeness of Character*

81 Put on the character of Christ.
82 Seek God's will and live by it.
83 Pray for wisdom and walk in wisdom.
84 Be pure.
85 See through God's eyes by developing the mind of Christ.
86 Do not be covetous, greedy, or lover of money.
87 Clothe yourself with humility.
88 Eagerly rejoice in right and goodness.
89 Endure suffering with faith, fortitude, grace, and courage.
90 Wage vigorous spiritual warfare.

10. COLOSSAE—*Build Mature Beliefs*

91 Be mature in your thinking and wise in doctrine.
92 Increase your knowledge of God.
93 Build on a foundation of Jesus Christ.
94 Love truth.
95 Do not be ruled by legalisms.
96 Do not be shallow of belief.
97 Walk with discernment.
98 Do not dispute over doctrine.
99 Do not be deceived.
100 Equip yourselves for fitness to teach spiritual completeness.

11. EPHESUS—*Exemplify Unity and Servanthood in Church Life*

101 Do not be anxious to teach or place the immature in leadership.
102 Older men and women, teach younger men and women.
103 Pursue and emphasize what builds up the body of Christ.
104 Encourage one another.
105 Be sensitive to the weak in faith.
106 Use your gifts wisely.
107 Do all things decently and in order.
108 Deal with body conflicts in the church.
109 Don't neglect fellowship with your brothers and sisters.
110 Maintain unity.

12. ROME—*Evidence Discipleship in the World*

111 Live quiet peaceable lives.
112 Live in harmony with all.
113 Honor and submit to authority.
114 Honor, respect, and give your best to your masters and employers.
115 Be modest in dress, manners, and demeanor.
116 Aim at what is honorable in men's eyes as well as God's.
117 Work diligently and do not be slothful or idle.
118 Live your faith with zeal, good cheer, and steadfastness.
119 Consider your witness.
120 Recognize yourselves as a people set apart.

Made in the USA
Columbia, SC
16 January 2026

77076018R00193